PRUDENT REVOLUTIONARIES

PRUDENT REVOLUTIONARIES

Portraits of British Feminists between the Wars

BRIAN HARRISON

CLARENDON PRESS · OXFORD
1987

Oxford University Press, Walton Street, Oxford OX2 6DP

Oxford New York Toronto Melbourne Auckland
Delhi Bombay Calcutta Madras Karachi
Petaling Jaya Singapore Hong Kong Tokyo
Nairobi Dar es Salaam Cape Town

Associated companies in Beirut Berlin Ibadan Nicosia

Oxford is a trade mark of Oxford University Press

Published in the United States
by Oxford University Press, New York

© *Brian Harrison 1987*

British Library Cataloguing in Publication Data

Harrison, Brian, 1937–
Prudent revolutionaries: portraits of
British feminists between the wars.
1. Feminists—Great Britain—Biography
2. Feminism—Great Britain—History—
20th century
I. Title
305.4'2'0922   HQ1595.A3
ISBN 0–19–820119–2

Library of Congress Cataloging in Publication Data

Harrison, Brian Howard,
Prudent revolutionaries.
Bibliography: p.
Includes index.
1. Feminists—Great Britain—Biography. 2. Feminism—
Great Britain—History. I. Title.
HQ1595.A3H37 1987 305.4'2'0941 87–5498
ISBN 0–19–820119–2

Typeset by Cotswold Typesetting Ltd, Gloucester
Printed in Great Britain by
Butler and Tanner Ltd
Frome and London

TO MY MOTHER
MARY ELIZABETH SAVILL
in gratitude and affection

ACKNOWLEDGEMENTS

MANY people have generously helped me to write this book; in some cases, it would be more accurate to speak of joint authorship rather than help. Especially with Chapter 2, which draws so heavily on two splendid interviews with Fiona Billington-Greig, who commented on an earlier draft of the chapter; for me, her approach to her mother attains the ideal standpoint of combining critical appraisal with affectionate understanding. Chapter 6 is a monument to the sharp memory and shrewd judgement of Barbara Strachey, who not only allowed me unstinted access to her rich family archive, but also gave me two memorable interviews and amply commented on an earlier draft. In writing Chapter 7 I enjoyed most generous hospitality not only from Dame Margery herself, but from her son and daughter-in-law Dr Michael and Mrs Pamela Ashby, who did everything they could to help me understand her personality and career.

Without enthusiastic collaboration from Naomi Lutyens, Henry Harben's daughter, I could never have attempted the memoir of him in Chapter 8; her busy life did not prevent her from giving me the utmost help in trying to bring her father to life. Chapter 9 owes a great deal to the kindness and honesty of the late Gladys Groom-Smith; I wish she could have lived to read it, if only because she always wanted justice done to the Pethick-Lawrences of whom she was so fond. Mrs Nita Needham, niece of Esther Knowles the Pethick-Lawrences' devoted secretary, not only gave me a valuable interview, but also carefully read this chapter in an earlier draft and made helpful suggestions. I use material from the Pethick-Lawrence papers by permission of the Master and Fellows of Trinity College, Cambridge. Chapter 10 is virtually a joint production between myself and Eva Hubback's three children, Rachel and David Hubback and Diana Hopkinson, together with Diana's husband David, all of whom gave me interviews, commented on drafts, and helped me in every possible way. One of the pleasures of conducting this research has been the excuses it has given me for getting to know people as helpful as these have been. In every case I have tried to prevent this kindness from distorting what I regard as the truth, and the responsibility for interpretation is entirely my own; but I will indeed be pleased whenever I and the relatives coincide in our view.

Eleanor Rathbone's collaborators Mrs Vera Schaerli and Mrs Helga Wolff gave me valuable interviews, and commented helpfully on Chapter 4; Mrs Rita Pankhurst gave me her recollections of Sylvia Pankhurst in Ethiopia, and she and her husband Dr Richard Pankhurst kindly commented on an early draft of Chapter 8. The late Mrs Molly Northey, Harben's eldest daughter, always undervalued her own comments on her father; I found my interview with her and her comments on an earlier draft of the chapter both sympathetic and penetrating. Catherine Joseph movingly recalled her cousin Eva Hubback for me, and took great trouble with an earlier draft of Chapter 10; Mrs Jenifer Hart commented helpfully on a later draft of this chapter. As the interviews (now in the City of London Polytechnic's Fawcett Library) were usually tape-recorded, I would like to record my debt to Christopher Storm-Clark of the University of York, who gave me wise and generous technical advice at an early stage.

History cannot be written exclusively from interviews, and I owe much to several archivists, especially those in the Fawcett Library; David Doughan has always been extraordinarily generous with his time and suggestions; Veronica Perkins was fertile in suggestions for illustrations, and most efficient in providing me with copies; and I have adopted all Meg Sweet's penetrating proposals for improving Chapter 2. Mrs Schreuder of the Institute for Social History in Amsterdam knows far more than I about Sylvia Pankhurst, and makes her extensive knowledge freely available to those who consult her. The archivists at the University of Reading were most patient with a very demanding customer during the weeks I spent there in 1980. So were the staff of that admirable institution the London Library; temporary membership saved me an immense amount of time because it enabled me to make off with their *Hansards* and work on them at home.

David Mitchell, who has done so much pioneering work in this area, made several suggestions for improving Chapter 8; he also gave me a transcript of his interview in 1980 with Margery Corbett Ashby. I gained much from the interviews Linda Walker sent me some years ago when we were exchanging transcripts of mutual interest. Dr Richard Trainor presented me with a xerox of Billington-Greig's lecture on birth-control, which I thought had been lost. The footnotes record many other debts, but special acknowledgement must be made to the Economic and Social Research Council. They financed the three-year interviewing project in 1975–8 which produced the interviews mentioned above; and their Personal Research Grant in 1980–1 gave me six months free of teaching duties, and so emancipated me for archival work. During that period the Nuffield and Wolfson Foundations met my travel and subsistence expenses.

I thank Virago Press for their permission to quote from *The Diary of Beatrice Webb* (eds. N. and J. Mackenzie). I owe many corrections and improvements to the alert eye of my former tutor, Keith Thomas, who somehow found the time, amid many pressing commitments, to read the proofs in their entirety. Lastly, this book's debt to the patience of David Cooper, Jennifer Hornsby and Frances White is fundamental in ways that they alone can fully comprehend.

I conclude by dedicating this book to my mother. Born in 1915, she joined none of the feminist organizations discussed here, yet in subtle ways her own life-story has strongly influenced me while writing this book. Though she herself experienced several of the difficulties encountered by the British women of her generation, she continues to demonstrate in her own life how courage, wisdom, and resilience can find in every setback a new starting-point, and in every disappointment a new opportunity.

CONTENTS

LIST OF ILLUSTRATIONS

ABBREVIATIONS

AEC   Association for Education in Citizenship: founded in 1934 to promote the study of democratic politics in schools and universities; disbanded in 1957.

IAW   International Alliance of Women: title of the IWSA after 1926.

ILP   Independent Labour Party.

IWSA   International Women's Suffrage Alliance: suffragist offshoot of the International Council of Women, founded in 1904 to hold triennial international suffragist congresses and renamed IAW in 1926.

LSWS   London Society for Women's Suffrage: direct descendant of the first women's suffrage committee formed in London in 1866, affiliated to the NUWSS from 1897 as the London organization of the non-militants. Renamed London Society for Women's Service in 1919, and London and National Society for Women's Service in 1926, it became independent of NUSEC in 1929. Ancestor of the present Fawcett Society.

NCEC   National Council for Equal Citizenship: feminist offshoot of NUSEC created when the Townswomen's Guilds became independent in 1932.

NUSEC   National Union of Societies for Equal Citizenship: feminist successor in 1919 to NUWSS. Bifurcated in 1932 into NCEC and Townswomen's Guilds.

NUWSS   National Union of Women's Suffrage Societies: federation of non-militant suffragist societies formed in 1897, renamed NUSEC in 1919.

WEF   Women's Employment Federation: offshoot from the London and National Society for Women's Service, formed in 1934 to promote careers for women, subsequently National Advisory Centre on Careers for Women.

WFL   Women's Freedom League: militant organization which broke off from the WSPU in 1907 out of distaste for its autocratic structure; disbanded in 1961.

WSPU   Women's Social and Political Union: Emmeline Pankhurst's militant suffragette organization, founded in 1903 and disbanded in 1914.

NOTE ON REFERENCES

ALL books in the footnotes were published in London unless otherwise stated. Full details of each item are included only at the first citation. Footnotes first identify quotations in their order of appearance in the text, then identify other items.

'It is very difficult, when we look at the honourable Lady the Member for the English Universities (Miss Rathbone), to think of her as a revolutionary, but she is, and it is her work, and her vision and courage, that have really brought us where we are today.'

(Lady Astor in House of Commons second reading debate on the Family Allowance Bill, 8 March 1945)

INTRODUCTION

FEMINIST ambitions for social change are revolutionary—in some ways more so than the ambitions of many class warriors. And to revolutionary aims the Edwardian suffragettes added what at first sight seem revolutionary methods. Yet heroism is not the only quality needed even for winning political reforms, let alone for getting full benefit from them; nor is militancy necessarily an index to intensity of commitment or consistency of principle. Most Edwardian suffragists were constitution-alist and non-militant, and some even thought that feminism was betrayed by the violence and authoritarianism that flowed from militant tactics. Feminist militancy vanished after 1914, and votes were extended to women over thirty in 1918 and to all adult women in 1928; the non-militants were free to carry their non-violent and democratic methods on to the national feminist stage. Enfranchised women could not spurn parliamentary methods, and between the wars political prudence seemed essential to feminist success.

Yet there were difficulties. The process of getting the vote helped to produce a mild inter-war anti-feminist reaction. Nor could inter-war feminists any longer content themselves with periodic extra-parliamen-tary campaigning on a single issue; they had to press male-created institutions continuously for a wide range of reforms. Would the relevant skills be forthcoming? Which feminist reforms should now head the list, and in what order? And should these take priority over other humanitarian objectives, and over class and national loyalties? Edwardian suffragism had united people who diverged markedly on feminist and other aims: could feminist unity survive the hard thought now needed on longer-term feminist objectives? Some pioneer feminists hoped enfranchised women would supplant the old party antagonisms with a new political harmony: would these hopes be realized? If not, should political parties be joined or shunned? These difficult questions had to be answered.

Little has so far been written about British inter-war feminists. This is partly because historians, like journalists, relish the dramatic, the flamboyant, the outrageous—whereas the leading British inter-war feminists shunned the limelight. Their story, like that of Oxford's stateswoman Annie Rogers, performing on a smaller stage, 'shows the

value of special knowledge and of being sure of your facts. It makes clear
the multitude of details and of side issues that have to be mastered; how to
act when your supporters disagree; when to wait and mark time . . . It
gives examples, also, of the importance of tact, of knowing when to keep
quiet, of learning by experience in apprenticeship; of the effectiveness of
quotation without comment; above all of the value of good temper, of
a sense of humour, and of cheerfulness in disappointment, of avoiding
the antagonizing of opponents, of keeping personal and official animos-
ities apart, of accepting temporary defeat without irritation or
disheartenment.'[1] Inter-war feminists tried to be unobtrusive, to cover up
their tracks, if only to prevent their triumphs from seeming too obviously
complete.

Yet historians—especially those who acknowledge the value and
complexity of the art of politics—will wish to ensure that such people are
not forgotten. British feminism between the wars faces the same need that
G. D. H. Cole detected in the Chartist movement when writing his
Chartist Portraits (1941): the need for an introductory survey of the key
personalities who were active in an important but neglected political
episode. Biography will help to arouse interest and to encourage further
research if the subject's life is set fully into context. As Sylvia Pankhurst
wrote, when introducing her fine study of the militant suffragists, 'no
history, whether of movements or of persons, can be truly expressed apart
from the social and economic conditions and thought currents of its time. I
have endeavoured to convey these not through the medium of statistics or
argument, but by incidents in the moving course of life.'[2] The approach
here, as with *Chartist Portraits*, is that of group-biography, which clarifies
the range of the talent available to the public life of a generation and
illuminates the interaction between its leading personalities. Each chapter
can be read on its own, but the many links between the chapters are drawn
tighter by the Introduction, the Conclusion, and the Index.

Most of my subjects reached their peak of influence between the wars,
but the feminist careers of Pankhurst and Fawcett began long before, and
profoundly influenced the next generation. On the other hand, the careers
of Corbett Ashby and Billington-Greig continued for long afterwards. I
have not confined myself to the best-known inter-war feminists. Of my
sixteen subjects, five published autobiographies, eight attracted biogra-

---

[1] C. F. Rogers, preface to A. M. A. H. Rogers, *Degrees by Degrees. The Story of the
Admission of Oxford Women Students to Membership of the University* (1938), pp. v–vi.
[2] E. S. Pankhurst, *The Suffragette Movement. An Intimate Account of Persons and Ideals*
(1931), p. vii.

phers, but six received neither; only eight of the fifteen who could have featured in the *Dictionary of National Biography* do in fact appear there. But others—Teresa Billington-Greig and Eva Hubback, for example—are now almost unknown, yet deserve to be remembered.

This book gives prominence to parliamentary activity—partly because of its intrinsic interest, partly because of parliament's great importance within a democratic society, but mainly because inter-war feminists were much preoccupied with parliament, and knew that women had much to gain from handling politicians skilfully. The inter-war feminist mood of political prudence is a theme that permeates much of what follows. Rare is the person who is temperamentally prudent from birth, or consistently prudent at any one time in all areas of life. Political prudence owes much to political culture, or is encouraged (perhaps only temporarily) by recent collective or individual political experience, and must always be located within its intellectual and social context.

Group-biography cuts across chronology, so it is first necessary to sketch in the essentials of British feminist effort in the period, aided by Figure 1. As a distinct and political movement, British feminism was launched in the 1860s, but the vote was never its sole concern. Victorian feminists reformed the property laws, extended women's educational opportunity, widened their access to careers, and achieved much else besides. The crusade against state-regulated prostitution upheld an equal moral standard, and was championed by Josephine Butler's Ladies' National Association, founded in 1869; a pioneer women's pressure group, the Association was particularly influential on the subsequent tone and tactics of British feminism. It triumphed over British legislation in 1886, but maintained a watching brief thereafter, and concentrated on international work. With two changes of name (to Association for Moral and Social Hygiene in 1915, and to Josephine Butler Society in 1963), it still exists.

Other late-Victorian women mobilized within organizations that were not overtly feminist. Religious women formed the Girls' Friendly Society in 1874 and the Mothers' Union in 1885; the Society had 237,000 members and associates by 1913 and the Union 300,000 members by 1910.[3] And with legislation against electoral corruption in 1883, the political parties felt the need to encourage voluntary help from their women supporters. The Primrose League and the Women's Liberal

---

[3] Statistics from my article, 'For Church, Queen and Family. The Girls' Friendly Society, 1874–1920', *Past and Present*, 61 (Nov. 1973), p. 109; M. Porter and M. Woodward, *Mary Sumner. Her Life and Work* (Winchester, 1921), p. 120.

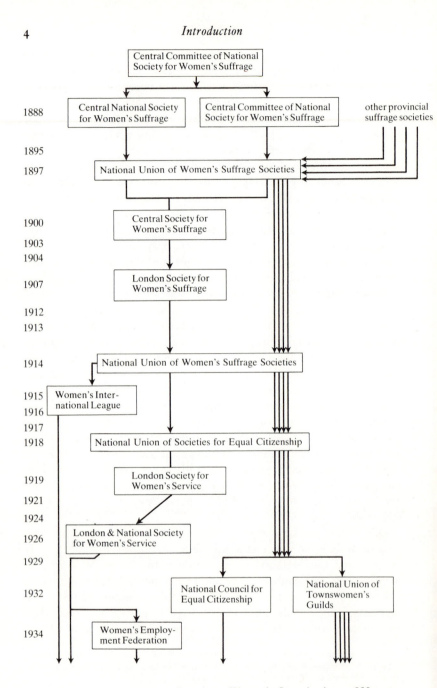

FIGURE 1. Prominent Women's Organizations, 1888–1934.

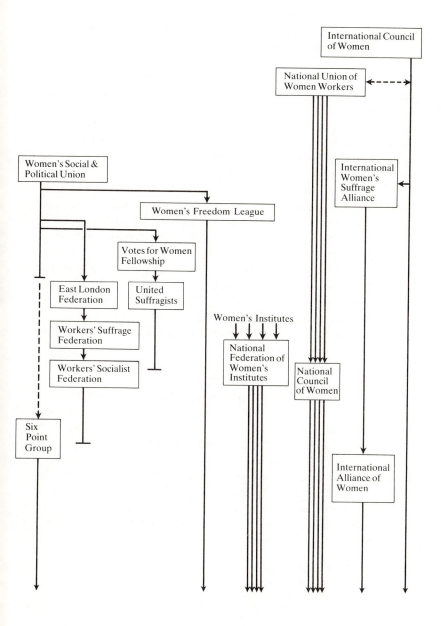

Federation brought women on to the political stage long before they won the vote, and women's organizations were important in creating the Labour Party. The Fabian Women's Group helped to mobilize the middle-class woman; as for working women, the Independent Labour Party (ILP) admitted women equally with men from the start. During the Edwardian period Mary Macarthur, Margaret Bondfield, and others mobilized women trade unionists in large numbers; by 1913 they totalled 356,963. Reinforcement came from that complex of semi-recreational bodies that helped to root socialism within the Edwardian working-class community—most notably from the Women's Co-operative Guild (founded in 1883) and the Women's Labour League (founded in 1906); the Guild had 521 branches and 25,942 members by 1910, the League 122 branches and 4,000 members by 1913.[4]

The better-off late-Victorian woman, too, was mobilizing. In 1895 women active in church work and philanthropy formed the National Union of Women Workers; it was renamed the National Council of Women in 1918, and still exists. A relatively conservative and never strongly feminist organization, it catered for the woman voluntary worker, especially in small towns and rural areas. Still, there were strong pressures within all Edwardian women's organizations, whether feminist or not, to commit themselves to women's suffrage. The Council espoused women's suffrage in 1902, but its international wing—the International Council of Women—moved more slowly; hence the foundation in 1904 of the International Women's Suffrage Alliance (IWSA), renamed the International Alliance of Women (IAW) in 1926, to hold triennial international suffrage conferences.

Edwardian suffragism grew apace, partly because the British women's suffrage societies had come together in 1897 to form a loose federation, the National Union of Women's Suffrage Societies (NUWSS). In 1903 Mrs Pankhurst's Women's Social and Political Union (WSPU) was formed to promote women's interests within the labour movement; its militant tactics gradually distanced it from the older suffrage societies and the labour movement, and steadily contracted its membership and regional scope. Those militants who disliked its increasing autocracy and its widening distance from organized labour broke off to form the Women's Freedom League (WFL) in 1907. Many other suffragist bodies grew up

---

[4] Figures from B. L. Hutchins, *Women in Modern Industry* (1915), p. 177; M. Pugh, 'Labour and Women's Suffrage', in K. D. Brown (ed.), *The First Labour Party, 1906–1914* (1985), p. 239; J. Gaffin and D. Thoms, *Caring and Sharing. The Centenary History of the Co-operative Women's Guild* (Manchester, 1983), p. 268.

between 1906 and 1914, but these three were the most important. This book follows Edwardian practice by applying the term 'suffragist' to any campaigner for women's suffrage, and 'suffragette' to any woman active in the militant sub-section of the suffragist category. By 1914 the non-militant NUWSS had 54,000 members; the publicity-conscious militants, by contrast, did not think they would gain by publishing their own membership figures. Mary Richardson, at the centre of militant activity in 1914, thought that by then 'the actual front-line militants numbered only one thousand odd.'[5] The war gave the Pankhursts an excellent excuse for abandoning an impossible strategy without too much loss of face, and the WSPU was disbanded as a suffrage organization. The non-militants remained active organizing wartime relief work, and played a crucial role in winning the vote in 1916–18. As for the WFL, it survived till 1961.

The war brought further complexities. Those non-militants who wanted the NUWSS to embark on peace work broke off in 1915 to form the British section of the Women's International League for Peace and Freedom, which still exists. Once women had won the vote, many feminists (Kathleen Courtney, for example, or Helena Swanwick) moved off into pacifist and internationalist work, and partly for this reason domestic feminism went into gradual decline. In 1919 the suffragist NUWSS broadened out into the National Union of Societies for Equal Citizenship (NUSEC), which campaigned for several feminist causes in the 1920s. Also in 1919 the Union's London section—the London Society for Women's Suffrage (LSWS)—renamed itself the London Society for Women's Service. Making itself expert on women's employment questions, it gradually resumed its autonomy from NUSEC, and in 1929 became entirely independent. In 1934 it channelled off its careers work into the Women's Employment Federation (WEF), later renamed National Advisory Centre on Careers for Women, which still exists; the parent-body also survives as the Fawcett Society. Small but forceful and interesting was the Six Point Group, founded by Lady Rhondda in 1921. Like NUSEC it campaigned for a package of feminist causes, but its rather strident tone jarred with an inter-war generation of women who wanted organizations of a more recreational and utilitarian kind.

For inter-war Britain gradually unravelled much of the feminist commitment that women's organizations had acquired since the 1880s. Much more popular with inter-war women than the overtly feminist bodies were two organizations that catered for women who acquiesced in

[5] M. R. Richardson, *Laugh a Defiance* (1953), p. 189. NUWSS figures from Pugh, 'Labour and Women's Suffrage', p. 240.

their conventional domestic role but wanted to broaden out their relevant interests and skills. With government help, the non-feminist Women's Institutes spread rapidly after 1915 to help countrywomen during the First World War; their Federation soon became the largest organization for British women. Strongly influenced by the Institutes, the non-feminist Townswomen's Guilds grew up within NUSEC during the late 1920s to perform a similar role for urban and suburban women. So successful were the Guilds that in 1932 NUSEC bifurcated into the National Union of Townswomen's Guilds and the National Council for Equal Citizenship (NCEC). The Council carried on NUSEC's residual feminist work but faded out after the Second World War, whereas the Union went from strength to strength. By 1939 it had 54,000 members in England and Wales, as compared with the Women's Institutes' 238,000.[6]

The feminist lives described in this book were lived within this organizational context. Chapter 1 immediately launches the book on one of its major purposes: to prevent the First World War from artificially separating Edwardian from inter-war feminism. With women's history, as with labour history, it is misleading to place pre-war and post-war history in separate compartments. Neglect of the Edwardian inheritance makes much of what happened between the wars difficult to comprehend; the memory of the Edwardian split between militant and non-militant suffragists hung over British inter-war feminism. Hence the need at the outset to juxtapose the two styles of leadership which provide inter-war feminists with their political exemplars, Millicent Fawcett and Emmeline Pankhurst.

Rare at any time is the individual with all the qualities the effective reformer needs; reforming movements must concentrate and focus many diverse talents, and deploy the right skills at the right moment. Given the divided inheritance of inter-war feminism, this was particularly difficult after 1918, and British feminism failed fully to deploy the talents of Teresa Billington-Greig, the subject of Chapter 2. In an important respect she does not belong in the book at all, for, as her daughter rightly says, 'under no circumstances can I imagine attaching the adjective "Prudent" to my mother'.[7] She is included because her imprudent career illuminates the prudent qualities needed for inter-war political success. She was imaginative, intelligent, and energetic, yet her life-story contains elements of frustration, tragedy, and waste. On the other hand, distance from the

---

[6] Figures from *Townswoman*, July 1939, p. 91; National Federation of Women's Institutes, *22nd Annual Report, 1938–9*, p. 57.

[7] Author's collection: Fiona Billington-Greig to author, 1 Aug. 1984.

political process can sharpen theoretical focus and clarify vision on long-term objectives; she may herself have in some sense failed after 1911, but she penetratingly criticized the successful for the rest of her life. It is the historian's privilege to rescue neglected talent from the enormous condescension of contemporaries.

With Nancy Astor in Chapter 3 we turn to a feminist lacking Billington-Greig's intellect but enjoying all the publicity she was denied. As the first woman to sit in parliament, Astor was very much in the public eye. She has much in common with Pankhurst, yet she worked closely with Fawcett's non-militant disciples; the feminist dimension of her career should be taken seriously, together with its substantial impact on inter-war attitudes to women. Astor was an erratic parliamentarian, yet she supplied things the inter-war feminists badly needed—zest, wealth, vigour, social influence, political connections, humour, and publicity.

If this book has a heroine, she appears in Chapter 4. Eleanor Rathbone was by far the most distinguished feminist of the period—perhaps the most distinguished British feminist the twentieth century has so far seen. She transcended the narrowness that is so often encouraged by campaigns and causes, and made a lasting contribution to British public life. She epitomizes the best qualities of late-Victorian suffragism—seriousness, dedication, rationality, and self-abnegation. Chapter 5 moves into the very different world of organized labour, which took a less individualist and less sex-segregated view of women's interests than many feminist organizations. On some definitions Margaret Bondfield, Susan Lawrence, and Ellen Wilkinson do not qualify as feminists at all, yet their careers reveal even more effectively than Astor's how much women could achieve through party loyalty. They deserve a chapter to themselves because none has so far received an adequate biography, and because their collective parliamentary impact was important and has been neglected.

The remarkable partnership of Pippa and Ray Strachey in Chapter 6 guides the book firmly back into the feminist mainstream; once the vote was won, feminists naturally turned to widening women's job opportunities. The joint campaign of Pippa and Ray for this highlights the inter-war importance of feminist partnerships, together with inter-war feminist skill in the arts of extra-parliamentary politics. This chapter also introduces the new and important theme of feminist historiography. Each generation finds its bearings by re-evaluating its predecessors; re-evaluation was particularly important for inter-war feminists moving towards direct political influence. Ray Strachey was the leading figure here, though always closely monitored from the militant suffragist and labour viewpoint by Sylvia Pankhurst. The inter-war feminist generation did much to get British feminist history on its legs; three of my subjects (Fawcett, Ray Strachey, and Sylvia Pankhurst) published on the history of British feminism, five (Bondfield, Fawcett, Emmeline Pankhurst, and the Pethick-Lawrences) published autobiographies, three (Billington-Greig, Corbett Ashby, and Harben) intended to write them, and two (Billington-Greig and Corbett Ashby) made considerable progress in doing so.

Chapter 7 on Margery Corbett Ashby highlights the importance of diplomacy and the international dimension. Corbett Ashby, Ray Strachey, and Eva Hubback shared Rathbone's best qualities, yet as mothers they faced greater difficulties. With their marked sense of proportion they were able to balance off conflicting obligations and ensure that in their case idealism produced practical achievement.

Chapter 8 makes a different kind of contribution. This book focuses on the pragmatic type of reformer whose idealism is compatible with short-term political effectiveness; yet the pragmatic and the utopian reformer inevitably interact—sometimes fruitfully, sometimes not. Henry Harben the Etonian Communist and Sylvia Pankhurst the champion of Emperor Haile Selassie can no more be described as 'prudent' than Billington-Greig, but their short-term political ineffectiveness did not prevent them from influencing the prudent of their own and later generations. Short-term political influence would have attracted them if it could have been enjoyed on their own terms; in its absence they had no choice but to employ their imagination on keeping alive their ideals for the benefit of posterity, while at the same time trying to prevent present-day compromises from becoming too lukewarm. Other feminist utopian candidates for inclusion were Christabel Pankhurst, Charlotte Despard, Catherine Marshall, Henry Nevinson, and Dorothy Evans; but there are now biographies of the first two, and too little is known about the inter-war careers of the last three. With Sylvia Pankhurst and Henry Harben, however, we have just the right mix: their inter-war careers have an inherent fascination, and interviews can complement documentary material. Sylvia Pankhurst's inclusion also has the advantage of reintroducing the social class theme raised in Chapter 5 and the historiographical theme raised in Chapter 6.

Harben's career introduces one further dimension: the importance and complex situation of the male feminist. No pantheon of British feminists could omit John Stuart Mill, Leonard Courtney, George Meredith, Lord Robert Cecil, and Arthur Henderson, and I have already analysed

Bertrand Russell's feminism elsewhere.[8] Harben's feminist career was confined to his brief but ardent support for suffragism between 1912 and 1914, but he deserves sustained discussion both in his utopian capacity and because his career, like Russell's, illustrates the very limited implications of suffragist commitment for the private life of an inter-war progressive male. In Fred Pethick-Lawrence, Chapter 9 introduces a second Etonian male suffragist, far more consistent than Harben both over time and across the divide between public and private life. He was much more influential than Harben, and in his later career effectively yoked idealism to the art of the possible.

Pethick-Lawrence's career is interesting for another reason: his marriage to Emmeline Pethick revealed the mutual regard and tolerance that are possible within a good marriage. Of my sixteen subjects, six were unmarried, three were widowed for most of their feminist career, and only three—Corbett Ashby and the Pethick-Lawrences—epitomize the potential for happiness of a lifelong partnership between the sexes. Chapter 9 experiments with that most difficult of tasks, portraying the essence of a marriage; it also highlights the mood of partnership between the sexes that has long dominated British feminism. It introduces one further theme: the importance to middle-class feminist achievement of (often female) servants and secretaries, whose labours lie beneath much of what Rathbone, Astor, and the Pethick-Lawrences achieved.

Chapter 10 draws the threads together by discussing that neglected figure Eva Hubback, the inter-war feminist who links up with most of the others, and whose fertile imagination and political sense achieved so much. She has perhaps suffered more than others in this book by her own self-effacement. Her career illustrates the many directions that an imaginative feminist could take after women won the vote, and she reconciled in a unique way the often-conflicting claims of family and feminism. The transition from her to the final chapter, which explores the parallels and linkages between the subjects of this book, is entirely natural.

The portraits cannot of course be exclusively concerned with feminist activity, which grows out of the subject's overall personality and objectives. Where feminism was but one phase within a lifetime's career, I discuss the career as a whole. Where feminism was but one among several reforming interests, I discuss these too. And where private life illuminates the public career, as so often with feminist leaders, I bring the two

---

[8] 'Bertrand Russell. The False Consciousness of a Feminist', in M. Moran and C. Spadoni (eds.), *Intellect and Social Conscience. Essays on Bertrand Russell's Early Work* (Hamilton, Ont., 1984), pp. 157–205.

together. But the portraits are inevitably not rounded or complete; I use each chapter simply to bring out a distinctive dimension of British feminism between the wars. Chapter 1, for instance, is primarily concerned with styles of leadership, Chapters 3 and 5 focus mainly on the parliamentary career, and Chapter 8 is preoccupied with utopianism; but I hope that the book will encourage further research. Much more needs to be known about the local electoral bases of Astor, Rathbone, Wilkinson, and Lawrence. More could be said on the religious interests of Ray Strachey, the Ethiopian adventures of Sylvia Pankhurst, the Labour Party career of Fred Pethick-Lawrence, and the trade-union dimension of Bondfield's life. Indeed the collective achievement of the women MPs between the wars needs fuller coverage than is possible here.[9]

This book omits many feminists with claims to inclusion, most notably Mary Stocks, whose robust common sense, dry humour, and decided Englishness stand out in the memory. Many will recall the combination of intelligence, honesty, courage, and wit that she brought to radio broadcasting in the 1950s; few then recognized how much these qualities owed to the far-off late-Victorian world of Fawcett and Lydia Becker. Yet she left behind two admirable volumes of autobiography, and she did not become a well-known public figure until her feminist career was almost over. Despite a fascinating conversation with her granddaughter, who described how curiosity led Stocks briefly to experiment with cannabis in old age, I eventually had to omit her. A non-militant of great distinction in international relations was Helena Swanwick; her rationalistic attitudes to feminism were courageous and intelligent, and are well documented in her autobiography *I Have Been Young*, but there is insufficient manuscript material for a rounded biography. For similar reasons I eventually decided to omit that progressive Cambridge feminist, Clara Rackham.

I omit Christabel Pankhurst because she became peripheral to British feminism after 1918; besides, her inter-war career has been ably chronicled in David Mitchell's interesting and pioneering book, *The Fighting Pankhursts*. Likewise Gervase Huxley's biography does justice to Lady Denman, who somehow managed to combine presiding over the Women's Institutes with helping to pioneer the birth-control movement. Lady Rhondda—proprietor of the feminist periodical *Time and Tide* and patron of the Six Point Group—perhaps deserved inclusion. Yet no personal papers or records of the Six Point Group survive to complement her revealing autobiography, *This Was My World*. Maude Royden's

---

[9] See my 'Women in a Men's House. The Women MPs, 1919–1945', *Historical Journal*, 29, 3 (Sept. 1986), pp. 623–54.

pioneering work for women in the church was both imaginative and courageous, but Sheila Fletcher's projected biography will assign her far more space than I could afford. Then there is Grace Hadow, who charmed so many of her contemporaries, and whose quiet but substantial achievement set a notable example to professional women. Her relatives were generous with their recollections, but the documentation on her is thin, and in the end she had to go.

Chapter 5 should arguably be complemented by a collective portrait of Conservative MPs, especially as Astor was a decidedly maverick Conservative back-bencher. Their inclusion would be essential if this book aimed to analyse the overall inter-war impact of women, rather than the impact simply of feminists, for Conservative indifference or even hostility to feminism helps to explain why so many women support the Party; Conservative women's contributions to political feminism are usually cautious, and seldom risk simultaneously offending the Party's conservatism about women's social role. The Duchess of Atholl was the best-known anti-feminist woman MP between the wars, but no substantial personal archive survives either for her or for the two other Conservative candidates for inclusion—Irene Ward and Florence Horsbrugh. Besides, Sheila Hetherington is writing Atholl's biography, and the careers of Ward and Horsbrugh continued long after the 1930s. In the end I decided to omit them all.

The last of these arguments for exclusion also applies to the most vigorous and adventurous feminist of all the inter-war women MPs—Edith Summerskill, whose distinguished parliamentary career did not begin till 1938, and who pioneered many late-twentieth-century feminist concerns: reform in family relationships, for example, in the use of language, and in health matters. I thought of including Margaret Wintringham, a keen feminist and prominent inter-war Liberal; her relatives were both tolerant and hospitable when I asked them about her. As the second woman to enter parliament she would have symbolized—in the premature end to her parliamentary career—the loss to British public life (and to feminism) that resulted from the quite unnecessary inter-war split between Liberals and Labour. But in the end I thought Corbett Ashby's eight election defeats as a Liberal candidate made the point eloquently enough.

One comment on method by way of conclusion. 'Oral history' as a technique of historical investigation was perhaps over-sold in the 1970s; the phrase is itself misleading, because no historian relies solely on interviews if other sources can complement them. Interviews with politicians can seldom illuminate the political process, because the politician is too preoccupied with the short term, too self-conscious, too adept at creating images, to make a good informant. Yet the current reaction against the historical fashions of the 1970s should not go too far. After conducting two hundred interviews on women's history since 1974, I remain convinced that tape-recorded conversations, for all their dangers, can be invaluable to the historian; the biographies which follow owe a great deal to them.

Interviews are especially valuable when the informant can describe events that made a deep impact at the time; 'it must all have happened very quickly', wrote Mary Richardson of slashing the Rokeby Venus at the National Gallery in 1914, 'but to this day I can remember distinctly every detail of what happened'. Alone among my informants, Corbett Ashby observed the inter-war feminist world closely and directly, and could talk about it vividly. Her busy life during her nineties did not prevent her from giving me six interviews. Fortunately she did not share the outlook of Mrs Blanco-White, who—covered in rugs and looking rather pale and ghostly at the age of 96—announced her belief 'that posterity has no claims whatsoever', and forbade me to switch on the tape-recorder.[10] If I had only been sufficiently aware at the time, I could have met that extraordinary person Henry Harben; but my preference would be for Teresa Billington-Greig (who died in 1964) and Pippa Strachey (who died in 1968). I am not at all sure that I would have liked Teresa, but their recollections of British feminist history, laced with shrewd analyses of British women's current situation, would have been memorable.

I suspect that both would have relished the opportunities the tape-recorder has now opened up. The autobiographical fragments Billington-Greig left behind in the Fawcett Library show how desperately in old age she wanted to tell her story. It would have been a classic autobiography, yet she found nobody to help her compile it. One reason for welcoming the growth of 'oral history' is that it will prevent such misfortunes in the future. As for Pippa Strachey, she was a delightful personality—witty, highly intelligent, yet also sympathetic. I wish I had been able to hear at first hand the Strachey voice, with its heavy emphasis and unusual modulation of pitch. Pippa was also the most penetrating critic of the militants, and fascinated all who heard her on the subject, yet she never published her thoughts.

Interviews can make a second type of contribution. Beatrice Webb

---

[10] Richardson, *Laugh a Defiance*, p. 168; cf. P. Thompson, *The Voice of the Past. Oral History* (1978), p. 103. Author's interview with Mrs Blanco-White, 11 Feb. 1977, at 44 Downshire Hill, London, NW3.

pointed out that 'it is . . . almost axiomatic with the experienced investigator that the mind of the subordinate in any organization will yield richer deposits of fact than the mind of the principal'.[11] Interviews at one remove from events—with secretaries, employees, and offspring—can vividly illuminate how a person seemed to close colleagues. I have received most generous help from the children of Billington-Greig, Ray Strachey, Corbett Ashby, Harben, and Hubback, and from secretaries and colleagues of Rathbone and Ray Strachey. Among the points that can be illuminated by informants of this sort are dress, household management, and daily office routine. A grasp of these topics is integral to understanding feminist achievement. Dress was often one of the few ways in which inter-war women could express their individuality, and feminists disagreed interestingly about it. As for daily routine, this presented ambitious women with special difficulties.

Another secretary to whom I owe much is the late Gladys Groom-Smith, who died of cancer a few months after she had given me a most full, honest, and sympathetic portrait of the Pethick-Lawrences. She had the greatest affection for them, and gave them dedicated and lifelong service as a secretary who defined her duties in the broadest terms. Yet this did not lead her to think that loyalty required secrecy or biased recollection, and I am sure they would have shared her view. All these tape-recorded interviews, which were financed by a grant from what is now the Economic and Social Research Council, can be consulted (with the interviewees' consent) in the City of London Polytechnic's Fawcett Library, Britain's Mecca for students of women's history. More specific acknowledgements appear on p. vii and in the footnotes.

Although the chapter-headings place each feminist in some sense in a category, all would have bridled at the thought of being neatly pigeon-holed. None was a stereotype, and the historian must struggle to recapture their unique combination of qualities. People are ultimately interesting less for what they achieved than for what they are—and at least two of my subjects (Billington-Greig and Harben) achieved rather little in relation to their talents. If the biographies have been written primarily for what they reveal about trends, pressures, and movements, they also possess an intrinsic interest. For it has rightly been said that 'one of the deepest lessons of oral history is the uniqueness, as well as representativeness, of every life-story. There are some so rare and vivid that they demand recording, whatever the plan.'[12]

[11] B. Webb, *My Apprenticeship* (2nd edn., n.d.), p. 362.
[12] Thompson, *The Voice of the Past*, p. 129.

PLATE I. Millicent Garrett Fawcett (National Portrait Gallery).

I

Two Models of Feminist Leadership

MILLICENT FAWCETT AND
EMMELINE PANKHURST

No generation makes a fresh start in politics. British inter-war feminists were deeply influenced by the memory of Edwardian suffragism, whose strikingly contrasted leaders—Millicent Garrett Fawcett and Emmeline Goulden Pankhurst—shared objectives and strategy, but memorably diverged on tactics. During the 1920s both were admired by their followers and occasionally appeared in public, and both died towards the end of the decade. The NUSEC, post-war descendant of Edwardian non-militant suffragism, embodied Fawcett's cautious statesmanship; Rhondda's Six Point Group carried forward Pankhurst's flair for combative publicity. This polarity even influenced inter-war writing on feminist history; books and reviews by Ray Strachey and Mary Stocks emphasized non-militant suffragist achievement, while Sylvia Pankhurst's books and lawsuits kept the suffragette memory green.

Feminists of the 1920s could regularly have seen Fawcett—a small, slightly bent figure—walking with rather short, quick steps from her home in Gower Street. As she approached the busier Holborn streets, she nimbly negotiated the traffic and astonished passing taxi-drivers with her dexterity. Who would have thought that she had been born as long ago as 1847? She did not look her age; her bright eyes, alert manner, and genial expression reflected her infectious enjoyment of life, her receptiveness to new ideas, her wide interests, and her many hopes for the future. No deep furrows lined her face; instead, her complexion was laced with a network of fine wrinkles.[1] This quietly spoken, equable, and good-humoured woman (nicknamed 'Foss' by her intimates) was welcome in many circles; she loved her many relatives and shared her home with her sister Agnes.

---

[1] This description owes much to my tape-recorded interview with Baroness Stocks, 30 Apr. 1974, at Aubrey Lodge, Aubrey Road, London, W8. See also *Woman's Leader*, 15 Nov. 1929, p. 316, and the undated extract from the *Daily Chronicle* in John Rylands Library, Manchester, Suffragette Collection, Box 1 (Harold Begbie's interview with Fawcett).

Everyone relished her delicate sense of humour. Reciting Kipling one day on the female of the species being more deadly than the male, she came to one of its more blood-curdling comments on woman and delighted her audience by interjecting: 'That's me.'[2]

Inter-war reputations were moulded by one's conduct during the First World War. Fawcett was deeply patriotic, and thought a wholesome internationalism could rest only on a wholesome nationalism; 'without national identity there is no art', wrote Turgenev in a quotation she admired, 'nor truth, nor life nor anything'. Her pronounced Englishness charmed Ray Strachey, her half-American biographer, who once told Fawcett of her affection for England in a moving and affectionate letter and received a heartfelt response. During the Boer War Fawcett braved hostility from progressive friends, and refused to criticize her country; during the First World War, as we shall see, her patriotism embroiled her in painful conflict with much-respected colleagues.[3] But she was no flag-waving jingo; she opposed the idea of giving white feathers to men who were thought to be shirking their duties, regretted the subsequent need for conscription, and repudiated vulgar anti-German feeling.[4]

Yet all this gives too bland an impression, for as a young woman Fawcett's views were so advanced as to seem incongruous in someone who looked so respectable; and although in the year of the Diamond Jubilee she published a sympathetic biography of Queen Victoria, in 1870 she had contemplated joining a Republican Club.[5] Her rugged and quarrelsome self-made father Newson Garrett, wealthy from brewing and malting in Suffolk, had always aimed to do his best for his daughters. Millicent married the rising young radical Henry Fawcett, who triumphed over blindness to become Postmaster-General in Gladstone's second government. He encouraged in her all the middle-class virtues of independence, self-improvement, and self-discipline, and she shocked the more conventional with her progressive ways. Like so many mid-Victorian feminists she was much influenced by the Broad Churchman F. D. Maurice,

---

[2] R. Strachey, *Millicent Garrett Fawcett* (1931), pp. 132–3, discusses her attitude to family. For Kipling, see *Time and Tide*, 16 Aug. 1929, p. 979.

[3] Catherine Marshall MSS, Box 23: Fawcett to Marshall, 18 Feb. 1918; cf. Strachey, *Fawcett*, pp. 139, 203. See also Smith Archives, Oxford: Strachey to Fawcett, 18 Feb. 1918; Fawcett to Strachey, 20 Feb. 1918; I am most grateful to Barbara Strachey for allowing me to quote from this archive, both here and elsewhere in this book.

[4] Strachey, *Fawcett*, pp. 279–80; cf. *Common Cause*, 25 Sept. 1914, p. 453.

[5] City of London Polytechnic, Fawcett Library Archive, 89/1: Helen Taylor to Fawcett, 9 Nov. 1870.

and carried into social questions much of the energy and enthusiasm that earlier generations (including her mother, a strict Evangelical sabbatarian) had devoted to religion. It was a background that nourished self-discipline and public spirit so completely and so early in life that by the 1920s these qualities seemed integral to her personality. Her marked fear of displaying emotion—tried and tested while struggling to cope with her husband's early and unexpected death in 1884—was shared by many non-militant suffragists; it reflects the harsh choices present in a society that never felt really secure from poverty and suffering.

Her faith in British parliamentary institutions and in the basic good sense of the people now seems congenial; less so is her firm and complementary commitment to political economy. This doctrine, too, grew out of Victorian scarcity, and she published a textbook on it in 1872. Throughout her life she nerved herself to shun the easy, sentimental, and self-indulgent remedy, and her stoical outlook on the world was easily misunderstood. She thought that only a sturdy, upstanding, and independent people would escape poverty and guarantee progress. Free education might rescue the pauper's child from the stigma of poverty, she argued in 1870, but it would also weaken the father's incentive to work and his sense of responsibility for his family. There might be a feminist case for family allowances, she admitted in the 1920s, but they might come to resemble those corrupting state hand-outs that the workhouse had curbed after 1834. She felt so strongly about this that, when Rathbone, her successor as president of NUSEC, incorporated family allowances into its programme, she resigned from the board of directors of the Union's periodical, the *Woman's Leader*.[6]

There was nothing meek and mild about Fawcett's feminism; moderate tactics by no means indicate lukewarm commitment. For her, suffragism was almost a religion, and she saw women's emancipation as steadily spreading, like Christianity in the third century. Tolerance was impossible towards anti-feminists, who were pushed firmly beyond her pale. Her feminism reflected all the fierce middle-class commitment to an opportunity society, all the strenuous Liberal faith in liberty and progress, that had motivated the nineteenth century's anti-slavery and free-trade crusades. As she argued in 1868, on the need for improved women's

---

[6] On free education, see her letter to *The Times*, 14 Dec. 1870, repr. in H. and M. G. Fawcett, *Essays and Lectures* (1872), p. 62. For her view of family allowances, see *Woman's Leader*, 30 Jan. 1925, p. 3. For her resignation, *Woman's Leader*, 10 Apr. 1925, p. 84.

education: 'let all, both men and women, have equal chances of maturing such intellect as God has given them.'[7]

Her feminism burned with resentment at the waste and frustration produced by traditional views of women, and was fuelled by two mid-Victorian conversations that she overheard as a young woman. In the first, two guests were dressing for a dance at her parental home. 'Look how he dresses her!' they said, unable to comprehend how a friend could be estranged from a husband who spent so much on her; sixty years later she recalled her reaction: 'I fumed inwardly, but said nothing. I thought I would like to try to make that sort of talk impossible.' In the second, two clergymen's wives in Ipswich station waiting-room were discussing what they were making to sell for charity. Asked which items she found sold best, one of the wives replied, 'Oh! things that are really useful, such as butterflies for the hair.'[8]

Fawcett profoundly affected British feminist strategy in three respects, each deserving brief discussion: she wanted feminists to work closely with men, operated on a very broad front, and shunned any close party connection. On the first point she was firm from the start. She and her sisters owed much to her father's encouragement, and she was deeply influenced by Maurice and Mill. Her husband sedulously encouraged her public work, and in 1872 they jointly published a volume of essays on feminist and other topics. For her, women's suffrage 'was not exclusively a woman's question. The interests of men and women were not opposed . . . if one member suffered, all the members suffered.' The leading Edwardian non-militant suffrage organization, the NUWSS, over which Fawcett presided for so many years, saw itself as a humanitarian rather than feminist body, always welcoming support from men. In March 1910, at the height of the suffrage campaign, she was still preaching the same message: 'I never believe in the possibility of a Sex War. Nature has seen after that: as long as mothers have sons and fathers daughters there can never be a sex war.'[9]

The sheer length and breadth of Fawcett's feminist career must not be forgotten. It was in 1859 that the famous conversation took place when Emily Davies selected women's higher education for herself, leaving the medical profession to Elizabeth Garrett, and the vote to her younger sister

---

[7] M. G. Fawcett, 'The Education of Women of the Middle and Upper Classes', *Macmillan's Magazine*, Apr. 1868, p. 513. For the religious analogy, see Strachey, *Fawcett*, pp. 239–40, and see p. 141 for her conduct towards anti-feminists.

[8] M. G. Fawcett, *What I Remember* (1924), p. 117.

[9] *Women's Suffrage Journal*, 1 Jan. 1872, p. 4. Fawcett Library Autograph Collection, IHi/6895: Fawcett to Lady Frances Balfour, 5 Mar. 1910.

Millicent. Yet Fawcett never focused narrowly on the vote. To the end of her life she was not afraid to attack trade unions and politicians who discouraged women from seeking paid work. She subscribed to the Society for Promoting the Employment of Women in 1867, and always encouraged the young women who wrote for advice on careers, urging them to hold out against family pressures. She herself experienced such pressures, for as early as 1872 London gossips alleged that she was neglecting her daughter Philippa, born four years before.[10]

From the first she recognized the importance of education and health to women's self-realization. In 1868 she repudiated the trivial education then received by so many middle-class girls, which had the effect of confirming anti-feminist belief in women's intellectual inferiority. Only her overriding concern for the vote caused her to turn down the idea, floated in 1884, that she should become Mistress of Girton.[11] As a young wife in Cambridge she went regularly to the local gymnasium, skated, and rode; in later life she relished overseas travel. She grumbled in 1921 about the women's pages of newspapers, with their 'inane observations on the length of skirts or the shape of sleeves'; this was not the complaint of a seventy-year-old indifferent to dress, but the objection felt by a well-dressed and lifelong feminist to mistaken priorities.[12] As for the double standard in morality, she discovered a precursor in Mary Wollstonecraft, to whom (she said) British and American feminism owes as much as political economy owes to Adam Smith.[13] Her introduction of 1891 to Wollstonecraft's *Vindication* is rather a *tour de force*; passing hastily over the morals of the Wollstonecraft circle by which 'one is sickened for ever . . . of the subject of irregular relations', and focusing only on the book's contents, she converts Wollstonecraft into a paragon of Victorian domesticity— repudiating the double standard of morality, elevating women's domestic role, and thus saving British feminism from the 'excesses and follies' witnessed elsewhere.[14]

Fawcett's patriotism and feminism reinforced one another: her recommendations on divorce reform to the royal commission in 1910 assume that Britain leads the world in elevating male to female standards of sexual behaviour. She carefully dissociated suffragism from birth-control and free love. She told Mrs Elmy that her pregnancy before

---

[10] For Philippa, see Strachey, *Fawcett*, pp. 62–3.
[11] Ibid., p. 106.
[12] Smith Archives, Oxford: Fawcett to Ray Strachey, 4 Sept. 1921.
[13] *Vindication* (1891 edn.), p. 30; cf. p. 26.
[14] Ibid., p. 23.

marriage disqualified her as secretary to the Married Women's Property Committee and that she must resign.[15] Like Mrs Butler, 'the greatest woman our country has ever produced', Fawcett opposed state-regulation of prostitution because she thought it endorsed the double standard, but she did not publicly support Mrs Butler's movement for repealing it because she did not want suffragism to make unnecessary enemies.[16] In 1885, though, unlike her sister Elizabeth, she openly championed W. T. Stead for so boldly publicizing the scale of London's white slave traffic; 'I cannot find words to say how I honour and reverence you', she told him, 'for what you have done for the weakest and most helpless among women'. She later braved unpopularity by publicly branding a candidate for parliament as a seducer.[17] When suffragettes in 1912 claimed that non-militant tactics had achieved nothing before 1906, her unfamiliar note of asperity was surely justified.[18]

She reached her non-party standpoint only gradually. When she embarked on public life, political economy and women's suffrage were predominantly Liberal causes. Distaste for Irish nationalist intimidation and resentment at Gladstone's coolness towards her husband caused her to desert the Liberals over Home Rule in 1886. For a time she remained a Liberal Unionist, but her free-trade convictions prevented her from drifting towards Conservatism, and henceforth she was non-party. A non-party post like that of NUWSS president suited her, she said, 'for I could not be a Conservative, because I was not a Protectionist, nor a Liberal, because I was not a Home Ruler, nor a member of the Labour Party, because I was not a Socialist'.[19]

Mill's equal franchise strategy of the 1860s fitted well with her non-party standpoint and was still moulding feminist strategies in the 1920s. It was obviously worth trying to unite suffragists from all parties, and there were two major advantages in the simplicity of a one-clause private member's Bill which would remove the sex-discrimination from the existing or future male franchise: it would preserve the feminist flavour of suffragist campaigning, and it seemed the best way to make progress within a parliament whose time was increasingly monopolized by party-based governments. Yet by the 1880s the equal franchise strategy suffered

[15] Strachey, *Fawcett*, p. 139. Fawcett Library Autograph Collection, IIB/9047: Fawcett to Elmy, 10 Dec. [1875] (copy).

[16] *Common Cause*, 28 Nov. 1913, p. 162. See also Strachey, *Fawcett*, p. 52.

[17] Fawcett Library Autograph Collection, XI: Fawcett to Stead, 9 Nov. 1885. See also Strachey, *Fawcett*, pp. 111, 118, 120.

[18] *Irish Citizen*, 31 Aug. 1912, p. 115.

[19] *Woman's Leader*, 22 Feb. 1924, p. 26. Strachey, *Fawcett*, pp. 125, 128, 152.

from the major drawback that it cut across mounting party loyalties. Conservatives might be happy merely to duplicate the anomalies of the existing property-based franchise, but they disliked the progressive mood of feminism; besides, they feared that a Conservative equal franchise measure might push Liberals towards enfranchising individuals rather than households—that is, towards adult suffrage. Given the Liberal Party's widening working-class connections, this fear was justified, but feminists disliked adult suffragism because it tied women's suffrage too firmly to what then seemed an extreme form of democracy, and distracted suffragists into campaigning simultaneously to enfranchise more men.[20]

Fawcett failed to adapt to this changed situation. Instead of issuing a resolute democratic challenge, she tried to win friends for the equal franchise Bill by diluting it. In the 1880s, for instance, she acquiesced in specifically excluding married women from the suffragists' Bill, and during the suffragist split of 1889 she stood out against those who wanted to strengthen suffragist links with the Liberals.[21] By the Edwardian period the labour movement was beginning to push the Liberals, and even some non-militant suffragists, towards adult suffrage, but she stuck to the old non-party equal franchise strategy.[22] She eventually acquiesced in an alliance of convenience after 1912 between the NUWSS and the Labour Party as the party most sympathetic to women's suffrage, but when wartime coalition changed the political climate she was happy to drop the connection.[23]

Wartime coalition removed these partisan obstacles to women's suffrage; women over thirty gained the vote in the democratic package of franchise reforms for both sexes enacted in 1916–18. By this time, coalition had also come to suit Fawcett's temperament; 'it is such an immense satisfaction to my non-party frame of mind', she told Sir John Simon in December 1918, 'that we owe the suffrage to no one party but to all the parties combined'. At the general election in the same month she praised Lloyd George for what he had done for women, and said that if she

[20] For a fuller elaboration of this argument, see my 'Women's Suffrage at Westminster, 1866–1928', in M. Bentley and J. Stevenson (eds.), *High and Low Politics in Modern Britain* (Oxford, 1983), pp. 80–122.

[21] See, e.g., Fawcett Library Autograph Collection, IA/6617: Fawcett to Edmund [Garrett?], 21 Feb. [end 1885]; *Women's Suffrage Journal*, 1 Jan. 1889, pp. 10–11; 1 May 1889, p. 67.

[22] McMaster University, Hamilton, Ontario, Bertrand Russell Archive, VI, 1: Russell to M. Llewelyn Davies, 27 May 1908, 5 June 1908. Fawcett Library Archive, 89/41: Fawcett to Miss Phillips, 12 Sept. 1909.

[23] Manchester City Library, M50/2/8/1: NUWSS Election Fighting Fund Committee Minutes, 14 July 1915, p. 3.

had twenty votes she would give them all to him.[24] When resigning from the NUWSS as president in 1919 she claimed that 'much of the value of our work has depended on' a non-party standpoint. Proportional representation seemed the natural sequel, for without it she thought the vote would lose much of its value; she therefore urged the Union to make it one of its six objects.[25] Her non-party outlook continued to mislead feminists in the 1920s in so far as it deterred them from adjusting to the restored two-party system after 1922.

Fawcett's feminist leadership was anything but charismatic. Her followers grew to love her, but she discouraged hero-worship and (as her rather pedestrian autobiography shows) she was not interested in herself. Somebody once asked whether she was often told that her speech had changed their lives; 'no, never,' was her prompt reply to what she no doubt regarded as a sentimental and silly question. When asked whether she enjoyed public speaking, she replied: 'no, I do not like it at all. I never like speaking; what I would like to do would be to sit down all day with my books.' Yet she managed to conceal the fact that stagefright brought on 'cold spasms' and even illness, and spoke in public for several decades.[26]

Eloquence requires passion. Fawcett possessed only reason; or, more correctly, she had trained her reason over many years to control her passion. She once told Ray Strachey, who had written a book about American religious fanaticism, that she was glad it had not crossed the Atlantic. Fawcett's straightforward, unadorned speeches were rarely inspiring. Perhaps she prepared them in the wrong way; it was all too deliberate, too systematic, too factual. First she worked over her raw material at her desk and arranged her ideas; then she sat down somewhere with her needlework and (as she put it) stitched them firmly into her mind.[27] It was as though she was writing an article rather than working herself up to inspire. Yet if her speeches did not excite when delivered, they were influential when printed, and it was in propagandism that her major contribution lay. She well knew the need for it, for before 1914 she consistently opposed a referendum on women's suffrage because she knew the feminists would lose it.[28]

Fawcett somehow found time to publish several books, many periodical

[24] Fawcett Library Archive, 89/149: Fawcett to Simon, 9 Dec. 1918.

[25] *Common Cause*, 10 Jan. 1919, p. 467. For proportional representation, ibid., 28 Mar. 1919, p. 619.

[26] *Common Cause*, 9 Apr. 1914, p. 6. Strachey, *Fawcett*, p. 131.

[27] Smith Archives, Oxford: Fawcett to Strachey, 2 Oct. 1927. Strachey, *Fawcett*, p. 229.

[28] See my *Separate Spheres. The Opposition to Women's Suffrage in Britain* (1978), p. 159.

articles, and numerous letters to the editor. She accumulated cuttings on women's suffrage, and became adept at spotting immediately the word 'women' when reading a column of *The Times*. She then marked up and annotated her extracts and sent them on to colleagues.[29] Only intense self-discipline and planning of time made all this possible. She was always punctual, rose early, and replied promptly to letters. Her ideas were not original, but their repetition over a long period made feminist ideas seem familiar. 'You have been a great help to us all through,' wrote Mrs K. W. Sheppard from New Zealand in the year when its women won the vote; 'we have had your addresses to quote from, and your clear logical writing in various papers and journals, and, if you will pardon the personality, we have been able to point to you as one of the "womanly" women, whenever it has been said that advocates of the Suffrage were "Wild Women".'[30]

Fawcett's long years of leadership must often have been a strain, yet she never grumbled, even in her memoirs. Perhaps her wide interests—her love of music, her extensive reading, her travels, and her enthusiasm for painting—enabled her to rise above the short-term and the unimportant, single-mindedly guiding her followers towards a long-term goal. Her calm rationality gave her the courage to guide the NUWSS over many hurdles, the undeviating purpose that rises above disputes. She deployed her common sense, humour, and sense of proportion to moderate the quarrels of others. She knew where wounded pride needed to be salved, when to defuse dispute by producing one of her humorous red-herrings of an anecdote, and how to alleviate low spirits by bringing out her list of hopeful developments. She was sceptical of passion and sentiment, yet her faith never wavered. She was rock-solid in a crisis, calm in the most discouraging situations. Many years later a colleague recalled how a serious setback had once plunged a suffragist committee into gloom; then Fawcett arrived 'outwardly serene and unperturbed, as if nothing had happened', and the committee spontaneously broke into cheering. 'By her complete self-control we were reminded that nothing was changed by our disappointment—that we had simply to continue our long struggle towards a goal as clear and compelling as it had ever been.'[31]

For suffragists aiming to prepare the rank and file for citizenship, this

---

[29] *Woman's Leader*, 15 Nov. 1929, p. 315.

[30] Manchester City Library, M50/2/1/204: K. W. Sheppard to Fawcett, 4 Oct. 1893; cf. Fawcett Library Archive, 90/211: Vida Goldstein to Fawcett, 20 July 1920.

[31] *Common Cause*, 8 June 1917, p. 97; cf. p. 99. See also *Woman's Leader*, 5 Dec. 1924, p. 361; M. Stocks, *My Commonplace Book* (1970), p. 72.

inability to fascinate, this refusal to domineer, had its virtues. Further-more Fawcett's long political experience and high political standing gave her access to the governing élite. Like her sister Elizabeth, she defused hostility with her self-control and her conformity on family matters and dress. 'She is a very nice attractive ladylike little person', wrote Gladstone's private secretary in 1882, 'and bears no trace of the "strong-minded female" about her'. She also contributed more tangibly: she did not hesitate sometimes to request specific sums from sympathizers on her lists, and she herself gave generously to London feminism in the early 1920s.[32]

A feminist whose humane outlook grew out of mid-Victorian Liberal optimism might have been expected utterly to repudiate suffragette militancy, especially when her own influence was challenged by Pankhurst's provincial and relatively inexperienced eruption on to the London suffragist stage. Yet in October 1906 Fawcett confessed that the suffragettes had done more in the last twelve months to make women's suffrage practical politics than the non-militants in the same number of years.[33] Subsequent suffragette depreciation of her past achievement and obstruction of her current work could well have goaded her into petty retaliation; yet she never lost her dignity, gave credit where it was due, kept up the suffragist pressure on the government, refused to break feminist ranks, and quietly encouraged her followers in their own methods.

Not until July 1908, when the suffragettes moved on to stone-throwing, did she repudiate their tactics as setting a bad example to the London 'roughs', and as threatening the civilized parliamentary government from which women had so much to gain; instead of citing male precedents for violence, she argued, women should set a better example.[34] Even after 1908 she was moved by suffragette martyrdom and frequently refused to condemn militancy. Compelled at last to do so, she blamed government insensitivity for bringing things to this pass. She reproached the Asquith government in deputation after deputation: by failing to reward non-militant tactics it fomented the militancy it subsequently repressed.

---

[32] *The Diary of Sir Edward Hamilton, 1880–1885* (ed. D. W. R. Bahlman, 1972), i, 287; cf. Swanwick, *Time and Tide*, 16 Aug. 1929, p. 979. For Fawcett's skill at fund-raising, see R. Strachey, *Women's Suffrage and Women's Service* (1927), pp. 34–5. For her personal generosity, *Woman's Leader*, 27 July 1923, p. 214.

[33] A. Rosen, *Rise Up, Women! The Militant Campaign of the WSPU, 1903–1914* (1974), p. 75; cf. pp. 79–80.

[34] Fawcett Library Autograph Collection, IC/6755: Fawcett to Miss P. Strachey, 12 Oct. 1908. See also *The Times*, 9 Mar. 1912, p. 7.

'Statesmen are the physicians of the body politic', she said in 1913, 'and a wise physician will treat not only the symptom, but its root and cause.'[35]

The First World War challenged her liberal optimism still more directly, and at first seemed likely to postpone women's suffrage indefinitely. In the early months, she later recalled, 'I was more miserable than I had ever been before in my life. I almost wished myself dead with all those I loved who had died, and for the first time felt thankful that they had died and had thus been taken out of the intense misery into which the country was plunging at that time.'[36] Yet she made the best of things by encouraging the non-militants to help the war effort; for her, women's interests required liberty and democracy to prevail over Prussianism.

In these difficult years her powers of leadership were tested more stringently than ever before—first by a split within the National Union, and then by government offers of a compromise settlement on franchise reform. In 1915 leading colleagues wanted the Union to repudiate the old diplomacy, but this roused all Fawcett's determination born of an outraged patriotism and an offended common sense. Diplomacy had not failed, she said; Germany had repudiated it. A women's peace congress at the Hague could never transcend national rivalries, whereas 'a *Peace Congress of Women* dissolved by violent quarrels would be the laughing stock of the world'. Suffragists must not be seduced into taking up tangential causes.[37] Helped by relative newcomers to the Union like Ray Strachey and Mary Stocks, she forced her opponents to secede into the Women's International League. But the dispute aroused strong feeling, and critics who later made friendly private overtures to her encountered the unforgiving and unyielding side of her nature.[38]

In 1917 the government offered to enfranchise all adult men and most women over thirty. Fawcett saw at once that this was a moment to accept half a loaf instead of no bread, and worked with Lloyd George to outmanœuvre three unhelpful groups: the anti-suffragists, the followers of Emmeline and Christabel Pankhurst (who saw women's suffrage as a side-issue at this point in the war), and arch-democrats like Sylvia Pankhurst, for whom nothing short of 'human suffrage' would do. When

[35] *Common Cause*, 28 Feb. 1913, p. 801.

[36] Ibid. 21 Mar. 1919, p. 606.

[37] Fawcett Library Autograph Collection, IK/7086: Fawcett to Mrs Catt, 15 Dec. 1914. See also *Common Cause*, 12 Feb. 1915, p. 712; Catherine Marshall MSS, Box 20: Fawcett to Marshall, 6 Mar. 1915 (roneo'd copy).

[38] Fawcett Library Archive, 89/124: Fawcett to Miss Leaf, 3 Nov. 1916 (copy). Catherine Marshall MSS, Box 20: Swanwick to Marshall, 22 Mar. 1915, and unknown correspondent to C. Macmillan, 15 June 1915 (copy); Box 23: K. D. Courtney to Marshall, 5 Mar. 1918.

women's suffrage at last got through the House of Lords in 1918, Ray Strachey went off to bring Fawcett the good news, and found her sitting by the fire in a dressing-gown; as Ray told her mother, 'we couldn't either of us believe it was true'. Fawcett told a colleague she was so relieved that it seemed like a dream.[39]

Fawcett did not immediately cease feminist work on resigning as president of the NUWSS in the following year; she continued to attend NUSEC council meetings and social functions, and saw her life's work completed when the franchise was equalized in 1928. In retirement she reaped admiration from her non-militant colleagues; for them she was to women's enfranchisement what Wilberforce had been to anti-slavery or Mazzini to the rebirth of Italy. And as Ray Strachey told her, 'you have not only done the thing, but shown how such things should be done: and the way has been as important as the end.'[40] Quite apart from her role in getting the vote, her long and democratically organized suffragist campaign had itself built up a powerful feminist structure; if women's victory had come as quickly and easily as in some other countries, British inter-war feminism would have been the weaker.

Yet there were dissenting voices. 'Fawcett is all brains but utterly without *heart*', wrote an exasperated militant in 1909, 'and that is why she has been fifty years getting the vote.' Harold Laski told former suffragettes in 1932 that 'no reason makes its impact upon public opinion until men are driven by the circumstances in which reason presents itself to pay attention to the causes that reason seeks to promote'; Fawcett had merely stated the case, whereas others had forced politicians to act upon it, and her contribution towards winning votes for women had been 'small indeed'.[41] Ray Strachey's biography drove Vera Brittain almost to distraction: 'the reader longs almost with desperation for Mrs Strachey to become violently critical or Dame Millicent to burst the bonds of her habitual commonsense and moderation, and exhibit unreasonable passion on any subject whatsoever,' but 'neither of these desirable surprises occurs'.[42]

[39] Smith Archives, Oxford: Strachey to her family, 11 Feb. 1918. Museum of London, Helen Fraser Collection: Fawcett to Fraser, 28 Feb. 1918.

[40] Smith Archives, Oxford: Strachey to Fawcett, 18 Feb. 1918. See also *Common Cause*, 10 Jan. 1919, p. 467.

[41] B[ritish] L[ibrary], Arncliffe-Sennett Collection, VIII: Mrs Arncliffe-Sennett's endorsement on letter of 25 Sept. 1909 received from Fawcett. Museum of London, Suffragette Collection, Z6061: H. Laski's typescript on 'The Militant Temper in Politics', pp. 9, 8.

[42] Reviewing Strachey's *Fawcett* in *Week-End Review*, 18 July 1931, p. 86.

PLATE 2. Emmeline Pankhurst leaves a London station for the provinces, c.1910 (London Museum).

We must now turn to a very different style of feminist leadership, at least as green in the inter-war feminist memory—Mrs Pankhurst's. The two women might have been born for contrast. The subversive firebrand who announced in 1912 that 'the argument of the broken pane of glass is the most valuable argument in modern politics' was imprisoned fourteen times, hunger-struck, and frequently emerged from prison haggard and fainting. She was a woman of dramatic gestures, exciting incidents, police raids, cloaks and daggers; her sudden shifts of policy took the Edwardians' breath away, and in 1912 she likened the suffragette struggle to the Mexican civil war. 'I incite this meeting to rebellion', she told a suffragette meeting in the Albert Hall amid 'tremendous applause and great enthusiasm'.[43]

Yet whereas Fawcett was more revolutionary than she appeared, the reverse applies to Pankhurst, whose interest in clothes, zest for window-shopping, and love of Paris bring her much closer to the Edwardian female stereotype. In small matters she was essentially a conformist, with natural good manners and a concern for her appearance—a woman who walked out of a socialist meeting in 1890 because she found a bug on her glove. Her personal fastidiousness enabled her, after hours of travel, to 'arrange herself' in two minutes and emerge from a train looking impeccable.[44] Some even saw her as reflecting the female stereotype also in her impulsive irrationality. Hers was a temperament of storms and sunshine—a mind that did not deliberate calmly, but leapt to sudden conclusions.[45] Yet more than once she rightly emphasized that she was by nature a law-abiding person. How ever did such a woman become leader of such a movement?

Partly from family tradition. Her grandfather had fled before the militia at Peterloo, and she was so influenced in childhood by *Uncle Tom's Cabin* that fifty years later she could recall its stories as freshly as if they had been the news of the day.[46] The Gouldens' English radicalism was reinforced by early exposure to French radicals, for as a fourteen-year-old she accompanied her father to Paris. There she embarked on a thirty-year friendship with the Communist's daughter Noémie Rochefort; she

[43] *Votes for Women*, 23 Feb. 1912, p. 319. *Suffragette*, 25 Oct. 1912, p. 17. For Mexico, see P[ublic] R[ecord] O[ffice] HO 45/231366/29: P. C. Renshaw's shorthand notes on the meeting at Chelsea Town Hall on 21 Feb. 1912, p. 2.

[44] See the excellent portrait of Pankhurst in *Votes for Women*, 14 June 1912, p. 601. See also E. S. Pankhurst, *Suffragette Movement*, pp. 90, 111.

[45] C. Pankhurst, *Unshackled. The Story of How We Won the Vote* (1959), p. 17; cf. T. Billington-Greig, *The Militant Suffrage Movement. Emancipation in a Hurry* (Frank Palmer, n.d.), p. 197.

[46] E. Pankhurst, *My Own Story* (1914), p. 2.

acquired a lifelong taste for things French, learned to speak the language fluently, and returned to Manchester wearing her hair and clothes like a Parisian. Then she married Dr Richard Pankhurst, whose views seemed extreme even to the radicals of late-Victorian Manchester.

Pankhurst often denied that her suffragism originated in personal suffering, yet as a young woman she undoubtedly resented some of women's disabilities. She witnessed the storms when her mother produced household bills for her father to pay. She was furious with him for refusing a dowry when she fell in love with a Frenchman, and later broke permanently with her father when he failed to keep his promise to endow her with property on marrying Dr Pankhurst, of whom he disapproved; for the rest of her life she thought the dowry the best way to give married women a measure of independence.[47] Her marriage to Dr Pankhurst was very happy, and we owe a fine description of it to her second daughter Sylvia. 'He was always her lover,' Sylvia recalled half a century later; 'I can see him, with the eye of memory, holding her at arm's-length and with a joyous admiration, to view, at her demand, some new or transformed dress'. 'Where's my lady?' he would say, on returning home from work; and when she had been away and was late in returning, he would pace to and fro, 'whistling always a single valse tune which had tender associations with his courtship, and from which, as his impatience grew, the melody would fade away'.[48]

So fond of him was she that, when in prison long after his death (in 1898) she dreamed that his kind face was looking down on her. Her late-Victorian radicalism was reinforced by the conviction that his political opponents had treated him unfairly, and her radical connections in their turn alerted her to the sufferings of poorer women. She told Philip Snowden in 1905 that she longed to get the suffrage question settled so that women could get into real social work: 'I am so weary of it and the long long years of struggle[,] first against ridicule and contempt and now of indifference and apathy.'[49] Her suffragette speeches often recall her days as a poor law guardian and registrar of births and deaths. There were the low-paid but respectable aged women condemned to the workhouse only

---

[47] E. S. Pankhurst, *Suffragette Movement*, pp. 55, 68. E. S. Pankhurst, *The Life of Emmeline Pankhurst* (1935), p. 14. R. West, 'Mrs Pankhurst', in *The Post Victorians* (1933), pp. 482, 484.

[48] E. S. Pankhurst, in Countess of Oxford and Asquith (ed.), *Myself When Young. By Famous Women of To-day* (2nd edn. 1938), p. 260. C. Pankhurst, *Unshackled*, p. 34. E. S. Pankhurst, *Suffragette Movement*, p. 4.

[49] P. Snowden, *An Autobiography*, i (1934), p. 283. See also E. S. Pankhurst, *Suffragette Movement*, pp. 64, 74, 77, and her *Emmeline Pankhurst*, p. 132.

because unable to save for old age; there were the frequent conspiracies between doctors and husbands to conceal from the wife that her baby had died of inherited syphilis; there was the judge of assize found dead in a brothel, an incident which she insisted on mentioning during her trial at the Old Bailey in 1913, despite the judge's warning that she was 'doing herself no good' thereby; and there was the pregnant thirteen-year-old with venereal disease whom she had seen playing with a doll—'Was not that enough', she asked suffragettes at the Albert Hall in 1912, 'to make me a Militant Suffragette?'[50]

One further nagging and lifelong personal deprivation lay behind Pankhurst's suffragism: shortage of money. But for this, her manners, looks, and personal distinction would have enabled her to shine socially. She was not extravagant or grasping, but she had little business sense, and her continuous financial worries during married life worsened in widowhood. In this her early life contrasts markedly with Fawcett's; it caused her later life to diverge still further, because the impecunious provincial middle-class wife of a failed radical candidate could mount London's suffragist stage only through adopting unorthodox tactics. When she made an unsolicited intervention during a suffragist deputation to MPs early in 1904, suffragists saw her as an impertinent interloper who made enemies for the cause.[51] For their London début to succeed, the Pankhursts needed to parade their Manchester-based irreverence in a theatre of their own.

At her trial in 1912 Pankhurst recalled the time when she was wondering whether to base her WSPU on London. 'What is there in our power to do?' she had asked her eldest and favourite child Christabel; 'We are not rich people. We are already doing without a great many of the things which we hitherto thought necessary. Few people have hitherto helped us with money. How can we expand our work?'[52] At this point, Christabel's influence becomes decisive, for Emmeline Pankhurst found in her the ally she needed to replace her husband. Their strange relationship involved a mutual dependence that was psychologically damaging to Christabel and in the end physically damaging to her mother.

At first destined for the ballet, Christabel had eventually opted for a law degree—a training unlikely to soften the personality of an assertive and opinionated child. Mother henceforth deferred to daughter on short-term strategy, crediting her with political genius and tolerating no criticism of

[50] *Suffragette*, 11 Apr. 1913, p. 422. *Votes for Women*, 25 Oct. 1912, p. 58.
[51] E. Pankhurst, *My Own Story*, pp. 39–40.
[52] *Votes for Women*, 24 May 1912, p. 532.

her; daughter deferred to mother on long-term objectives, while ruthlessly exploiting her mother's talents for the cause. Each admiringly used the other for her own purposes in an almost proprietorial manner, warding off rivals for affection, whether political or personal. Each relished the other's company, and Emmeline Pankhurst delighted in those brief intervals between militant episodes when she could stay with Christabel in her Paris flat, tidy her up, visit the theatre, and go window-shopping. Within this formidable partnership, the mother was the extremist, the idealist whom those in the know nicknamed 'enfant terrible', whereas the daughter was cautious, calculating, and in some respects cynical.[53]

Allegations that the Pankhursts made money from suffragette agitation were unfair, for it soon deprived Emmeline of her post as Registrar; nor did her finances at first improve when her crusade moved to London. But the Pethick-Lawrences helped her set a mass movement on its feet, and as the children grew up her personal needs became less pressing. In old age her problems returned with a vengeance; her testimonial fund in the early 1920s did not reach £3,000—much less than Fawcett's—so that her last days were spent in furnished accommodation above a barber's shop in the Ratcliffe Highway, Wapping. Sylvia describes her flinging wide her arms within her cramped flat 'with the old, impetuous cry: "I hate small rooms!"'[54] During her last illness begging letters were sent to Astor, and Christabel was eventually enabled to isolate her mother from her London friends into the Hampstead nursing home where she died; at her death her entire estate amounted to only £73.[55]

In their looseness to party attachment, Fawcett and Pankhurst are at one—Fawcett moving from far left to centre, Pankhurst moving from far left to far right. Their suffragist strategy is also similar; although Pankhurst in the 1880s was less inclined to compromise, and repudiated expedients such as excluding the married woman from the vote, she too preferred the equal franchise to the adult suffrage strategy. Both feared a repetition of events in 1884, when feminist campaigning had merely been followed by an enlarged male franchise. Pankhurst's WSPU was at first designed as an appendage to the Labour Representation Committee (precursor of the Labour Party), and she originally wanted it to promote

---

[53] Bodleian Library, Oxford, MS Eng. Misc. e 618/1: Nevinson Diary, 23 Dec. 1913. E. Pethick-Lawrence, *My Part in a Changing World* (1938), p. 278.

[54] E. S. Pankhurst, *Emmeline Pankhurst*, p. 174. See also D. Mitchell, *The Fighting Pankhursts. A Study in Tenacity* (1967), p. 125; E. Smyth, *Female Pipings in Eden* (1933), p. 266.

[55] Mitchell, *Fighting Pankhursts*, pp. 198–9. University of Reading Library, Nancy Astor MSS 1416/1/1/509: Miss Kerr to Mrs Deacon, 29 Apr. 1928. Smyth, *Pipings*, p. 271.

social as well as political causes; but she soon began to diverge. Philip Snowden told Ramsay MacDonald in November 1903 that she was quite unreasonably demanding freedom to say what she liked from the platform at the ILP's Free Trade Hall meeting; she was 'simply a monomaniac at present', he grumbled, 'engaged actively in an organized attempt to alienate the women fr[om] the ILP on the Woman Question'. The labour movement's commitment to the adult suffrage mode of enfranchising women edged Pankhurst rightwards.[56] Here she lost a much larger opportunity than Fawcett ever sacrificed, for an adult suffrage strategy could have drawn progressives and feminists together. Not till 1913–14, by which time militancy had seriously distracted and alienated opinion, did her daughter Sylvia begin to get the suffragists back on to politically practicable lines.

Yet Pankhurst made one important advance on Fawcett's strategy. She came to despise the annual charade whereby allegedly sympathetic yet in reality do-nothing back-benchers contented themselves merely with assuring Fawcett's non-militants of their sympathy; she saw that back-benchers would never unaided get a simple removal of the sex discrimination from the franchise, and demanded a government measure. Yet she did not go far enough. Instead of recommending women's suffrage in the adult suffragist mode that a Liberal government could espouse, she thought militancy could intimidate it into the equal franchise measure that it saw as undemocratic. Pankhurst was too eager for the fray, too prone to the dramatic gesture, to grasp the realities of the parliamentary situation. 'It is the Government alone that we regard as our enemy', she declared in 1912, 'and the whole of our agitation is directed to bringing just as much pressure as necessary upon those people who can deal with our grievance.'[57] Such a strategy might at first publicize the cause, but it ultimately produced a sequence of pseudo-revolutionary gestures which made enemies without instilling fear, and which eventually cut her off from the labour movement.

The First World War gave her a prize excuse for climbing down from an impossible strategy, but in doing this she and Christabel abandoned much else besides; whereas Fawcett kept women's suffrage firmly in view, Pankhurst allowed the cause to slip slowly down her list of priorities. She had disliked the Germans ever since visiting France in the 1870s, and her

---

[56] PRO 30/69 (MacDonald papers), 1147/155: Snowden to MacDonald, 13 Nov. 1903; cf. BL Add[itional] MSS 47453 (Elmy Papers), fo. 210: Elmy to McIlquham, 9 Dec. 1903. E. S. Pankhurst, *Suffragette Movement*, pp. 180–1.

[57] E. Pankhurst, *My Own Story*, p. 234.

wartime oratory quickly identified France as the feminine state threatened by 'the over-sexed, that is to say over-masculine, country of Germany'.[58] No doubt feminism required the defeat of Germany, but Pankhurst's energetic pursuit of victory blinded her to the domestic opportunities whose uniqueness Fawcett rapidly grasped. At first Pankhurst blocked the suffragist road by having it announced in parliament that her Union would not use the women's demands to block servicemen's votes. It is not surprising that in April 1917 Ray Strachey, organizing a crucially important suffragist deputation to Lloyd George, found that 'one and all objected to Mrs Pankhurst, and I had to go and see her and make an arrangement by which she came in, but was not part of, the deputation.'[59]

In the manifesto of the Women's Party, for which Christabel was the sole candidate at the 1918 general election, women's claims come low down on the list. Pankhurst was equally unhelpful in the campaign to equalize the franchise in the 1920s. She told the Six Point Group in 1925 that such a dangerous period in the world's history was not the time to campaign for more women's votes,[60] and it was Fawcett's disciples who ultimately won votes for women between twenty-one and thirty in 1928. Pankhurst's wartime preoccupations had drawn her still closer to the Conservatives, and on 3 May 1926 she told Astor she wanted to help organize relief work during the General Strike. 'How I wish that I could do what I did at the outbreak of war,' she wrote, 'that is set a whole organization to work . . . Do use me if you can.' She was adopted as Conservative candidate for Whitechapel and St George's in the following year. By now her concern for empire, her distaste for socialism, and her support for Baldwin had displaced feminism from her list of priorities. Baldwin wanted to conciliate Astor (a restive centrist at this time) and believed in letting bygones be bygones; besides, Pankhurst despite her age could help the Party cultivate a progressive image and so attract votes from women and former Liberals. To her left-wing daughter Sylvia all this seemed 'utterly amazing, infinitely sad'.[61]

The disillusion was mutual. Shortly before marrying, Pankhurst had proposed dispensing with legal formalities so as to show independence of

---

[58] *Suffragette*, 23 Apr. 1915, p. 26; cf. *Daily Sketch*, 23 Mar. 1915, p. 4. See also West, 'Mrs Pankhurst', p. 496.

[59] Smith Archives, Oxford: Strachey to her mother, 1 Apr. 1917. Bellairs, H[ouse of] C[ommons] Deb[ates], 16 Aug. 1916, c. 1960.

[60] Mitchell, *Fighting Pankhursts*, p. 156.

[61] Nancy Astor MSS 1416/1/1/507: Pankhurst to Astor, 3 May 1926. E. S. Pankhurst, *Emmeline Pankhurst*, p. 172.

spirit and solidarity with the sufferings of unhappy wives.[62] She did not repeat such boldness; henceforward on moral issues, like Fawcett, she knew it was important not to offend too many susceptibilities at once. In the early 1920s she went on lecture-tours in Canada to promote higher moral standards, and her distress in 1928, when Sylvia publicized the birth of her illegitimate child, reflects what must have seemed a double-dyed betrayal. 'She felt the disgrace on her husband's name', wrote her solicitor Arthur Marshall, 'and the dread of taunts from Communist interrupters when she spoke from the platform.' Ethel Smyth thought Sylvia's conduct had helped to strike down her mother at a moment of physical weakness, for she died shortly afterwards.[63]

So Pankhurst's strategic advance on Fawcett did not go far enough, and between 1912 and 1914 her militancy actually held back the cause. And whereas Fawcett never allowed suffragism to slip among her priorities, there are times (some of them crucial) when suffragism fell almost below Pankhurst's horizon. While Fawcett was if anything too stolidly consistent in her political outlook, Pankhurst was almost cavalier in her political inconsistencies, looking only to the present and the future. Yet to leave the matter there would be greatly to underestimate Pankhurst's stature and achievement, for the essence of her style of leadership has yet to be discussed. She remains a major figure in the British feminist revolution as much for her personal qualities and for the myth she became as for what she achieved during her lifetime.

What H. W. Nevinson called 'that mingled look of pathos, appeal, the sorrow of the world, a courteous refinement, and an indomitable resolve' continued to haunt her admirers long after her death.[64] Suffragettes who discussed her with me in their extreme old age were still haunted by her outstanding qualities of leadership. Many young people no doubt projected on to her the qualities they admired, or erected her into the guiding figure they felt they needed in their lives—for this was a time when values and institutions were changing even more rapidly than usual, yet when established figures were losing their traditional authority. 'She was a lovely, motherly woman,' Mrs Cohen, the Leeds suffragette, told me; 'after my own mother, in my eyes, she had a heart; she was typical to me of a lovely woman.' Several politicians were disgusted at the way she seemed to be leading young girls astray and exploiting their idealism

---

[62] E. S. Pankhurst, *Suffragette Movement*, p. 56.

[63] Nancy Astor MSS 1416/1/2/49: Marshall to Smyth, 4 July 1928; cf. ibid.: Smyth to Astor, 4 and 6 July 1928; Mitchell, *Fighting Pankhursts*, p. 197.

[64] *Votes for Women*, 31 May 1912, p. 565.

when, as an older woman, she should know better. The career of Mary Richardson, who slashed the Rokeby Venus in the National Gallery, illustrates well the devotion Pankhurst could inspire; Richardson's almost personal fealty to her leader caused her to interpret a command from Pankhurst, however distasteful, almost as a personal honour. 'I want women that can't be spared,' Pankhurst would say at London suffragette meetings, and she won them.[65]

What was her secret? When asked, half a century later, to sum her up in a word, the suffragette Jessie Kenney replied 'dignity'.[66] She was not a large or intimidating woman; slight in build, she long retained the capacity, also possessed by her daughter Sylvia, of looking strangely young. But she was regal in bearing, a great actress whose father had been well known on Manchester's amateur stage, and whose sister Mary had longed to take up acting as a profession. Pankhurst knew how important were quite small matters of presentation: suffragette organizers' clothes, for instance, and the detailed staging of her public meetings. She wore her clothes with style, and preserved her dignity in the most impossible situations. Prison warders quailed at the thought of forcibly feeding her, and in the famous photograph outside Buckingham Palace, where she is being gripped round the waist by a burly policeman, she still somehow manages to seem triumphantly majestic. For the Pankhursts, politics and theatre were never distinct; they knew how to capture the headlines, though without always distinguishing between publicity and notoriety.

Rhetorical tricks were not Pankhurst's secret. She used little gesture beyond occasionally stretching out both hands, as in her statue at Westminster. Nor does her magnetism lie in the content of her speeches, which were not powerfully reasoned, and usually involved no more than appealing to familiar experience and common humanity. Her impact at meetings stemmed from the combination of personality, appearance, and expression with what Sylvia called 'her wonderful voice, poignant and mournful, and shot with passion'. She did not use notes, and at the age of seventy she spurned the microphone when addressing a mass meeting in the Albert Hall.[67] Her voice was quiet and low in tone, but it was also flexible, and she knew how to vary emotions and pitch. A single speech was

---

[65] Author's tape-recorded interviews with Mrs Leonora Cohen, 26 and 27 Oct. 1974, at 9 Whitehall Road, Rhos-on-Sea, North Wales.

[66] Museum of London, David Mitchell Collection, 73.83/48: Mitchell's interview with Jessie Kenney, 24 Mar. 1964.

[67] E. S. Pankhurst, *Emmeline Pankhurst*, p. 54. See also David Mitchell Collection, 73.83/36(f): D. Spencer to Mitchell, 4 Jan. 1965.

enough to ensure that another great actress, Sybil Thorndike, was (as she told me in extreme old age) 'bouleversée' into the movement. 'One never thought of her as an advocate in her own cause,' wrote H. N. Brailsford; 'she was Maternity pleading for the race.'[68]

Non-militants noted Pankhurst's close rapport with suffragette audiences; by sharing their prison experience she did wonders for rank-and-file morale. It was exhilarating to find women of all classes, ages, and situations collaborating in a crusade that was always exciting and sometimes dangerous. Pankhurst took pride in those she described as 'my splendid ones', and many non-militants, including Stocks, later admitted to being spellbound by her oratory, even if her arguments did not tempt them into militancy.[69] At her greatest moments—during the court case of 1908, for example, or during her Old Bailey speech of 1912—she held even her critics spellbound; to this day, the sheer eloquence of her speech at her trial in 1912 rises out from the printed page.

But she was also a woman of action, with all the necessary courage and resource. Sylvia recalled her presence of mind even in the Manchester days; she had always been good in a crisis—quickly putting out a fire by tearing down burning window curtains, for example. 'Swift in impulse and intuition,' writes Sylvia, 'she was at her best when occasion demanded immediate action.'[70] Revolutionary ideals inspired her to transfer these qualities to the public stage; not for nothing had Carlyle's *French Revolution* been her favourite childhood reading. The labour movement nourished her unusual combination of martyrdom, self-advertisement, and defiance of the law; but only the suffragette movement fully mobilized the dare-devilry of her zest for action and drama. She may have lacked a sense of humour, but she certainly possessed a sense of fun. 'This is what I call life!' she said, dismissing Sylvia's alarm at her apparent over-excitement while privately declaiming about woman's suffrage; later, when visiting Sylvia in the East End, she confessed to being 'thrilled by the sportingness of it'. Long afterwards Despard recollected being surprised at this aspect of Pankhurst's personality during a militant raid on the House of Commons. Pankhurst was lying on the marble floor with two

---

[68] Author's tape-recorded interview with Dame Sybil Thorndike, 2 Dec. 1975, at 98 Swan Court, King's Road, Chelsea. H. N. Brailsford, 'Mrs Pankhurst Joins the Immortals', *Daily Herald*, 5 Mar. 1930, p. 4.

[69] Stocks, *Commonplace Book*, pp. 67, 71.

[70] International Institute for Social History, Amsterdam, Sylvia Pankhurst Collection: undated typescript (carbon copy) 'special to the *Star*', headed 'My Mother', p. 1; cf. C. Pankhurst, *Unshackled*, p. 17.

policemen over her; 'horrified, I rushed to her assistance, to be met with a brief glance from a fearless and rather amused pair of eyes'.[71]

Reforming agitation is no less sincere for being enjoyed, yet militancy also entailed pain. It took courage for an Edwardian middle-class woman simultaneously to breach the conventions of class and sex, and, by incurring physical assault, to risk sacrificing comfort, income, reputation, and family life. Then there was the humiliation of the prison search, which caused her briefly to break down in court when defending herself at Bow Street in 1908, and the miseries of the prison-cell, with its boredom, confinement, and eventually its starvation. The Pankhurst legend, still such a force with critics of government everywhere, does not ultimately stem from her militant tactics or flamboyant gestures: it grows out of her unique and extraordinarily powerful combination of angry defiance and unstinting self-sacrifice. There was truth, yet also a crass lack of perception, in Asquith's claim that these sufferings were self-inflicted.[72] Though Sylvia went to even greater extremes of self-sacrifice, she somehow lacked her mother's righteously indignant fire; and though militancy owed much to Christabel's shrewd dedication and resourcefulness, she never attained her mother's dignity, nor did she ever court martyrdom on such a scale.

Pankhurst's courage was yoked to impulsiveness. As a child she had always enjoyed romantic and idealistic tales, and rather disappointed the serious-minded Sylvia with her continuing taste for novels. Not for her the tedium of steady application and routine. She would turn the pages of a newspaper impatiently, running her eyes hastily down the columns,[73] and found it difficult to express herself on paper. Even her autobiography was ghosted, and—as Christabel later realized—riddled with errors.[74] She knew her own defects, and tried to remedy them with a systematic course of study early on in marriage, but did not persevere. Hence her limited influence within the suffragette machine, which rested primarily on Christabel's close collaboration with the Pethick-Lawrences. Pankhurst at

---

[71] E. S. Pankhurst, *Suffragette Movement*, p. 181; *Emmeline Pankhurst*, p. 137. Despard, *Vote*, 22 June 1928, p. 193.

[72] *Daily Telegraph*, 26 Oct. 1908, p. 8; cf. E. S. Pankhurst, *Emmeline Pankhurst*, p. 76. For Asquith, see R. Postgate, *Life of George Lansbury* (1951), p. 124. On the dynamic behind militancy generally, see 'The Act of Militancy. Violence and the Suffragettes, 1904–1914', in my *Peaceable Kingdom. Stability and Change in Modern Britain* (Oxford, 1982), pp. 26–81.

[73] E. S. Pankhurst, *Suffragette Movement*, p. 57. *Votes for Women*, 14 June 1912, p. 601.

[74] See the interesting correspondence of 1932 between Miss Pepper, Grace Roe, Ray Strachey, and J. R. H. Weaver on Mrs Pankhurst's entry in *Dictionary of National Biography* in Smith Archives, Oxford.

first acted as the itinerant evangelist who inspires the rank and file, but later became the martyr, forever moving in and out of prison.[75]

She could be ruthless, and several times severed apparently close relationships with family and colleagues. After breaking with her father she never saw him again, and saw her mother only after both had been widowed. Her suffragette commitment accentuated this trait; like Christabel, she subordinated her personal life to the single-minded pursuit of an idea. Sylvia loved her mother, was continuously tormented after 1906 by the maternal neglect that stemmed from her fanatical dedication, and criticized her for going off to America on a lecture-tour when her son Harry was dying from infantile paralysis. When Sylvia's son Richard was born many years later, she wrote to inform her mother but received no reply.[76]

On three notable occasions Pankhurst brusquely discarded colleagues to whom she owed much, uncompromisingly and apparently without regret: the founders of the WFL, who deployed the constitution against the leadership in 1907; the Pethick-Lawrences, who diverged on militant policy in 1912; and Sylvia, whose democratic crusade in the East End she branded as schismatic in 1914. 'You are unreasonable,' she told Sylvia in a letter from Paris in 1914, 'always have been and I fear always will be.' After the split of 1912, the Pethick-Lawrences never saw or heard from her again. Emmeline Pethick-Lawrence thought she sacrificed her soul to the movement. 'The worst of these politics of revolution', wrote Burke in another context, 'is this; they temper and harden the breast, in order to prepare it for the desperate strokes which are sometimes used in extreme occasions.'[77]

Impulsiveness, ruthlessness, and a taste for drama united to produce authoritarian leadership. As a young mother, says Sylvia, she 'demanded implicit obedience, and would tolerate "no likes and dislikes"'. It was the same woman who dramatically repudiated the WSPU's constitution when the founders of the WFL used it to enhance rank-and-file participation. 'I shall never forget the gesture with which she swept from the board all the "pros and the cons" which had caused us sleepless nights,' Emmeline

---

[75] F. Pethick-Lawrence, *Fate has been Kind* (n.d.), p. 75. E. S. Pankhurst, *Emmeline Pankhurst*, p. 71.

[76] E. S. Pankhurst, *Suffragette Movement*, pp. 154, 320, 324. See also the interview with Sylvia in an undated cutting from the *News of the World* early in 1928 in David Mitchell Collection, 73.83/20(f).

[77] Sylvia Pankhurst Collection, Amsterdam: undated [1914] letter from Mrs Emmeline Pankhurst to Sylvia, and E. Pethick-Lawrence to Sylvia, 17 Dec. 1929. E. Burke, *Reflections on the Revolution in France* (Pelican edn., Harmondsworth, 1968), p. 156.

Pethick-Lawrence recalled. '"I shall tear up the constitution," she declared.'[78] Her followers' loyalty was so complete that she could in theory have preserved both the constitution and her authority; yet militancy requires secrecy, and secrecy makes for authoritarian structures. Likening her Union to the Salvation Army, she pointed out in 1915 that 'when an army is in the field there is no time for procrastination and delay'.[79] Dissidents were free, after all, to depart, and the WFL's rather unsuccessful history perhaps retrospectively justifies her stand.

Yet authoritarianism dangerously insulated the leaders from new ideas, from rank and file opinion, and ultimately from political realities. Critics became traitors, loyalty was prized above intellect and independence, those who were not with us were against us. Commenting on Pankhurst after her death, Fawcett noted how she gradually shed all her leading colleagues except Christabel; 'she was very able but very impossible to *work with*'. By contrast, voluntary collaboration was integral to the philosophy of the non-militants, who saw themselves as preparing women not only to obtain the vote, but to use it. Committees abounded within the NUWSS, whereas Pankhurst, refusing to join a committee for advising the government on munitions work in 1915, pronounced it 'a mistake to have committees if one wishes effective work to be done'.[80]

Encouraging leader-worship was no preparation for democratic politics. 'She wishes women to have votes,' said Swanwick, 'but she will not allow them to have opinions'. Yet this argument should not be pushed too far; at lower levels, militancy allowed participation in many forms. Norah Balls, the Gateshead suffragette, organizing a meeting for Pankhurst, had never chaired a meeting before. Pankhurst swept aside her diffidence: 'I was *terrified*', she told me, 'and when she said afterwards "you did very well", if you'd given me a million pounds, you know, you couldn't have thrilled me more. So that was . . . really my baptism of fire.'[81] Pankhurst could also advise individual members sympathetically and sensitively. 'Well, my dear, you know your own business best,' she told Lady Ricardo, refusing to press her into risking a prison sentence through militancy. Pankhurst was particularly alert to the professional woman's conflicting priorities; as she told Letitia Fairfield, 'you're much

---

[78] E. S. Pankhurst, *Suffragette Movement*, p. 101. E. Pethick-Lawrence, *My Part*, p. 176.
[79] *Weekly Dispatch*, 5 Dec. 1915, p. 7.
[80] Smith Archives, Oxford: Fawcett to Ray Strachey, 15 May 1928. House of Lords Record Office, Lloyd George MSS D/11/2/9(b): Mrs Pankhurst to Sir James Murray, 25 July 1915.
[81] Swanwick, *Jus Suffragii*, 1 Apr. 1914, p. 89. Author's tape-recorded interview with Miss Norah Balls, 16 Apr. 1977, at Crewe Lodgings, Bamburgh Castle, Northumberland.

more useful to us as a doctor doing a new job than you possibly could be in any demonstration'.[82]

It was, of course, absurd for Pankhurst to argue that the British public, let alone its government, would enfranchise women simply to rid itself of a militant nuisance; the suffragette leaders' strident tone towards politicians reflects weakness and inexperience. But as Christabel once pointed out, women needed to 'grow their own backbone', and suffragette militancy at least exposed flaws in the anti-suffragists' argument that women's inferior physical strength disqualified them from political power. Pankhurst saw that citizens' large-scale withdrawal of consent could disrupt the modern state quite as much as any physical-force rebellion. 'Civilization was so complicated', she declared at Ipswich in 1913, 'that a very little thing could put everything out of working order'.[83]

In 1930 Vera Brittain asked herself why a statue had been erected to Pankhurst but not to Fawcett. She found the answer partly in the inter-war British desire to bury old controversies; those who honour Pankhurst, she wrote, 'by canonizing the heretic . . . close the door on the uncomfortable past'. She might have added that Pankhurst's reputation benefited from the sort of shorthand whereby we relieve ourselves, in a busy world, of the need to grapple firmly with the complexities of the past. Pankhurst had so obviously possessed courage, imagination, and flair for publicity that to credit her with winning votes for women conserved intellectual and emotional energy and was even, for some, politically expedient. 'If Mrs Pankhurst did not make the movement,' said Baldwin, when unveiling her statue, 'it was she who set the heather on fire'.[84] But Brittain offered a second explanation: society rewards those who offer it a touch of drama. Ray Strachey admitted, when writing about Fawcett, who contributed so much more than Pankhurst towards winning the vote, that she was a difficult subject for the biographer: 'nothing sensational remained so in her atmosphere. It was all level and quiet and eminently reasonable.' By contrast, Pankhurst saw herself in a historic role; she was angry when Sylvia and Keir Hardie deterred her from creating a disturbance in the House of Commons: 'you have balked me—both of

---

[82] Author's tape-recorded interview with Lady Ricardo, 29 Nov. 1974, at Woodside, Graffham, Petworth, Sussex. Linda Walker's interview with Dr Letitia Fairfield, 28 Mar. 1976, at 60 Beaufort Mansions, Beaufort Street, Chelsea.

[83] BL Add. MSS 58226 (Harben Papers), fo. 36: C. Pankhurst to Harben, 7 Aug. 1913. *East Anglian Daily Times*, 12 Feb. 1913, p. 5; cf. her speech at Chelsea, *Suffragette*, 28 Feb. 1913, p. 309.

[84] *Manchester Guardian*, 5 Mar. 1930, p. 8. Baldwin in *The Times*, 7 Mar. 1930, p. 13.

you! I thought there would have been one little nitch [*sic*] in the temple of fame for me!'[85]

Sceptics can point to the element of vanity and even humbug that the pursuit of martyrdom entails. They can emphasize that Pankhurstian militancy recklessly squandered the humanitarian and democratic capital accumulated by previous generations, whereby disputes that had once been resolved violently were settled peacefully by voter and politician. They can even draw out the ironies of a militancy which championed a sex with everything to gain from the non-violent settlement of disputes—of a militancy which damaged the parliament that women were struggling to enter. Those who deal in might-have-beens may even regret Britain's lack of a composite feminist leader who could unite Fawcett's reason with Pankhurst's fire; indeed, in an earlier generation Josephine Butler came near to attaining just such a combination. In the event, British inter-war feminists inherited a divided legacy. Pankhurst was, as Emmeline Pethick-Lawrence pointed out, 'great in her littleness, human in her greatness, and superb at moments of crisis'. It is she, and not Fawcett, who now symbolizes for ordinary British women the claim of their sex to fair treatment. Mrs Pethick-Lawrence, the close collaborator whom Pankhurst treated so badly, yet who remained an admirer from afar, should perhaps have the last word: 'I sometimes think that she will live in memory not so much as a great reformer (as, of course, she was) but rather as a great *woman*—worker of magic—creator and destroyer—the Woman whom men all down the ages have dreaded and loved.'[86]

---

[85] Smith Archives, Oxford: Strachey to her mother, 5 Feb. 1930. E. S. Pankhurst, *Suffragette Movement*, p. 209.

[86] Sylvia Pankhurst Collection, Amsterdam: E. Pethick-Lawrence to Sylvia, 17 Dec. 1929. E. Pethick-Lawrence, *My Part*, p. 343.

PLATE 3. Fred and Teresa Billington-Greig holidaying in Scotland, about 1922, with Fiona in front and Dorothy Aiken, a family friend, holding a racquet (Fiona Billington-Greig).

2

Woman of Ideas

TERESA BILLINGTON-GREIG

ANYONE searching in 1906 for a feminist with a future would have alighted upon Teresa Billington, 'a leader who loves the joy of battle, and means to win'.[1] Intelligent, self-confident, and not yet thirty, she was a powerful speaker who looked striking on the platform—yet now she is forgotten; like many Edwardian militant suffragists, she seemed to fade out after 1914. Yet she has several claims to inclusion in this book. Unsuccessful careers illuminate the nature and causes of success, and Billington-Greig (unusually among the unsuccessful) wrote memoirs which have survived. The reasons for her failure are interesting in themselves; as with Henry Harben, the other failure in this book, she was her own worst enemy, and her failure originates in childhood experience. Furthermore failure so distanced her from inter-war feminism that she was able to set its achievements into perspective and speak more frankly about them than most of her feminist contemporaries. Above all she wrote *The Militant Suffrage Movement* [1911], the most penetrating contemporary comment on the suffragettes, distinctive for its rare mix of intelligent analysis and participant-observation.

The book clarifies not just the suffragette legacy, but also the origins of a significant feminist body that survived till 1961, the WFL, and in effect it pioneers the study of what we now describe as Fascist government. This analogy was drawn by Emmeline Pethick-Lawrence in 1938; aspects of the suffragette movement, she says, 'bore certain resemblances to the dictatorships so common in the world to-day'. The historian Roger Fulford, also accepting the analogy, drily confesses that Fascist leaders 'would not have relished the comparison with a woman'.[2] Nor would suffragettes have relished the parallel, for democracy was their aim, and most of them later strongly resisted Fascism. Yet Fascism can arrive by

[1] F. Pethick-Lawrence, *Labour Record and Review,* July 1906, p. 97.
[2] E. Pethick-Lawrence, preface to *My Part;* cf. Mary Stocks, in *Woman's Leader,* 31 Oct. 1924, p. 321. R. Fulford, *Votes for Women. The Story of a Struggle* (1958), p. 266.

unexpected routes, and is by no means always consciously desired by those who hurry it forward.

In her memoirs written in old age, Billington-Greig richly evokes the flavour of the Blackburn she knew as a child. The knocker-up man rattled his umbrella wires against the windows of the millhands who paid him to wake them up, and factory horns and buzzers parcelled out the hours of the day. Then, she says, 'the march of the clogs would begin and resound in all the industrial parts of the town—a great army in the grey morning . . .'. Teresa's mother Helen hated the place; as a Preston woman pursuing a handsome but lost legacy, she thought Blackburn's manners inferior, its accent coarse. To Blackburn people she was 'the Duchess' or 'the little saint', and as a Catholic she felt her beads, murmured prayers as she moved about the house, and softly sang hymns at any time of day. In her prudishness she sandpapered the nude bottoms off the cherubs on the tea-service her children bought her, and snipped out the murders, divorces, and police-court cases from the newspaper before releasing it. She was often moody and withdrawn, and her long meditations with eyes closed helped to make the young Teresa feel rejected, and later to view her mother as 'a spoiled nun' whose ten years of convent life had ruined her outlook on sex.[3]

Helen helped to cause the failure of her own marriage. Her husband Bill Billington was a big, handsome, jovial shipping clerk with strong Liberal views and a taste for travel. Railwaymen instantly recognized his beautiful handwriting, and he nearly took up an operatic career when an impresario spotted his talents as tenor solo in a local church choir. Yet he was ill-educated and a poor earner, childishly generous yet also selfish and greedy—a man who could cut an open tart crossways so as to appropriate the middle piece with the smallest proportion of crust. Teresa despised him for being insincere in his Catholic allegiance and for not appreciating his wife's calibre.[4] Helen had four miscarriages, and did not want Teresa to be born at all; she twice ran away from her husband with Teresa, once before she was born and once in early infancy, but was brought back. The young Teresa, born in 1877, sat on the stairs in her flannelled nightgown as her parents quarrelled, restraining herself from rushing down to defend her mother; then 'as the storm died down', she writes, 'I would slip back to

    [3] City of London Polytechnic, Fawcett Library Archive, B[illington-]G[reig] Papers: files on 'childhood' and 'social and feminist awakening'.

    [4] Rosen, *Rise Up Women!* pp. 44–5. Author's tape-recorded interview with Miss Fiona Billington-Greig, 24 Aug. 1974, at 146 Dora Road, Wimbledon, London SW19. B.-G. Papers: file on 'family background'.

bed generally weeping and chilled to the bone'. She had no teenage illusions about home sweet home, and grew to loathe the narrowness lurking beneath Blackburn Catholics' prized sweetness and humility.[5]

She rebelled against both parents. As the only chestnut-haired, green-eyed member of a blonde blue-eyed family, she had already been told she was ugly, and despised the weak character of her brother Stan who was so proud of being the only boy.[6] At thirteen she asked her mother how to reconcile divine benevolence with the local advent of a deformed baby, and was not appeased when told that the sins of the fathers are visited on the children. 'I became the critic, the questioner,' she later recalled, 'the flyer of the wild kites of free thought'. She was now in revolt against Catholicism, and for five years thrashed out her doubts with priests whose ignorant arguments she came to despise.[7]

Only later did she speak out; as a teenager she confided only in close companions, and throughout her life retained the habit of lapsing into silence; 'a single word can start me,' she wrote in old age, 'an odd look, a silence, anything, even a year-old smile can imprison me so that there is no possibility of speech'. History reinforced her rebellion—English democratic traditions, a Catholicism that distanced her from the English hierarchy, French and Polish precedents, and her agnostic and Chartist grandfather W. S. Billington. Her family's money worries forced her to leave school at thirteen, and she was apprenticed to a milliner, but she feared becoming a shop-girl and family drudge, and fled to relatives in Manchester. She was now determined to become a teacher, became a monitor at seventeen, and, with the aid of hard study in the evenings and a Queen's Scholarship, took the customary route upwards into the teaching profession. Her liberation went further when she joined the labour movement and Manchester's University Settlement, with its relatively liberal and tolerant outlook on religion.[8]

It was not Teresa's feminism that first brought her into contact with Emmeline Pankhurst, but her labour connections and her distaste for religion—for as a young schoolteacher she thought it hypocritical to explain away the Bible's more cruel passages. A public protest was her first

[5] B.-G. Papers: file on 'childhood'.

[6] Author's collection: F. Billington-Greig to author, 19 Jan. 1975; interview, 14 Aug. 1974.

[7] B.-G. Papers: files on 'childhood' and 'social and feminist awakening'. Author's tape-recorded interview with Miss Fiona Billington-Greig, 19 Sept. 1984, at 70 Bayford Road, Littlehampton, West Sussex, BN17 5HN.

[8] B.-G. Papers: file on 'childhood'; see also file labelled 'Miscellaneous, Personal Background. Biographical Article'.

idea, but Pankhurst, who was on the local education authority, advised discretion; she must make sure of getting her science degree. The interview made such an impact that she recalled it in precise detail half a century later; her problem was solved by going to a largely Jewish school where Jews gave the religious instruction.[9] At this time she acted as honorary secretary to the Manchester teachers' Equal Pay League and to the Associates of the Ancoats University Settlement; in 1905 Pankhurst helped get her appointed as one of the ILP's two paid organizers. Then in spring 1906 Teresa threw in her lot with the WSPU, and helped to launch it in London. In June she created a stir by using a dog-whip on stewards who tried to eject her from one of Asquith's meetings, and was arrested outside Asquith's house for a technical assault on a policeman. Refusing to recognize the court, she was imprisoned until someone paid her fine; in October she was arrested again after a House of Commons demonstration, again refused to recognize the court, and was again imprisoned. All this put paid to the science degree, but her ambitions were now opening out.

Everybody who knew Teresa (or 'Tess' as she then liked to be called) emphasizes her impact. She 'certainly . . . found a great zest and enjoyment in life', says Sylvia Pankhurst, 'and was vastly interested in herself and her doings. She was one of the "new" young women, who refused to make any pretence of subordinating themselves to others, in thought or deed.' A large, powerfully built woman with a round pleasant face, she adopted a Grecian hairstyle with plaits woven round her head.[10] Her oratory did not scale the heights of emotion, but she pushed her arguments forcefully home, and aspiring suffragist speakers admired her for annihilating opponents with what Annie Kenney called the 'sledge-hammer of logic and cold reason'. Mary Gawthorpe at Leeds admiringly 'noted . . . most carefully with what effective control she commanded breathing space between sentences', and profited from the example. Men, too, admired her. She was engaged in 1903, but later broke it off; and her second fiancé, acquired in 1906—a working man on the University Settlement committee who 'bestowed on her a dog-like devotion'—was discarded during 1907 in favour of Frederick Louis Greig, whom she married in that year.[11]

[9] B.-G. Papers: files on 'Social and Feminist Awakening' and 'Family and Early Years'.

[10] E. S. Pankhurst, *Suffragette Movement*, pp. 187–8. See also Helen Moyes (née Fraser), *A Woman in a Man's World* (Sydney, Australia, 1971), p. 29.

[11] A. Kenney, *Memories of a Militant* (1924), p. 27. M. Gawthorpe, *Up Hill to Holloway* (Penobscot, Maine, 1962), p. 235. E. S. Pankhurst, *Suffragette Movement*, p. 188; cf. B.-G. Papers: MS on 'The Birth of the Women's Freedom League. Jubilee Year Memories 1907–57' in file labelled 'Personal Records and Comments'.

Her romances irritated the Pankhursts, busy with their rapidly growing organization. Early in 1904 she had prepared the democratic first draft of its constitution—complete with voting members, elected officers, and an annual conference—but such formalities seemed redundant at a time of rapid growth; the leaders' informal meetings coped well enough, and nobody seriously questioned the Pankhursts' decision to shift the WSPU's base from Lancashire to London. Still, trouble was piling up for the future: the Pankhursts were shedding their labour connections, and Emmeline Pankhurst created 'considerable sensation' at the ILP's Derby conference in April 1907 by repudiating conciliatory moves from her more left-wing followers.[12] A body like the WSPU, democratic in origin, with members democratic by temperament, inevitably became restive: pressures mounted for democracy within as well as without.

Personal ambition inflamed matters; given the WSPU's rapid growth, which leaders should remain close to power in London? Annie Kenney and Sylvia Pankhurst solved this problem for themselves when they bowed before Pankhurstian autocracy; Teresa would not. Already she had twice diverged from the Pankhursts. In 1905 she had questioned (incorrectly, as she later admitted) whether good publicity would result from interrupting Sir Edward Grey's Manchester meeting in 1905; and in 1906 she was overruled when, rational as always, she advocated reserving suffragette questions at public meetings till question-time. No trouble resulted, if only because there was so much else to do. But by summer 1907 Teresa (now working in Scotland) found that the London leaders were ignoring her suggestions, excluding her from national publicity and even eroding her Scottish following.[13] The time for action had come, and she would use the WSPU's democratic constitution as her weapon.

Christabel Pankhurst was alarmed; 'by instinct and reason, I was apprehensive of the entrance of "politics" into our Union', she recalled. Preparing her ground carefully, she told her sister Sylvia that 'T.B. is a wrecker'. Emmeline Pankhurst was equally determined: 'the time has come to act,' she told Sylvia, 'I wish we had done it long ago . . . we have just to face her and put her in her place.' Many years later Billington-Greig contrasted the Pankhursts' greatness with the occasional littleness of their political devices, with their tactical wiliness, and their astute flair for

---

[12] *Labour Record*, Apr. 1907, p. 29.
[13] For divergence on policy, see her *M[ilitant] S[uffrage] M[ovement]*, [1911] pp. 35–6, 41, 43; for mounting friction, see B.-G. Papers: 'Birth of the WFL', p. 4.

publicity.[14] These devices helped to oust her from the WSPU in autumn 1907. She then formed what was in effect her own organization, the WFL, under Despard's presidency, and attracted many of the WSPU's labour sympathizers into it; but the Pankhursts denied it publicity and retained WSPU funds, and so prevented the League from matching her ambitions.

She later came to think that democracy need have posed no threat to the Pankhursts, given their popularity. Still, 'if we are fighting against the subjection of woman to man', she told the WFL's launching conference, 'we cannot honestly submit to the subjection of woman to woman'. Leaders are fallible, she pointed out, and must be made accountable.[15] There might at the outset have been a case for autocracy, she thought, but this could not fairly be imposed later by *coup* upon members who had joined a democratic body. Besides, suffragists could not plausibly condemn the Liberal government for autocracy while failing to practise democracy themselves; the vote must be sought only through a democratic campaign. For her, as for J. S. Mill, 'a democratic constitution, not supported by democratic institutions in detail, but confined to the central government, not only is not political freedom, but often creates a spirit precisely the reverse, carrying down to the lowest grade in society the desire and ambition of political domination'.[16]

The Pankhursts pointed out that nobody had to belong to the WSPU, and that, whatever its structure, it helped to develop its members' self-confidence and political awareness;[17] seven splits and numerous individual secessions from it between 1903 and 1914 show that dissidents were indeed free to depart. Billington-Greig could fairly have replied that unquestioning obedience to leaders was a poor training for democracy, that the WSPU's capacity for emotional blackmail made the members' freedom to leave often merely nominal, and that the cost of militancy was too high: a widening gulf between suffragism and the labour movement. The Pankhursts might have replied that tactical (as distinct from mass) political violence requires speed, discipline, and secrecy—all hampered by

[14] C. Pankhurst, *Unshackled*, p. 81. Sylvia Pankhurst Collection, Amsterdam: C. to S. Pankhurst, 19 June 1907; Emmeline Pankhurst to Sylvia, 22 June 1907; the second of these letters was mis-dated 23 June in E. S. Pankhurst, *Suffragette Movement*, p. 264. See also Fawcett Library Autograph Collection, XX, Pt 2: Billington-Greig to Jessie Kenney, 5 June 1961, p. 2.

[15] WFL, *Report of the Second Annual Conference . . . October 12th, 1907*, p. 4; cf. *MSM*, pp. 87–8.

[16] J. S. Mill, *Principles of Political Economy*, ed. W. J. Ashley (1909), pp. 949–50. See also B.-G. Papers: 'Birth of the WFL', p. 8, and separate pencilled MS on the 1907 split, in file labelled 'Personal Records and Comments'.

[17] C. Pankhurst, *Unshackled*, p. 81.

a democratic structure. Billington-Greig's problems within the WFL soon demonstrated the point, though in persisting with tactical violence she showed that she had not grasped it.

The Pankhursts were also vindicated in a more personal way, for the WFL split was only the first of many storms in Billington-Greig's public life. As her daughter Fiona told me, she put great energy into many organizations during her lifetime, but 'from all of them she withdrew because she had come to disbelieve in the methods that were being used to promote them—usually. Because, apart from her firm belief in complete democratic participation, she was also quite unable to accept that the end justified the means, the means had to be impeccable. And of course they very seldom are in any successful organization or political party. So most of these efforts ended in some kind of quarrel or breach.' Warnings from her family were of no avail, for she 'had a sort of innocence. She believed the best of everybody until it was absolutely *proved* that that was not the case'. She was blind to this recurring pattern in her life, and Fred and Fiona were too tactful to mention it.[18]

The WFL disappointed her from the first; though claiming to be the WSPU's true heir it allowed the Pankhursts to retain its name, funds, and prestige. It also refrained from criticizing them, and at first reacted so strongly against their styles of publicity that it seriously neglected the press. Its austere truthfulness left its members 'shivering and naked', she later wrote; they soon 'fled back to the warm corners of self-satisfaction' provided by the WSPU.[19] Its continued militancy prevented the WFL from fully capitalizing upon Billington-Greig's rationality, and it rejected her suggestion that rational questions should be asked at public meetings and confined to question-time. Indeed, the League's participatory structure hindered its leaders from embracing any definite policy; it had originated in debate about the constitution, and could hardly deny its members the right—exercised from its president downwards—to abstain from any aspect of its work. So it was beset by internal arguments from the start, and Billington-Greig began to envy the Pankhursts their autocracy.[20] The League could, therefore, only palely imitate the WSPU's exciting exploits, and failed to establish any distinctive public image.

During 1910 the League's internal disagreements exploded. Billington-Greig had been its dynamo from the start, preparing its propaganda and guiding its political strategy, but at least one insider found her 'extremely

---

[18] Interviews, 24 Aug. 1974, 10 Sept. 1984.
[19] *MSM*, p. 102.
[20] Ibid., pp. 102–3.

autocratic and overbearing in Committee'. At the annual conference of 1911 Despard referred to the past year's 'moments . . . of almost intolerable strain and tension'.[21] Minute-books usually conceal such disputes, but by May 1910 Billington-Greig was complaining about the League's inconsistency and disunity on policy, and resigned as honorary secretary; a compromise was patched up, but she resigned again in October. Her faith in militancy was shaken in November when the WSPU resumed 'raids' on parliament; these she thought seriously counter-productive. She left the League in December and accused it of deferring unduly to the Pankhursts, who were placing the vote before women's wider emancipation. The League had 'ceased to be governed by reason and conviction', she wrote, and had 'yielded itself up to emotion'; henceforth she would be a freelance, 'because I cannot otherwise be true to myself, cannot otherwise express myself freely'.[22]

At this point she published her book, *The Militant Suffrage Movement.* Its importance is threefold: it illuminates her personality and methods, both then and later; it clarifies the structure and mood of the two leading militant suffrage organizations, and therefore clarifies further the inter-war feminist inheritance; and its analysis of militancy's organizational implications has permanent value. We may well owe it to the train accident in Belfast that left her 'suffering very seriously from nervous shock' in March 1910; the doctor prescribed complete isolation in a nursing home for at least six weeks. Until 1910, she said, her thoughts on militancy had not matured, but 'a year of more or less enforced leisure has given me time to go back to the beginning again and revisit the land of promise; it has given me an opportunity of seeing the movement from without and fighting things out with my own soul'.[23]

The *New Age* published long extracts during January 1911 and the book was announced for February. Dedicated to 'the women who know me and will understand', it is in effect a huge public sigh of relief that she can at last speak freely. At last she has escaped the shrugged shoulders and raised eyebrows that greet inside criticism of militant policy; at last she can abandon the hypocrisies, the quibbles, the evasions, and the discretion required from leaders obliged to enthuse their followers; at last she can break out of a heated and emotional militant atmosphere which prevents

[21] BL Arncliffe-Sennett Collection, XIII, p. 7 (MS notes on Billington-Greig's *New Age* article). WFL, *Report . . . for the Year 1910*, p. 5.

[22] Resignation letter in *Vote*, 21 Jan. 1911, p. 159. See also Fawcett Library Archive: WFL Minutes, 28 May, 20 June, and 31 Oct. 1910.

[23] *Vote*, 5 Mar. 1910, p. 218. *MSM*, pp. 147–8.

one from seeing straight. 'I wish to see reason substituted for hurry,' she writes, 'growth for eruption, cool courage for hot frenzy.'[24] The book's thirteen chapters and 219 pages are arranged chronologically; after a personal foreword she describes the origins of militancy, moves on to its growth and to the split of 1907, and thence to a critique of WFL ineffectiveness and WSPU autocracy.

The book deploys a clear, trenchantly expressed, tripartite argument. She first explains that she does not oppose militancy as such: 'I am a feminist, a rebel, and a suffragist,' she writes, '—a believer, therefore, in sex-equality and militant action.' Insurrection against unfreedom is 'a sacred duty', and Pankhurstian militancy is defective because too timid. In seeing that modern parliamentary conditions require a government franchise measure rather than a private member's Bill, the Pankhursts have revived suffragism and have stolen a march on the non-militants. But their strategy entails too much collaboration with the Conservatives; in courting support from the rich, the WSPU abandons the poor. What had begun as a movement of mass protest, an outcrop of the labour movement, now contemplates accepting franchise extension in the most limited form; working people slip down its list of priorities, and it retreats into that pre-announced and purely tactical militancy—that merely simulated revolutionism—which waves a red flag only from the drawing-room. WSPU militancy aims only at bluffing its way into publicity, and 'is always so arranged as to produce the maximum of effect for the minimum of work done'.[25]

In the second stage of her argument she analyses the implications of tactical militancy for styles of leadership. Government retaliation against militancy sends the WSPU into a 'double shuffle between revolution and injured innocence'; its pained pose of martyrdom sacrifices the dignity that could have been won through the sort of genuinely democratic and unashamed rebellion that takes its punishment on the chin. Women have quite enough real grievances without any need to invent them, and a purely tactical militancy generates impetuous and mutually glorifying leaders who can work up their servile disciples to individual symbolic protest; moral intimidation, charm, magic, and 'pageant fever' generated inflated hopes and blind loyalties.[26] She claims that, 'as with all emotional degradations, its victims glory in it', and 'the personal liberty of women, the integrity of women, the self-respect of women, the mind and spirit of

[24] *MSM*, p. 8; cf. pp. 138, 212.
[25] Ibid., pp. 1–2, 129; see also pp. 13, 112–14.
[26] Ibid., pp. 4, 155; see also pp. 73–4, 129, 131.

women, their warm hearts and their rebel souls . . . are . . . sacrificed for a piece of machinery, a mere tool of government.' Their self-subjection is 'not less objectionable than the more ordinary self-subjection of women to men, to which it bears a close relation'. Even WFL rationality succumbs before this political revivalism, this 'bemused Salvation-Army-cum-*Daily Mail* falsity and humbug', she complains; yet these beloved leaders are in effect betraying their rank and file, which 'has given itself to a thousand servitudes to win one small symbol of liberty'.[27]

The argument's third stage sees militancy as obstructing feminism. In this atmosphere of worked-up emotion, 'facts and figures, serious investigation, considerations of principle and consistency' succumb before 'the atmosphere of hurry'. Emmeline Pankhurst's 'divine impatience' rejects the adult's rationality for the childish impulsiveness of the politically immature, and ensures that 'noise and show . . . come to be the accepted substitutes for argument. . . . The impetus of emotion and numbers has taken the place of reason.'[28] A threefold threat to British feminism results. Suffragists cease to think seriously about feminism, as the militants' silly speeches demonstrate. Suffragism becomes vindictive, anti-male, and absurdly woman-worshipping, and so antagonizes male politicians. And suffragist inexperience in democratic procedures will prevent the vote from benefiting women even if they win it; 'a slave woman with a vote will still be essentially a slave'. Billington-Greig especially dislikes militancy's impact on the rank and file who suffer so much, yet advance so slowly in democratic awareness. Militancy escalates in its 'search for a new thrill for the public and a new claim for the women who pay the price'.[29]

It is a powerful book, combining logic with a trenchant honesty. Billington-Greig detests the distortion of the political process by modern journalists and by the reformers who play up to them; she resents reason's retreat before mistaken loyalties, wishful thinking, emotional attachments, and capricious leadership. She is the ideal participant-observer, combining theory with practice, generalization with detail. She grasps nuances in the relationship between the mood and structure of political organizations; she is well informed, observant, and intelligent; and she brings a broad and often comparative outlook to bear on her theme.

---

[27] *MSM*, pp. 114–16. *Freewoman*, 14 Dec. 1911, p. 70; cf. a non-militant's very similar account of a WSPU meeting in *Common Cause*, 30 Dec. 1909, pp. 515–16.

[28] *MSM*, pp. 173, 154. T. Billington-Greig, 'Emancipation in a Hurry', *New Age*, 19 Jan. 1911, p. 270. See also *MSM*, pp. 196–7.

[29] *MSM*, pp. 173, 142; see also pp. 3, 165–6, 213 for her repudiation of attacks on the male sex.

'I do not willingly make this book a personal document,' she writes; '. . . it shall be as impersonal as it is in my power to make it.'[30] Certainly her underlying argument is abstract and structural in nature; she abstains from personalities, and even finds grounds for admiring the Pankhursts. Yet the book's apparent rationality is powered by passion at more than one level. On the surface there is her strong commitment to freedom, feminism, and political progress, and her relief that she can at last ventilate views long suppressed. Beneath this lies frustrated personal ambition, a fierce resentment that Pankhursts who have outwitted her continue to enjoy apparent success, and that nobody seems to realize the damage they are doing. Deeper still there is the penitent who reproaches herself for involving herself earlier in mistakes that have retarded a beloved cause; in this confessional between boards, Billington-Greig criticizes herself as well as others. Yet repentance mixes with subtle self-regard, for she nurtures her own personal integrity and consistency, and 'cannot keep silent longer without self-contempt.'[31] Buried deepest of all is the teenage daughter shaking off the hated religion of her mother: after investing so much emotional capital in throwing off the old faith, she is hardly likely to embrace a new.

Her phrasing is revealing. She likens the WSPU's mood to revivalism, for instance, and sees herself as exposing false idols. Her trenchancy, even her occasional bitterness, denote the disillusioned insider who criticizes former friends more fiercely than present enemies. 'A defrauded rebel', she admits, 'is naturally the bitterest opponent of leaders who exploit rebellion'. Abundant are those epigrams, neat antitheses, and paradoxes that an alert intelligence applies to contrasts between appearance and reality, between what people say and what they do; ardent feminists enslave women, for instance, and a self-proclaimed emancipatory movement curtails freedom. There are occasional flashes of the rather mordant humour that springs—not from tolerance and a sense of proportion—but from high hopes dashed against disappointing reality. Discussing the self-advertising fraudulence of WSPU militancy, for instance, she grimly comments that at least it 'has one advantage over murders and accidents in that one is always informed beforehand when and where to come and see it'.[32]

Yet for all its merits, the book has three major defects: it is misleading as history, its scope is too narrow for effective propagandism, and its mood is

[30] Ibid., p. 8.
[31] Ibid., p. 1; cf. her resignation letter in *Vote*, 21 Jan. 1911, p. 159.
[32] *MSM*, pp. 211, 140; see also pp. 129–30.

too negative. Each of these defects deserves analysis. Billington-Greig as feminist historian has not yet jettisoned enough of the militants' excess baggage. She focuses as narrowly as any militant on the purely political dimensions of women's emancipation, and accuses the non-militants of promoting 'forty years of futile agitation' before 1905; wasn't militancy the appropriate response, she asks, when Gladstone excluded women from his Reform Bill of 1884?[33] Yet this grossly underestimates the non-militant achievement; it also exaggerates Gladstone's command over policy and ignores the mid-Victorian transformation in the relationship between public opinion and political party.

Billington-Greig tries harder than most Edwardian suffragists to understand the politician's situation and the Liberal Party's needs, and she improves on the Pankhursts with her belated but refined perception of how militancy affects public opinion. But she does not move on to the perception that suffragists must now work through political party instead of cutting across it. In 1911, as in 1907 when debating with Bondfield, she sees the demand for adult suffrage as being 'obviously raised to postpone our equality measure', rather than as the obvious route to women's suffrage for democratic Liberals keen to consolidate their alliance with Labour.[34]

Secondly, the book's limited scope denied it propagandist impact. Billington-Greig knew that the popular press would not grasp its complex and often subtle argument, and to judge from its present-day scarcity its sale was small; someone should reprint it. Yet she need not have narrowed her readership quite so far. She wanted to shift public opinion towards feminism, yet her theme could interest only that open-minded subsection of the militant section of the suffragist wing of the feminist movement. Instead of sketching out a feminist programme for the future, she refought old suffragist battles. Anti-suffragists thought that the book's critique of militancy was merely stating the obvious, while noting that her argument 'cannot fail to have its effect, and we dare say . . . will end some delusions'.[35]

She probably expected more attention from suffragists; 'to those in the militant ranks,' she writes, 'there can be imagined no worse crime than this I am now committing—to go over to the anti-suffragists would be a venial

[33] *MSM*, p. 26; see also pp. 22, 62, 150, 152, 161.

[34] Ibid., p. 25; cf. p. 141 and *Verbatim Report of Debate on Dec. 3rd 1907. Sex Equality (Teresa Billington-Greig) versus Adult Suffrage (Margaret G. Bondfield)* (Manchester, 1908), p. 8.

[35] *Anti-Suffrage Review*, Feb. 1911, p. 29, on her article in *New Age*, 12 Jan. 1911.

offence by comparison'. She even prepared herself for a mild form of martyrdom, envisaging 'condemnation varying in degree from mild to vindictive, from the great majority of women in the movement'.[36] In her Introduction she steels herself to hear the truth she has spoken twisted by knaves to make a trap for fools. Yet her book fell rather flat even among non-militant suffragists; with them, too, she seemed merely to be stating the obvious. Nor would their hearts warm to her history and critique of the non-militants, still less to her claim that suffragism can now rest securely on a popular basis, and that non-militants should have repudiated WSPU militancy in November 1910.[37]

The WFL had even more cause for resentment—not simply at the fact of her resignation, but at its manner. The book's non-militant reviewer thought the justification for publishing information obtained during a confidential relationship with colleagues 'a matter of nice ethical balance . . . The common conscience holds that except for grave reasons of public advantage the lips of old associates should be sealed concerning the secrets of their former communion'; an unintentional dishonesty lurked beneath Billington-Greig's patent but naive honesty. Although the WFL made no public rejoinder, its minutes show that it was privately corresponding with the book's publisher Frank Palmer in April 1911 on a matter of breached confidentiality; perhaps this arose out of the book.[38]

Her rejoinder is implicit in her statement that 'my personal experience and effort alone entitle me to speak with any authority'; the larger loyalty must transcend the smaller. But need she have been so contemptuous in her resignation? 'I do not any longer believe in the potentialities of the Freedom League', she declares, for it 'has dropped steadily to a position of mediocrity.' How could she write like this about colleagues so recent and close? She had already embarked on her lifelong strategy of uncompromisingly burning her boats; 'one might as well have not spoken at all', she writes, 'if one did not speak strongly'.[39] Yet ultimately she was reckless of consequences; like a more famous critic of the Papacy, when it came to the point of decision, she had no choice: she could do no other.

She was at least as forthright in condemning the WSPU; 'I shall write in vain', she admitted, 'for seven out of every ten of the women with whom I have worked during the last six or seven years'—yet surely three or four of

---

[36] *MSM*, pp. 5–6, 8.

[37] Ibid., p. 117.

[38] *Common Cause*, 6 Apr. 1911, p. 852. See also Fawcett Library Archive: WFL Minutes, 24–5 Apr. 1911.

[39] *MSM*, pp. 8–9, 108, 90, 211.

the ten would give tongue? She rightly predicted 'hot anger or the laughter of ridicule' among militants.[40] The journalist and militant sympathizer H. W. Nevinson thought her attack 'treacherous' and inspired by 'jealous vanity and hatred', and Mrs Arncliffe-Sennett, a keen suffragist, felt that Billington-Greig, 'not being able to herself lead . . . turns round and tries to tear down the Pankhursts of whom she is blindly jealous'.[41] But these comments were only private; in anticipating a public assault on her book, Billington-Greig underestimated three incentives to suffragist reticence: the strength of mutual loyalty within and between suffragist organizations, the Pankhursts' perennial distaste for mulling over the past, and their ruthless, almost cynical skill at manipulating public opinion. She herself had noted how the WSPU disliked debate and discussion. No official WSPU rejoinder was ever published.

Some who did comment publicly claimed that she was making too much fuss about her own departure, or that her criticisms were too personal, or that they would have been made more effectively from within. She could have replied that a personally motivated criticism is not thereby rendered untrue, and that her attempts at inside criticism had already failed; persistence in them would merely provoke a schism, which in turn would escalate controversy.[42] Besides, her criticism of militancy was intelligent and important; in a democratic society it deserved public discussion. Yet it did not receive it, for she had committed what is commonly called an indiscretion, an error of judgement. Historians may relish such events, but contemporaries do not; a democratic society's appetite for free discussion is in principle broad, but in practice narrow. Not only had she supplied almost every relevant section of public opinion with good reason for remaining silent; in her rationality she had forgotten that loyalty is due to persons as well as to principles.

Her rebuttals of her few open critics were too shrill, for in retrospect she could simply have pointed to the diminishing impact of enhanced militancy after 1911, to mounting Pankhurstian autocracy, and to the vote's limited inter-war impact on women's situation. Yet after 1911 she commented neither publicly nor privately on the book's reception, subsequent vindication, or impact on her own career. Perhaps the memory was too painful; but prudence would also dictate silence between the wars when she resumed her WFL connection; besides, people are not loved for

---

[40] *MSM*, pp. 6, 7.
[41] Bodleian Library, Oxford MS Eng. Misc. e 616/3 (Nevinson Diary), 17 Jan. 1911. BL Arncliffe-Sennett Collection, Vol. 13, p. 7 (MS notes on a *New Age* article).
[42] *MSM*, p. 105. See also the correspondence in *Vote*, 4 Feb. 1911, p. 183.

advertising the subsequent vindication of their views. Her later career suffered not from the memory of her indiscreet book, but from her continuing capacity for self-sabotage.

Her book's third defect, its negative mood, also contributed to its subsequent neglect. 'I am convinced that the best women concerned in this struggle stand in deadly need of criticism, sympathetic and merciless criticism,' she wrote;[43] effective future policy does, of course, require intelligent reflection upon the past, but criticism is not enough. It is not even clear that some of her suggestions on past policy would in fact have promoted the cause, and on the future she is vague indeed. She is clear on the need for democracy and collaboration with men, but what structures will be set up, by whom, and how will they be financed? She merely bows out: 'for the time I must work alone,' she writes; 'it would be unfair to saddle such a movement with a responsible official so generally execrated—and dare I say feared, since unanswered?—as myself.'[44]

As for future feminist policy, she finds suffragists in 1911 either divided or silent on 'every question of grave importance' relating to women's future except on the need for the vote. Militancy ensures that 'there has been no study, no constructive activity, no criticism, no analysis', so there is 'no system of feminist economics, but shreds and patches of many systems in a medley of many colours, unclassified, unselected'.[45] Yet what guidance does she herself provide? 'Feminists . . . will certainly regard the book as very good for excited suffragettes', said one reviewer, 'but not a great help to themselves.' She offers only 'a free feminist platform in every town and city' with 'organized lectures, discussions and debates on a free platform' as precursors to 'a vigorous rational development in feminism'.[46] She knows that effective feminist legislation requires prior education of the public, that feminist policy must take more account of 'the home-women', that attention must move away from the vote towards women's economic and sexual roles, especially towards birth-control, and that it is 'more important to get sex equality than to get the vote'.[47] But these desirable things will emerge neither from an organizational vacuum, nor from an unfocused inquiry.

Was she wise to go freelance in 1911? One critic stressed that women

---

[43] *New Age*, 12 Jan. 1911, p. 246.

[44] *MSM*, p. 217. *New Age*, 30 Mar. 1911, p. 525.

[45] *New Age*, 26 Jan. 1911, p. 294. *Daily Chronicle*, 15 Aug. 1911, p. 4.

[46] D. Triformis in *New Age*, 6 Apr. 1911, p. 12; 30 Mar. 1911, p. 525; cf. *Common Cause*, 20 Apr. 1911, p. 26.

[47] *MSM*, p. 217. *Common Cause*, 20 Apr. 1911, p. 26.

must combine to be effective.[48] Collaboration is necessary even to thought and research, let alone to ensuring that these result in action, yet Billington-Greig now distanced herself from suffragist, feminist, and party structures. Here she echoes the contemporary fashion for depreciating parliament; her book refers to 'the hollowness of the party sham, and the ineffectiveness of governing machinery,' and hopes that votes for women will produce 'a clean sweep of present ineptitudes and stupidities'. By December 1911 she is condemning party dominance, cabinet secrecy and back-bench impotence; feminists, instead of pursuing equality inside such a system, must concentrate on rendering it more democratic.[49] Yet co-operation with others is integral to democracy, and, for all her talents, her inability to work with others was to be ultimately her undoing. So the rest of her public career is in some respects only an extended epilogue to the dramatic events so far described.

Her short book, *The Consumer in Revolt* [1912], shows that she was also moving away from the labour movement. It displayed a pioneering interest not only in consumerism, but in linking it with feminism. Women's segregation into families, she argues, denies them their full economic influence; furthermore the labour movement concerns itself solely with producers, neglects the interests of the brain-worker, and sometimes conspires with employer against relatively unorganized consumer. Labour's revolt 'has been as narrowly sectional as the system it attacked'; the profiteer can be curbed only through complementing labour's limited vision with a separately organized consumers' movement. Here again she shows vision, independence, and imagination, but again she spurns the instruments lying ready to hand. She brushes aside existing consumer organizations—the Christian Social Union, the Women's Industrial Council, the Consumers' League—as ineffective, yet proposes no alternative structures.[50] Once again there is no route-map to guide her readers towards her destination. In 1937 she was still urging woman the consumer to mobilize, and in her eighties she lived to see consumerism in vogue,[51] yet its prosperity owed little to her.

In 1912 she publicized her contempt for strengthening the law on the seduction of girls, and rejected Josephine Butler's belief—virtually an article of faith among feminists after the 1860s—that feminists must reject state-regulated prostitution. She thought the moralists of 1912 shared

[48] *Vote*, 4 Feb. 1911, p. 183.
[49] *MSM*, p. 213. See also *Freewoman*, 21 Dec. 1911, pp. 85–6.
[50] T. Billington-Greig, *The Consumer in Revolt* [1912], p. 10; cf. p. 91.
[51] WFL, *Bulletin*, 5 Feb. 1937, p. 3.

suffragette emotionalism, and lowered women's reputation for political judgement. Refraining as usual from mincing her words, she attacks 'these dabblers in debauchery by word of mouth', and ridicules their breathless indignation, their cavalier approach to facts, their exaggerated faith in legislation, and their sentimental idealization of woman. One non-militant thought her bitter tone rendered her views 'wholly unworthy of serious consideration', but Billington-Greig's irritation once again reflects proximity, not distance. She too wanted feminists to concern themselves with women's sexual role; indeed, she had earlier wanted the WFL to be more active in the police courts.[52] Yet by now she was criticizing the WSPU's wastefulness and unreality from afar. 'Stretching out after more and more pitiable and effective immolations' had not arrested the decline of a movement which 'now has no more interest than a puppet-play, pathetic, pitiful, heroic, ridiculous, but a play only.'[53]

Why didn't she join Sylvia Pankhurst after 1911 in reuniting feminism and labour on an adult suffrage basis? Both regretted the WSPU's divergence from labour; 'the London mob could have been won in two years,' wrote Billington-Greig, 'but . . . only . . . through the working classes'. And Sylvia too had first acquiesced in Pankhurstian militancy and had then broken free; 'I realized how supremely difficult is the holding of calm thought and the sense of perspective at such a time,' she wrote later, in phrases that could have been Billington-Greig's, 'how readily one daring enthusiast influences another, and in the gathering momentum of numbers all are swept along'. Yet two such forceful personalities could never have collaborated—though this would not have deterred either from plunging in. Furthermore, even Sylvia's strategy was now impossible for Teresa, who was becoming disillusioned with all organizations; in 1912 she speaks of 'a common fault in our reform movements: they are prone to work only along lines, to be of one dimension, to have no breadth, no capacity for seeing more than one aspect of a problem'.[54] Besides, she had now removed herself to a home in Glasgow.

She now faced many of the obstacles hindering the women of her generation: shortage of money, family distractions, health problems, and the need to put her husband's career first. By what she saw as 'the maddest paradox', money worries came in to replace suffragist entanglements as

---

[52] T. Billington-Greig, 'The Truth about White Slavery', *English Review*, June 1913, p. 445. *Common Cause*, 20 June 1913, p. 168. See also *MSM*, pp. 136–7.

[53] T. Billington-Greig, 'Militant Methods. An Alternate Policy', *Fortnightly Review*, Dec. 1913, p. 1099.

[54] *MSM*, p. 141. E. S. Pankhurst, *Suffragette Movement*, p. 316. Billington-Greig, *Consumer in Revolt*, p. 16.

curbs on her freedom.[55] Fred Greig had early experience of poverty, for he was the son of a saddler in Aberdeen who moved up from errand-boy to insurance-agent. Like Teresa he was largely self-educated, and read a lot of philosophy as a young man. He retained his trade-union sympathies longer than his wife, and was a gentle, rather academic but sociable man with a quiet, wry sense of humour, who wrote a play in the Doric that was produced on the Glasgow stage. He became manager of the Glasgow branch of Burroughs and Watts, the billiard-table manufacturers, and in 1920 republished in his *Billiards in Mufti* the humorous articles that had earlier appeared in *Punch* and elsewhere; these included dialogues with 'Minerva' (Teresa), a bystander who makes rational but inappropriate comments about the game.

Theirs was a love-match from the start. Because Teresa expected it also to be a complete marriage of minds, she discussed everything with Fred, including her feminist work. She hated disagreement on anything; though convinced she was right, she wanted all disagreement rationally resolved, and tried persistently to argue him round. Fred knew the limits to argument as an aid to understanding, and retreated into silence. By the standards of the time he was helpful in the home—bathing Fiona, pushing her out in the pram, and getting the meals on Sunday. He complemented Teresa's seriousness with fun, and Fiona affectionately recalls a father who really enjoyed children, and knew how to tell stories and invent games.[56]

Teresa designed 'The Myth', her new but decidedly chilly Glasgow bungalow—with its numerous windows, wide views, and large garden. Relatives also took up her time, despite the claim in her memoirs that during her teenage rebellion 'I abolished all my relatives at seventeen, retaining only those whom I love as friends'. As Fiona points out, 'she had a dramatic romanticism, the obverse of her passionate rationality' which sometimes led her to exaggerate.[57] In reality she remained in lifelong regular touch with her parents, brother, and younger sister. At this time she also took into her house the two teenage daughters of her elder sister Beatrice in order to give them a high-school education, but this later

[55] Dora Marsden MSS (in the care of Mrs Elaine Bate, Cedar Cottage, 15a Gronant Road, Prestatyn, Clwyd LL1 99DT): T. Billington-Greig to Dora Marsden, 26 Jan. 1912.

[56] This portrait of the marriage owes much to the two tape-recorded interviews with Miss Fiona Billington-Greig cited in notes 4 and 7 above, and to my tape-recorded interview with Teresa's niece Mrs Blackman, 19 Sept. 1974, at Flat 4, 78 Salisbury Street, Blandford Forum, Dorset.

[57] B.-G. Papers: file labelled 'Social and Feminist Awakening'. Author's collection: F. Billington-Greig to author, 3 Sept. 1984.

produced a breach with Beatrice, who claimed that Teresa had stolen the affections of one of them.

Then there were the distractions of running a household (moderated till the Second World War by a resident housekeeper); of bringing up her only child Fiona, who arrived unplanned during the First World War; and of leading an active social life in leftish Glasgow circles. Teresa was capable in the house, quite skilful at hat-trimming, dressmaking, and covering chairs, and keen on carpentry. Her diverticulitis and difficult menstrual periods did not prevent her from leading a busy life; she sallied forth from her well-appointed study at 'The Myth' to publish and organize. She launched a non-profit-making organization to gather Glasgow young people (especially Glasgow university students) for weekend cultural activity in rented houses near lochs or the sea, and found time to publish her lecture of 1914 on *Commonsense on the Population Question* [1915].

Here again she strikes a note of personal liberation, at several levels. There is first her freedom at last to discuss the forbidden subject; 'too many of us remain deeply ashamed of sex', and some 'are almost disabled from rational discussion of its problems because of our sense of shame in experiencing its emotions'. Then there is a delight at distancing herself still further from the Catholicism of her childhood. By facilitating earlier marriage, birth-control can reduce suffering and disease at the same time as making it possible to plan family size; reason can at last dismiss the self-interested clergyman and doctor who batten on maternity. 'We are regimented by conventions,' she writes; 'habits and customs and ideas persist amongst us and control us because we do not submit them to trial by our commonsense.'[58]

The lecture also breathes a vigorous feminism, and no doubt owes something to memories of her mother's sufferings. 'Consciously-desired motherhood', Billington-Greig had written in 1908, 'is the only motherhood that is fair either to the mother or to the child'. In the lecture she regards every undesired baby as 'a terrible infringement of the personal rights of the mother'; the woman must always have the last word on whether to bear a child.[59] Once again her published views distance her from other feminists, for whom in 1915 birth-control remained a dangerous topic. And, as in her book on the consumer, her eagerness to

---

[58] T. Billington-Greig, *Commonsense on the Population Question. The Substance of a Lecture delivered to the Glasgow Clarion Scouts on December 13th, 1914* (Malthusian League [1915], xerox copy), pp. 3, 6; see also p. 4.

[59] T. Billington-Greig, 'The Rebellion of Woman', *Contemporary Review*, July 1908, p. 6. *Commonsense*, p. 13.

'get rid of cant and face facts' widens her distance from the labour movement. She claims that the working classes produce more children than is good for their health and comfort. Birth-control will enable labour supply more precisely and rapidly to match demand than any trade-union restriction; voluntary birth-control will achieve far more 'than . . . the creation of any great Moloch of a Socialist State'.[60]

The First World War disrupted the careers of both Fred and Teresa. In 1914 she opposed the war, but she was soon providing hospitality for Belgian refugees and war-workers, and, while Fred acted as fuel controller in Glasgow, she managed Burroughs and Watts for him. When Fred became the firm's joint managing director in the 1920s the family moved to North Finchley, and thence to Northwood, Hampstead, and lastly Wimbledon. These frequent moves—together with Teresa's lack of any full-time employment or independent income—rendered a cumulative career and impact still more elusive.

On moving south she became active in the Sports Fellowship, which aimed to encourage sport among young people, partly because she wanted to involve more girls. Although she had no business sense, her restless intelligence busied itself in analysing the science of billiards; watching the men at play, she worked out the mathematics of the game, prepared diagrams, organized classes for women through the Women's Billiards Association, and promoted the career of Ruth Harrison, who taught women from the firm's Birmingham headquarters. A dispute in the 1930s caused Fred to lose his job; he ran a small and not very successful stationer's shop for a time in Carnaby Street, and then the London Rotary Club made him their secretary for the rest of his life.

Teresa's personality remained a difficulty. 'She was quite without small talk', Fiona told me, 'and she couldn't tell white lies, and she couldn't hide the fact that she was bored'; people who repeated themselves were informed of the fact. She made controversial remarks, not always appreciated, about topics of the day to her husband's business associates. There followed a sequence of enthusiasms, all eventually ending in disputes and disappointment. She 'couldn't work with people for long', Fiona told me, 'because she couldn't compromise . . . She was quite sure what was the right thing to do, and *nothing* else would do.'[61]

Despite the events of 1911, the WFL became her major inter-war instrument. On meeting Despard at her birthday celebrations in 1924, she was relieved to hear her name uttered three times 'in accents of love';

[60] *Commonsense*, pp. 8, 14.
[61] Interview, 14 Aug. 1974.

thereafter she regularly attended WFL reunions. In 1928 she briefly resumed feminist activism; at a special conference on women candidates for parliament, she urged the League to undertake 'a determined propaganda' and to put up woman candidates at every by-election. But she lost her motion, and vanished from the scene as suddenly as she had arrived.[62] The same theme reappears in 1937 when once more she suddenly bursts upon the WFL scene. Women's enfranchisement had at first seemed to free her for work on other things, she said, but now it was clear that 'there was a great deal to be done before women secured their full emancipation. Our hard-won political power had not brought us the full equality of women with men, which was still our aim.' Speaking on 'new tactics for new times', she urged feminists to be more constructive and preventive in outlook: 'we should take things more in our own hands, assume and seize equality all along the line rather than protest if we do not get it.'[63]

For a few months the WFL minute-book hums with her resourcefulness and energy. She planned to revive the League with lecture-lunches, systematic regional coverage, and closer co-ordination with other feminist bodies. Feminists must collaborate on a joint newspaper, mobilize women's consumer-power, and capture the young in schools and universities. She revived the Women's Election Committee, which had lapsed since the mid-1920s, and as chairman persuaded the League's conference on women parliamentary candidates in 1937 to endorse proportional representation. She still wanted women candidates put forward at every by-election, and the Central Women's Electoral Committee was set up in February 1938. Yet in September, citing illness as her reason, she suddenly resigned from both WFL Executive and Electoral Committees.[64]

During the Second World War she helped the London County Council to evacuate children, accompanying them to reception areas and helping to settle them in. She set up an air-raid shelter near her home, and invited parties of RAF cadets and nurses to dinner every Thursday. She briefly resumed paid schoolteaching—at King Alfred's, the Hampstead progressive school—and the war extended her long list of organizations joined or formed, energetically promoted, and then abandoned. She supported

[62] B.-G. Papers: file labelled 'Charlotte Despard', typescript entitled 'Postscript on the Birthday'.
[63] WFL *Bulletin*, 12 Feb. 1937, p. 5; 5 Feb. 1937, p. 3.
[64] Ibid., 29 Oct. 1937, p. 2. Fawcett Library Archive: WFL Minutes, 8 May, 2 and 23 Oct. 1937; 12 Mar., 29 and 30 Apr., 24 Sept. 1938.

Richard Acland's Common Wealth Party, and was active in Women for Westminster, which campaigned to get more women MPs. Henceforward she was as prominent as she had ever been in the feminist world, but she made less national impact because organized feminism had itself lost impetus.

She worried a great deal about this. In an undated manuscript she blames women's deeply inculcated mood of grateful acquiescence; in accepting the vote and seats in parliament, women had exaggerated their progress and had become 'the easy dupes of politicians already in possession'; inexperienced in parliamentary tactics, they had accepted male political priorities. Influence is gained by linking up with the governmental structure, but there is then the danger that the desire to challenge it will wither; women thus become 'the unconscious artificers of their own continued subordination'.[65]

She also detected wider reasons for this parliamentary failure. Women lack skills in engineering and training in logic, she says; they are poorer than men, and lack control over family finances; hence her support for the Married Women's Association. She wants child allowances, equality for women within the family, trained and paid housewives; 'the community should recognize the work of the housewife and mother as a form of social service', she says, 'and should recompense her for it'. Edith Summerskill was alone among women MPs in promoting such a range of feminist causes in parliament at this time. Juanita Frances, a colleague from these years, recalled Billington-Greig as being forthright, confident, and logical, but also as being memorably severe on a member whom she accused of wasting the committee's time. Again there was trouble. I was told more than once in the 1970s about her overbearing manner and about methods which were misinterpreted by opponents as unscrupulous—as when she tried to amalgamate Women for Westminster with the Women Citizens Association. Likewise her attempt to merge the Married Women's Association with the Six Point Group (highly desirable in itself) failed amidst much bad feeling.[66]

Fred and Teresa gave Fiona what she now regards as a secure and intellectually stimulating childhood. Teresa provided good plain cooking and always made visitors feel welcome. She pursued reason in Fiona's upbringing; every decision had to be argued about and discussed. Fiona

---

[65] Fawcett Library Archive, Box 241 (material on Women for Westminster): undated manuscript headed 'The Full Measure of Dual Government', pp. 20, 4.

[66] WFL, *Bulletin*, 6 Sept. 1943, p. 1. Author's tape-recorded interview with Mrs Juanita Frances, 14 Nov. 1974, at 87 Redington Road, Hampstead. Private information.

found this frustrating because she sensed that those who can argue best are not always right, and when pressed she took refuge in tears or silence. But reason stopped short at sex, where Teresa, who disliked the increasingly permissive mood of the 1950s, showed all her mother's reticence. Her parents did not push Fiona towards any particular career, but did their utmost to help her to choose. They wanted her to go to university, but educationally she never quite lived up to their high expectations. As for Teresa's feminism, Fiona remembers feeling acutely embarrassed as a child at WFL gatherings when asked 'what is it like to have such a wonderful mother?' As she says, 'there's no answer to that, is there?' Not surprisingly, she did not take up her mother's feminist interests.[67]

Teresa wrote far more than she ever published. She tried to write murder stories, partly to make money, but never finished them. Once or twice she went off on her own for several weeks to write, but nothing came of it. In later life she came to think that 'the quality of clear speech, of piercing with words a little deeper than the common, of seeing further round a problem and putting it under verbal analysis is the only really valuable endowment that I have had to offer'.[68] Like her mother, she snipped out newspaper cuttings, but for quite different reasons, and sorted them carefully by topic into drawers. There flowed forth a mass of miscellaneous manuscripts, none published, many now in the Fawcett Library. In 1949 she told the Fawcett Librarian, Vera Douie, that she was now urging 'the use of the Pen at every level as a major weapon in the current struggle', and was herself writing pamphlets on equal pay and on women candidates for parliament. She longed for a comprehensive history of the suffrage movement. 'Do you not feel', she asked Douie, 'that while we are still alive, who took some part in it—a move should be made to get, if not a detailed record, at least an accurate condensed presentation made by the right person—or the right group of persons?'[69]

She amassed much material for a biography of Despard, but more important are her autobiographical manuscripts—comprehensive, penetratingly introspective, vividly evocative of places and people. 'The autobiographical writing is going very slowly', she told Douie in February 1951, 'and the condensation I'm finding really difficult—I remember far too much!'[70] Historical inquiries led her to correspond with Christabel

[67] Interview, 19 Sept. 1984.

[68] B.-G. Papers: file entitled 'Childhood'.

[69] Fawcett Library Archive: uncatalogued letter from Billington-Greig to Vera Douie, 17 June 1949.

[70] Ibid: Billington-Greig to Douie, 9 Feb. 1951.

Pankhurst in 1956. Predictably they talked past each other; Christabel— overbearing as ever—thrust forward her religious views, accused Teresa of neglecting present-day feminist causes, and questioned the value of historical work. For once Teresa restrained herself, quietly pointing out that 'to build at all soundly we have to know and use the foundations laid by workers in the past'; a British feminism soundly based on accurate history would, she said, reap a harvest 'less meagre, less delayed'. But suffragette historiography revives some of her old fire: 'the picture in the common mind is altogether too petty,' she writes. 'Just to hear the speeches at the Suffragette Fellowship meetings, and to read the various volumes dealing with the movement shows how utterly they lack what is needed. The purely personal story on "I–went–to–prison" lines is re-told *ad nauseam* without historical or political background, philosophy or principle.' No wonder Roger Fulford, compiling his *Votes for Women* in the mid-1950s, found her a stimulating informant.[71]

An active person's final years are in some ways saddest of all; the past contrasts all too vividly with the present, and a strong will no longer commands a failing body. Earlier in life Teresa had enjoyed gardening, but now she read more thrillers and biographies; she and Fred enjoyed the radio and went to the Aldwych farces. She became more critical of the Labour Party than Fred, and felt that consumers would benefit if employers controlled their employees more firmly. When her house was being redecorated in 1962 she grumbled about 'the sloths' who took such an age over the work.[72] In later life she voted for the woman candidate regardless of party.

In the 1950s Fiona drove her parents through the parts of Derbyshire where their courtship had taken place fifty years earlier; Teresa had always loved the countryside, and when they recognized places of emotional significance or natural beauty they would get her to stop the car. For all her outward aggressiveness, for all Fred's capacity for prolonging silences 'for days on end', Teresa leaned heavily upon him; Fiona told me that in 1961, when he died, 'nobody guessed that she was over eighty . . . but she became an old woman in a week'. Her final years were not at all happy. At times she felt that her life had been wasted, and she sometimes said she wished she had concentrated on her work instead of marrying or having

[71] Museum of London, David Mitchell Collection: Billington-Greig to C. Pankhurst, 8 Jan. 1957 (copy). Fawcett Library Autograph Collection, XX, Pt 1: Billington-Greig to C. Pankhurst, 26 Oct. 1956.

[72] Hunkins-Hallinan Collection, 45 Belsize Park Gardens, London NW3: Billington-Greig to H. Hunkins-Hallinan, 3 Jan. 1962.

Fiona. She missed Fred badly, worried about money, and decided to take a lodger into her Wimbledon house. Then (as Fiona puts it) she 'had eighteen months of knowing and six months of hell' with cancer.[73]

She said nothing now about her earlier clash with the Pankhursts. Even in 1911 she said she had probably seen 'more of the finer and more intimate of their virtues than the ordinary suffragist who is their unending adorer'. In the 1950s she admitted that Christabel had been right to distance the WSPU from the Labour Party, given its indifference to women's suffrage.[74] She remained continuously fascinated by Emmeline Pankhurst, and sensitively recalled their first encounter in detail; in 1960 she described her as 'in my mind the greatest woman of her generation'.[75]

In her final years she made one last effort to get British feminism on to the right lines by giving general encouragement to Mrs Hunkins-Hallinan, Chairman of the Six Point Group, which she wished she had supported earlier. She also sent her some important letters on feminist policy. 'The future of the Feminist Societies gives me much worry', she wrote in 1958, 'and the only ways likely to help much are increasingly debarred to someone growing old.'[76] She was no doubt depressed by the WFL's demise in October 1961, if only because she knew its work was by no means done. 'Now that so much is disintegrating about our movement', she wrote in December, 'could you not consider some form of amalgamation other than [with] that deadly slow Status of Women Group?' In the following months she welcomed the idea of addressing a Six Point Group conference: 'there is so much I want to say to feminists while there is yet time.'[77] A sudden illness prevented her from going, but after apologizing she said: 'I still burn with anxiety to "deliver my message" while I am still capable of doing so.' She wanted the Group to appoint a small committee 'so that the possibilities of my ideas may be considered before I die'.[78] Her money worries did not prevent her from sending three guineas towards the conference expenses; she also sent two most interesting sets of questions for the Six Point Group to discuss—questions which anticipate many feminist concerns of the 1970s.

Apologizing for their rough-hewn quality, she continued: 'please,

[73] Interviews, 24 Aug. 1974, 19 Sept. 1984.

[74] *MSM*, p. 10. See also B.-G. Papers: file labelled 'Writings II'.

[75] *Guardian*, 11 May 1960, p. 8. Her account of her first meeting with Emmeline Pankhurst is in B.-G. Papers: file on 'Family and Early Years'.

[76] Hunkins-Hallinan Collection: Billington-Greig to Hunkins-Hallinan, 23 May 1958; see also same to same, 19 Dec. 1961.

[77] Ibid.: same to same, 19 Dec. 1961; 3 Jan. 1962.

[78] Ibid.: same to same, 6 and 8 Mar. 1962.

believe me, that I am so deeply committed to these questionings of policy. They have always been there—but for years now I have refrained from voicing them—because there was prejudice enough against me and what I said—and because the idea of our movement gradually dying would not have been accepted. Now it cannot be denied.' She sees no future for feminist organizations if they merely promote 'a sort of patchwork repair service' of legislative and legal change. 'The whole atmosphere of our lives is honeycombed with the theory and practice of inequality,' she argues; voting every five years can hardly alter this. Feminists must be more ambitious, and root out anti-feminism by moving into broader questions such as language, religion, and child-rearing. 'All these inequality usages permeate the mental atmosphere from infancy,' she writes. 'We leave them to their evil work—and when the child . . . has become an adult we proclaim equal citizenship. I think we have been cowardly and blind and have deserved the partial failure that we have won.'[79]

In 1962 as in 1911, she was trying to guide feminists away from politics and towards society. Education and communication are crucial. Among Christians, for instance, 'there is no Goddess. There is a masculine God, three male gods in the trinity, all the old Testament prophets are male, the whole Jewish records are permeated with male dominance and Jesus had no women apostles, and scorned his earthly mother when he was "about his father's business"'. Then there is the wording of the marriage service and the practice of assigning the husband's initials to the widow. As for language, she goes on, 'I could fill you a book with thousands of examples of masculine priority, many of them used every day in common speech and all assuming that the woman is inferior'. Dons, journalists, and lecturers frequently offend in this way, she says, 'and reveal thus that they are definitely *inequality-minded*'. The Group's committee could also discuss 'how equality can be translated into our common speech, how the Churches can be influenced, how the idea of inequality can be eliminated from our common speech, and prevented from corrupting generation after generation of young minds'.[80]

It was a huge and imaginative agenda, quite beyond her own powers, and nothing more seems to have come of it. She knew she had not long to live, and was desperate to preserve her thoughts, sometimes getting up in the middle of the night to record them. 'She always had paper [and] pencil wherever she was', her niece Mrs Blackman told me of this period in her life; 'if she was in the kitchen, if she was in the bedroom, she had paper and

---

[79] Hunkins-Hallinan Collection: Billington-Greig to Hunkins-Hallinan: 21 Feb. 1962.
[80] Ibid.

pencil beside her and was writing . . . She was all burned up about it, and doing it almost feverishly.' But this only carried further a rooted habit, for as Fiona says, 'all my life I remember her stopping what she was doing to write something down.'[81] She would herself have appreciated the irony of the fact that she died (in 1964) at just the time when a revived feminist movement rediscovered many of her ideas, without the reticence on sexual questions which had always constrained her feminism.

An individual's success requires opportunity. Many of Billington-Greig's difficulties were shared by most women in her generation: household commitments, child-bearing, lack of cumulative employment when the wife accompanies the husband in his career-moves. Illness also hindered her, including her difficult periods as a young woman, her diverticulitis, and the recurrent appearance on her neck of seborrhoeic dermatitis, which was sometimes bad enough to preclude public work, but vanished in her seventies. Most important hindrance of all, perhaps, was the climate of the time. With Billington-Greig—as with Charlotte Perkins Gilman, who also placed the vote low among feminist objectives—ideas, however progressive, are powerless unless people are ready to receive them. Given the slow pace of feminist advance between the 1920s and the 1960s, and the distractions offered by social class, political party, and foreign affairs, perhaps only the most exceptional woman with her ideas could have prevailed. Nor could Billington-Greig reap the rather different kind of success that completing her autobiography, a minor masterpiece in embryo, might have brought.

She had foreseen it all. Few suffragists really wanted the complete emancipation of women, she wrote in 1911; when enfranchised they would turn out to be conservative 'in politics and social and sexual affairs'. Perhaps she then underestimated the status value of the vote, a mistake not made by Christabel Pankhurst, but she knew it would not alter things very much. Women untrained in how to use their vote, she wrote, 'will be easy prey for political adventurers of both sexes'. She also foresaw her own lifelong isolation: 'I shall be a militant rebel to the end of my days,' she wrote.[82] The full range of qualities required for political success is seldom present within a single person, and a democratic society must generate institutions that will foster collaboration between people who collectively possess the right mix. More is involved here than the familiar difficulty of uniting theory to practice; Billington-Greig was strong on both counts.

---

[81] Author's interview with Mrs Blackman, 19 Sept. 1974. Author's collection: F. Billington-Greig to author, 3 Sept. 1984.

[82] *MSM*, p. 175. *Daily Chronicle*, 15 Aug. 1911, p. 4. *MSM*, p. 3.

Her problem was rather her inability to compromise with those who did not share her views. Evan Durbin thought 'a tolerant disposition and a willingness to undertake responsibility' essential in the democratic citizen; democracy, he wrote, 'demands a certain kind of *emotional* life and character in individuals before it can exist or survive in society'.[83]

For all her passionate belief in freedom and democracy, Billington-Greig lacked the co-operative personality needed to bring action out of ideas. Her recurrent and often bitter disputes damaged her influence, with consequent loss to herself and society. She later recognized some of her own defects; she knew that she had sometimes allowed anger to submerge her reason, and that 'instead of demonstrating truth one finds oneself lashing the untrue'. Fiona says that she 'could feel more guilty about more things than anybody I've ever met'; she also retained the childhood habit of searching for and recording her own shortcomings, but could now find no confession or absolution to discharge her guilt. Hence the long and painful sequence of quarrels; 'she was an extremely vulnerable person,' Fiona told me, 'I always thought she had one skin too few'.[84]

In a revealing autobiographical passage Billington-Greig notes that throughout her life she has been 'dissatisfied with many things and so dissatisfied with myself that a great part of my life has had to be spent in efforts to make myself over—and of regretting and repenting the repeated failures of such efforts'. Perhaps she foresaw these disappointments in the rather wistful conclusion to her *Militant Suffrage Movement*. Bracing herself in its last paragraph for the obscurity that results from repudiating self-advertisement, she predicts that 'we shall drop to the level of the common-place and do our common-place work'. Yet she consoles herself with two concluding questions: 'who will count the plaudits at the end? If we do our work as well as we can, what else matters?'[85]

---

[83] E. F. M. Durbin, *The Politics of Democratic Socialism. An Essay on Social Policy* (1965 edn.), pp. 258, 257; cf. p. 241.

[84] B.-G. Papers: file on 'Childhood'. Interview with Miss Fiona Billington-Greig, 24 Aug. 1974; cf. Author's Collection: F. Billington-Greig to author, 19 Jan. 1975.

[85] B.-G. Papers: note in file on 'Family and Early Years'. *MSM*, p. 219.

3

Publicist and Communicator

NANCY ASTOR

'THE writing of your life is no task for an anaemic don,' Nancy Astor was told when a biography was being contemplated in 1956.[1] She had all too little of Billington-Greig's intellect, and, as the first woman to sit at Westminster, she calls to mind Pankhurst's eager pursuit of publicity rather than Fawcett's stolid rationality. One MP saw her first election campaign, the Plymouth by-election of 1919, as 'more like a circus than a Parliamentary Election', and journalists had a wonderful time. The artificialities of a New York academy for young ladies provoked her into a lifelong desire to shock people, and her taste for sparking off hecklers is reminiscent of Christabel Pankhurst, whose smart answers she sometimes quoted. As MP she kept on good terms with former militants in the flamboyant Six Point Group, and once told feminists that she would readily vacate her parliamentary seat to Emmeline Pankhurst if she only knew how.[2]

Yet her career draws together both halves of the fractured Edwardian feminist legacy, for as MP she also skilfully harnessed the tactical and legislative expertise of Fawcett's followers, and mixed freely with the non-militants of NUSEC, whence came her secretaries. Most notable among these was Ray Strachey, at three points in her career. 'Strach', as Astor was calling her by 1931—aided by Eva Hubback and Pippa Strachey—possessed an alert political sense and a deep knowledge of the feminist world which helped to keep Astor on the parliamentary rails. It is a pity that Ray Strachey never acted on her intention of writing Astor's biography,[3] for she would never have allowed Cliveden's surface glitter to conceal Astor's serious political and feminist purposes. Astor's prudent but firm and consistent feminism and her career's major impact on inter-war

---

[1] Nancy Astor MSS 1416/1/6/88: Andrew Scotland, Director of Education, Plymouth, to Astor, 23 Jan. 1956.

[2] *HC Deb.* 27 Feb. 1920, c. 2095 (Leng-Sturrock). For Emmeline Pankhurst, see *The Times*, 4 Mar. 1926, p. 16.

[3] Smith Archives, Oxford: Ray Strachey to her mother, 7 Apr. 1935.

PLATE 4. Nancy Astor and Mrs Wintringham outside Mrs Wintringham's home at Tealby, Lincolnshire (Mr and Mrs Leslie Smith, Tealby).

attitudes to women demand her inclusion in this book. Three of her many roles require consecutive discussion here: as feminist, as Conservative, and as parliamentarian.

By spring 1921 Astor was entertaining members of women's organizations at her house in St James's Square. During her American tour of 1922 she studied the Women's Joint Congressional Committee; this seems to have been the model for the Consultative Committee of Women's Organizations she set up in that year to co-ordinate women's political work. All feminists later praised its evening receptions. You ascended to the first floor, and after an introduction from the butler you met Astor at the door. It was a stand-up occasion with food and non-intoxicating drink, so you were free to circulate; within the big L-shaped drawing-room you made useful cross-party contacts within the worlds of politics, government, feminism, and reform.[4] Mutual disagreements and a non-political outlook among inter-war women's organizations caused the Consultative Committee to be disbanded in 1928, but for several years it offered women a most valuable forum.

As MP, Astor took up many questions affecting women. For the purpose of analysing parliamentary debates, women's questions can be defined as embracing equal franchise, women's rights and status, women's employment, family law reform, family allowances, equal pay, birth-control, sexual morality, and women's war service. On size of debating contribution in this area per sessional day as MP, Astor comes fifth among the thirty-eight women MPs between 1919 and 1945, and provides one-sixth of all that they said on these topics at Westminster; only Rathbone surpassed her total parliamentary contribution in this area, and the percentage of inter-war women MPs' total debating contributions assigned to women's issues is at its height in the early 1920s when Astor and Wintringham were struggling to alter the political priorities of a male assembly.

More important than quantity of speaking is its content and influence. On equal franchise in the mid-1920s Astor privately pressed the Baldwin government while simultaneously restraining extra-parliamentary feminists from counter-productive agitation;[5] her confidence that Baldwin would resist his die-hards on the issue was not misplaced. Women's

[4] Author's tape-recorded interview with Mrs Gertrude Horton, 13 Apr. 1977, at 315 The Greenway, Epsom, Surrey. *Woman's Leader,* 18 Jan. 1924, p. 410.

[5] Nancy Astor MSS 1416/1/1/261: Astor's pencilled note on letter from Lady Rhondda, 5 Nov. 1925; 1416/1/1/634: Astor's secretary to Mrs Wintringham, 14 June 1926; 1416/1/1/263: Astor to E. Rathbone, 24 Nov. 1927 (copy). *HC Deb.* 9 Feb. 1927, c. 206.

employment took up a tenth of her debating contribution during the 1920s, but rather less later, though during the Second World War she pressed government to make fuller use of women. She spoke up for equal pay in 1936, and rebuked Baldwin behind the scenes for giving in to his die-hards on the question;[6] and in 1944, when the government was embarrassed by defeat over equal pay, hers was one of the dissident Conservative votes that government needed to reverse it through making the question one of confidence. She repeatedly recommended women's appointment to public bodies, whether at home or overseas. Her first parliamentary intervention was to urge women's involvement in India's political system, and, although she strongly supported the India Act in 1935, she opposed clauses that seemed unduly to restrict Indian women's political influence. On this as on so much else she diverged from the Duchess of Atholl who, she once said, 'never sees straight about women'; in 1931 she warned the National Government's leaders against giving the Duchess a government post, and recommended Mary Pickford instead.[7]

Astor's moralistic variant of feminism reflects her religious outlook and late-Victorian Virginian background. Strongly influenced as a young woman by Archdeacon Frederick Neve, she wrote to him monthly for forty years. Morning and evening between the wars she read her Bible and her books on Christian Science, which she recommended to other women MPs. Herself sexually frigid, she was often quoted as saying that she could not tolerate seeing two birds mating without wanting to separate them.[8] She saw child assault as 'one of those things which makes one either see red or weep tears of blood', and told MPs that her husband became a supporter of women's suffrage because he thought the courts punished this offence too mildly by comparison with theft.[9] Like Fawcett and Pankhurst she hoped that women electors would produce a wave of moral reform, and was keenest on causes that would elevate personal morality—temperance, the attack on prostitution and gambling, and the protection of children. Also like them, she thought women were best protected through tightening, rather than relaxing, the divorce laws.

Her hopes were disappointed. The twentieth century has indeed moved towards equalizing the double moral standard, but through what the

[6] Nancy Astor MSS 1416/1/1/1330: unsigned private and confidential note to Baldwin, presumably from Astor, 18 Apr. 1936.

[7] *HC Deb.* 8 Apr. 1935, c. 937. See also Nancy Astor MSS 1416/1/1/1124: Astor to MacDonald, 29 Oct. 1931 (copy).

[8] On Astor's frigidity, see M. Collis, *Diaries. 1949–1969* (1976), p. 98. See also R. Harrison, *Rose. My Life in Service* (Futura paperback edn. 1976), pp. 88, 98.

[9] *HC Deb.* 12 July 1923, c. 1655; see also 12 Feb. 1932, c. 1226.

nineteenth century would have seen as lowering standards of female morality rather than through elevating male standards. Also misplaced were her high hopes for women's political influence; temperance in Britain did not move forward to prohibition, and moral reform did not turn out to be among the women MPs' major concerns. But this was not for lack of effort on her part. Her files of the 1920s bulge with campaigns to expand the women police—a cause which united her twin enthusiasms for improved morality and wider employment for women. The Geddes Axe and anti-waste movement blocked progress soon after she entered parliament, but she and Wintringham did their utmost to protect the women's police against them. Throughout the 1920s she saw the leading Home Office officials as a rock of Gibraltar vulnerable only to the biggest political guns.[10] During the second Labour government her parliamentary jousts with Labour MPs, then at their most vigorous and frequent, did not prevent her from collaborating on women police with Labour's Wilkinson and Picton-Turbervill.

Like most other feminists, Astor thought venereal disease best tackled through elevating male moral standards. At the general election of 1922 she firmly opposed the position of the rival Conservative candidate Dr Wansey Bayly, who thought contraception the best cure, and in a broadcast of 1928 she pronounced Josephine Butler 'the greatest woman and most inspiring personality the nineteenth century produced'.[11] This firmly aligned her with the Association for Moral and Social Hygiene; so numerous were her donations and personal kindnesses in the 1930s that its secretary Alison Neilans once described her as 'my dear Fairy Godmother'.[12]

Her moralism might well have caused Astor to reject birth-control, which moralists still associated with lax morality, especially as reticence on sexual matters was still expected from women in public life. Yet in mid-career she became cautiously helpful to the birth-controllers. In 1928 she refused to 'bring in measures in Parliament which are ahead of the articulate desires of the electorate', and two years later she declined a vice-presidency of what is now the Family Planning Association.[13] But she gave money to the cause, and was one of only three inter-war women MPs to

---

[10] *HC Deb.* 28 Nov. 1930, c. 1712; see also 11 July 1934, c. 370.

[11] Nancy Astor MSS 1416/1/1/60: typescript of her talk, p. 10 (copy); see also 1416/1/1/290: correspondence on the 1922 general election.

[12] Nancy Astor MSS 1416/1/2/175: A. Neilans to Astor, 23 June 1937.

[13] Nancy Astor MSS 1416/1/1/309: Astor's Political Secretary to Mrs Thurtle, 20 Dec. 1928 (copy); see also 1416/1/1/311: Astor to Hubback, 8 July 1930 (copy).

speak in parliament on a subject which she described (when presenting the anti-abortion argument for contraception) as 'not so easy or so pleasant'. Discussing the birth-control clinic she supported in Plymouth in 1933, she told Lady Goodson that 'when I see those poor mothers with too many children and dreading another pregnancy, I cannot help feeling that it is right to save them'.[14]

Astor's feminism was prudent, and was by no means her sole motive for entering Westminster; her other preoccupations affect both the tone and the priorities of her comments on women's issues. Her feminist style is never merely sectarian, negative, or uncompromising. Many of her political alarums and excursions reflect her attempt to combine two standpoints always in tension within a two-party system—commitment to a cause and loyalty to a party. Still more difficult, she was trying to reconcile two positions that then diverged: the demands of feminism and the current perceived interests of women. Her failures need to be judged against the scale of the task she attempted.

Her approach to dress reflects the caution that moulded her challenge to women's conventional role. To modern eyes the inter-war press seems absurdly preoccupied with the clothing of the early women MPs, and when Astor took up her seat in 1919 she found the small room reserved for women full of hats sent by hopeful milliners; on 28 November the *Daily Express* allowed itself the headline 'COMMONS BOUDOIR FOR WOMEN MPs HAT PROBLEM STILL UNSOLVED'.[15] For ten years she wore the sort of black dress with white lace that any woman MP could afford, but this did not prevent her from taking great trouble with her appearance. Files of correspondence with dressmakers swell among her papers, and she eventually relaxed her austerity; in 1928 she made a dramatic entry into the House of Commons wearing a red hat and dress, progressing in 1931 to a rich white silk ball dress flowing down to her ankles.[16] Furthermore she was quite prepared to capitalize on her femininity; Clement Attlee likened her to Queen Elizabeth I—sharp-tongued and tender by turns, ranting or sobbing to get her way, but watching you all the time out of the corner of an eye.[17]

Nor did Astor's feminism lead her to repudiate three roles convention-

---

[14] *HC Deb.* 17 July 1935, c. 1135. Nancy Astor MSS 1416/1/1/1037: Astor to Lady Goodson, 7 Nov. 1933 (copy). For her donations, see 1416/1/1/845: E. How-Martyn to Astor, 10 Mar. 1930, and National Birth Control Association, *3rd Annual Report, 1931–2.*

[15] *Daily Express,* 28 Nov. 1919, p. 1. See also *Leicester Daily Mercury,* 25. Feb. 1939, p. 11.

[16] *Daily Dispatch,* 5 Dec. 1928, p. 8. *Evening News,* 8 May 1931, p. 6.

[17] *Observer,* 3 May 1964, p. 23.

ally performed by upper-class women: motherhood, moral crusading, and political entertaining. She entered parliament through a decidedly non-feminist route as the first successful British example of 'male equivalence', whereby women progress in politics by stepping into male shoes. Her husband's peerage created the vacancy for the Plymouth constituency which she held continuously from 1919 till she retired in 1945. In parliament she did not thrust herself forward. She knew she would give offence by too obviously intruding into a male club and, protected by her temperance views, avoided the smoking rooms and bars. In her early days as MP she rarely ate in the dining-room, and spent her time either in the debating chamber or in the room where her secretaries worked.[18]

Her cautious variant of feminism assumed that the woman's place was at home with her children, and in 1922 she felt she must temporarily leave Westminster to join her seriously-injured eldest son. In her first speech at the 1919 by-election she denied that she should stay at home to mind her children, but in terms that merely carried the family's separation of spheres into national politics: 'I feel someone ought to be looking after the more unfortunate children. My children are among the fortunate ones'.[19] She espoused the type of inter-war 'welfare feminism' that in effect acquiesces in young mothers leaving breadwinning to the husband and staying at home. She made a major speech on widows' pensions on 6 March 1923 and showed continuing enthusiasm for nursery schools. Welfare questions (defined as education, housing, public health, rating, welfare benefits, and the relations between the state and industry) account for 41 per cent of her contribution to debate. This is below the average (49 per cent) for women MPs between 1919 and 1945, but it is high for a Conservative, and was maintained over the entire period—though she did not support the Beveridge Report in 1942–3.

She championed the employment of married women as civil servants, but argued that most would withdraw from paid work on marriage. And although in 1930 she argued strongly that educational maintenance grants should be paid to the mother, this was because she thought the mother responsible for educating and feeding the child.[20] In reality it was the very mild feminism of the Women's Institutes that attracted her, and she aimed to mobilize opinion among 'the real women, not the sort that is neither

---

[18] Collis, *Diaries,* p. 107. M. Collis, *Nancy Astor. An Informal Biography* (1960), p. 77.

[19] C. Sykes, *Nancy. The Life of Lady Astor* (1972), p. 190. See also *HC Deb.* 3 Dec. 1941, c. 1205 and her annual report to Plymouth Conservative and Unionist Association in Nancy Astor MSS 1416/1/1/621.

[20] *HC Deb.* 29 Apr. 1927, c. 1197; 15 Apr. 1930, c. 878.

male nor female; I mean the real old-fashioned, courageous, sensible, solid, cup-of-tea women'.[21]

Astor's wider political purposes in some ways limited what she could do for women. She would have liked to unite all women MPs, and she was unobtrusively thoughtful in her kindnesses to women MPs of other parties—to Wilkinson and Wintringham, for example. Sharing much of the non-party attitude long prevalent among British feminists, she saw party only as a 'necessary evil'; she wanted women MPs to see themselves as women first and as party members second.[22] But, as Bagehot said of parliament, party is 'bone of its bone, and breath of its breath', and between the wars party was reinforced by strong class loyalties. Her lunch for the women MPs elected in 1929 soon ran into trouble; the Labour women made it clear that sex equality was but one dimension of their political creed, and that union could go no further.[23] On three notable occasions during the 1930s the women MPs drew together—in November 1930, on the need for feminist reforms of the nationality law; in 1932, when eleven out of fifteen women MPs opposed restrictions on married women's right to claim unemployment benefit; and in the divisions of 1936 on equal pay, when all the women who voted were solid for the reform except Atholl. Yet far larger issues existed in the 1930s to draw the women MPs apart.

Astor's feminism gradually became less salient for two reasons: her other commitments cut across it, and as MP she inevitably reflected the reduced salience of feminism within the nation as a whole after the early 1920s. Up to 1931 women's issues contribute about a fifth of her debating contribution, but from then to 1939 the figure falls to an eighth; questions of women's war service cause it to rise again thereafter, but she was slower than some women MPs to exploit the feminist opportunities presented by the war. She did not attend the woman-power debate of 20 March 1941 or speak in either the woman-power debate of 5 March 1942 or the Beveridge Report debates of February 1943. She was not prominent in the important controversy over equal compensation for war injury, and completely neglected the wartime opportunity for promoting her favourite cause, nursery schools—perhaps because blitzed Plymouth had by then become a cause in itself. She was in fact always more than a single-issue MP, and comes no higher than eleventh among the inter-war women MPs when

[21] *Maidenhead Advertiser,* 30 Apr. 1930, p. 6.

[22] *The Times,* 12 Mar. 1932, p. 9. See also *Daily News,* 18 Oct. 1924, p. 3.

[23] W. Bagehot, 'The English Constitution', in his *Works,* ed. N. St.-J. Stevas, v (1974), p. 295. For the lunch, see Sykes, *Nancy,* pp. 304–5.

judged on the proportion of her total debating contribution assigned to women's questions.

In her second role, as Conservative politician, social class was central. The Astors enjoyed what now seems an almost legendary life-style. Before the First World War Cliveden employed between forty and fifty gardeners, and Walter Elliot likened tea there between the wars to a Bedouin encampment. The town house in St James's Square—with its chandeliers, pearl-studded harps, and marble busts—was a sight to see, and the family also had houses in Plymouth, in Sandwich, and on their sporting estate in the Hebrides. And, although the servants ceased powdering their hair after the First World War, they wore an elaborate livery for years after that; Frank Copcutt, the gardener at Cliveden, prepared a daily buttonhole for Lady Astor, and dispatched it by post if she was away in London.[24] Like many women in public life between the wars, she owed a great deal to servants; indeed, she was spoiled by them. At a time when class feeling moulded party attitudes more strongly than ever before, why wasn't she firmly located on the right?

Partly because her kindliness shunned any narrow pursuit of self-interest. Memories of poverty in early life never left her, and her servants resented the impostors and spongers who so often took her in. Harold Laski, in a very critical article, said that 'if good intentions could solve the problems of the universe, Lady Astor would have solved them long ago'. When she made a radio appeal for help to the miners' children, Lord Londonderry said this would merely prolong the miners' strike. On the contrary, she replied: caring for expectant and nursing mothers and children under five would create a better spirit. She invested much time and energy in this work, and surveyed South Wales for herself; 'I should be a red hot communist in their conditions,' she said.[25]

Her informality also drew her away from the right; she lacked class feeling, and by the mid-1920s everyone called her Nancy. Laski's article dilated upon the skills of the British aristocracy—their sense of timing, their charm, and so on. True, the public imagination was caught by Churchward, her Dickensian coachman, wearing a rosette the size of a soup-plate during her by-election campaign of 1919. Yet a mistress of Cliveden who chewed gum and lifted her skirt to warm herself at the fire could strike a precarious balance between mobilizing the deference voters and fascinating the rest. It was her populist repartee more than any deference appeal that throughout the 1920s brought frequent requests for her to speak in the open air on behalf of Conservative candidates pursuing working-class votes.[26] Responding to one such request in 1926, she told Thomas Inskip that 'as a matter of fact, it is the poorer working women that I like talking to, far better than your highbrows'. Her speeches during the Kelvingrove by-election of 1924 were much interrupted, with rival groups singing the Red Flag and the National Anthem. But her most memorable election performance occurred five years later in the courtyard of one of the worst tenements in Plymouth's worst street; 'so you are a pack of Bolshies, eh?' she said, standing alone and pointing her umbrella accusingly at Labour women clustering in the balconies above.[27]

Astor's informality stems from a transatlantic valuation of individual achievement and belief in the classless society. She stressed the wealth-creating potential of capitalism and wanted building societies to diffuse property ownership; nothing in parliament infuriated her more than Labour's emphasis on conflicts of class interest. She saw woman as the reconciler within both nation and family, and her affection for the Women's Institutes owes much to their socially integrating role. Repudiating class-conscious argument on one occasion, she angrily insisted that 'a mother is the same in all walks of life'. Her relations with Labour may have limited her feminist impact in some ways, but they broadened it in others. She was free to attack trade-union restrictiveness towards women; 'the reason why we need to have factory legislation', she announced in 1927, 'is because the trade unions have never stood up for women'.[28]

Paradoxically it was because she was politically so close to the Labour MPs that she became one of their most combative back-bench critics; she was competing with Labour for the moral advantage, and in the 1920s she could be excused for not foreseeing the Party's moderating role on class issues within a two-party system. Sharing a highly moralistic view of politics, each felt the need to submerge the other. Both wanted ethical progress, but, whereas Astor sought it directly through campaigning to

[26] Joyce Grenfell, in BBC2 television programme on Lady Astor, 28 Nov. 1979. *Yorkshire Observer*, 7 Nov. 1919, p. 8.
[27] Nancy Astor MSS 1416/1/1/807: Astor to Inskip, 10 Dec. 1926 (copy). *Daily Express*, 28 May 1929, p. 1.
[28] *HC Deb*. 3 Apr. 1925, c. 1735; 9 Feb. 1927, c. 207. See also her speech at Leeds, wrongly located in *Yorkshire Observer* in Nancy Astor MSS 1415/1/7/42, p. 30.

uphold personal morality, Labour preferred an environmentalist route towards moral progress, and conducted a highly moralistic critique of the entire social and economic order. Rebutting Wilkinson's attacks in 1929, Astor angrily felt the need to stress that 'one does not have to be poor to have a heart. Women who have money are just as much interested in infant welfare in this country as any other people.'[29]

By 1924 her exchanges with Labour MPs were regularly developing into parliamentary scenes and wrangles. Culminating during the 1929 government, these persisted to the end of her debating career, which appropriately concluded in 1945 with a supplementary question combating alleged 'Socialist stories' at the same time as she was urging continuance of the wartime coalition. 'I always know when I have said something that is true,' she once remarked, 'because Hon. Members opposite rise like trout.'[30] Labour MPs' hostile interruptions readily diverted her from the point, and so made her speeches even more rambling. Lifting her white-gloved finger in half-humorous warning, she would conclude the exchange with a round of repartee, but lacked the intellect to deploy the precise argument or accurate information that would finally unhorse the enemy.

She got under the skin of Labour MPs because she liked puncturing their claims to moral superiority. She thought they exaggerated the suffering in depressed areas like South Wales, and her doubts about the alleged virtues of Stalin's Russia were irritating. 'Don't you wave the Red Flag at me', she told one such enthusiast; 'I prefer the Union Jack or the Stars and Stripes any day.'[31] In a speech of 1925 she promised to pay the passage of any British worker unwise enough to want to live in Russia; the offer was taken up by a Liverpool ironmoulder Jim Morton, who set sail with his wife at Astor's expense in the following year. She enjoyed harping upon Labour's failure in office to implement its allegedly fraudulent promises in opposition, and spoke with feeling because the 1929 election brought her nearer to defeat than any other; she won only 211 more votes than the Labour candidate, and a lower percentage of the votes cast than at any stage in her career. After 1931 she repeatedly emphasized that Labour, even with Liberal and Conservative offers of support, hadn't nerved itself even to raise the school-leaving age.[32]

[29] Ibid. 23 Jan. 1929, c. 200.
[30] Ibid. 14 June 1945, c. 1772; 11 Mar. 1937, c. 1441.
[31] Nancy Astor MSS 1416/1/2/127: Astor to H. P. J. Marshall, 4 Aug. 1934 (copy). For Wales, see *HC Deb*. 16 Nov. 1926, c. 1760; 13 Mar. 1929, cc. 1187–8.
[32] e.g. *HC Deb*. 30 July 1943, c. 1963.

In the late 1920s clashes on welfare questions between Conservative and Labour women MPs became more frequent. They culminated when Lawrence rebutted Astor's attack on corruption in West Ham's local authority: she was 'like a child . . . She flings accusations about just like a child. She repeats words she hears and uses them without . . . any real reflection.'[33] After Labour took power, Astor took her revenge; she relished reminding MPs of Lawrence's claim in opposition that within three weeks of taking office Labour, simply through administrative acts, could appreciably ease the plight of the unemployed. In November 1930 the Labour MP Marion Phillips complained that Astor mounted strong attacks on Labour's women MPs when they were absent, yet absented herself when they spoke.[34] This party split among women MPs reappears with Wilkinson's scorching assaults on appeasement in 1938–9 as a class-interested policy; but perhaps partly because she had benefited personally from Astor's kindness, these exchanges did not become personal.

Somehow Astor managed to assault Labour without giving undue offence, perhaps partly because she was known to be fighting on two fronts: against the Labour MPs, but also against Conservative die-hards. She readily supported the Lloyd George Liberal-Conservative anti-socialist coalition when it was in its progressive phase, but like Baldwin her leader she later pursued the same objective by a different, single-party, route. Also like Baldwin she combined defending capitalism with conciliating the individuals who rejected it, and got on well with Labour's trade-unionist MPs while disliking its intellectuals; indeed in 1935 Herbert Morrison warned new Labour MPs against being corrupted by her invitations.[35] Her capacity for entertaining the House of Commons, like Baldwin's soothing interventions, often helped to mute its conflicts, and after the most clumsy of attacks on one issue she could rise to the parliamentary occasion on another, and show the utmost good feeling. Her assaults on Labour did not reflect personal rancour, and the *Clarion* in 1934 saw her as 'the tomboy of British politics' who is 'always quarrelling and always making it up'; not surprisingly, when the House of Commons debated its new building in 1943, she advocated a circular seating plan in the hope of removing the polarity between government and opposition.[36]

She was always on the left of her Party; during the 1920s, like Lord Randolph Churchill half a century earlier, she recognized that Conserva-

[33] *HC Deb.* 23 July 1929, c. 1245.
[34] Ibid. 28 Nov. 1930, c. 1723.
[35] *Manchester Guardian*, 7 Dec. 1935, p. 13; cf. F. Brockway, *Inside the Left* (1942), p. 201.
[36] *Clarion*, 19 May 1934, p. 9. See also *HC Deb.* 28 Oct. 1943, c. 417.

tives must pursue the new electors. In 1918 the Party realized that it would have to mobilize women. It adapted the women's tariff reform association for the purpose, renamed it the Women's Unionist Association, and got it to promote lectures, house-to-house visits, and class harmony. Astor did her utmost to arouse Conservative women in her consituency. Even before the First World War she was encouraging working women to participate in Plymouth Conservatives' social functions, and in the 1920s she tried at the local level what J. C. C. Davidson, the party chairman, was doing at the national level—countering the Labour threat by encouraging women to help the party machine. More women candidates would come forward, she said, if the Party ceased expecting them to give funds to the local party.[37]

Astor did not consciously operate within a Disraelian Conservative tradition, and had no inclination or talent for elaborating a political philosophy; her standpoint was always personal and pragmatic. Yet she was a Tory Democrat in practice, cultivating both its populist and social reform dimensions. Her national stance grows out of her constituency situation. The Labour vote in Plymouth (Sutton) rose continuously between 1918 and 1923, and reached its inter-war peak in 1929; Labour's percentage of the votes cast reached its inter-war peak in 1923. By contrast the Conservative vote, and the Conservative share of the total vote, fell consecutively in 1919 and 1922. A Liberal-Conservative alliance seemed the best way to fend off Labour. Liberal candidates had stood in 1918 and 1919, but a liberal Conservative candidate might end this by tempting Liberal voters rightwards. Alert to Plymouth opinion during the early 1920s, the Astors pursued a local variant of Baldwin's centrist Conservative strategy for the nation as a whole.

So temperance, Astor's earliest parliamentary cause, was less a personal whim than the progressive policy that promised to unite local Liberals to Conservatives. Its chances were improved by the fact that Astor was no temperance fanatic: she avoided the more sectarian policies of temperance organizations, recommended generous compensation to the drink trade, and distanced herself from Britain's sole parliamentary prohibitionist, Edwin Scrymgeour. In 1923 she got the Liberal Wintringham to endorse her at Plymouth, and made strong complaints in 1924 when the Conservatives failed to reciprocate in her constituency at Louth.[38]

---

[37] Sykes, *Nancy*, p. 149. Nancy Astor MSS 1416/1/1/623: Astor to Mrs Cunningham, 18 Jan. 1924. *The Times*, 16 May 1930, p. 13.

[38] Nancy Astor MSS 1416/1/1/1747: Astor to Wintringham, 16 Nov. 1923 (copy); 1416/1/1/615: Astor to H. Wilson Harris, 12 Dec. 1924 (copy); 1416/1/1/813: Astor to Maxse, 13 June 1924 (copy).

Reform versus revolution was Astor's cry: voluntary concession from individual employers and Conservative governments was her programme. She wanted to pre-empt extra-parliamentary agitation by piecemeal reforms, especially on behalf of groups reluctant to organize: women, domestic servants, West country fishermen, and so on. The ruthless employer and the Conservative die-hard were, she believed, allies of Bolshevism; she repeatedly repudiated Labour's polarity between capital and labour, and told Robert Boothby in May 1929 that 'social reform is better than the Socialism of the extremists or the stagnation of the reactionaries.'[39]

Her parliamentary career is that of a centrist who possessed all the consistency and courage and much of the flexibility that this political standpoint requires. On entering parliament she at once plunged into a rather personal vendetta against the die-hard back-bencher Sir Frederick Banbury. Factory legislation, housing reform, and the attack on unemployment were all among her early parliamentary enthusiasms. For her, social reform took priority over party politics, and she preferred non-party causes like education, temperance, and the defence of the family. Unlike several of the more silent Conservative women MPs, she strongly supported welfare measures, was pragmatic on the role of the state, and responsive to the nonconformist conscience. Yet with Labour making rapid strides, such views were not popular with Conservative activists. She made more enemies in December 1923 with an indiscreet letter (delightedly advertised by the drink trade[40]) to *The Times;* she was shocked, she said, by Conservative indifference to women's questions—no wonder women voters would not support such a party! She was privately very cross with Baldwin for not giving Fawcett an honour in 1924: 'I don't feel that I can go on long with such a collection,' she told Mrs Lyttelton, '—no vision, no strength.'[41]

After Baldwin's election victory of 1924—which in Plymouth at last reversed Labour's rising total of voters and percentage of votes cast—it looked as though Conservative plans for digesting Liberals were going well. Astor joined Margaret Wintringham and Maude Royden during the General Strike in writing to *The Times* on 12 May to urge a compromise settlement. She resisted vindictive legislation against the trade unions, but

[39] Nancy Astor MSS 1416/1/1/73: Astor to Boothby, 6 May 1929 (copy); cf. *HC Deb.* 4 Mar. 1924, cc. 1328–9.

[40] *Morning Advertiser*, 13 Dec. 1923, p. 6.

[41] Nancy Astor MSS 1416/1/2/35: Astor to Hon. Mrs Alfred Lyttelton, 11 Feb. 1924 (copy).

Baldwin's victory over the strikers temporarily held back progressive Conservatism, and during 1927 she was almost in despair. Attacking Atholl's economies at the Board of Education, she told parliament that 'sometimes I wonder whether I am in the right party'. Earlier in the year she had privately described herself as 'in a state of political suspended animation', loose to party loyalty.[42] All this brought her close to the rising young Conservative back-bencher Harold Macmillan, who told her in February that her leadership had been 'a great help and inspiration . . . during the short time I have been in politics'; in the November debate on unemployment insurance, she too recommended a middle way between reactionary government and socialism, and urged Conservatives to respond more constructively in the face of socialist pressure.[43]

The National Government in 1931 cleared the way once more for centrist Baldwinite Conservatism. 'All my life I have wanted a National Government,' she said in March 1932; here she spoke for many women voters, and she remained its staunch defender.[44] In Plymouth the election gave her by far the largest vote of her career, and her percentage of the total votes cast almost rivalled her husband's figure of 1918. There was no Liberal candidate; Isaac Foot said he would vote for her, no doubt partly because she'd never relished the Conservatives' protectionist panacea. The absence of a Liberal candidate in 1935 gave her a comfortable victory again, but the presence of one in 1945 would probably have guaranteed her defeat, and she reluctantly took her husband's prudent advice and retired.

She saw the National Government as simultaneously protecting Britain against Communism and Fascism, but this required it to take 'a big national view'. In 1933 she therefore warned Neville Chamberlain against a partisan adjustment of co-ops' taxation, and repeatedly attacked government subsidies to the sugar-beet industry; most Conservative voters, she emphasized, live in towns. 'Governments need kicking,' she declared in 1934, opening a bazaar for Macmillan at Stockton, and in the same year she claimed that, if the National Government 'would take a really progressive line about little children, they would have the mothers of the country behind them'.[45] She longed for an ambitious government

---

[42] *HC Deb.* 26 July 1927, c. 1081. Nancy Astor MSS 1416/1/1/508: Astor to Maxse, 15 Mar. 1927 (copy).

[43] Nancy Astor MSS 1416/1/2/38: Macmillan to Astor, 9 Feb. 1927. See also 1416/1/2/86: Macmillan to Astor, 29 Dec. 1931; *HC Deb.* 9 Nov. 1927, c. 267.

[44] *Yorkshire Herald*, 3 Mar. 1932, p. 3; cf. the manifesto, which she signed, in *The Times*, 14 June 1934, p. 16. See also J. Ramsden, *The Age of Balfour and Baldwin, 1902–1940* (1978), p. 327.

[45] *HC Deb.* 12 May 1932, c. 2154. *North Eastern Daily Gazette*, 16 Nov. 1934, p. 12. Nancy Astor MSS 1416/1/1/1168: Astor to Baldwin, 5 June 1934 (copy).

scheme which would tackle unemployment, especially among young people, and co-ordinate the educational, health, and welfare aspects of government policy; she wanted the school-leaving age raised to fifteen, restrictions on working hours extended, cuts in unemployment benefit restored, smallholdings promoted, housing improved, and, above all, nursery schools provided.

On nursery schools, her centrist purposes coincided with her undoubted love of children, who inject real passion into her speeches whenever their sufferings are discussed; 'there is no more pitiable sight in life than a child which has been arrested for playing in the street', she said, in a debate on recreation in 1926. In a debate on children in 1932 she described how she had watched a page-boy from a nearby hotel walking down St James's Square. 'He was very smart. He took a comb out of his pocket and began to comb his hair. There was something tragic in that little fellow all dressed up. No doubt he was associating with all the "toffs". His [working] hours might have been anything. What will be his future? I will not dwell on it, because I feel too strongly about it.'[46]

Nursery schools in the late 1920s were her panacea to replace the fading appeal of temperance, and promised to attain many of the same long-term objectives, but with more hope of Conservative backing. Her affectionate correspondence with Margaret Macmillan on the subject is full of enthusiasm, if only because this was one of several policy areas where Plymouth could operate pilot schemes for national policy. Her hopes were almost millennial, for she thought nursery schools could simultaneously grapple with problems of health, housing, education, and poverty more efficiently and less controversially than other schemes. Nursery-school children learn to socialize early, she pointed out in 1934, and the system 'eliminates greed, fear and disease'; subsidies should be channelled away from agriculture, she argued, and surplus milk should go to needy children and expectant mothers.[47] Yet the Astors' strenuous efforts failed to rouse opinion on the question.

This was partly because Astor was not a skilful parliamentary advocate; the contrast with Rathbone's approach to family allowances is instructive. Whereas Astor wearied parliament in and out of season with repetitive speeches on her pet subject, Rathbone first built up the intellectual case for her reform, then unobtrusively won influential friends for it. Only rarely did Rathbone devote an entire parliamentary speech to family allowances; instead she used debates on other topics to demonstrate their broad

[46] *HC Deb.* 28 Apr. 1926, c. 2155; 12 Feb. 1932, c. 1229.
[47] Ibid. 30 May 1934, c. 249; see also 7 June 1934, cc. 1204–6.

relevance. Though Astor possessed the vision, energy, and courage necessary for successful parliamentary advocacy, she lacked the necessary intellectual agility, command of information, and self-discipline. She is a transitional figure between the Victorian moral reformer and the mid-twentieth-century advocate of public welfare, and was continuously tempted forward in that transition by the self-effacing and scholarly efforts of her husband. For her, the politician's decision to act resembled the individual's impulsive decision to donate to a charity, not the careful weighing up of priorities that is required when spending the money of others. Sometimes her advocacy could verge on absurdity—as when she recommended juvenile unemployment centres in a debate of 1927 by describing how in Plymouth 'a boy came in waving the red flag, but . . . went out reading Shakespeare'.[48] So MPs came to regard her, and she even came to regard herself, as a person with a bee in her bonnet.

Yet however Astor had behaved, her position within the Conservative Party would always have been difficult because—like Lord Randolph Churchill or J. E. Gorst before her—she favoured policies that were more acceptable on the left. The party conference was furious in 1939 when she wanted flogging abolished; 'too often in this hall have I been howled down', she shouted into the microphone, 'and in four or five years you have regretted your action'. Yet Conservative leaders in a two-party system must guard their Party against opposing inevitable changes, and pressure from centrists like Astor can help them here; as Astor told a Primrose League banquet of 1933, the Conservative Party had 'always done its best work under liberal leaders—Disraeli, Chamberlain and Baldwin'.[49] Unfortunately for her, the Conservatives' need to make concessions to the left diminished with Baldwin's success in 1926, and his willingness to resist his right-wingers on India limited his scope for leftward concessions on social policy.

It is no surprise that Astor was one of Neville Chamberlain's most enthusiastic followers. Ever since 1923 she had been praising his social policy; as a housing reformer he had 'a heart as large as any Hon. Member on the other side of the House, and a head far better'. As Minister of Health he was 'a treasure', and she credited him in 1939 with transforming policy on state care for children.[50] When he embraced a foreign policy

---

[48] Ibid. 29 Nov. 1927, c. 360.

[49] *Daily Herald,* 11 Apr. 1939, p. 5. Nancy Astor MSS 1416/1/6/28: notes for speech at Primrose League Banquet, 16 Nov. 1933.

[50] *HC Deb.* 7 June 1923, c. 2471; 28 June 1923, c. 2618; cf. *Saturday Evening Post,* 4 Mar. 1939, p. 78.

that borrowed many ideas from the left she was hardly likely to resist. An attack on the Versailles settlement of 1919, integral to her support for appeasement in the late 1930s, fitted admirably with her distaste for the post-war parliament which she had found so unwelcoming. Devoting only 3 per cent of her parliamentary speaking to foreign policy—far less than the average (14 per cent) for women MPs between 1919 and 1945—she is none the less lodged in the national memory for supporting appeasement.

Like so many supporters of the Munich settlement, she passionately wished to avert a second world war. She told parliament in a navy debate of 1927 that she would 'never forget an Australian boy of about 23 who came into the Royal Naval Hospital at Plymouth, who had gone mad as the result of his service, and the struggle we had to bring him round'.[51] The Plymouth dockyards made her keener to speak in defence debates than most women MPs, though more often about sailors' welfare than about naval strategy. To judge from her inter-war speeches, her policy seems to have involved a centrist free-trading internationalism which rested upon Anglo-American naval collaboration. She was neither jingo nor pacifist, and often emphasized that pacifist and non-pacifist diverge only on how best to win peace. On India she strongly backed the National Government, and classified Atholl as a die-hard for opposing the India Bill of 1935. In the following year she backed the government on avoiding war over Abyssinia, but she also favoured rearmament. 'I think it is a woman's job to be always on the side of peace,' she said on 4 May 1936, 'but I believe this time that a strong England means world peace.' Her outlook on foreign policy can best be described in her own words of 1937: 'internationalist . . . but . . . also . . . realist.'[52]

A romantic, trusting, or rationalistic idealism may well have inspired some supporters of the Munich settlement, but Astor was among its many pragmatic supporters; she doubted the French will to resist Hitler, profoundly respected the statesmanship and motives of Neville Chamberlain, and deeply distrusted Winston Churchill. Her feminist and reforming career makes her attitude to these two statesmen entirely comprehensible. Churchill greatly disliked women's advent to the House of Commons; she later claimed that he did not speak to her for two years after her arrival there. And they diverged on many policy issues—from education cuts to betting, from conciliation during the General Strike to

---

[51] *HC Deb.* 14 Mar. 1927, c. 1759.
[52] Ibid. 4 May 1936, c. 1429; 4 Mar. 1937, c. 622.

devolution in India. In November 1935 she privately urged Baldwin not to put Churchill in the government.[53]

Although she spoke in the debate on the naval estimates in 1938, she made no parliamentary speech on foreign policy during the year, and made no contribution to the Munich debate beyond interrupting Churchill's speech. It was her social role, not her parliamentary speeches, that identified her so firmly with appeasement. By December 1938 Aneurin Bevan had swallowed the myth of the Cliveden Set, and impugned her faith in democracy in a grossly unfair article. Ray Strachey then set about organizing an exculpatory interview for her. The myth conflicts with all that we know about her character: 'I am too impulsive', she said, 'to plot or even to plan long ahead.' Nor does it accord with her feminism: 'how anyone who is a feminist and has seen the effect of the women's interest upon public affairs could believe in dictators,' she said, 'I can't conceive.'[54]

None the less, her position on Munich—like Irene Ward's or Florence Horsbrugh's—turned out to be one of those political leaps in the dark that crucially affect reputations and careers, decisions the politician sometimes lives to regret. Yet in 1940 she faced facts. She and Mavis Tate had supported Chamberlain in the Munich division of 6 October 1938, but they seem to have played a crucial role on 8 May 1940 by encouraging Labour to divide against him.[55] In the division of 2 July 1942 on the confidence motion about the management of the war, no woman spoke and no woman MP voted among the 25 who opposed the government, but Astor did not join the 475 who supported it; she abstained. Throughout the war she welcomed the revival of all-party coalition—now at last genuine and complete—which she had twice championed before. Thereafter her regular refrain was to encourage Churchill away from party government; and when coalition had to end in 1945, she shared all Churchill's regrets.

Astor's feminist and party roles were deeply affected by her role as parliamentarian. This was spent entirely as a back-bencher, and to judge from her public statements she did not aim at office, though several feminists thought Baldwin should have preferred her to Atholl in 1924.

[53] M. Gilbert, *Winston S. Churchill*, v (1976), p. 686. Nancy Astor MSS 1416/1/1/1378: proofs of an article for the *Strand Magazine*, 1935, p. 3.

[54] *Saturday Evening Post*, 4 Mar. 1939, p. 6. See also *Tribune*, 2 Dec. 1938, p. 5. Smith Archives, Oxford: Ray Strachey to her mother, 15 Dec. 1938.

[55] On this episode, see A. J. P. Taylor, *English History, 1914–1945* (1965), p. 472 n. 2; P. Brookes, *Women at Westminster. An Account of Women in the British Parliament, 1918–1966* (1967), p. 131.

She seems to have toyed privately with the idea of office, but Lord Eustace Percy argued that her influence stemmed from independence, and would diminish if she came to be seen as a disappointed politician.[56] Her unsuccessful joust with Sir John Anderson at the Home Office in 1929 over Mrs Westlake's pension vindicates Percy, for there she showed a decidedly non-governmental—indeed, breathless—approach to a complex administrative question. Several hints in her speeches of 1941 suggest that her ambitions had revived. But when on 11 June she claimed that Horsbrugh, parliamentary secretary at the Ministry of Health, did not understand children, the Minister was roused. Next day he came down to the House and demolished her accusations in the most humiliating fashion, advertising her irresponsibility and lack of constructive ability for all to see.[57]

Was Astor a natural back-bencher? The necessary energy, flair for publicity, and suspicion of red tape were all present, and her wealth and social connections supplied ample information and assistance. And in some ways she was a good constituency MP, whose close local connection is more reminiscent of American than of British politics; only Wilkinson at Jarrow rivals it among inter-war women MPs. Astor made the city a testing-ground for national policy on educational, housing, and planning questions, and frequently blew Plymouth's trumpet. Yet a controlled, powerful, and coherent parliamentary speech was beyond her, and the light-heartedness and inconsequence of her parliamentary contributions no doubt reinforced anti-feminist doubts about women's logical powers. Cyril Asquith once claimed that Margot Asquith 'abjured logic and attained truth—or error—with a single hawk-like swoop of divination'; Thomas Jones thought this applied also to Astor.[58] She contributed to debate with the frequency and informality that are normally justifiable only in a minister. Over-emphasis and repetition caused even her maiden speech to be interrupted towards the end—a rare event. She so relished repartee that all too often she allowed interruptions to divert her still further from her point, if she had one.

Her spontaneity made her a lively parliamentary performer, but she tended self-indulgently to 'fire off' at either government or opposition, without supplying constructive or practical suggestions. Neither her

[56] Nancy Astor MSS 1416/1/1/624: Lord Eustace Percy to Astor, 23 Nov. [1924]. See also *Time and Tide*, 28 Nov. 1924, p. 1170.

[57] *HC Deb.* 12 June 1941, c. 393. For Mrs Westlake, see the correspondence of 1929 between Anderson and Astor in Nancy Astor MSS 1416/1/1/941.

[58] T. Jones, *A Diary with Letters, 1931–50* (1954), p. 59; cf. Sykes, *Nancy*, p. 460.

husband nor Ray Strachey could coax her into better habits. By the late 1920s she was regularly on automatic pilot, responding predictably to stimuli, and her longer speeches had begun to disintegrate. Even on her favourite causes—temperance and nursery schools, for instance—she offered one-line, unargued, and only half-serious interventions, apparently designed only to remind MPs that neither she nor her cause had gone away. 'She has a mind like a rag-bag,' said Bevan unkindly in 1938, '. . . she speaks by free association, giving utterance to any ideas that come into her head.'[59]

As early as 1921 she was publicly confessing her defects as a speaker;[60] these defects pained friends who knew the excellence of her intentions and the potential for good in her wealth, connections, and energy. Worse, she seemed unable to obey the rules of parliamentary debate. She never learned that MPs must not be addressed by name, and the Speaker continued to rebuke her in vain about this till 1945. The press condemned her emotionalism in 1923 when Banbury tried to block her temperance measure—conduct he later adduced when opposing women's admission to the House of Lords.[61] Between 1919 and 1941, in every session except her first, she was among the top hundred MPs for the number of oral and written parliamentary questions asked. *Hansard* records an average of sixty-four parliamentary questions a year; but she undermined herself by using the supplementary question either illegitimately or frivolously, and again seemed unable to learn from the Speaker's rebukes.

Still more irritating to MPs, because discourteous, was her almost continuous fire of interruption. She comes third among the thirty-eight women MPs between 1919 and 1945 for the number of her interventions in debate per sessional day in parliament, but she had far less excuse for such abundance than the two women who surpassed her, because both Bondfield and Lawrence held office. She leads the field for the percentage (49 per cent) of her debating contributions devoted to interruptions (as distinct from speeches and questions) and comes thirty-sixth for her average length of debating intervention. The *Daily Mail* claimed that she uttered 161 'hear, hears' during the equal franchise debate of 1920, sometimes at the rate of three times a minute.[62] This is but the tip of her

[59] *Tribune*, 2 Dec. 1938, p. 5.

[60] Nancy Astor MSS 1416/1/6/88: notes [1921] of an interview on 'My First Year in Parliament', p. 6.

[61] *Morning Advertiser*, 30 June 1923, p. 4. H[ouse of] L[ords] Deb[ates], 21 May 1925, c. 435.

[62] *Daily Mail*, 28 Feb. 1920, p. 3.

interruptive iceberg, for *Hansard* identifies only audible verbal interruption, whereas many of hers involved a shaking of fists, a making of faces, a
wagging of the head, and a pointing of the finger. She persisted to the very
end. 'The Noble Lady gabbles and gabbles all the time,' Bevan
complained in 1945; 'we really ought to have some protection'. Her verbal
St Vitus Dance was but one dimension of that lifelong restless activity
which one shrewd biographer saw as 'an opiate for some kind of secret
unrest, an unrest arising perhaps from a fundamental distaste for a close
communion with anybody, male or female'.[63]

As if this was not enough, she often gave offence by commenting on
speeches she had not heard, and by departing from debates immediately
after speaking—for she was lax in the unglamorous but necessary business
of attending the division lobbies; the session of 1923 saw her highest inter-
war peak, when on this count she came 345th among the 615 MPs, but in
other years she was often well below that. Furthermore, so talkative a
back-bencher inevitably dropped bricks. She repeatedly embarrassed her
friends by publicly urging their claims to promotion, and sometimes made
wounding public comments about her own family. She ignored her
husband's warnings and gave great offence by attributing Australia's
cricketing victory of 1930 to the relative sobriety of her team. She gave
double offence in 1934 by failing to substantiate her claim that the drink
trade bribed MPs and ministers, and by disclaiming responsibility for
letters her secretary had written on her behalf. And in 1942 she made
things worse with her indiscreet and untimely assault on Roman
Catholics.[64]

How could such a person retain any hold on the House? Partly through
the remarkable tolerance shown by a great debating assembly, but partly
because major virtues counterbalanced her defects. She soon acquired that
first qualification for parliamentary popularity—affection for the House.
Her breaches of procedure paradoxically reflect the fact that she felt
completely at home there, and in 1945 she hated leaving. Furthermore she
retained to the end a surprising capacity for rising to the occasion; after a
sequence of trivial and lowering interventions, she could suddenly capture
the mood of the House and make a major impact with her sincerity and
courage. As Rathbone noted on 11 April 1940, when Astor had
courageously criticized Chamberlain's appointments policy, she had
'struck a note which needed to be struck'. Her maid thought she reached

[63] *HC Deb.* 24 Jan. 1945, c. 896. Collis, *Diaries*, p. 113.
[64] Sykes, *Nancy*, pp. 322, 359. *HC Deb.* 9 Feb. 1934, cc. 1533–4. Smith Archives, Oxford:
Ray Strachey to her mother, 14 Feb. 1934. *HC Deb.* 17 Feb. 1942, cc. 1751, 1758.

her full stature during the blitz, when she embodied the national will to victory, and memorably boosted local morale when things were at their worst by turning cartwheels in an air-raid shelter or cavorting on the Hoe.[65]

Her achievement must also be judged in the context of the immense barrage of publicity she faced; the world of entertainment has since frequently demonstrated how corrupting this can be. To this was added an indulgence from a long-suffering husband and an army of servants that would have destroyed a woman of weaker character. She was perpetually providing articles about her life and ideas, making speeches, giving interviews, being photographed—continually moving about from one place to another, from one sphere of life to another, and always at risk of being tripped up by sceptical bystanders. Even in her by-election of 1919 she complained that the press made a stunt of her campaign.[66] She fascinated the media, not only as a pioneer woman MP, but also as a rich and beautiful hostess with an aristocratic life-style and forthright opinions. Of course she enjoyed publicity, but her different worlds must often have exposed her to conflicting demands.

Then there is the sheer quantity of work she managed to get through as mother of one son by her first marriage and of five children by her second; as organizer of several large houses, amply staffed; as well-dressed hostess at numerous, often extravagant, social functions; as philanthropist, reformer, feminist, and politician with a huge correspondence. Like other early women MPs she had to respond, not only to constituents, but to demands from women throughout the country; by 1922 she was receiving an average of between 1,500 and 2,000 letters a week. Ray Strachey was amazed at the perpetual whirl of her life, and admiringly reported it in letters to her mother.[67]

Her papers reflect the elaborate secretarial apparatus all this required. Political diaries were compiled, reminders were sent, digests even of short letters were prepared, carbon copies kept, newspaper clippings pasted, background documents worked up, volumes of press comment preserved, briefs for speeches typed, phone calls made, pressmen interviewed, beggars warded off. Her regular exercise and daily cold bath may have preserved her good health, but credit must also go to the staunch backing she received and the stability her breathless life acquired from a husband

[65] *HC Deb.* 11 Apr. 1940, c. 762. Harrison, *Rose*, p. 175; cf. p. 189.

[66] *Daily News*, 8 Nov. 1919, p. 6.

[67] Nancy Astor MSS 1416/1/1/621: annual report of Plymouth Conservative and Unionist Association, 1922. Smith Archives, Oxford: Ray Strachey to her mother, 19 Nov. 1931, 3 Dec. 1932.

who can only be described as a saint, and who in later life seems to have endured something close to martyrdom at her hands.[68]

Her gross debating contribution was the largest of any woman MP before 1945, and among her twenty-one parliamentary sessions between 1920 and 1939 only that of 1936–7 shows her annual debating contribution falling below that of MPs in the top quartile. Her speeches, for all their defects, familiarized politicians and the public with women's new parliamentary role and prepared the way for successors whose quality surpassed her quantity. Her role was particularly important in the early 1920s when she held the fort alone or in partnership with Wintringham. Rathbone acknowledged this in 1922 when publicly praising her for the number of speeches made and questions asked.[69]

Astor was criticized from the start for taking her inauguration as 'a huge joke', and for talking animatedly throughout to all and sundry;[70] her unblushing Americanism irritated a nation half-conscious of its own international decline. Yet she was well able to laugh at herself, and could be disarming about her faults; 'no matter what I start with,' she once told MPs, 'I always get back to beer'. MPs also warmed to her humour. The House appreciates light relief and, as A. G. Gardiner wrote in 1925, 'wherever Lady Astor's "view halloo" is heard there is the assurance of sport'. Like her well-known temperance predecessor Sir Wilfrid Lawson, she was a decidedly cheerful puritan.[71] Politicians do not enter parliament merely to deliver learned and judicious speeches, and parliamentary government would soon languish if the worlds of politics and entertainment moved too far apart. If sober legislators entirely crowded out 'characters' with a popular following, political controversy would soon take unsavoury directions.

When the much-feared Clydeside MPs could not make themselves understood, Astor's mimicry in 1924 enabled her to translate their broad Scots dialect into English, and also to translate the English replies into broad Scots. Irene Ward thought her informality sometimes excessive—as when she sat in the Conservative front row, put in her false teeth, and bowed to the opposition.[72] Yet this only publicized what she frequently did at home, for she presided over much gaiety and boisterous play-acting

[68] Harrison, *Rose*, pp. 62, 144–5. Collis, *Diaries*, p. 98. Sykes, *Nancy*, pp. 444, 451, 489.

[69] *Liverpool Daily Post and Mercury*, 30 June 1922, p. 6.

[70] *Yorkshire Observer*, 2 Dec. 1919, p. 9.

[71] *HC Deb.* 7 June 1934, c. 1202. *Daily News*, 4 Apr. 1925, p. 6; cf. J. Johnston, *Westminster Voices* (n.d.), p. 190.

[72] Nancy Astor MSS 1416/1/6/88: draft chapter on 'The House of Commons and the Party System' for autobiography, p. 3. Author's tape-recorded interview with Baroness Ward, 6 July 1977, at the House of Lords.

within her family circle, where her special set of false teeth for taking off Margot Asquith gave much pleasure. She was adept at organizing children's parties, and Ray Strachey recalled her simultaneously handling two utterly different adult parties on the terrace of the House of Commons—one for retired servants of the House, the other for an American delegation—and brilliantly darting from one to the other.[73]

But she was more than a mere entertainer. Her wit was designed to ward off intrusion; the House knew both that her purposes were serious, and that she stood for important traditions in British public life. Besides, her defence of parliamentary government was direct; she repudiated Mosley at a time when democracy was in danger, yet when parliamentarism was integral to feminist objectives; in 1935 she told a National Government rally that the British people 'could not stand Fascism—it was too farcical, and if ever it came we should all die laughing'.[74] Like Pankhurst she was at her best in a crisis, and A. G. Gardiner saw pluck as the one quality in her that shone out above all others.[75] Courage was integral to her achievement as pioneering woman MP. In later years she often recalled being shouted down in the 1919 parliament when she stood up to ask questions affecting women and children; she never forgot the kindness of the Labour MP Will Thorne, who gave her the seat in the House which others refused.[76]

Her wit, courage, and energy enabled her to survive in an assembly whose rituals, clublike atmosphere, timetable, and combative mood were—and to some extent still are—uncongenial to women,[77] and needed to be challenged. Feminists needed to repudiate male pomposity, but whereas Virginia Woolf's assault upon it in *Three Guineas* is bitter and narrow in tone, Astor's parliamentary assault reflects an American's refreshing spontaneity, approachability, classlessness, and disrespect for tradition. One day in 1943 Harold Nicolson told his wife that Astor had been even more irritating than usual, yet he could not leave it there. 'But you know,' he added, 'tiresome as she is, there is something in her. A flame somewhere.'[78]

[73] M. Astor, *Tribal Feeling* (1963), p. 75. Harrison, *Rose*, pp. 100–1. *Leicester Daily Mercury*, 25 Feb. 1939, p. 11.

[74] *Kilmarnock Standard*, 6 July 1935, p. 6; cf. Nancy Astor MSS 1416/1/1/1328: Astor to Josiah Wedgwood, 14 Sept. 1934 (copy).

[75] *John Bull*, 13 Jan. 1945, p. 8.

[76] For examples of her attacks on the 1919 parliament see *HC Deb*. 29 Mar. 1928, c. 1452; 15 May 1935, c. 1821. For Thorne, see Sykes, *Nancy*, p. 220; *Stratford Express*, 10 Feb. 1939, p. 11.

[77] E. Vallance, *Women in the House. A Study of Women Members of Parliament* (1979), pp. 107–8. R. Butt, in *The Sunday Times*, 30 Oct. 1977, p. 16.

[78] H. Nicolson, *Diaries and Letters, 1939–1945* (1967), p. 333 (8 Dec. 1943).

PLATE 5. Eleanor Rathbone addressing a feminist meeting on 13 July 1925 with the old non-militant suffrage banners behind her (Fawcett Library).

4

Constructive Crusader

ELEANOR RATHBONE

During the Family Allowance Bill's second reading in 1945, its leading advocate Arthur Salter located Eleanor Rathbone 'in the great tradition of English humanitarian reformers, and the great line of English women reformers, from Florence Nightingale down'.[1] To her younger colleagues between the wars she seemed drawn from an earlier generation, a true Victorian who used an old-fashioned vocabulary, wore old-fashioned clothes, and moved about in a rather formal and dignified manner. Her booming, emphatic, and rather slow voice dominated conversations that were punctuated with mysterious initials such as 'NU' and 'FE'. Marjorie Green, a colleague of the 1930s, remembered her as rather portly and motherly-looking, but with beautiful white hair; her thoughtful eyes and forceful brow impressed people not just for their own sake, but because they reflected her intensity of purpose.[2] You thought twice before making a joke in her presence, for her dedication to her causes was complete.

Her biographer Mary Stocks says she possessed 'that rare capacity for mental concentration which is inaccurately designated "absence of mind"'; she could remove herself from immediate distractions and concentrate single-mindedly on the problem in hand. This discomfited those who failed to win her full attention; invited to tea when Rathbone had just come away from a worrying interview with Jan Masaryk, Green received no food and thought it best after twenty minutes to get up and leave. This curtailed the reverie. '"Oh, my dear child, my dear child. I've forgotten to give you any tea," she said, and then she set to, and I can see her still, put jam on the bread and cut it all up for me like a little girl'.[3]

[1] *HC Deb.* 8 Mar. 1945, c. 2322.

[2] Author's tape-recorded interviews with David and Diana Hopkinson, 15 Feb. 1976, at Missenden House, Little Missenden, Amersham, Bucks.; with Mrs Marjorie Soper (née Green), 22 Feb. 1977, at New Hall Farm, London Road, Harlow, Essex, CM17 9LU; and with Mrs Doris Cox and Mrs Vera Schaerli, 22 Mar. 1977, at 6 Vicarage Drive, Eastbourne. D. Hopkinson, *Family Inheritance. A Life of Eva Hubback* (1954), p. 105.

[3] M. D. Stocks, *Eleanor Rathbone. A Biography* (1949), p. 40; cf. p. 75. Author's tape-recorded interview with Mrs Soper, 22 Feb. 1977.

Rathbone often mislaid letters and parcels, and her papers and books on public questions were stuffed into the apparent chaos that lurked within her large and ubiquitous cheap bag; her two strings of pearls were so frequently left behind in taxis that the police came to know them quite well. She would make her points effectively in humanitarian committees while simultaneously littering the floor with her papers, leaving colleagues patiently to gather them up. Like several inter-war feminist leaders she had no interest in clothes, and wore only black and white. Her companion Elizabeth Macadam would check to see that her stockings were in order before she went out, and if she removed her hat at a committee meeting, people made sure she replaced it the right way round before leaving.[4]

Behind the drive and imagination of Rathbone's public work lies a personal austerity that now seems remarkable. She often had to be reminded to take meals, cared little about their quality, and was dissuaded only with great difficulty in the mid-1930s from personally testing the British Medical Association's minimum diet necessary for health. She could sleep at any time, in any posture, and never seemed to be ill. Despite her wealth and position she never travelled first class, and holidays were mere intervals for thought, periodic launching-pads for reinvigorated campaigning. The one indulgence she abundantly allowed herself, originally perhaps for feminist reasons, was the cigarette; she somehow never found a reason for giving it up.[5]

Though happy in her own life, she hated the thought of suffering in others; emotion many people channel into close personal relationships she reserved for generalized causes. She disliked talking about herself, and her secretaries vividly recall her reticence on sexual matters. She once told Vera Schaerli, a wartime colleague in humanitarian work, that she had been brought up to avert her eyes at nakedness even in small children; yet when seeing some children playing semi-naked in a sandpit recently she had been surprised at how charming they looked. She used the word 'sin' to hint at homosexuality in the Isle of Man's wartime internment camps, and she continually worried about whether Schaerli's necessarily informal relations with aliens were entirely above board.[6]

All this made her rather frightening to work for, if only because she

---

[4] Interviews with Mrs Cox and Mrs Schaerli, 22 Mar. 1977, and with Mrs Soper, 22 Feb. 1977. Interview with Mrs Gertrude Horton, 28 Feb. 1977, at 315 The Greenway, Epsom, Surrey. Stocks, *Rathbone*, p. 121.

[5] Stocks, *Rathbone*, pp. 39, 59, 119–20. Interview with Mrs Soper, 22 Feb. 1977.

[6] Interview with Mrs Cox and Mrs Schaerli, 22 Mar. 1977. Author's tape-recorded interview with Mrs Schaerli, 19 Sept. 1984, at Glebe Cottage, 37 Vicarage Drive, Eastbourne BN20 8AP; cf. Stocks, *Rathbone*, p. 181.

assumed that subordinates shared her own dedication. Her humane outlook paradoxically made her in some respects a very hard woman, stringent in her demands of people, impatient with self-pity or weakness of character. Schaerli, depressed by long and continuous involvement with refugee miseries, once requested a short holiday; Rathbone's more variegated life as a politician blinded her to Schaerli's problem, and at first she contested the need. Her single-mindedness could not easily be diverted on to her employees' welfare—though once alerted to it, nobody could have shown more concern; by 1944, when Schaerli had to leave her employment, Rathbone wanted her to provide adequately for old age, gave her a substantial sum from her own pocket, and took pains to advise her on how best to invest it.[7]

Stocks's biography, published in 1949 shortly after Rathbone's death, unites sympathy with close knowledge and critical appraisal in just the right measure; this unusual personality clearly intrigued Stocks, who wrote about her with verve, wit, and penetration. 'It made me weep onto my waistcoat,' Gilbert Murray said of the biography's moving final page.[8] If Rathbone has been so well portrayed already, and if most of her personal papers have vanished, why include her here? Because her career highlights a nonconformist reforming tradition that was once a significant influence on British public life and feminism; besides, no study of British inter-war feminism could possibly omit its most distinguished exponent.

Rathbone entered British public life through steadily broadening out her spheres of influence from the Rathbone family of Liverpool, with whose nonconformist idealism and public spirit everything began. She scrutinized the tradition closely as biographer of her father William Rathbone, a social reformer and Liberal MP for many years. Her biography shows much interest in his ancestors; the careers of the three William Rathbones, she says, seem 'but for the incidents of birth and death . . . to be but a single life extended over three generations'.[9] Eleanor's biographer must extend that figure to four, so strong was her father's influence. Not only is the biography affectionate in tone; its preoccupation with her father's political methods illuminates the many parallels between father and daughter. Both combine qualities seldom united; simultaneously preoccupied with the ideal and the practical, they

---

[7] Interview with Mrs Schaerli, 19 Sept. 1984. Author's tape-recorded interview with Mrs Soper and Mrs Cox, 15 Mar. 1977, at New Hall Farm, Harlow. Author's tape-recorded interview with Mrs Helga Wolff, 31 Aug. 1977, at Hemstal Road, London NW6 2AB.

[8] Bodleian Library, Oxford, Gilbert Murray MSS 100, fo. 70: Murray to Stocks, 7 Nov. 1949 (copy).

[9] E. F. Rathbone, *William Rathbone. A Memoir* (1905), p. 53.

both join independent-mindedness to collaboration, firm principle to an alert eye for compromise. As reformers, both are constructive in outlook, thorough in preliminary inquiry, politic in method, and, when necessary, unobtrusive in diplomacy.

Social reform activism eased, because it partially concealed, the transition of Eleanor's generation from religious to secular concerns; as Stocks puts it, she assumed the burdens of Christianity without accepting its consolations, whereas 'with most of us it is . . . the other way about'. Nineteenth-century provincial nonconformity remained psychologically distant from Whitehall and Westminster, Oxford and Cambridge; personal austerity, social responsibility, stewardship for wealth and power, distaste for honours and formality—all ensured that Rathbone politics could not be predicted from Rathbone wealth. Advocating higher taxation of inherited wealth in 1930, Eleanor pointed out that whereas the poor do not get the chance to realize their full stature, the heirs to business wealth throw their chances away.[10]

Her gateway to a wider world was Somerville College, Oxford, where she went in 1893. Its students' varied background broadened her perspectives, and its academic training—most notably its discussion-group, the Associated Prigs—sharpened up her formidable intellect. After taking her degree she thought of doing joint philosophical work on personality with Hilda Oakeley, but in an interesting correspondence she eventually dismissed the idea. Arguing that empirical scientific research was more likely than metaphysics to solve the problems in question, she turned instead to social work; she could not afford the luxury of a lifetime's study, she said, amid a world 'with all its wrongs shouting in one's ears,.[11]

She later pointed out that the Edwardian suffrage campaign provided 'an invaluable apprenticeship to the arts and crafts and qualities of the political engineer'.[12] In the 1870s the Rathbones had supported the movement for women's higher education, and by 1900 Eleanor's suffragist work in Lancashire got her on to the Union's executive committee. She remained there almost continuously until 1919, when she became president of NUSEC, the successor organization. She brought thoroughness and precision to the work, as we can see from her letter of July 1910, which elaborately calculates how many campaigners are needed to get a given number of signatures on a suffragist petition; each campaigner can get

---

[10] Stocks, *Rathbone*, p. 259; cf. p. 314. *HC Deb.* 16 Apr. 1930, c. 2990.

[11] Stocks, *Rathbone*, p. 53.

[12] E. Rathbone, 'Changes in Public Life', in R. Strachey (ed.), *Our Freedom and its Results. By Five Women* (1936), p. 26.

seven signatures per hour, so that if 150 branches place an average of six members in the work for twelve hours per week, a million signatures can be obtained in about thirteen and a half weeks.[13] Her time was not wholly taken up with the vote; in 1912 she published ideas on family allowances that she had first elaborated eight years before, and in Liverpool she remained active in local government and social questions, forming the Liverpool Women Citizens' Association in 1913 to educate women in public affairs.

The First World War accelerated her feminist promotion in rather unusual circumstances. Early in 1914 she offended the NUWSS leaders by mobilizing opposition to the Union's alliance with the Labour Party; hurt at being accused of disloyalty, she resigned from the executive. Yet she returned within a year, because the champions of the Labour connection had by then themselves resigned after failing to push Fawcett into supporting the women's peace conference at The Hague. Rathbone's timely aid to Fawcett at this point was crucial not only to her own feminist career, but also to preserving the Union as a broad church for feminists of many types. Partly in the hope that the Women Citizens' Associations would join the Union after the war, NUSEC (as the NUWSS became in 1919) allowed its initial statement of objects to remain ambiguous as between feminism and social reform. When standing for the NUSEC presidency in 1919, Rathbone made it clear that if elected she would feel free to promote her own ideas on policy, and this she ably did; she remained president from 1919 to 1928, and stayed on the executive committee till 1931. Through NUSEC she made her major contribution to British feminism— encouraging it in hard thought about long-term objectives.

In a presidential speech of 1925 which Stocks thought 'one of the great speeches of her career', Rathbone claimed that NUSEC was 'approaching a stage in its existence when its work will be less obvious and clearly defined . . . than it has been during the last five years', and that 'the time has come to take stock and decide what next';[14] amid much excitement, she went on to persuade NUSEC to adopt family allowances. Four of the seven committee-members who launched the family allowance movement in 1917 had been non-militants, and when Rathbone developed her ideas further in *The Disinherited Family* (1924), non-militants contributed all three of those who 'helped . . . with many criticisms and suggestions':

---

[13] Fawcett Library Autograph Collection 1Hii/6936: Rathbone to Mrs Ward, 23 July 1910.
[14] Stocks, *Rathbone*, p. 117. E. F. Rathbone, *Milestones. Presidential Addresses* (Liverpool, 1929), p. 28.

Hubback, Stocks, and Macadam.[15] Stocks thought the book the most substantial contribution made by a woman to economic thought, producing 'a revolutionary change' in the subject, stamping it 'with an indelible feminist mark'; one reviewer saw it as 'perhaps the most important feminist text since Mill's *Subjection of Women*'.[16]

This new feminist campaign placed Rathbone at the centre of the important but now somewhat forgotten debate of the 1920s between the 'old' feminists who wanted the Union to concentrate on individualist and egalitarian reforms and the 'new' feminists who favoured discriminatory welfare reforms as the way of bringing 'real' equality to woman in her distinctive role as mother. Rathbone's 'new' feminism wanted to move beyond a mere shedding of the fetters, beyond what Kathleen Courtney called 'me too feminism', beyond the sort of feminism which thinks only 'in terms of men' and therefore betrays an inferiority complex. Instead, women should cease seeing their problems through men's eyes, cease discussing them in men's language. The 'old' feminist's pursuit of wider career opportunities was criticized for 'belittling the home claims which in fact prevent the majority of married women from entertaining that wish', whereas the 'new' feminist insisted that women have distinctive legislative needs, and promoted family allowances to reward the family woman.[17]

Rathbone carried weight within NUSEC not only because of her formidable intelligence and wealth (twice during the 1920s she gave £100 to rescue the Union's periodical) but because she could mobilize friendship and paid or unpaid help from other women. During the 1920s she settled down to live with Macadam in Romney Street, and although Rathbone always wanted her to persist with her own career in social science, Macadam eventually took over the domestic department of Rathbone's life. Below Macadam was that 'terrific personality', the cockney housekeeper Mrs Wilson, with whom Macadam conducted a long-running struggle for supremacy within the household.[18] Rathbone also greatly valued two friendships with leading members of the Union: Stocks she regarded almost as a daughter, and Hubback she saw as 'a

---

[15] E. F. Rathbone, *The Disinherited Family* (1924), p. xi (introduction).
[16] *Time and Tide*, 18 Mar. 1927, pp. 267–8. *Woman's Leader*, 28 Mar. 1924, p. 72.
[17] Rathbone in R. Strachey (ed.), *Our Freedom*, p. 57; cf. pp. 74, 76. *Time and Tide*, 12 Mar. 1926, p. 254. Rathbone in R. Strachey (ed.), *Our Freedom*, p. 61. See also Rathbone, *Stocks*, p. 116.
[18] Interview with Mrs Soper and Mrs Cox, 15 Mar. 1977. See also Stocks, *Rathbone*, p. 93. Interview with Baroness Stocks, 30 Apr. 1974, at Aubrey Lodge, Aubrey Road, London W8.

strong tower to lean against in time of trouble'.[19] Rathbone's influence and presence were nicely complemented by Stocks's incisive intelligence and literary skill and by Hubback's marked organizing ability as the Union's parliamentary secretary.

These distinguished women enabled the Union to get equal franchise and several reforms of family law enacted during the 1920s, despite the Six Point Group's grumbles about its cautious and unobtrusive methods. 'We were backwoodsmen in pre-war days,' said Rathbone, justifying NUSEC's methods in her presidential address of 1926; 'now we need to be skilled artisans'. Some of the Union's many successful activities budded off into distinct organizations: into the Family Endowment Society and the Townswomen's Guilds, for example. Rathbone contributed much to both, but at least as much to another feminist development of the 1920s: promoting women's welfare in India. In 1927 Katherine Mayo's *Mother India* issued what Rathbone saw as 'a challenge loud enough to waken the dead', and helped tempt her on to parliament's larger stage as an Independent MP.[20]

Only a university seat, with its highly educated electors and proportional representation, could have given her such a platform; she had stood unsuccessfully as an Independent at East Toxteth in 1922, obtaining 40 per cent of the votes cast, but the seat was invulnerably Conservative at all elections between 1918 and 1945. When she stood for the Combined English Universities' two-member constituency in 1929 she won only a third of the first-preference votes cast; but as the top candidate reached the quota, Rathbone was able to win the second seat through the redistributed second preferences of his surplus supporters, and held it for the rest of her life. Time gradually weakened her Liverpool connection; when setting out for London after the First World War she stopped taking a return ticket, and during the 1920s her changed domestic circumstances at both ends increased London's attractions still further. In 1935 she did not offer herself for re-election to Liverpool city council because she felt she had been neglecting her duties there.[21] But she never lost the Rathbones' serious-mindedness, their continuous awareness of suffering, and their sense of personal responsibility for relieving it.

Her relationship with her university constituents was happy; she regularly sent them bulletins, praised them and often quoted them in

[19] Eva Hubback Papers (in the care of her daughter, Diana Hopkinson): Rathbone to Hubback, 2 Sept. 1941.
[20] Rathbone, *Milestones*, p. 32. *Woman's Leader*, 26 Aug. 1927, p. 231.
[21] Stocks, *Rathbone*, pp. 77–8, 92–3, 194.

parliament. Her election results show that the respect was mutual. She won 3,331 first-preference votes in 1929, 5,096 in 1931, was unopposed in 1935, and won 11,176 in 1945. She consistently won first-preference votes from about a quarter of the constituency's expanding electorate, and obtained a rising percentage of the total first-preference votes cast (53 per cent of them in 1945). As an Independent in a two-party system she could never be a model for aspiring women politicians—though if her wish for proportional representation had been granted her type of career might have become more common. NUSEC included this reform among its objects in 1919, and she eloquently defended it in parliament more than once in the 1930s; but during the Second World War she came to see it as better suited to local than to national politics.[22]

Feminists disliked the British party machines partly because they had opposed women's suffrage, and the rationality of suffragist outsiders to the system led some to hope that the women's vote would render redundant the rival machines that mobilized opinion at the national level. In her first presidential address to NUSEC Rathbone explained that she 'must not be a bottled vintage bought at the party wine-shop',[23] and carried these attitudes into parliament. She always stressed the all-party nature of support for family allowances, and as sole Independent MP she often felt free to take a distinctive line, or to speak more frankly than others on some issues. In April 1940, for example, she urged Chamberlain to prune incompetents more ruthlessly from his administration, and in November 1944 she wanted a general election postponed until the war was won.

Rathbone had been launched on social reform by the Charity Organization Society, which thought sheer strength of will in donor and recipient could eliminate poverty if only enterprise and self-provision could be protected against sentimental and indiscriminate hand-outs. Like many of its members, Rathbone outgrew its principles but retained its preoccupation with cultivating character at every social level. She referred directly to the Society in 1929 when opposing the sort of means test that would undermine honesty; it was important, she said, to uphold the Englishman's reputation for truthfulness overseas and to strengthen character, 'the greatest asset of this country'.[24] As housing reformer she felt concern for the poor family whose payment of high rents precariously kept it out of the slum, and therefore prevented it from benefiting by slum-clearance schemes. And because she thought the much-abused working-

[22] *HC Deb.* 23 Jan. 1945, c. 714.
[23] NUSEC presidential address, 1920, in Rathbone, *Milestones*, p. 3.
[24] *HC Deb.* 13 Nov. 1929, c. 2097.

class mother honest and best-informed on her own affairs, she opposed cuts in women's national insurance benefit, and urged that family allowances be given in cash rather than (through school meals) in kind.

All this locates her among the many twentieth-century Liberal social reformers who moved only reluctantly towards the class politics of organized labour. She condemned the Labour government for its lack of feminist impact during 1924; to a feminist seeking women's wider occupational opportunity, organized labour seemed fully capable of tyranny and selfishness. She also worried about a class differential in the birth-rate that was apparently boosting the working-class proportion of the British population. For their part, trade unionists thought family allowances might undermine the concept of the standard wage, and so threaten collective bargaining procedures; age-group and gender might then dethrone social class from priority in the public debate about the distribution of wealth.

Repudiating the 'pretence and humbug' whereby politicians conceal their real feelings on class issues, Rathbone said that Britain had avoided a dictatorship of the proletariat only because working-class voters had not yet chosen to exercise their full power. In a revealing parliamentary speech of 1931 she recommended university seats and proportional representation as safeguards; by ensuring representation for geographically scattered professional occupations, the university seats complemented a constituency-based electoral system which over-represented more concentrated groups, and brought into the House of Commons 'something of that atmosphere of impartiality and unprejudiced outlook upon the truth that has always been characteristic of the universities themselves.'[25] Given Labour's advent as a distinct and major party, a Liberal label would have been too limiting, yet a Liberal she was; 'I regard you as one of the finest Liberals I know,' Lady Violet Bonham-Carter told her in 1945, '—and I only wish you were one in name as well as in fact'.[26] In 1931 she supported the National Government as the only way out of the immediate crisis, but her free-trading convictions and distaste for the cuts made this painful; she later joined the Next Five Years Group and supported Lloyd George's 'call to action'.

She was now fully launched into politics, and her parliamentary speeches make it possible to recreate her outlook across the whole range of policy from welfare to war. Given her family background, constituency,

[25] *HC Deb.* 23 May 1931, c. 2015; 26 Feb. 1936, c. 511; see also 17 Jan. 1945, c. 306.
[26] Liverpool University Library, Eleanor Rathbone Papers, XIV.3.3 (33): Bonham-Carter to Rathbone, 9 Feb. 1945.

and cast of mind, one might have expected educational policy to attract her, for her father had helped found university colleges at both Liverpool and Bangor. But although alert to opinion within the provincial universities, she focused instead on the larger aim of upholding the sort of society within which universities could flourish. In some ways she remained a scholar throughout her life, retaining an academic innocence and even gullibility in areas where she was ignorant. An academic appetite for clear, empirically based, and impartial analysis invariably pervaded her speeches; she was always well briefed on social surveys, and was among the earliest MPs to cite opinion-poll evidence. Her role as MP for a university constituency was entirely appropriate, and her bond with her constituents was close; yet her intellect was never used to blunt her sense of responsibility for the world around her, nor did it tempt her into that timid variant of impartiality that is more accurately described as concealing one's opinions.

At first housing reform seemed likely to be her cause. She was puzzled that so much inter-war political effort went into subsidizing house-building for private or public ownership, so little into helping the poorer families who rented from a private landlord; far from catering for the poorest groups, local authorities were as keen as any private landlord to attract the better tenants. Her experience as a Liverpool councillor convinced her that many council-house tenants could well afford to buy or rent a house, and were 'cheating the poor and using money which was never intended for them'. Wouldn't it be cheaper to subsidize the person rather than the house? Couldn't rent rebates (she asked in her maiden speech) readily be geared to family size? Greenwood's Act of 1930 went some way along this road, but not far enough, and although she was still pressing this approach on Bevan as late as November 1945, other causes soon claimed her.[27]

She devoted a quarter of her parliamentary debating contribution to welfare questions, less than the average for women MPs (46 per cent) during her time in parliament. Yet for her there was no clear line between welfare and feminist issues, and she contributed twice as much on family allowances per sessional day in parliament as any other woman MP. In 1928 NUSEC's council resolved to back better provision for maternity in the National Insurance Acts; if differential scales of contribution or benefit were needed, it felt that these should be based on rates of pay, not on sex or age. Throughout the 1930s Rathbone complained that women were

[27] *HC Deb.* 29 July 1931, c. 2379; cf. 20 June 1934, c. 447; see also 29 Nov. 1945, c. 1739.

lumped together with men in the national insurance system only when it suited the men; unemployment benefits, where women claimed less than the men, were pooled—but not health benefits, where women claimed more. She also wanted a fairer national insurance policy for married women in paid work; if they gave up work, the family income was no larger than a bachelor's, but if they continued working they were accused of poaching jobs from men and from unmarried women.

She had worked out her case for family allowances before 1914, and was not alone in the field; but wartime administration of separation allowances briefed her fully on working-class family finance and convinced her that her reform might become politically viable. The family allowance committee formed in 1917 gained impetus in 1924 from her *Disinherited Family*, a landmark in the literature of social administration which illustrates how a society's practical needs can sometimes stimulate major intellectual advance. She claims that economists, when discussing the family, make 'statements of a vagueness, an ineptitude, a futility' of which elsewhere they would be ashamed.[28] Closely argued, fertile in practical suggestions, strenuous in meeting likely objections, impatient with sentimentality in any form, the book draws upon sociologists' latest information, and ranges broadly over time and space for its evidence.

Her historical introduction claims that at the same time as nineteenth-century factory legislation subordinated women to the male head of the family, economists' textbooks divorced wage-structure from family need. In fighting for better wages, she says, male adults hide behind the petticoats of women and children, as they had earlier done when curbing factory hours. As long as wage-rates reflect the assumption that every adult male (though not every adult female) has a family to support, national resources will be lavished on the unmarried or childless male at the expense of dependent mothers and their children. At least since Wollstonecraft, feminists had been criticizing 'the selfish coxcomb, who lives but for himself, and who is often afraid to marry lest he should not be able to live in a certain style', and in other contexts Rathbone more than once condemned teenagers' irresponsibility and extravagance; it is hardly surprising that Liverpool bachelors began mobilizing against her at the general election of 1922.[29] What she calls 'the Turk complex'—the husband's pride (sometimes fostered by the wife) in being responsible for 'dependants'—can and must succumb. With family allowances as with

[28] Rathbone, *Disinherited Family*, p. 272.
[29] M. Wollstonecraft, *A Vindication of the Rights of Woman*, ed. C. W. Hagelman, Jr. (New York, 1967), p. 252. For 1922, see *Woman's Leader*, 24 May 1929, p. 123.

housing policy, she goes on, poverty can be relieved far more cheaply; the flat-rate principle must be abandoned in both cases, and payments must be adjusted to the needs of the individual.

Eugenic arguments reinforced her case, for she shared the public alarm of the late 1930s at the falling birth-rate, and feared that Britain's lack of a population policy could be remedied even less easily than her failure to rearm. She wanted to preserve British world influence by boosting the national birth-rate, and to rectify the situation whereby 'the unfittest parents and homes are receiving the largest numbers of children'. She argued that universal family allowances would reduce family size only among the very poor whose improvidence flourished on despair and ignorance; among the better off, her reform (perhaps upwardly graded with increase in family income) would reduce the marginal cost of children.[30] So her *Disinherited Family* advocates a state-administered, non-occupational, universal, and compulsory scheme.

Fond of small babies, Rathbone never really wanted to reduce their number; she was always delighted when a new Rathbone child was born, and the news of anybody's new baby always brought out what Schaerli calls the 'shy warmth' of her personality. Yet she thought birth-control could help family allowances to emancipate motherhood. Feminists had been unable to advocate it before getting votes, she wrote in 1924, 'but now that those irrevocable gifts have been given, we can afford to speak our minds'.[31] She wanted government health clinics to provide birth-control information, gave regularly to the precursor of the Family Planning Association in the early 1930s, and was one of only three inter-war women MPs to advocate birth-control in parliament.

She promoted family allowances skilfully, relying not on bulk of discussion—the subject takes up only 17 per cent of her debating contribution between 1940 and 1945, when the question was most alive—but on ingenuity and timeliness; she slipped the subject into debates on related social problems. For example, during the General Strike and in the early 1930s she claimed that family allowances would boost purchasing-power precisely among those most hit by the trade cycle's downswing. Likewise the preoccupation of the 1930s with nutrition produced her Children's Minimum Campaign Committee, which from 1934 tried to guarantee the minimum diet necessary for health with a welfare package

[30] Rathbone, *Disinherited Family*, pp. 242, 239. *HC Deb*. 25 Mar. 1938, c. 1574; 3 Nov. 1944, c. 1174.

[31] Interview with Mrs Schaerli, 19 Sept. 1984; cf. Stocks, *Rathbone*, p. 94. Rathbone, *Disinherited Family*, p. 246.

which included family allowances, free school meals, and free milk for children and pregnant mothers.

Family allowances arrived late on the parliamentary scene; there was no substantial discussion until 1936, and only after 1939 did the parliamentary discussion become annual. The war came to her rescue: morale must be boosted and national resources must be conserved, so pressures built up for the reformed structure of welfare she had always wanted. War also made it politically feasible to do this through the non-contributory method, and so win over the trade unions; and government came to welcome universal family allowances as a way to relieve poverty without eroding the parent's incentive to seek work. In the first full-dress parliamentary debate on 23 June 1942, several speakers noted the marked recent advance in opinion on the subject.

One penetrating historian of the family-allowance movement denies that it was crucial in getting the reform introduced; it provided no more than a forum, he says, for debates 'which would have taken place anyway'. Such determinism is not echoed by the politicians who praise Rathbone's achievement during the debate on the Family Allowance Bill's third reading on 11 June 1945. Nor is it the mood of Beveridge's epilogue to the 1949 re-issue of *The Disinherited Family*; there he gives full credit to Rathbone for educating public opinion on the issue, and for writing the book which had produced his own 'instant and total conversion' to the idea in 1924.[32] The family-allowance movement would in fact have been unusual among pressure groups if it had determined the detailed administrative outcome, or even the prevailing political climate, at the last stages of the campaign. Rathbone herself told the Beveridge Committee in 1942 that the Family Endowment Society had switched only recently from advocating a general principle towards considering its detailed application.[33] Movements of this kind encourage the tree to grow; they cannot be expected to determine the precise timing and flavour of its fruit.

Feminist arguments are not prominent in Rathbone's speech of 23 June 1942 and rare in the debate as a whole. But she hoped family allowances would dignify motherhood as a service to the community and therefore insisted, against government opposition, that they be paid to the mother. They would also prevent equal pay from driving women out of

[32] J. Macnicol, *The Movement for Family Allowances, 1918–45. A Study in Social Policy Development* (1980), p. 217. W. Beveridge, 'Epilogue', in E. Rathbone, *Family Allowances. A New Edition of 'The Disinherited Family'* (1949), p. 270.

[33] PRO CAB 87/77, fo. 312: Hubback and Rathbone's evidence to the Beveridge Committee from the Family Endowment Society.

employment: adequately rewarded mothers would rarely undercut the husbands of other women in the labour market; those women, feeling more secure, would stop nourishing their husbands' fears; then women's labour, 'neither boycotted nor preferred because of its cheapness, might be allowed to find its natural level'.[34] This is not the sole instance in twentieth-century welfare history where state intervention has advanced with the aim of ensuring the successful operation of the free market.

In the first parliamentary debate on equal pay (in 1936) Rathbone diverged from many feminists, and incongruously allied with the anti-feminist Atholl. Rathbone thought advocates of the change should 'look at the motives of their male allies'; equal pay without family allowances would simply throw women out of work. Hence trade unionists implicitly favoured equal pay; the British Union of Fascists in 1934 was explicit—it would 'bring about a natural functional reorganisation of industrial labour, women turning again to those occupations and followings for which they are constitutionally better fitted than men'.[35] In the equal pay division of 28 March 1944, however, family allowances were on the horizon, so Rathbone felt able to support equal pay, and abstained when the government made the question one of confidence.

She expected much from family allowances, and astonished some French feminist women in the 1920s by saying they could make more difference to women's status and children's welfare than any event since Christianity began.[36] Family allowances have produced no such transformation; the initial scale of benefit was smaller than she wished, nor has its real value kept up with inflation. For this she can hardly be blamed, but many feminists would now reject its premiss: that most married women, if given a real choice, would or should withdraw at least temporarily from the labour market into a family role. They see 'welfare feminism' as conservative on women's social function, and share the egalitarian and libertarian priorities of the 'old feminists'.

Yet Rathbone promoted these too; she easily leads inter-war women MPs for size of debating contribution on women's rights and status per sessional day in parliament. After only a few months as MP, she bravely spoke out against female circumcision in Kenya. On women's nationality in 1933 she for once refused government offers of half a loaf; she thought

[34] Rathbone, *Disinherited Family*, p. 262.

[35] *HC Deb.* 1 Apr. 1936, c. 2034. A. Raven Thompson (Deputy Director of Policy), reply to questions from the London and National Society for Women's Service, 1 Aug. 1934 (consulted when in the care of Miss Halpin, of 5 Chagford Street, London NW1).

[36] Rathbone, *Disinherited Family*, p. 193.

acceptance might tempt the authorities to treat the subject as closed, but, as she would in other circumstances have predicted, the result was that she got no bread. Her Wills and Intestacies (Family Maintenance) Bill tackled what she described as 'the meanest thing that can be done'—the evil whereby people (usually men) omitted from their wills the dependants (usually women) who had cared for them.[37]

In the early 1930s British feminists championed the rights of Indian women. Rathbone felt acutely responsible for their welfare; she toured India for six weeks and told parliament in 1933 that 'for the last four years I have lived almost night and day with this question'. Civil service obstruction on this and other colonial feminist issues made her really angry; 'in all my life I have never been so completely up against a dead wall as in this business of Indian women', she complained in 1935; she later claimed to feel 'really . . . bitter' on the subject.[38] She helped to widen the India Bill's concessions to women electors, but failed to get safeguards for women's civil rights. Given her loathing of inhumane Indian practices towards women, her support for Indian devolution was an act of somewhat precariously-held faith.

Here, as in overseas matters generally, her feminism was linked to broader perspectives. Her faith in colonial devolution was consistent, and in March 1933 she thought that the best way forward in India was to collaborate with Gandhi's section of the Congress movement. Such a standpoint did not come easily to her, for her profound patriotism distanced her from what she saw as Fenner Brockway's sentimentality and even gullibility towards Indian criticism of the British authorities. She also resented Indian nationalist exploitation of Britain's wartime difficulties, and she could sometimes treat Indians tactlessly, with insufficient regard for their self-respect. None the less she held firmly to the liberal belief that conciliation and self-government ward off violence, and urged Churchill towards both during the Second World War.[39]

To judge from their debating careers, the early women MPs regarded foreign policy as a male sphere, and while Rathbone was in parliament they assigned it only 5 per cent of their total debating contribution; her figure was 16 per cent, and was surpassed by only one of the women MPs between 1919 and 1945, Marjorie Graves, 90 per cent of whose short speaking career went on foreign policy. Rathbone was the first woman MP

---

[37] *HC Deb.* 22 Jan. 1937, c. 530; see also 9 Nov. 1933, c.390.

[38] Ibid. 28 Mar. 1933, c. 941; 8 Apr. 1935, c. 918; 15 May 1935, c. 1819.

[39] Ibid. 28 Mar. 1933, c. 949. Stocks, *Rathbone*, pp. 138–9, 155, 297. *HC Deb.* 1 Aug. 1941, cc. 1738–9.

to express concern in parliament at Hitler's advent, which on 13 April 1933 she saw as 'an omen for the rest of the world'. Neither she nor Graves (the next woman MP to express concern in parliament, on 5 July) included feminism among their motives for doing so, either at this or any other time; it was too obvious to need mentioning. After Hitler's bloody coup later in the year, Rathbone found it difficult 'to get the stench out of one's nostrils, the sights of horror out of one's mind, or to feel at first as if anything else mattered'.[40]

Already by May 1933 she was sounding a note that became frequent during the next few years: the need for a defensive political and cultural league of the free democracies. She simultaneously urged better overseas propaganda for democracy, opposed disarmament, and virulently condemned Nazism. She thought the Hoare–Laval Pact had originated 'not in conscious treachery, but in the moral and intellectual weakness of the Government—its lack of courage and foresight, its divided aims, its inconsistent motives, its internal dissensions'; British abandonment of Abyssinia made her think nothing in the future 'could happen to make us feel more ashamed or more wounded in our racial pride'. Pleading on 5 November 1936 for collective security through the League, she longed for a Fox or a Gladstone who would go beyond uttering pious opinions and mount 'a campaign which would sweep the country and create a movement of all those right-minded people who care for peace'.[41]

Rathbone's feminism frontally repudiated a traditionalist chivalry, yet a fierce belief in chivalrous conduct is integral to her case for building up a democratic alliance against the dictators. Her fervent patriotism—deeply moralistic and libertarian in tone, never crudely chauvinist—made her think national honour and decency were at stake. She felt humiliated when Britain repeatedly betrayed democrats abroad; this would not only fail to avert war, but would inflate the dictators' pretensions and leave Britain friendless in Europe, with the second-rank status of a Sweden or a Denmark. Hence the change in the pace of her parliamentary career in 1936. Hitherto she had made on average nine major speeches a year; she often prepared the ground for these with her parliamentary questions, and supplemented them with about ten shorter speeches—except in 1935 when the India Act seemed to require more short contributions. But after 1935 foreign affairs swing the balance of her contributions towards parliamentary questions and away from long speeches, whose annual

[40] Rathbone Papers, XIV.3.4: circular letter to constituents, Mar. 1934, p. 1.
[41] E. F. Rathbone, *War Can Be Averted. The Achievability of Collective Security* (1938), pp. 47, 49. *HC Deb.* 5 Nov. 1936, c. 337.

average falls to six. And whereas till 1936 she had asked an average of thirty-seven oral and written parliamentary questions a year, this figure rises to 155 for the rest of her career. In the late 1930s she therefore became one of the top forty MPs for asking oral questions.

By summer 1937 she had become really angry at British feebleness abroad, and spent the summer recess writing *War Can Be Averted* (1938). The book reflects three of her best qualities: the courage that leads the lay person to spice with common sense discussions that are too readily left to experts: the combination of idealism with down-to-earth appreciation of political realities; and the consequent linkage of means to ends. She therefore warns her political friends against giving way to their perilous desire for clean hands. The sharpness of her criticism here springs from proximity rather than distance, for she fully shared the aims and comprehended the mood of the pacifist world. Her book's prime message is that collective security can avert war, given 'the belief that it can be done and the will to do it'. Her chapter on 'the defeatism of the left' voices the alarm felt by 'anyone with the temperament and experience of a pre-war Victorian' that the inevitability of war should be so widely assumed.[42] Pacifists, she complains, seem to pursue peace primarily through vivid but enervating descriptions of the horrors of war. On several occasions, she argues, the National Government has shown itself squeezable by outside pressure. Mobilize, then, for collective security through the League, and seek allies—even Conservative and Soviet Communist ones—wherever they can be found!

In summer 1937 and 1938 she even worried about leaving the Chamberlain government unsupervised by parliament during the recess.[43] After the Munich settlement, which she opposed, the Molotov–Ribbentrop Pact of 1939 came as no surprise, for her book had already predicted that Russians left too long in the lurch might outbid the democracies in seeking Nazi friendship; after all, she writes, 'there is far more ideological affinity between the Nazi–Fascist *bloc* and Bolshevism than between Nazi–Fascism and Western democracy'.[44] Events in 1939 apparently vindicated her line since 1933, so during the Norway debate of 8 May 1940 she experienced none of Astor's need to change horses; once again she could consistently vote against Chamberlain.

After 1933 she combined attacks on Fascism with concern for its refugee victims. She devoted 6 per cent of her total debating contribution

[42] Ibid.
[43] *HC Deb.* 21 July 1937, c. 2198; 26 July 1938, c. 3021.
[44] Rathbone, *War Can Be Averted*, p. 93; cf. *HC Deb.* 24 Aug. 1939, c. 34.

to refugees—nine-tenths of all that was said on the subject by woman MPs before 1945. Her humanitarian concern was consistent throughout her career, but its direction changed according to need. Her first parliamentary question on the subject, on 13 April 1933, concerned British policy on refugees from Germany, but by summer 1937 Spanish refugees from Franco had become her priority; by 1939 she wanted British and Commonwealth entry restrictions relaxed, claiming that these had been 'among the least generous of civilized States in contributing towards a solution' to the refugee problem. British policy towards the dictators made her feel a special responsibility in 1939 for Czech and Spanish refugees; she told parliament that she was one of those who 'feel guilty of every bit of evil in the world which they or their nations . . . fail to prevent, provided it was possible to prevent it or try to prevent it without creating a greater evil'.[45]

War once more altered her humanitarian priorities. She joined a very disparate group of politicians in defending the aliens interned in the Isle of Man; 'we were inundated with cries for help', Schaerli recalled. But the aliens' defenders faced a double difficulty: they wished neither to embarrass an over-pressed government nor to provide Hitler with propaganda against British democracy: 'this is a question which affects our prestige as a nation,' said Rathbone on 10 July 1940, at last nerving herself to protest, 'and we do not want to let it go out that our land is a land of oppression and not a land of the free'.[46] This unleashed her flood of parliamentary questions on the matter; why intern people who had more reason than most to loathe Hitler? A third of her debating contribution during 1940 and 1941 went on their welfare—far more than was contributed by any other woman MP.

Once the aliens had been cared for, she could return to European refugees. Humanitarian considerations apart, it seemed merely foolish to exclude them when Hitler's lunacy gave Britain the chance of 'skimming the cream of European culture'. She formed the National Committee for Rescue from Nazi Terror, keeping her own role in the background; by 1943 she had developed a network of refugee contacts so broad that she felt as expert on the subject as any civil servant, and continually pestered ministers to help. Government moved slowly, especially Herbert Morrison. His response to one deputation made her so angry that she

---

[45] E. Rathbone, 'A Personal View of the Refugee Problem', *New Statesman*, 15 Apr. 1939, p. 568; cf. *HC Deb.* 4 Aug. 1939, c. 2893.
[46] Interview with Mrs Cox and Mrs Schaerli, 22 Mar. 1977. *HC Deb.* 10 July 1940, c. 1220.

uncharacteristically refused to round it off with conventional politeness: 'she felt that she had nothing to thank him for, as he had not made a single concession of any sort . . . To thank him under these circumstances would be merely an empty formality and she did not propose to do so.'[47]

'Have I sounded too bitter?' she asked, in the debate of 19 May 1943 on European refugees; 'I tell you . . . there is not one who would not feel bitter if he or she had my postbag and read the letters I receive by every post from agonised people who feel that the one chance left for their relatives is slipping from them and that they may soon have to take that awful journey to the Polish slaughter-house and who beg me to rescue them, not realising how impotent I am.' The horrors of the concentration camps nourished in her the Zionism she had first developed on a visit to Palestine in 1934; Jewish sufferings rested on her conscience day and night, and she came to think that in cultural and intellectual matters the world owed far more to the Jews than to the Arabs.[48]

Yet her humanitarianism did not stop at national boundaries: when the tide turned and the Germans themselves became refugees, they too benefited from her concern. 'What is the use of university representation', she asked in December 1944, 'if university representatives cannot speak the truth as they see it?' Politicians seemed to wink at Soviet deportation of Germans, and she later expressed shock when the Czechs did the same. She knew more than most about German war crimes, yet she insisted on distinguishing clearly between Germans and Nazis, and braved inevitable misunderstanding in November 1944 when she urged that after the war the Germans themselves should be left to try Nazi crimes against Germans.[49]

Her lifelong humanitarianism restlessly changes direction according to need but is unendingly resourceful in its methods; an ample reserve of new causes boils and bubbles below her surface, awaiting the chance to erupt. Almost at the end of her career, she urges MPs to 'remember that all suffering is individual suffering', that 'there is no such thing as collective suffering', and that 'all responsibility is individual responsibility, that everyone in the world is responsible for every calamity that happens in the world, if he or she has left undone anything he could have done'. She

---

[47] *HC Deb.* 16 July 1943, c. 561. Typescript report (carbon copy) of undated deputation from Archbishop Temple and others to Morrison on the refugee question, p. 4 (in the care of Mrs Schaerli); cf. *HC Deb.* 19 May 1943, c. 1141.

[48] *HC Deb.* 19 May 1943, c. 1142. See also Stocks, *Rathbone*, pp. 214, 216; *HC Deb.* 14 Dec. 1943, c. 1472; 20 Aug. 1945. c. 365.

[49] *HC Deb.* 15 Dec. 1944, c. 1512; See also 26 Oct. 1945, c. 2414; 10 Nov. 1944, cc. 1728–9.

champions oppressed minorities when they are at their most vulnerable—
Spanish republicans in 1937–9, British-interned aliens in 1940, European
Jews in 1942–3, deported Germans in 1944–5. Her variant of feminism
promotes not only the interests of women, but companionship and
collaboration between the sexes. 'It is not a question of feminism . . .', she
once said of Indian women's rights, 'it is a question of life and death.' In
August 1945 she foreshadowed future humanitarian concerns by claiming
that Japan should have been allowed more time for decision before the first
nuclear bombs were dropped.[50]

Behind all this humanitarian effort lies a passionate commitment to
defeating Hitler. Briefly she wavered at the start of the war. On 9 October
1939 she suggested a British statement of war aims; negotiation with
Germany might reassure the public that everything possible had been
done to avert war. But she did not hesitate again, and so completely did the
war come to fill her mind that she of all people became one of the most
ardent champions of Churchill, the anti-feminist opponent of the India
Act—praising him in August 1939 for accurately predicting so much,
furiously rebuking Bevan in 1943 for attacking him unfairly, deeply
reluctant in 1945 to criticize his policy on aid to refugees. 'My admiration
for him is such, that I hate to differ from him in anything,' she said,
'because I believe that he will go down in history as the man to whom not
only this country, but the whole world, owes more than to any other
British statesman who ever lived.'[51]

We have already seen how her patriotism advanced her feminist career
in 1915; 'I can see her at the [NUWSS] conference,' Fenner Brockway
recalled many years later, '—fury personified, bushy black eyebrows over
flashing eyes, a mass of black-grey hair, her face red with patriotic
fervour'. In the Second World War her patriotism remained undimin-
ished, and lent her national stature. All her humanitarian causes merged
with the one great aim of defeating Hitler. In September 1941 she told
Hubback that she would hate to die without knowing the outcome of the
struggle: 'it would be such an agonizing anxiety . . . Even if I knew or
believed it would be defeat, I should want to see it through and struggle to
the last.'[52]

She racked her brains for ways of accelerating Hitler's defeat, devoting

[50] *HC Deb.* 26 Oct. 1945, c. 2417; 10 May 1935, c. 1304. For bombs, see 22 Aug. 1945,
c. 607.
[51] Ibid. 20 Aug. 1945, c. 302. See also 24 Aug. 1939, c. 35; Stocks, *Rathbone*, p. 302.
[52] Brockway, *Inside the Left*, p. 49. Eva Hubback papers: Rathbone to Hubback, 2
Sept. 1941.

well over twice as much of her debating contribution to war questions than other women MPs. Her patriotic zest for national austerity is worthy of her nonconformist ancestors. Urging yet more national economies on behalf of suffering Europeans, she asked parliament towards the end of her career in November 1945: 'are we such a nation of greedy beasts that we want to be reminded of the significance of Christmas by getting a few extra ounces of sweets?' Self-denial on this scale was by no means always popular. War temporarily demotes even her precious freedom of speech among her priorities. She urges Chamberlain in April 1940 to broaden the base of his administration, struggles to think of new forms of salvage and thrift, presses for propaganda in Europe that will rear up a German fifth-column against Hitler, urges women's mobilization, scathingly dismisses Kirkwood's class-war rhetoric as irrelevant to victory in a far more deadly contest. Couldn't advertisements be limited to save paper? Wouldn't shipping space be saved if smokers are encouraged to cut down their consumption? Shouldn't more be done to dissuade people from using cosmetics, drink, and luxury items? Is the BBC using aliens to the most effect? Endlessly her suggestions flow.[53]

It is now time to draw the threads together, for she died in 1946. What are we to make of this consistent and passionate humanitarian, gazing out at Smith Square from her comfortable study in Romney Street? Her many privileges—education, money, influential connections, dedicated secretaries, a devoted companion—never blunted her humanitarian purpose, and her parliamentary speeches are consistently impressive in quantity and quality. For size of debating contribution per sessional day in parliament, Bondfield comes first among the women MPs before 1945 and Lawrence second. Yet these were office-holders with short parliamentary careers; Rathbone's sixteen back-bench years do not prevent her from coming third. In only one of the eleven sessions for which we have figures does she fall below the top hundred MPs in the size of her contribution to debate. An Independent MP, though, could not be coerced into the division lobby, and at no stage in the 1930s does she come higher than 241st among MPs for her voting record in divisions; for most of the time she is well below that.[54]

At first sight, the pattern of her later debating career—with its frequent questions and infrequent major speeches—resembles Astor's. But her debating interruptions were rare indeed by comparison; she is only

[53] *HC Deb.* 16 Nov. 1945, c. 2592. For Kirkwood, see 22 May 1940, c. 169.
[54] For information on division lobby attendance, see the *Parliamentary Gazette* for each session.

seventh among the women MPs for the proportion of her contributions to debate, and parallels with Astor vanish completely when quality of contribution is taken into account. From her maiden speech onwards her longer speeches reach a high standard; her vigour springs from conviction, her common sense from long practical experience, her grasp of factual detail from scholarly training and connections. She was sometimes over-serious, lacking a sense of occasion; but the times were dangerous, and her offence often lay simply in saying what others dared not say, yet what needed to be said.

Rathbone soon became a parliamentary institution like Astor; she too loved the House, but unlike Astor she had no problems with parliamentary procedure. As an Independent she of course made only a half-entry into the political process, and she thereby disqualified herself for the politician's apotheosis, governmental office. The back-bencher's role still contains an element of that protest from without, that shirking of responsibility, which was so common among her nonconformist predecessors. Yet the vigorous and independent critic of government is integral to democracy, and Rathbone became one of the great parliamentarians of the twentieth century, constructively critical of the front bench, yet zealously upholding the rights of the benches at the back.

In all this she achieved much for women, whose status could only benefit from effectiveness in the early women MPs. She never apologized for or denied her feminism, unlike some women speakers in the woman-power debate of 20 March 1941; 'I am a feminist, a 100 per cent feminist', she declared, 'who has been working for the large part of my life in trying to secure equality of citizenship between men and women'.[55] She contributed far more than any other woman MP to debates on topics affecting women (a fifth of their total up to 1945); furthermore she led the field for contribution in this area per sessional day in parliament, despite reaching Westminster only after the crest of the feminist wave had passed. True, feminist issues became less prominent in her later parliamentary career, but this was partly because her feminism was broad and self-confident enough unobtrusively to penetrate other areas of policy; besides, any feminist of the 1930s had to make Hitler's defeat the first priority.

Stocks found it difficult to bring out the full diversity of Rathbone's daily concerns: 'again and again must one evoke the symbolical figure of the juggler with his leaping balls.'[56] Her reforming career, in repudiating

---

[55] *HC Deb.* 20 Mar. 1941, c. 369; 1 Apr. 1936, c. 2033.
[56] Stocks, *Rathbone*, p. 184.

specialization by subject-matter, resembles those high-minded nineteenth-century crusades her forebears championed. But she had moved on from there, and displayed none of the Victorian crusader's intellectual fragmentation, lack of detailed knowledge, or indifference to the practical. Her father had already shed the protest-mindedness of Victorian provincial nonconformity, for example when repudiating the more sectarian aspects of the temperance movement in the 1870s; here, as elsewhere, she followed him.

Her pragmatic approach to the state reflects the twentieth century's broadening interaction between volunteer and paid administrator. She repudiated that exaggerated individualism which visits the sins of the fathers upon the children, but when Labour politicians condemned voluntarism in 1936 she vigorously counter-attacked. Citing Sidney Webb's comment that public authorities 'have no fingers, but only thumbs', she wanted volunteer and local authority to advance together; 'the work of the voluntary organizations is on the whole now as fully organized, and as free from the spirit of patronage and interference with the private lives of those they employ as the work of the local authorities'. She not only originated and managed a sequence of reforming bodies, but frequently did much to finance them; as Marjorie Green told me, she 'was very much the Family Endowment Society, both in the sense that she largely financed it and . . . directed it'.[57]

Rathbone was not a specialist in Beatrice Webb's sense of promoting single-minded research and theorizing on a limited body of empirical material. She promoted a sequence of reforms, one at a time, for which—always excepting family allowances—she acted as advocate rather than as theorist. Her speciality lay less in subject-matter or empirical inquiry than in reforming technique, and she acquired the sort of expertise absent from Beatrice Webb's Edwardian campaign against the poor law: skill at working up sufficient and timely support in the right places. She somehow managed to show compassion without censoriousness, and championed minorities without minority-mindedness. Her career radiates a belated afterglow of nineteenth-century radical nonconformity at its best, passionately committed to personal freedom, pervaded by humane values, instinct with the personal initiative and resource that flows from an abiding and anxious civic concern. 'Meantime let no one say: "we are not responsible",' she urged, in a peroration defending refugees in 1943. 'We

---

[57] *HC Deb.* 30 Apr. 1936, c. 1195. Interview with Mrs Soper, 22 Feb. 1977.

are responsible if a single man, woman or child perishes whom we could and should have saved.'[58]

In 1936 she outlined five rules for reforming success, and by way of conclusion each can be illustrated in operation from moments in her own career. Firstly there was 'concentrating effort on the maximum achievable rather than on the ideal, while never forgetting to keep that in mind as the ultimate objective'. When preached to Nehru in 1941 her maxim 'not the optimum, but the achievable optimum' seemed somewhat patronizing, but when applied to suffragist, feminist, and humanitarian campaigns it produced results time and again, not least in India itself. She once described how energetically the feminists lobbied behind the scenes before debates began on the India Bill in 1935, and how this made it possible to estimate the maximum concession feminism could hope for. Some Indian women thought this involved asking for too little, yet merely harping on the ideal would have done no good: 'the actual result was that we did manage to secure very substantial concessions,' she wrote, 'more in number and extent than any other group which was working to amend the Bill in a democratic direction.'[59]

Her approach to the India Bill also illustrates her second rule: 'the importance of being early in the field if you want to influence legislation'— getting at the ministers and civil servants while legislation is being drafted. Her wartime work for aliens and refugees elicited a backstage assiduity sometimes so forceful as to alarm the type of civil servant and minister who, public-school-trained in politeness, discovers that soft words do not always suffice. Harold Nicolson said he had often seen government ministers 'wince in terror when they observed that familiar figure advancing towards them along the corridors; they would make sudden gestures indicating that they had left some vital document behind them . . . and scurry back to their rooms'.[60]

Her third rule was 'the importance of meeting your opponent's case as it looks to him, not as it looks to you, at least if the opponent matters'. Her *Disinherited Family* shows this in full operation; 'facts are the best of all allies,' she writes, and in her last presidential address to NUSEC she recommended to her successors 'the faculty of regarding obstacles through the eyes of those that raise them, and then seeking to cut away from the

[58] *HC Deb.* 19 May 1943, c. 1143.

[59] Rathbone in R. Strachey (ed.), *Our Freedom*, p. 72. Stocks, *Rathbone*, pp. 113, 360. E. Rathbone, 'The Harvest of the Women's Movement', Fawcett lecture, Bedford College, 29 Nov. 1935, p. 14—copy in Fawcett Library, shelfmark 396.1(42).

[60] Rathbone in R. Strachey (ed.), *Our Freedom*, p. 72. Nicolson quoted in Brookes, *Women at Westminster*, p. 84.

obstacle everything that serves to clothe it in a vesture of reason and respectability'.[61] It was important not only to make friends by deploying the relevant facts—but to avoid making enemies through using counter-productive methods.

Her conciliatory approach was more than merely tactical; it reflects her deepest political convictions, for it is essential to peaceful persuasion and freely chosen collaboration.

'Slowly and stumblingly, through the generations [she once pointed out], the British people have discovered the truth of this paradox, that the best way of arriving at the truth is to allow complete freedom for the propagation of error, and the sister paradox that no one can be called good who has not been given a free choice between good and evil, because, as John Milton put it, the scanning of error is necessary to the confirmation of truth. Those are hard sayings, and I do not think, even in the days of John Milton or in the present, there is more than a small minority of people who really believe them, but, fortunately, that minority has always included many of the leaders of thought and action, and they believe it with such white hot intensity of conviction that they have succeeded in impressing their belief upon the mould not only of thought but of legislation in this and every other country which has inherited its legal traditions from the Anglo-Saxon race'.[62]

Fourthly there was 'the importance of infinite perseverance—the perseverance of Sisyphus, Bruce's spider, the Ancient Mariner, and the Importunate Widow, all rolled into one'. Tedious this might be, but in a democratic society the education of public opinion is the only route to change, perseverance the only way to make change effective and permanent. In her last presidential speech to NUSEC she summed up the Union's special contribution as 'pertinacity and constructiveness'. She could have cited in illustration her own ingenuity at introducing family allowances into debates on related subjects, or her speech of 23 June 1942 in the first of the family-allowance debates, where she cites Beatrice Webb on how it usually takes nineteen years in Britain for a new idea to germinate and bear fruit.[63]

Stocks saw her as possessing 'a stubborn Victorian belief in the reality of individual responsibility and the efficacy of individual attack'. Not for her the 'divine impatience' of Emmeline Pankhurst, which created in the WSPU what Billington-Greig condemned as its 'spirit of hurry', for Rathbone

---

[61] Rathbone in R. Strachey (ed.), *Our Freedom*, p. 72. Rathbone, *Disinherited Family*, p. 315. Rathbone, *Milestones*, p. 46.

[62] *HC Deb.* 2 Nov. 1934, c. 582.

[63] Rathbone in R. Strachey (ed.), *Our Freedom*, p. 73. *Woman's Leader*, 9 Mar. 1928, p. 36. See also *HC Deb.* 23 June 1942, c. 1862; 3 Nov. 1944, c. 1168.

thought improvement in a parliamentary democracy could prove lasting only if won without intimidating fellow citizens.[64] She dismissed the fashionable idea of the 1930s that revolution is inevitable; her fear in 1931 that the mass franchise would produce single-class domination may now seem mistaken, but this is partly because she helped to falsify her own predictions by eroding class-consciousness. 'What is needed is merely more knowledge, more scientific planning, as to the ends, and more faith and energy in pursuing them,' she said in 1933. 'There is no case for a revolution in this country.' Conversely, her resolute libertarianism helped to falsify her fears of an opposite danger, right-wing revolution imposed from above. Her speech against the Incitement to Disaffection Bill of 1934 is memorable for its stout commitment to arousing 'tens of thousands of English men and women to the value of the liberties that were fought for by their forefathers'.[65]

None of this entailed self-advertisement or flamboyance. The success of her Inheritance (Family Provision) Act in 1938 shows how unobtrusive she could choose to be if this seemed prudent; so also does the smooth passage of so much feminist legislation while she was president of NUSEC. In a revealing letter to Hubback on equal franchise in 1927—breathless with phone calls, backstage meetings with the influential, and discreet forms of pressure—she admits that 'of course the result of getting all these things done in other people[']s names is that we shall get no credit for it. But it seemed the surest way of getting them done.'

Yet Rathbone's final rule stresses 'the importance of knowing when the time has come to allow your followers to let loose their emotions and become explosive', for she knew that 'very few reforms have been won by rational methods alone'.[66] The emotional weapons in the reformer's armoury she rarely deployed, partly because her earlier years had seen feminism damaged by Emmeline Pankhurst's neglect of timeliness and proportion when deploying emotion; this helped to ensure that the inter-war climate was rarely ripe for feminist emotionalism. Nor was emotionalism to Rathbone's taste; besides, others would readily cater for the demand when it arose, whereas reformers with her own combination of qualities are rare indeed.

---

[64] Stocks, *Rathbone*, p. 315. Billington-Greig, *Militant Suffrage Movement*, p. 154.

[65] Rathbone Papers, XIV.3.11: notes for a speech to the AGM of the Proportional Representation Society, 10 May 1933, p. 7. *HC Deb.* 2 Nov. 1934, c. 586.

[66] Eva Hubback papers: Rathbone to Hubback, 28 Apr. [1927]. Rathbone in R. Strachey (ed.), *Our Freedom*, p. 73. See also Stocks, *Rathbone*, pp. 184–6.

5

Class Politics

MARGARET BONDFIELD, SUSAN LAWRENCE AND ELLEN WILKINSON

So far we have been moving primarily among feminist organizations, yet on some definitions of feminism important things were happening within the inter-war labour movement. And whatever one's definition of feminism, these three distinguished women MPs did much to advance women's interests, and made a considerable individual and collective impact on parliament. Of the thirty-eight women MPs before the general election of 1945, Bondfield comes fourth for the size of her debating contribution, Wilkinson fifth, and Lawrence sixth; collectively they contributed nearly a third of what was said in parliament by women MPs up to 1945. Their parliamentary impact is the theme of this chapter.

The Labour Party's outlook on feminism was ambiguous, to say the least. British feminism was launched as a political movement in the optimistic mid-Victorian liberal mood of emancipation and free trade, and reflected predominantly middle-class interests and attitudes. This posed no problem when labour's libertarian, anti-authoritarian, and humanitarian mood was to the fore. While collaborating with Edwardian Liberals in a progressive alliance, Labour favoured adult suffrage and welfare reforms that were very much in the interests of women. Its manifesto of 1929 rightly points out that the Party 'was advocating the cause of Equal Citizenship when the Tory and Liberal Parties were either utterly hostile or hopelessly divided on the question'.[1] During the 1920s the Party's liberal and feminist inclinations in some ways gained from its need to pursue Liberal voters and win recruits outside the organized working class.

On the other hand, feminists felt no necessary affinity with the collectivist, socialist and communitarian aspect of Labour, whose preoccupation with full employment and public welfare posed several

---

[1] F. W. S. Craig (ed.), *British General Election Manifestos, 1918–1966* (Chichester, 1970), p. 59.

PLATE 6. The Labour women MPs in June 1929 (back row, left to right: Marion Phillips, Edith Picton-Turbervill, Ethel Bentham, Mary Hamilton; front row, left to right: Cynthia Mosley, Susan Lawrence, Margaret Bondfield, Ellen Wilkinson, Jennie Lee—S. & G. Press Agency, Ltd.).

problems. Feminists urged equal opportunity of employment, but for two reasons trade unionists wanted discriminatory legislation on working hours and conditions: to protect the health of mother and child, and to promote the full employment of men at a 'family wage'. Both strategies discouraged women from paid employment, so while Labour MPs attacked Conservatives during the 1920s for excluding women from the vote and from the professions, Conservatives attacked Labour for excluding women from the labour market.[2]

Furthermore, integral to working-class life in areas of heavy industry where the early Labour Party was strongest was the practice of separating the spheres of the sexes. Labour's manifesto of 1918 bids for the women's vote because 'the Labour Party *is* the Women's Party. Woman is the Chancellor of the Exchequer of the home.' This separation seemed inevitable for working people before housekeeping had been simplified by birth-control, relative affluence, prepared foods, and mechanization of the home. Feminist priorities on employment seemed scarcely relevant to the day-to-day realities of life in places whose main occupation called for physical strength and endurance; only in the textile areas did the community revolve round the assumption that married women would work.[3] Where men on shift work are returning home and requiring attention night and day, man and woman must work as a team, and 'the whole economy of the house turns on the skill, industry and devotion of the housewife'. During the 1950s the wife's main object in Yorkshire mining villages was still to send her husband to work with a good meal and to greet him with another on his return.[4] Trade unionists tended to see the basic social unit as the family, not the individual, and saw no inequality in a common-sensical and traditional separation of roles. All this encouraged Labour to place the domesticated woman at the centre of its welfare programme; her task was taxing and laborious, and the state must help her carry it out.

This situation inevitably affected politics in the trade-union and party branch. The trade-union movement—the miner's major political instrument, central to the growth of the Labour Party—was inevitably male-dominated. If women went out to work at all, they usually did so only before marriage and in under-unionized trades, so they accounted for only

[2] See, e.g., Fawcett, in *Woman's Leader*, 6 Feb. 1920, p. 4; Col. Greig, *HC Deb.* 27 Feb. 1920, c. 2137.

[3] Craig, *Election Manifestos*, p. 6; cf. Harrison, *Separate Spheres*, p. 59.

[4] Aneurin Bevan, *HC Deb.* 24 Oct. 1939, c. 1288. N. Dennis, F. Henriques, and C. Slaughter, *Coal is our Life. An Analysis of a Yorkshire Mining Community* (1956), p. 181.

about 16 per cent of total trade-union membership between 1918 and 1939.[5] At a Yorkshire mining community's Labour Party branch meeting in 1953 the women's contributions were diffidently expressed, subject to the husband's rebuke, and 'treated with amused tolerance by the men'. Teresa Billington, struggling between 1903 and 1906 to promote women's suffrage at trade-union meetings, protested against her item on their agenda being squeezed out by administrative preoccupations, and more than once reminded the men that she had travelled specially from Manchester to raise the matter; conduct like this helped to distance Edwardian feminists from trade unionism.[6]

Still, Labour's democratic and egalitarian mood and desire for solidarity at work demanded women organizers and speakers. Enid Stacy, Kate Conway, and Caroline Martyn were pioneer socialist propagandists, and women contributed 17 per cent of the Fabian Society's members in 1893, 43 per cent in 1912.[7] Socialist crusading gave a new scope and meaning to the unmarried woman's traditional philanthropic role, and a political partnership between spouses inevitably grew out of their domestic partnership; they collaborated closely within the close-knit local network of labour organizations—from Women's Co-op Guild to ILP and trade-union branch, from Labour church to Workers' Educational Association. Within such a world almost the whole of Edwardian working-class life could be lived.

Edwardian women rapidly organized in Mary Macarthur's National Federation of Women Workers, and a national committee of women's industrial organizations grew out of the need to help women under the national insurance legislation of 1911. The Women's Labour League, founded in 1906, was the only political organization of working women represented at Labour Party conferences before 1918, when its branches became Women's Sections of the constituency labour parties. During the 1920s the Party's elaborate branch, regional, and national structure of committees, conferences, and summer schools enabled women simultaneously to participate collaboratively and separately;[8] at the same time, Henderson and Morrison tempted women voters into the Party, though

[5] N. C. Soldon, *Women in British Trade Unions, 1874–1976* (Dublin, 1978), p. 104.

[6] *Coal is our Life*, p. 165; cf. p. 207. B.-G. Papers: Box labelled 'Mrs Charlotte Despard: Material for a Biography', small notebook labelled 'WSPU and WFL'.

[7] M. Currell, *Political Woman* (1974), p. 12. See also E. J. Hobsbawm, *Labouring Men. Studies in the History of Labour* (1964), p. 257.

[8] For good discussions of this see *Woman's Leader*, 13 Feb. 1925, p. 19, and *Vote*, 8 Feb. 1929, p. 45. See also R. McKibbin, *The Evolution of the Labour Party, 1910–1924* (1974), p. 141.

sometimes they did little more than make the tea and wash up.[9] Labour's women candidates at general elections consistently outnumbered those of other parties, so the number of women MPs increased with each swing to the left—in 1923, 1929 and 1945.

The routes taken by Bondfield, Lawrence, and Wilkinson into parliament reveal the Edwardian Labour Party's rich potential for growth. Three broad influences drew Bondfield into the Party: her respectability, her trade unionism, and her search for companionship. She gave the labour movement the loyalty which her upright, radical, and inventive father had devoted to his employer; and labour returned to her the respect which her mother's good sense, truthfulness, and strong grip on the facts had won from a smaller community. Mrs Bondfield was an active Congregationalist, a pioneer woman canvasser at elections; Margaret (born in 1873) made her own distinctive contribution both to religion and politics, and long retained much of the countrywoman's freshness and simplicity.[10] In 1929 her small, neat appearance, with bright sharp eyes and ruddy-brown cheeks, reminded one observer of 'the exterior of a very well-preserved apple'. Convalescing from an accident in the same year, she enjoyed looking out at the apple trees and flowers in a friend's garden; 'for the first time for years', she told Ramsay MacDonald, 'I can really watch the birds, and the myriad life in a garden. That is my great compensation in this disaster.'[11]

Like so many respectable artisans, Bondfield's respectability was highly evangelical. It gave her the means of rising within the movement— the ability to read, write, speak, and organize, the self-discipline to make the most of opportunity—and at the same time impelled her towards the welfare reforms that promised to make respectability more widely feasible. Unwittingly accepting some alcoholic drink from a friend in youth, she went out into Kensington Gardens and soon found herself drunk and incapable; she 'clung to the Park railings in deep humiliation for what seemed like a long time' and, she adds, 'never since have I tasted strong drink'. She later published a lecture on Joseph Livesey, the pioneer of teetotalism. Not for her the immediate resort to the collectivism of prohibition: 'it is through the individual, the family, and the community', she said, 'that we must work to prepare a moral foundation of conduct

---

[9] As Mrs Betty Fraser complained in Labour Party, *Report of the 35th Annual Conference* (*1935*), p. 144.

[10] M. A. Hamilton, *Margaret Bondfield* (1924), pp. 29–33.

[11] *Time and Tide*, 14 June 1929, p. 716. PRO 30/69 (MacDonald Papers) 672/2/85: Bondfield to MacDonald, 6 Sept. 1929.

upon which we can safely impose such regulations and restrictions as are for the benefit of the community as a whole.'[12]

As a shop-girl newly recruited to town life, she was shocked by the moral outlook of girls 'living in'; such girls, she said, 'are ridiculed when they come up fresh from the country, because they blush at lewd jokes, until they become perfectly hardened'. A shop-girl's life involved long hours, continuous rush and clatter, poor diet, sordid conditions, and lack of privacy. She later recalled as 'positively unendurable' the atmosphere built up from the East End shops' dust, gas fumes, and customer smells after six in the evenings. When boarded out in Brighton for three years she shared a room with a girl who had tuberculosis and with 'a woman of mature age who led a life of a most undesirable kind'. In another post she found herself sleeping with three other girls in a room whose fireplace was boarded up, and whose window could not be opened in winter without the girl beneath it getting too cold. 'Sometimes I would personally insist on having the window thrown up for a little while to clear the room', she recalled, 'and then somebody would want it down again in five minutes' time'; by the morning the room's atmosphere was 'abominable'.[13] Respectability was almost impossible in such conditions, and she favoured shop hours legislation for the same reason that she later favoured unemployment insurance: both would promote the worker's independence and self-respect.

Religion protected her from the perils of city life. Dr W. E. Orchard, of the King's Weigh House Church, opened up for her, she said, 'a new world of adventure'. Her religion is inseparable from her politics; socialism promises ethical progress. Morality is involved at every level in the trade relationships she discusses in her booklet on *The Meaning of Trade* (1928), for co-operation will restore the employee's sense of responsibility to consumer and employer. 'It is essential to the success of the coming new order', she writes, 'that every one of us should also develop interior control and personal responsibility.'[14]

Trade unionism was her instrument; she joined after reading the newspaper that contained her fish and chips—giving up her Sundays to executive committee meetings, and writing surreptitiously at night for the

[12] M. Bondfield, *A Life's Work* (n.d.), p. 64; *Joseph Livesey. A Man of Destiny!* (Sheffield, 1933), p. 14.

[13] Departmental Committee on the Truck Acts, Minutes of Evidence, *Parl[iamentary] Papers* 1908 LIX (Cd. 4442), Q. 13445. Select Committee of the House of Lords on Early Closing of Shops, *Parl. Papers* 1901 VI (369), Q. 2601. Truck Acts Committee, QQ. 13216, 13325, 13271.

[14] Bondfield, *Life's Work*, p. 354.

union journal while her fellow employees slept.[15] In 1899 the *Economic Journal* published her attack on the living-in system, founded on investigating house rules and living conditions in six selected firms. So dedicated and selfless a woman did not preen herself on becoming the first woman cabinet minister in 1929: 'I am what I am,' she said, 'not out of any personal virtue, but because all my life has been in the training ground of corporate bodies and of different organisations, and I am merely the product of the work of hundreds of thousands of unknown names.'[16] Her parliamentary defence of trade unionism in 1927 reflects her deep sense of the movement's long history in raising working-class living standards, her recognition that it had produced 'a singular growth and development of order, of discipline, and of self-control among the workers'.[17]

The labour movement offered companionship; her dedication to trade-union work was, she recalled, 'undisturbed by love affairs', and in her early twenties she thought 'the love of comrades, of friends' too much neglected by comparison with the wife's love for her husband. She developed a close bond with Mary Macarthur, beginning as her teacher and ending as her disciple. She later credited herself with 'a natural inclination for team work', and found fulfilment in a crusade which united men and women, an experience which profoundly influenced her attitude to feminism.[18] Bondfield, Lawrence, and Wilkinson were all unmarried; all three found companionship in their dedication to the movement. Only a third of Labour's women MPs before 1945 were married, and several entered parliament because they had married their party; by contrast, several Conservative women MPs, half of whom were married, got there because they had married their husbands. Bondfield advanced within her union, and therefore within the Party, not because she was a woman, or because of women's votes, but because colleagues valued her combination of dedication, courage, and practical common sense. As Beatrice Webb pronounced in 1925, Bondfield was 'an extremely competent instrument within a limited range'.[19]

Lawrence's background could hardly have been more different. Her career illustrates the Party's attraction in those days not only for underprivileged groups, but also for university-trained women, who contributed more women MPs to Labour than to the Conservatives.

[15] Ibid., p. 28.
[16] *Scotsman*, 19 July 1929, p. 9; cf. Bondfield, *Life's Work*, p. 277.
[17] *HC Deb.* 24 May 1927, c. 1883.
[18] Bondfield, *Life's Work*, pp. 36, 354. Hamilton, *Bondfield*, p. 52; cf. p. 97.
[19] S. and B. Webb, *Letters*, iii, ed. N. MacKenzie (Cambridge, 1978), p. 247.

When the Webbs were analysing the twenty non-cabinet ministers and under-secretaries in the Labour government of 1929, they classified her (with Fred Pethick-Lawrence) among the eight drawn from the 'old governing class'—as compared with the nine ('a poor lot!') drawn from the manual workers and the three drawn from the 'lower middle class brainworkers'.[20] Lawrence was born into a wealthy London family, her father a prominent solicitor and her mother the daughter of a judge. The privileged and educated woman's self-confidence gave her a standing within the labour movement which she might not have enjoyed elsewhere.

When reading for the maths tripos at Newnham College, Cambridge, Lawrence was a formidable figure, 'tall, upright and dignified, with a disconcerting habit of looking at her interlocutor through a lorgnette', and exercising herself on a bicycle with a Dalmatian for protection. Her political destiny could hardly have been predicted, for in the College Political Society she led the Conservatives, selected Byron and Shaftesbury as her heroes, and eloquently defended Church and Empire. On going down from Cambridge she went to live with her mother, and was elected to the London County Council for the safe Conservative seat of Marylebone. What drove her into the labour movement was Conservative indifference to low wages and bad conditions of women cleaners in the London schools.[21]

Her masculine and austere appearance, close-cropped hair and highly intellectual manner puzzled the factory girls she now began to address; adorning their eyes with pennies to imitate her monocle, they allowed them to fall to the ground 'with devastating clatter'. But in 1924 Margery Corbett Ashby was struck by her practical, alert, and experienced manner and her 'striking face full of humour'; she had vigour and a sense of fun.[22] Besides, her sincerity and integrity commanded respect. She paid for Mary Macarthur, dying of cancer, to have a car during her last years, and in 1921 she was imprisoned for five weeks with twenty-seven other borough councillors for refusing to collect Poplar's poor rate; to local Labour supporters she became 'our Susan'.[23] Experience in local government prepared the way for constructive national achievement; as she told the Party Conference in 1927, Labour's rank and file were already in power at the local level even if their national leaders were still in

[20] B. Webb, *Diaries, 1924–1932*, ed. M. Cole (1956), p. 210; cf. p. 223.

[21] C. D. Rackham, 'Susan Lawrence', *Fabian Quarterly* (Spring 1948), p. 20.

[22] Ibid. City of London Polytechnic, Fawcett Library, Corbett Ashby Papers: Margery Corbett Ashby to her husband, 25 Jan. 1924.

[23] *The Times*, 25 Oct. 1947, p. 6. Rackham, 'Susan Lawrence', p. 23. Linda Walker, tape-recorded interview with Dr Letitia Fairfield, 28 Mar. 1976.

opposition. For her a municipal socialist policy involved encouraging municipal enterprise, acting as a model employer, and preventing hunger, cold, and primary poverty.[24]

Her political work was so single-minded that she regularly lost her possessions, and snatched her food and sleep at any time of day. She was so indifferent to clothes that as a junior minister she raised her head from her papers for only a minute to point with her pencil at the favoured choice among the half-dozen inexpensive dresses she had sent for.[25] She too found in the labour movement companionship and an outlet for emotions. Admired and liked by Sidney Webb, during the mid-1920s she inevitably came under close scrutiny from Beatrice, who classified her (with the other two Labour women MPs) as lacking the temperament of the lover, and then used this to explain the daredevil element in her attitude to life; only her tough intellect, thought Beatrice, kept Lawrence's revolutionary temperament within bounds. 'Virago intacta' was a phrase applied to her which Beatrice thought 'as witty as it was true'; Lawrence was heroic in style, and 'as a woman chieftain she would have led her people into battle and died fighting'. During the General Strike Lawrence seemed almost in a state of exaltation, addressing her constituents as 'comrades' and declaring that the world 'would never be the same again'. Beatrice thought it all rather unreal, and saw her as the cultivated woman telling her working-class audiences what she incorrectly thought that they wanted to hear. None of this endorses Sylvia Pankhurst's view of Lawrence as climbing to power through cultivating a reputation for moderation while 'leaving the noisy work to other people'.[26]

Wilkinson's route to parliament differs again. Her respectable origins, located on what we would now see as the margin between middle and working class, gave her much in common with Bondfield, but instead of working her way up slowly within the trade-union movement she was a meritocrat; of the four Wilkinson children, three went to college, of whom two won university degrees. Her mother took care to whiten the front doorstep with regular stoning, and her father had become a teetotaler in reaction against his heavy-drinking Irish parents. Wilkinson recalled how completely his ambitions were satisfied by chapel life: 'there he was taught

---

[24] Labour Party, *Report of the 27th Annual Conference, 1927*, p. 227. *HC Deb.* 13 Dec. 1927, c. 2163.

[25] Vallance, *Women in the House*, p. 39. B. Webb, *Diaries, 1924–1932*, p. 24.

[26] B. Webb, *Diary*, iv, ed. N. and J. MacKenzie, 1985, p. 247. B. Webb, *Diaries, 1924–1932*, pp. 24, 58, 95–7. E. S. Pankhurst, *The Home Front. A Mirror to Life in England During the World War* (1932), p. 40.

134 *Class Politics*

to read, was lent books. It was his only contact with education, its pulpit his only means of self-expression.' For her as for Bondfield religion was an important influence, but more as an initial impulse than as a continuing inspiration. Born in 1891, she got up on a chair as a little girl while her parents were away at their Wesleyan Sunday evening services and preached a sermon to her grandmother. Public speaking was much talked about at home and often practised—through Band of Hope recitations, addresses to missionary meetings, school debates, and so on; she later accompanied her father to hear lectures on theological subjects. But perhaps more important was religion's indirect influence; in education and public life she sought the opportunities and idealism that her parents had found within the chapel.[27]

She was a rebel from an early age, refusing as a ten-year-old to push out her younger brother in his pram. At school she refused to work at the mathematics and drawing she disliked, discovered 'all too early that a clear decisive voice and a confident manner could get one through 90 per cent of the difficulties of life', and won a scholarship to university.[28] Her ambition flourished on indignation against the deprivation all about her, and feminism and socialism arrived early. By January 1910 she was cheerfully dodging missiles on a lorry while opposing the anti-suffragist candidate Hilaire Belloc at Salford's general election, and she soon became a full-time organizer for the NUWSS. Her socialism took fire when she read Blatchford's books and heard Mrs Bruce Glasier speak; she also knew that her mother's persistent illness stemmed from being unable to buy proper medical treatment at her own birth.[29]

In the First World War Wilkinson became a trade-union organizer, then Labour councillor for Gorton South. She briefly espoused Communism, and as Labour candidate for Middlesbrough at the 1924 election expressed impatience with small-scale patching-up reforms. She is Winifred Holtby's headmistress Sarah Burton in *South Riding*, who 'believed in action . . . believed in fighting. She had unlimited confidence in the power of the human intelligence and will to achieve order, happiness, health and wisdom.' She always found it difficult to refuse people, and was swept forward into journalism and a sequence of causes in an atmosphere of hurry, muddled paperwork, and missed deadlines. Eva

---
[27] Wilkinson, in Asquith (ed.), *Myself when Young*, pp. 401, 410–11. B. D. Vernon, *Ellen Wilkinson, 1891–1947* (1982), p. 2.

[28] Wilkinson, in Asquith (ed.), *Myself when Young*, pp. 403–4, 410. See also S. Davies, 'The Young Ellen Wilkinson', *Memoirs and Proceedings of the Manchester Literary and Philosophical Society*, 107 (1964–5), p. 35.

[29] Wilkinson, in Asquith (ed.), *Myself when Young*, pp. 406, 414.

Hubback's daughter Diana, working for her in the mid-1930s, found her informal to a degree—dropping everything to dash off somewhere unpredictably, and sometimes dictating letters from her bath.[30]

Like other women politicians, these three Labour MPs found it difficult both to get into parliament and to stay there. Bondfield stood unsuccessfully for Northampton in 1920 and 1922, was elected in 1923, but defeated in 1924. She returned to parliament in 1926 as MP for Wallsend, was re-elected in 1929, but defeated in 1931 and 1935. Lawrence stood unsuccessfully for Camberwell North West in 1920; then at North East Ham she was defeated in 1922, elected in 1923, defeated in 1924, re-elected in 1926 and 1929 but defeated in 1931, and failed to get in at Stockton-on-Tees in 1935. Wilkinson was defeated at Ashton-under-Lyne in 1923, represented Middlesbrough East from 1924 till her defeat in 1931, and then the Jarrow division of Durham from 1935 till she died in 1947.

The House of Commons gives no credit for outside distinction and takes its recruits as it finds them; these three women responded very differently to its stimulus. As parliamentary speaker, Bondfield was in some ways hindered by her earlier career; the House dislikes being addressed like a public meeting, and her 'harsh cascade of sound' was too fast and too high-pitched.[31] She was liberal on overseas questions, an experienced and loyal party member, and expert on labour issues; she usually spoke on unemployment and industrial relations. Her parliamentary speeches in opposition indicate compassion, practical ability, and even breadth of vision. They are not flamboyant, and they lack a precise over-arching economic framework, but they abound in well-informed and constructive suggestions.

She knows the country is 'in the backwash of a terrible catastrophe' whereby mechanization reduces millions to machine-minders with outmoded skills and increases the risk of unemployment. She herself had once been unemployed, and in 1929, when discussing its psychological consequences in parliament, she said 'it makes one feel almost heartbroken to go into areas such as the Tonypandy district'. 'Sometimes I feel I can hardly bear it,' she admits, when discussing unemployment in 1927.[32]

---

[30] W. Holtby, *South Riding. An English Landscape* (Fontana edn., 1954), p. 66. Author's tape-recorded interview with David and Diana Hopkinson, 2 Oct. 1984, at Huntingdon House, 23 Huntingdon Street, Bradford-on-Avon, Wilts. See also *Vote*, 4 July 1924, pp. 209–10; Vernon, *Wilkinson*, pp. 58, 64, 117.

[31] J. Johnston, *A Hundred Commoners* (1931), p. 110; cf. pp. 109, 111; *Westminster Voices*, p. 197.

[32] *HC Deb.* 16 Dec. 1929, c. 1140; 24 Apr. 1929, c. 1011; 29 Nov. 1927, c. 375.

Between 1926 and 1929 she wants government departments collaborating
more closely to deal with unemployment, relevant statistics more fully and
systematically collected, the school-leaving age raised, training schemes
promoted to encourage labour mobility, relief works, special efforts for the
teenagers, Commonwealth development and emigration fostered, trade
boards extended, working hours restrained by international agreement,
and a more positive role for labour exchanges, so as 'to develop that
manliness and independence which the British people are capable of
displaying'.[33]

Before 1929 she was not clear on whether a capitalist government can
gain control over the situation; in 1927 she argued that the government's
extended insurance role must logically involve it in trying to eliminate
unemployment, yet in the following year she claimed that 'under
capitalism you have no real solution for unemployment . . . we have
reached a stage in our development when competitive individualism
cannot function for the benefit of the community . . . because it cannot
secure for the people any certainty of a decent standard of life'.[34]
Henderson had long shown interest in her career, and in June 1929 he
wanted her in the cabinet;[35] at fifty-nine she became Minister of Labour.
Unfortunately for her reputation, her ministry was the eye of the storm
between 1929 and 1931. The problems she faced would have alarmed any
government, and the blame for failure lies as much with the labour
movement as a whole, and with the civil servants and the economists, as
with Bondfield herself. True, she lacked originality, but politicians can
rarely afford to run ahead of public opinion. She may have lacked subtlety
and magic, but such qualities are rare in an effective man or woman of
action.

She began by reviewing the whole system of unemployment insurance
and toured the various divisions to see it for herself. Serious as the
situation was, she knew that government insurance schemes against
unemployment had improved things since her young days.[36] Convinced
that the unemployed were not to blame for their unemployment, she
concentrated on getting the unemployment benefit properly financed. Her
aim was to end the policy of recurrent borrowing to bale out the
unemployment benefit fund; everything in her respectable upbringing

[33] *HC Deb.* 27 Feb. 1929, c. 2042; cf. 21 Nov. 1929, cc. 742 ff.
[34] Ibid. 30 Apr. 1928, c. 1462; see also 5 Dec. 1927, cc. 1008 ff.; 15 Nov. 1928, cc. 1231 ff.
[35] Bondfield, *Life's Work*, p. 253. P. Snowden, *An Autobiography*, ii (1934), p. 759.
[36] *HC Deb.* 4 Apr. 1930, c. 1732; cf. 23 July 1930, c. 2184.

made her dislike debts, and she wanted the fund's overall cost shifted away from rates and towards taxes. This involved her in promoting complicated financial reforms at the same time as dealing with what within six months had become an avalanche of parliamentary questions about mounting unemployment—questions aimed less at shedding light on the problem than at scoring Conservative party points and promoting protection.

Long-term strategic thought withers in such conditions, yet the situation demanded something more than a well-intentioned pragmatism. Bondfield was not in overall charge of the government's economic strategy, and all she could do was keep a cool head, administer her department efficiently, and hope that things would improve. She responded to questions in a stolid, unimaginative way, and already by December 1929 she features in Beatrice Webb's list of cabinet failures—tactless to deputations and entirely in the hands of her permanent secretary, Horace Wilson.[37] During the debates of 1931 she could do no more than speculate on whether the unemployment figures would cease to rise, and if so when. If others suggested remedies—a minimum wage, for example—she merely explained that such changes were impossible and apologized for having to bow her shoulders still lower. MPs became impatient with a minister who seemed routinely to occupy her post without hope for the future. It was a situation so difficult and painful that even Astor diverted her attacks elsewhere.

Bondfield voted with the majority in the cabinet to cut unemployment benefits and admired MacDonald's decision to form the National Government, but she did not join him.[38] Her support fell only slightly at Wallsend in the general election of 1931, but whereas in 1929 there had been four candidates, now there were only two, and the Conservative candidate Irene Ward won by a large majority. In 1935 Ward was again her sole opponent; the gap between them narrowed, but not by enough to get Bondfield returned. Thereafter she fades from political life, though she remained active in social and religious work. In 1940 Virginia Woolf was invited to be her biographer, but nothing came of it.[39] Bondfield's rather pedestrian autobiography published in 1949 is reticent on her brief period of cabinet office: her tenure was controversial, her precedent for her successors by no means happy, and the memory was no doubt painful.

Lawrence's parliamentary career was equally brief, but unlike Bondfield's it ended before she had reached her prime. In committees she

[37] B. Webb, *Diaries, 1924–1932*, pp. 230–1.
[38] D. Marquand, *Ramsay MacDonald* (1977), p. 648.
[39] V. Woolf, *Diary*, v (1984), p. 295.

was too single-minded and did not listen enough to others, but in parliamentary debate her specialization paid rapid dividends. Her speeches—mainly on local government questions such as housing and education—were expert, factual, and dry. To Laski she gave an impression of brusque efficiency 'in which nothing matters except the intelligent arrangement of details of the task in hand'. Eagerly instructing her parliamentary pupils like a schoolmistress, she was persistent and forceful; her confrontations with Astor in 1929 have already been discussed.[40] The House respected her clear head, knowledge, good sense, competence, sincerity, and hard work. In its precise grasp of relevant detail, her mind resembled that of the clever lawyer or accountant; party leaders find such talents indispensable. Within a year she was debating local government matters on equal terms with Neville Chamberlain, and conducted an almost personal dialogue with him over the Unemployment Insurance Bill in 1927; 'sometimes the Minister finds me out,' she said on 12 December, 'and sometimes I find him out. I admit that the Minister is right on this occasion.' Wilkinson later pointed out that 'if either can catch the other tripping on a fact or a figure, they feel they have done a good day's work'.[41]

'If you had asked me what I wanted,' she told MacDonald in 1929, 'I should have chosen this post, and this chief'; as Parliamentary Secretary to the Minister of Health she was on home ground. In her first week she revelled in the post, conjuring up 'visions of glorious changes'. Yet within a month she thought the government was neglecting its promises; the Webbs restrained her from resigning, but in summer 1931 she had no doubts, and prepared herself to resign whoever implemented the cuts.[42] At the general election of 1931 she too faced a united opposition, and, although her vote did not fall markedly, she was defeated.

In September 1935 Beatrice Webb found her 'obsessed with getting back into Parliament at the next general election'. At Stockton she increased Labour's vote against Harold Macmillan, despite the advent of a Liberal candidate, but not by enough; it was a sad waste of her talents, and disappointing too because she loved parliament. Her socialism remained undimmed, and in 1938 she dismissed the Popular Front because she thought it diluted socialism, and so achieved the reverse of its anti-socialist

[40] *Daily Herald*, 16 Aug. 1930, p. 8. See also Rackham, 'Susan Lawrence', p. 22.
[41] *HC Deb.* 12 Dec. 1927, c. 1944. E. Wilkinson, *Peeps at Politicians* (1930), p. 27.
[42] PRO 30/69 (MacDonald Papers) 1174/69: Lawrence to MacDonald, n.d., end. '[1929]'. B. Webb, *Diaries, 1924–1932*, pp. 201, 207, 211. F. Pethick-Lawrence, *Fate has been Kind* [1943], p. 165.

objective. In 1941 Hugh Dalton rejoiced in his diary when 'silly old Susan Lawrence' was ousted from the Party's executive committee: she should have retired gracefully 'years ago', he unkindly wrote. In her later years this tall, gaunt figure with piercing eyes could often be seen darting her finger at those with whom she eagerly conversed during Fabian summer schools, showing kindness to the shy or the newly recruited; Margaret Cole recalls that her talks on Labour personalities were popular for 'her racy anecdotes of the Great Ones'. For Beatrice Webb she belonged 'to the old order of irreproachable female celibates, which used to be an important caste in Victorian days, and which has no votaries among the younger generation'. Towards the end of her life she learned to transcribe books for the blind into Braille, and she remained keenly interested in public affairs till the day of her death in 1947.[43]

Younger than Bondfield and Lawrence, Wilkinson entered parliament at thirty-two, and was the first woman MP to wear a brightly coloured dress and shingled hair.[44] Her small size inspired men to protectiveness,[45] and she knew how to capture the mood of the House. She alone of the three under discussion seems to have capitalized as a parliamentary speaker on what were seen as her feminine qualities, whereas Bondfield and Lawrence both struck contemporaries as women who adopted a male approach to their task. Her detective-story, *The Division Bell Mystery*, played down the importance of parliamentary speeches, and claimed that a whispered word in the Members' cloakroom 'may sometimes have more effect than an hour's speech thundered in the debating chamber'.[46] Yet her energy and courage made her lively in debate, and she was soon nicknamed 'the mighty atom'. Beatrice Webb described her as 'amazingly vital and a first-rate debater . . . with her tiny lithe figure, delicate pale face, and brilliant red-brown hair and red brown eyes, she is . . . at times extremely pretty'.[47]

As the first woman MP to strike a note of class conflict, Wilkinson's oratory was eloquent and powerful but sometimes sharp in tone; in 1926, for instance, she vividly juxtaposed London's starving poor and opulent rich, and on another occasion she exhibited the coil of rope miners placed round their legs to drag tubs along. She was on the left of her Party, and

[43] B. Webb, *Diary*, iv. 247, 357. H. Dalton, *The Second World War Diary*, ed. B. Pimlott, 1986, p. 219. M. Cole, *Growing up into Revolution* (1949), pp. 206–7. See also *19th Report of the Conference of Labour Women . . . 1938* (n.d.), p. 44.

[44] Vernon, *Wilkinson*, p. 78.

[45] Ibid., p. 6. Johnston, *A Hundred Commoners*, p. 114.

[46] E. Wilkinson, *The Division Bell Mystery* (1932), p. 91.

[47] B. Webb, *Diaries, 1924–1932*, p. 132.

the distrust between herself and MacDonald was mutual; at the Party Conference in 1927 she thought the Party should go to the country next time 'with the boldest programme and the biggest demand . . . a fighting programme'; parliament, she said, was too conscious of the obstacles to reform.[48] Yet her lively sense of humour moderated her sarcasm; she knew how to spark off other members in debate, and her remarks are often very funny, even half a century later when read cold in the columns of *Hansard*. 'Really . . . !' she would exclaim, incredulous that Tories could hold such opinions—yet she was popular even with them.

From the start she was a fine constituency MP. In her first session she defended Middlesbrough against silk and lace duties and urged government to rationalize the iron and steel industry and open up trade with Russia. Her speeches regularly draw upon constituency experience, and usually aim—in her own phrase—at 'taking up the cudgels'.[49] Though often involved in parliamentary scenes, she was in reality helping to knit British society together by alerting parliament to her constituents' mood, and by alerting her constituents to parliamentary remedies.

By 1927 Beatrice Webb was predicting 'a big political career before her'. The social life of the House was 'taming her spirit', and her platform opinions had begun to diverge from her real beliefs; she was unconsciously being 'moulded for the Front Bench and eventually for office'. Beatrice did not think highly of her intellect; she thought Wilkinson lacked originality in argument or insight, and was rather too prone to follow political fashions, though clever at publicizing the views of others.[50] But Beatrice knew that intellect was not the only, or even the major, qualification for office. Wilkinson was not long in parliament before she showed how capably she could get up a case, and by 1930 she was working on the reform of hire-purchase law which she brought to fruition seven years later. As Lawrence's Parliamentary Private Secretary in the 1929 Labour government, she was muzzled as critic of the government, but she was becoming restive at Middlesbrough's rising unemployment. During the debates of 1931 she avoided big speeches and big issues, but she did not hesitate during the crisis in the summer. The Labour MP Edith Picton-Turbervill told her she intended to abstain on the confidence motion of 8

[48] Labour Party, *Report of the 27th Annual Conference (1927)*, p. 183. *HC Deb.* 16 Mar. 1926, c. 338; 29 June 1926, c. 1023. See also Vernon, *Wilkinson*, p. 82.

[49] *HC Deb.* 1 July 1925, c. 2626.

[50] B. Webb, *Diaries, 1924–1932*, pp. 132–3, 150. See also Johnston, *Westminster Voices*, pp. 194–5; *A Hundred Commoners*, pp. 113–14.

September; 'just like you middle-class people,' Wilkinson scornfully replied.[51]

The election hardly eroded her support at all, but she too now faced only one opponent—a Liberal, who doubled his vote of 1929 and defeated her. Even before Labour took office in 1929 she seems to have been experiencing personal difficulties; she writes to Astor in January of 'a nightmarish 5 weeks', and thanks her for a talk which has enabled her to sleep better. In July 1931 she asked Beatrice Webb whether a woman in public life who wished to remain single could be expected to remain celibate when a congenial friend was unhappily married; Beatrice assumed that this referred to her relations with J. F. Horrabin. After her defeat of 1931 Wilkinson came under the influence of Christian Science, and accepted money from Astor on behalf of a sick sister—not the last instance of timely help from this source. After visiting Germany in 1933 she told Astor that she had earlier put all her faith into socialism but now wondered who would ever implement it: 'the young people are driven out and embittered, and the old are corrupt with cynicism[,] the worst kind of corruption, I think . . . so much of my faith in *people* has been broken of late and I am struggling to find something to believe in, again.'[52]

In 1935 she recovered Jarrow for Labour; as MP in the mid-1930s she was on her best jauntily irreverent form, and combined uncompromising hostility to the National Government with strong respect for the House of Commons and sensitivity to its mood. She again displayed her skill at getting up a question—on hire purchase during 1937, and on the building society law which occupied so much of her time during 1939. But she was now best known for being an outstanding constituency MP; her skill at making Jarrow the symbol of national problems prevented her from ever seeming parochial. As she pointed out in 1938, 'nowadays any Member of Parliament for one of the distressed areas has become a kind of glorified commercial traveller for his area'.[53]

Jarrow vividly illustrated her attacks on unemployment; in 1936, for instance, she cited a local vicar as saying that its under-nourished men 'looked all right outside, but when they were faced with the infection and cold of the winter they just cracked like eggshells'. She was still trying to channel protest into parliament, though she found it 'extremely difficult

[51] E. Picton-Turbervill, *Life is Good, An Autobiography* (1939) p. 258.
[52] Nancy Astor MSS 1416/1/2/62: Wilkinson to Astor, n.d. [in envelope dated 28 Jan. 1929]. B. Webb, *Diary*, iv. 247. Nancy Astor MSS 1416/1/2/63: Wilkinson to Astor, '11 April'; 1416/1/2/215: Wilkinson to Astor, n.d. [in envelope dated 5 Aug. 1940].
[53] *HC Deb.* 28 Nov. 1938, c. 157.

for us who thoroughly disbelieve in all the assumptions on which the present system is built to make constructive suggestions for the better working of a system which is breaking down before our eyes'. In November she begged the House to allow the Jarrow marchers to appear at the bar: there could be no substitute for hearing directly what unemployment was like.[54] In *The Town that was Murdered* (1939) she sees Jarrow as 'an illustrated footnote to British working-class history'; it illuminated national problems in miniature, vindicated socialist objectives, and fuelled the argument for nationalization. The book reflects her admiration for the independence and skill of Jarrow people and her concern at the insensitivity of a London-based administration. It was a formidable work for a busy MP to write—drawing upon local newspapers, historical works, and official documents. Writing it was, she said, 'a race between Hitler and me—whether he would get his war before I finished my book. That race I won.'[55]

She bitterly opposed Chamberlain's foreign policy. As one of the few inter-war women MPs who spoke on foreign policy, she saw appeasement as linked to the privilege she loathed; Chamberlain was 'putting the narrow interests of his class . . . and of the rich, before the national interests', whereas he should be responding to Russian overtures. Her scorching and impressive attack of 24 August 1939 on appeasement seemed even to Harold Macmillan, who spoke next, incompatible with parliament's prevailing mood of national unity.[56] But as a junior minister in the Churchill wartime government, briefly at pensions and then at home security, she soon came to epitomize national unity in resisting Hitler, and showed both courage and energy in promoting civil defence and touring air-raid shelters throughout the country.

Office narrowed her debating front and tied her still more closely to Morrison's cause within the Party. By the time she won her great opportunity as Minister of Education in the Attlee government her health was failing; as the second woman cabinet minister, she faced problems almost as complex as Bondfield's fifteen years before. Even to implement Butler's Education Act of 1944 would take a generation, she said, and on top of this the government must raise the school-leaving age, expand the school meals service, and catch up on building and rebuilding schools. These major problems did not prevent her from working towards two

---

[54] *HC Deb.* 8 July 1936, c. 1269; 2 Mar. 1936, c. 1104; 11 Nov. 1936, c. 1000.

[55] E. Wilkinson, *The Town that was Murdered. The Life-Story of Jarrow* (1939), pp. 8, 188.

[56] *HC Deb.* 24 Aug. 1939, cc. 50, 52.

overall objectives: providing four years' secondary education for all children, and ensuring equal opportunity for the able regardless of parental wealth. She thought smaller classes essential and welcomed experiments with comprehensive schools, even though she did not promote them with the energy that hindsight has led some of her critics to recommend. In his tribute of February 1947, Churchill stressed the patriotism that had always lain beneath her class rhetoric; 'she always wished to see this Island great and famous', he said, 'and capable of offering a decent home to all its people'.[57]

The debating energy of these three women enabled the women MPs to surpass the men in the size of their average debating contribution between 1926 and 1931; otherwise only 1936 can produce such a contrast in the years before 1945. Bondfield and Lawrence were MPs for less than six years, and their promotion to office helps explain why they come first and second, respectively, of the thirty-eight women MPs before 1945 on size of debating contribution per sessional day in parliament, though Wilkinson's longer career does not prevent her from coming fifth. All three usually appear among the top hundred MPs for the size of their debating contribution in each session, and in the parliamentary sessions of 1928 and 1928–9 Lawrence comes thirteenth and sixth, respectively, among all MPs. Only one woman MP between 1919 and 1945 rose higher—Atholl, who came fifth in the session of 1934–5 when she opposed the India Bill with such energy.

As for the overall shape of their debating careers, office in 1929–31 caused Bondfield's annual contribution to shoot far above that of any other woman MP before 1945, whereas Lawrence reaches her peak in 1929 and declines thereafter. Wilkinson, too, peaks early in her career (in 1927) and then declines. When she returns to parliament in 1935 she again peaks early, surpassing in 1936 her peak of 1927; office in the wartime coalition curbed her debating role, but as Minister of Education after 1945 she had to speak more often, and her debating contribution reaches a peak for her entire career in 1946, the year before she died.

MPs who contribute frequently to debate are usually either experienced back-benchers or office-holders; they intervene to ask or answer parliamentary questions or to interrupt the speeches of other MPs. On total number of interventions only Astor, continuously in parliament between 1919 and 1945, surpasses Bondfield, who in her turn easily surpasses Rathbone at third position, with Wilkinson fourth and

[57] *HC Deb.* 6 Feb. 1947, c. 1984.

Lawrence eighth. For interventions per sessional day in parliament Bondfield easily leads the field, with Lawrence second and Wilkinson sixth; this reflects Bondfield's answers to her avalanche of parliamentary questions as minister—2827 in all—whereas Lawrence faced only 523; among ministers only Henderson faced more during Bondfield's first governmental session and only Graham in her second. Wilkinson intervenes frequently for a different reason: she was more eager than Lawrence and Bondfield to ask oral parliamentary questions when Labour was in opposition; assessed on this criterion, she falls below the top sixty MPs in only two of her nine sessions in opposition. For readiness to interrupt during debates, none of the three could approach Astor, but Lawrence and Wilkinson were lively enough to come fourth and fifth, respectively, though Bondfield trails behind at twenty-first. Bondfield, Lawrence, and Wilkinson come well down the list for length of contribution per debating intervention; it is usually the less experienced performers who speak only formally and at length. As for attendance in the division lobby, only Lawrence was at all assiduous; Wilkinson and Bondfield usually come well down among the MPs in the bottom half.

Particularly important for the purposes of this book is the pattern of preferred debating topics. All three focus on welfare issues:[58] whereas the average for the thirty-eight is 49 per cent—in itself a high figure—for Bondfield it is 82 per cent, for Lawrence 90 per cent and for Wilkinson 38 per cent. As anti-suffragists had long ago predicted, welfare expenditure would gain from votes for women. Office cannot explain the high percentage for Bondfield and Lawrence; the causal connection is really the other way round—they were assigned welfare posts because these reflected their interests when in opposition. If Wilkinson's subject-balance is more dispersed, this is because her career persisted into a period when welfare slipped among parliament's priorities; more of her energy therefore went into foreign policy (11 per cent of her total), commercial questions (8 per cent), and Second-World-War issues (10 per cent).

What does feminism owe to these parliamentary careers? Merely by getting into parliament and by operating efficiently there, whatever their views, these three Labour MPs helped to raise society's respect for women—as also did the anti-feminist Atholl. Women MPs apparently felt a special need to contribute when heavily outnumbered in the House; Wilkinson prefaces her comments on unemployment in 1925 by saying that 'as I am the only woman Member of my party in the House, I must say something on this head'. In 1928 she said she sometimes felt she was MP

---

[58] For definition of 'welfare issues', see p. 79.

for widows rather than for Middlesbrough, so amply did their letters fill her postbag.[59] Still more important for feminism was quality of debating contribution. No Conservative woman MP surpassed Bondfield, Lawrence, and Wilkinson for debating quality, and others among the period's sixteen Labour women MPs—Bentham, Hamilton, Lee, Manning, Phillips, Picton-Turbervill, and Summerskill—could have achieved as much if fate had allowed. Of the seventeen Conservative women MPs only Apsley, Atholl, Horsbrugh, Tate, and perhaps Irene Ward are in the same league.

For proportion of debating career spent on questions specific to women, all three rank low, Wilkinson with 8 per cent, Bondfield with 5 per cent, and Lawrence with 1 per cent; these figures place them twenty-first, twenty-second, and twenty-ninth, respectively, among the thirty-eight. Even when assessed on contribution to the area per sessional day in parliament, Bondfield comes only fourth, whereas Wilkinson is twelfth, and Lawrence twenty-third. This low ranking reflects Labour's outlook on women. Beatrice Webb was quite wrong in 1927 to claim that 'not one of the three seems to need emotional companionship', for all three found companionship within Labour's joint campaign of both sexes for social justice.[60] So Bondfield was impatient in 1931 when feminists pressed for women's presence on unemployment benefit tribunals; women in the labour movement, she said, often liked men to represent them; the argument was 'to some extent overstrained by those who . . . have this obsession about women'. Likewise she thought feminists unwise in attacking women's special protection under lead poisoning law; such efforts tended, she said, to come from outside the working class. Instead, she wanted the protection extended to men, saying that 'in all these matters we have to exercise commonsense'. She had rejected the Edwardian feminist campaign to equalize the franchise and preferred the joint campaign of both sexes for democracy—that is, for adult suffrage. Equal franchise in 1928 was for her the culmination of democracy, not of feminism: 'it is an entire mistake,' she said, 'and I always said it was a mistake on the part of some of the ultra-feminist suffragists, to argue the specific woman point of view in connection with political questions. I do not think that is the way in which we develop.'[61]

[59] *HC Deb.* 29 June 1925, c. 2123; 22 Feb. 1928, c. 1646.

[60] B. Webb, *Diaries, 1924–1932*, p. 151. For definition of 'questions specific to women', see p. 75.

[61] *HC Deb.* 21 July 1931, c. 1363; 19 July 1927, c. 246; 29 Mar. 1928, c. 1417. See also Bondfield, *Life's Work*, p. 82; *Verbatim Report of Debate on Dec 3rd 1907. Sex Equality (Teresa Billington-Greig) versus Adult Suffrage (Margaret G. Bondfield)* (Manchester, 1908), pp. 15, 26.

Her position on women's employment is similar; she devotes more of her debating contribution to it than any of the thirty-eight—but only because she spoke for her Party on the subject; she offers no cure for unemployment that is specific to women except to encourage them into the home—either as domestic servants or as family women. She wants training provided for domestic service, not just to improve the servant's status, but because no such training will be lost on women destined for domesticity. Her speeches frequently emphasize woman's family responsibilities, and in 1924 she created a stir by saying that she had 'little patience with the woman who wants to leave husband and children to the care of paid labour while she herself seeks outside work because it is more intellectual'.[62]

Like Bondfield, Lawrence did not see the world in feminist terms. She attacked the marriage-bar for London County Council teachers, but told the Labour Women's Conference in 1918 that 'women must combat the argument that women should organize themselves on a sex basis'. Her enthusiasm for welfare legislation did not involve distinguishing between the interests of the sexes, and as MP she was hardly involved in feminist concerns at all. For her, the struggle for social justice in a classbound society requires men and women to band together, and she is really indignant in 1929 when attacking the proposal to exclude male members of the Labour Party executive from speaking at the national conference of Labour women: 'she could not believe that the women who put forward that resolution meant anything so ridiculous.'[63] Only on a rather broad definition of feminism, then, do Bondfield and Lawrence enter the feminist pantheon. As for Wilkinson, she told the WFL, which campaigned for her at the general election of 1924, that it was 'a mistake for women candidates and women's societies to speak as though women MPs were in essentials different from the men, with special policies of their own'. Yet she approaches feminism more closely than Bondfield or Lawrence. In the late 1920s she joined Astor in campaigning for more policewomen; and in the debate of 1930 on reforming women's nationality law, Astor praised Wilkinson's speech with the comment: 'I only want to say "ditto" to every word that she said.'[64]

[62] Hamilton, *Bondfield*, p. 183; cf. pp. 171–2, 181. See also *HC Deb.* 10 Mar. 1924, c. 2082; 6 Nov. 1930, c. 1213.

[63] Lawrence quoted in H. Smith, 'Sex vs. Class. British Feminists and the Labour Movement, 1919–1929', *Historian*, Nov. 1984, p. 23. *Report of the 10th National Conference of Labour Women . . . 1929*, p. 33. See also London Society for Women's Service, *Annual Report, 1923*, p. 11.

[64] Wilkinson, *Vote*, 4 July 1924, p. 209. Astor, *HC Deb.* 28 Nov. 1930, c. 1710.

Wilkinson's feminism was, however, of the 'new' variety, and rejected any analogy between the professions' restraints on middle-class women's work and factory regulations' restraints on working-class women's work; 'the need in the case of industrial women . . .', she said in 1927, was 'not to secure opportunity (which they had), but to prevent their exploitation'. In 1928 she opposed including birth-control in Labour's programme on the ground that this was an issue on which there were no class differences, but her position probably stems mainly from fear of Roman Catholic constituents. In the 1930s she did much to advance equal pay; on debating contribution to the subject per sessional day she comes third of the fifteen women MPs who discussed it between 1919 and 1945.[65] Equal pay as a parliamentary issue did not come alive till 1935, and in 1936 she instituted an important debate. She was on her best form—lightly sarcastic, almost skittish, yet concisely wielding powerful arguments; by inflicting an embarrassing defeat on the government she gave life to the cause. The government was again defeated on the issue in 1944, but on that occasion her first priority (if only for feminist reasons) was Hitler's defeat, and her votes in the three divisions therefore helped the government to get parliament's decision reversed.

Whereas Wilkinson's career illustrates the linkage between feminism and the labour movement, the careers of Bondfield and Lawrence illustrate the tension. In the 1890s Lady Dilke had guided women trade unionists away from feminist resistance to regulating women's working hours, and the Women's Co-operative Guild between the wars kept aloof from feminist bodies. Tension was heightened by feminist disappointment with Labour's minority government of 1924. The Six Point Group included Snowden, MacDonald, and Henderson on its 'grey list'—that is, among men who had claimed to support feminism, but 'not only failed to do anything whatsoever to forward it when it was in their power to do so very easily, but have actually gone out of their way to obstruct it'. Rhondda said the government had done nothing to help equal franchise, had watered down Wintringham's equal guardianship proposals, and had not made birth-control advice available at government welfare clinics. For the WFL, Labour had failed to get peeresses into the House of Lords in their own right, acquiesced in a continued marriage-bar against woman teachers, failed to reform the law on women's nationality, and made no feminist tax reforms.[66]

[65] *Woman's Leader*, 11 Feb. 1927, p. 7. Smith, 'Sex vs. Class', p. 26. Vernon, *Wilkinson*, p. 98.
[66] *Vote*, 8 Aug. 1924, p. 254; 11 Apr. 1924, pp. 113, 117; 17 Oct. 1924, p. 332. Rhondda, *The Sunday Times*, 13 July 1924, p. 12.

This tension between feminism and labour lies behind the feminists' own internal disagreements during the 1920s. The traditional feminist doubts about welfare regulations specific to women were voiced by Astor, by the London Society for Women's Service, by Rathbone's opponents within NUSEC and by the Open Door Council—a forceful offshoot from NUSEC formed in 1927 and led by Elizabeth Abbott. When the Council asked for an interview with MacDonald in 1928, the Party's chief woman officer Marion Phillips strongly (and successfully) opposed the idea, pointing out that the Council 'consists of extreme feminists who have no industrial knowledge', and insisting that 'oblivion would suit it better than anything else'.[67] On the other hand, the 'new' or 'welfare feminists' drew the feminist and labour causes together: they aimed to reconcile the interests of spouses through enacting family allowances and humanitarian restraints on working hours and conditions that would tempt women voluntarily away from the labour market and into motherhood. The feminists' split on discriminatory welfare legislation was advertised in contrasting letters to *The Times* during February 1929. On the one side were feminists who took up an individualist libertarian position— Emmeline Pethick-Lawrence, Lady Rhondda, Vera Brittain, Elizabeth Abbott, Cicely Hamilton, and Chrystal Macmillan. On the other side were the interventionists—Beatrice Webb, Eva Hubback, Clara Rackham, Gertrude Tuckwell, Wilkinson, and Bondfield—who argued that 'women workers as a class do differ in some respects from men workers as a class' because relatively young, under-unionized and only temporarily active in the labour market.[68]

After the early 1920s feminism was submerged by class and foreign-policy issues that were central to party loyalties; feminist politicians were therefore dispersed to right and left, and sucked into the contest between Labour and Conservative for the Liberal Party's ambiguous libertarian legacy. In welfare debates of the late 1920s Labour women MPs like Lawrence and Bondfield found themselves embattled in parliamentary scenes against Conservative women MPs like Astor and Iveagh. At one point in a debate of 1930 on unemployment, Astor complained that Morrison had 'not said one single word about any scheme affecting women'; 'I do not think too much about men and women,' he retorted, 'I think about the human race'.[69]

---

[67] PRO 30/69 (MacDonald Papers) 1173/2/233-4: Phillips to MacDonald, 15 Feb. 1928.
[68] *New Statesman*, 1 Mar. 1930, p. 662. See also *The Times*, 1 Feb. 1929, p. 13; 11 Feb. 1929, p. 8; *Woman's Leader*, 20 Dec. 1929, p. 353.
[69] *HC Deb.* 4 Nov. 1930, c. 732; cf. c. 766.

Yet the complexity of Labour's relationship with feminism emerges from two facts: Morrison did more than most Labour leaders to promote women within his Party, and Wilkinson, his ally, was more than once able to bring the two movements together. And if party loyalties could sometimes divide feminists from one another, feminism could also sometimes unite feminists from all sides of the House. For example, no unbridgeable gulf on attitudes to women's family role separated the 'welfare feminist' on the left from the more traditionalist attitudes to family on the right. In their impatience with party politics—sometimes even with the political process itself—Edwardian suffragists were in some ways prophetic, for parliament fully exposes MPs to the complexities and compromises involved in policy-making, and these only the politically inexperienced are tempted to ignore.

PLATE 7. Pippa Strachey (National Portrait Gallery).

6

Two Organization Women

PIPPA AND RAY STRACHEY

SOCIAL reform often runs in families. New ideas readily catch on in small groups that meet regularly, if only because trusted relatives lend confidence to one another; and the reforming impulse can be concentrated by a family's traditions and religious commitment, as Liverpool's Rathbones, Darlington's Peases, and Birmingham's Sturges illustrate. Among British feminist families, the Garretts and the Pankhursts reign supreme, but the Stracheys follow close behind—most notably Lady Strachey, her daughter Pippa, and her daughter-in-law Ray—and it was from their social circle that many of Virginia Woolf's feminist writings emerged. In discussing Pippa and Ray, to whose careers family is of central importance, we return to the British feminist mainstream.

Pippa was born in 1872, the fifth of ten children born to Sir Richard Strachey and Jane Maria Grant. If birth-control had been fashionable fifty years earlier, this close-knit and deservedly famous family—whose size produced its distinctive mood, wide connections and intellectual vitality—might never have existed. The Strachey characteristics—'lucidity, good sense, balance, and order'[1]—had been cultivated in the sort of administrative post which, especially in India, brings the reality rather than the trappings of power, and leaves time for cultivation and even scholarship. Pippa's father was a distinguished Indian public servant, and she was alone among his children in really loving India.

She was the mainstay of the family—more tender than most Stracheys and more patient with bores, though capable of giving 'a severe nip' when provoked. Leonard Woolf, who first met her when she was twenty-nine, found her 'extremely intelligent, enthusiastic and highly critical, effervescing with ideas'; she 'seemed able to make everything possible and amusing'. At this time she had a vigorous line in Scottish reels, which she propagated among her friends. She once confessed that she liked things 'to be pleasant', and that she had never loved anyone very much outside her

---

[1] C. R. Sanders, *The Strachey Family, 1588–1932* (Durham, N.C., 1953), p. 4.

circle of family and friends. Ever understanding, ever helpful, she was particularly attached to Pernel and Lytton. It was she whom he asked to suggest a title for his latest book in 1922, she who nursed their dying mother night and day, she who nursed Lytton through several early illnesses and alternated with Carrington at his bedside during his last illness, never showing grief or thought of herself—she to whom Carrington clung when he died. 'I have never known anyone more profoundly and universally a person of goodwill than she was,' Leonard Woolf recalled.[2]

Her letters chronicle her family's domestic crises, household difficulties, illnesses, and deaths, yet they are delightful letters—whimsical, elaborately phrased, self-deprecating, alert to the ironies of social life and, like Pippa herself, curiously elusive. Like all Stracheys she eagerly exposes pomposity, humbug, or the cultural *gaffe*. High-pitched Stracheyan shouts of laughter greeted gossip and Rabelaisian repartee; voices varied and unpredictable in pitch but heavy with humorous emphasis mercilessly punctured sentimentality and pretentiousness, and Pippa's high-pitched cackle or screech contributed amply to the subsequent *mêlée*.

Her letters often reflect the intense love of music that her European travels aimed to gratify. A lifelong reader, she found blindness a special deprivation—her sole occasion for complaint when bedridden in her nineties. 'Beauties of Lisbon. Gold Medal Awarded', she inscribes in 1911 on a postcard from Portugal displaying a peculiarly hideous nude; 'Beauties of Lisbon—Architectural Dept. 1st Prize', she writes beneath a remarkably ugly building dispatched in 1913. Like so many middle-class correspondents of the day, she extracts humour from false gentility or lower-class malapropism and mispronunciation: 'my health has had a slight diminuendo,' she writes, 'perhaps caused by some piercing winds or perhaps by hysteria superindooced by the arrival of two thermometers.' Leonard Woolf was impressed by her unusual amalgam of unsentimental benevolence: 'her attitude was compounded of clear-sightedness, affection, tolerance, amusement, and scepticism.'[3] She employed her almost puckish sense of fun to ward off intrusions and safeguard her privacy; contemporaries think of her as an elf-like figure, always half-vanishing into the background.

[2] R. Strachey, *A Strachey Boy* (1980), p. 16. L. Woolf, *The Journey not the Arrival Matters* (1969), p. 120. B. Askwith, *Two Victorian Families* (1971), pp. 66–7. M. Holroyd, *Lytton Strachey. A Critical Biography*, ii (1968), pp. 447–8, 577, 699, 710.

[3] BL Add. MSS 60728 (Strachey Papers), fos. 55–6. Smith Archives, Oxford: undated fragment, possibly 1916, in file labelled 'Pippa'. L. Woolf, *The Journey*, p. 120.

She was birdlike in her quick movements, small and rather plain, but her strikingly circular brown eyes were set in a very mobile and expressive face that grew rather lined in old age. Like her siblings she wore pince-nez and her short-sightedness caused her to move towards you when she laughed, looking sideways with head slightly cocked. 'Why are you interested in our mother? Why are you interested in us?' she asked Elizabeth Boyd, an American writer studying the Stracheys in the 1960s; then 'she got out of her little chair and came over to put her face down close to mine, so that with her almost sightless big brown eyes she might be able to read my expression'.[4] Careless of appearances, she allowed her hair in middle age to hang in wisps and her stockings to gather in rings round her ankles. She was indifferent to dress or personal comfort. As with so many late-Victorian middle-class reformers, privilege was combined with austerity; domestic chores were quite beyond her. Yet, although she did not herself need to work, she spent a lifetime defending women less fortunately placed.

Her conversational silences were misleading; she might at first seem not to listen, yet unexpected interventions later revealed that she had been listening all along. The well-known 'Strachey pauses' in her conversation reflected both the familiarity which makes small-talk redundant and the liberty which holds that everyone must be allowed their own private trains of thought; but her young niece Ursula Wentzel found it agonizing at Gordon Square tea-parties when conversational gaps were left unfilled. Pippa's intelligence could also seem intimidating, reinforced as it was by a rather quizzical expression and an eyebrow frequently raised. None the less Irene Hilton's reaction was typical: 'from the very first moment when I met her and heard her, my reaction was "What a completely fascinating person!"'[5]

When shyness was set aside, nobody's conversation could be more entertaining; a flood of reminiscences, amusing stories, and witty remarks would flow. She was a good listener, hanging on the lips of any relative who brought news of self or family; with her intense interest in people, she could tempt life-stories out of engine-drivers when travelling, policemen while in procession, and nurses in her nineties. 'Ma'am, when you get the

---

[4] E. Boyd, *Bloomsbury Heritage* (1976), pp. 4–5. Author's interview with Mrs Mary Dunlop, 25 Nov. 1984, at 22 Cavendish Road, Oxford.

[5] Author's tape-recorded interview with Miss Irene Hilton, 24 Feb. 1977, at 12 Sydney House, Woodstock Road, London W4 1DP. Also helpful here was the author's tape-recorded interview with Cyril and Ursula Wentzel, 1 Mar. 1977, at 36 Compton Road, London SW19 7QD.

vote, you and I'll have a date,' a sympathetic policeman told her *sotto voce* when accompanying a suffragist procession; years later he fulfilled his promise and took her out to dinner; 'she was the kind of person to whom that sort of thing happened', Hilton recalled.[6] Yet Pippa's raillery concealed a serious-minded feminist, determined on long-term objectives, well able to connect means with ends. We should not allow her deliberate self-effacement to conceal either her delightful personality or her substantial practical achievements.

As secretary to the LSWS from 1907 to 1951 she shunned the limelight—displaying her fine memory, her acute political judgement, and her cool tenacity only to consenting colleagues in private. She preferred to avoid platform speeches and make her points through asking penetrating questions from the floor.[7] Unobtrusively she stage-managed non-militant suffrage demonstrations. Her brother James could surely not have refused her request for stewards at the suffragist procession of February 1907: 'bands, brakes and badges are provided,' she wrote; 'trained gymnasts with trumpet voices are engaged. Police in their thousands will attend us . . . But further assistants are much wanted . . . What a sell if only 30 females assemble! And the weather! Lor!!!' But her horizons ranged well beyond Edwardian suffragism; she is a key figure behind the information-gathering, employment-promoting role of feminist organizations in the next generation. When Pippa praised *Three Guineas* in May 1938, Virginia Woolf found it 'the last load off my mind . . . for I felt if I had written all that and it was not to her liking I should have to brace myself pretty severely in my own private esteem . . . Now I can face the music.'[8]

Ray's background was very different. Born in 1887, she and her sister Karin were daughters of the London Roman Catholic radical Frank Costelloe and Mary Pearsall Smith, of the Philadelphia Quaker family; but Mary departed in 1891 to join the art connoisseur Bernhard Berenson in Italy, and her reproachful mother, the well-known preacher and author Hannah Whitall Smith, was left to bring up the children. As the women were dominant in the Whitall family, and as Costelloe died in 1899, the strongest early influence on Ray was Hannah, who enjoyed life and thought children should do the same; to Ray she seemed 'a perfect

[6] Interview with Miss Hilton, 24 Feb. 1977. Author's tape-recorded interviews with Barbara Strachey, 5 Jan. 1977, at 15 Richmond Road, Oxford, and 22 Jan. 1977, at 12 Rowland Close, Wolvercote, Oxford.

[7] Moyes, *Woman in a Man's World*, p. 102.

[8] BL Add. MSS 60728, fos. 17–18: Pippa to J. B. Strachey, n.d. [envelope postmarked 4 Feb. 1907]. V. Woolf, *Diary*, v (1984), p. 147.

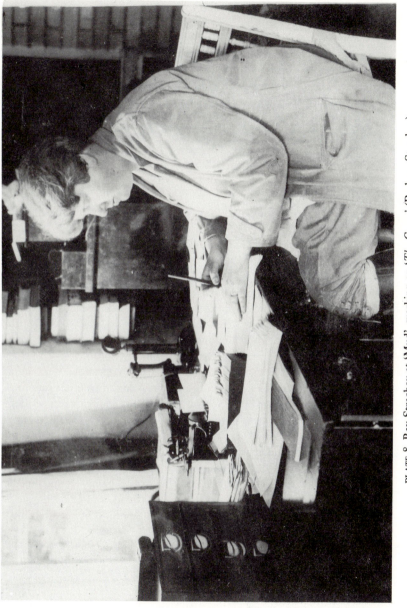

PLATE 8. Ray Strachey at 'Mud', working on 'The Cause' (Barbara Strachey).

grandmother'.[9] She gave Ray and Karin consistent sympathy and much freedom. Ray always felt she was on their side, and edited her papers. Her book about Hannah is less a biography than a compendium of Hannah's ideas on how to be a good grandmother. Throughout her life Ray remembered and acted upon Hannah's wise guideline—avoiding quarrels or jealousy, and never taking umbrage.

Mary intrusively tried to manipulate the lives of her two daughters, and in self-defence Ray became what the family called 'the oyster': 'I cannot stand being pumped,' she wrote in her youthful diary, 'I will not endure it.' Reason was Ray's protection against her mother's emotional self-indulgence; as she told her own children, 'you get as much affection as you deserve, and if you get less, be nicer'.[10] There were other sources of friction. Mary's feminism did not prevent her from acting upon Berenson's conventional expectations of woman; she became the elegant and cultivated but hypochondriac hostess at his famous Florentine villa I Tatti. Ray disliked the artificialities of this life—a dislike later reinforced by the Stracheys' contempt for Berenson's well-paid parasitism on artistic creativity; yet if she was to work for feminism, she needed Berenson's subsidy. Besides, the strong sense of duty inculcated by Hannah prevented any open breach; correspondence was copious, though cautious, and periodic visits were exchanged. Mary drew heavily on Ray's letters when writing her posthumous biography of Ray; its eulogistic tone suggests that she never really understood their relationship.[11]

Ray's marked ability survived her disrupted education—first in a convent school, then in a Lambeth board school, and then (after catching lice there) in Kensington High School. She was a good organizer, became head of school, abandoned Catholicism, and during her second year at Newnham College, Cambridge published a novel, *The World at Eighteen*. Her private diary's mood at this time is quite introspective, but facetious and not at all gloomy; she is alert to social situations and is already testing out her skills at manipulating people. Hers was a happy temperament which enabled her to eat well, sleep soundly at will, and enjoy physical exercise outdoors; she felt no older than twenty for most of her adult life.

[9] Introduction to R. Strachey, *A Quaker Grandmother. Hannah Whitall Smith* (1914), p. 9.

[10] Smith Archives, Oxford: Ray Strachey's Diary, 29 Mar. 1905. Interview with Barbara Strachey, 22 Jan. 1977. B. Strachey, *Remarkable Relations. The Story of the Pearsall Smith Family* (1980), pp. 199–200.

[11] This chapter's discussion of the personalities and careers of Pippa and Ray Strachey owes more to the interviews with Barbara Strachey specified in note 6 above, together with related correspondence, than can conveniently be acknowledged in individual footnotes.

Anxiety seldom troubled her, and her positive outlook on life enabled her to dismiss difficulties and emphasize enjoyments; 'at any rate, *that's* to the good,' she would say.[12]

Like Pippa, Ray rejected the purely personal type of success that could have come so easily. She was impatient with bores and refused to become one of Mary's admired 'charming, exquisitely dressed young girls, who curtsied to older women, and were elegant and at ease in society'. By 1905 she was already a pioneer woman driver; 'what Ray really liked . . .', her daughter writes, 'was lying in the muddy road underneath the machine trying to get it going again when it stopped'. Keynes made things worse by persuading her to read the unfeminine subject of mathematics at Cambridge. By 1909 even Hannah was concerned at her shabby dress and social isolation.[13]

Ray was almost predestined to inherit the Whittalls' long-standing feminism. Hannah praised Costelloe in 1887 for attending at Ray's birth; 'husbands ought always to do this,' she told her cousin Carrie, 'nurse says they ought to be pinned to the wall beside the bed and *made* to stay'. Ray's first novel was partly inspired by indignation at being patronized by an anti-feminist young male visitor to I Tatti; she welcomed the contrast provided in 1906 by Keynes and Geoffrey Scott, who were 'utterly unflirtatious' and talked to her as though she was a reasonable being.[14] By 1907 she was organizing enjoyably surreptitious open-air suffrage meetings during vacations, and during term was 'being very wiley' (as she herself wrote) at promoting suffragism among women undergraduates. Suffragism enthralled some of her Newnham contemporaries, and in 1908 Ray carried the Joan of Arc banner in a London suffragist procession. Hannah was disgusted at being unable to go; 'had I only had a Bladder that was alive to its female responsibility, I should have been in that Procession myself, being wheeled along in my Bath chair,' she told Mary. 'But instead I must stay at home and attend to my Bladder's demands, under a decided protest.'[15]

Ray loved mathematics but had little talent for it, and went down from Cambridge with a third. Her energies had gone into her suffrage work,

[12] Smith Archives, Oxford: Mary Berenson's typescript biography of Ray, i. p. 28.

[13] Ibid. i. 18. B. Strachey, *Remarkable Relations*, p. 232. See also Smith Archives, Oxford: Hannah's endorsement on Ray's letter to her mother dated 5 Oct. 1909.

[14] B. Strachey, *Remarkable Relations*, p. 95. Smith Archives, Oxford: Ray's diary, 21 June 1906.

[15] Smith Archives, Oxford: Ray to her family, 1 Dec. 1907; Hannah to Mary, 13 June 1908. B. Strachey, *Remarkable Relations*, p. 238, incorrectly describes this procession as the 'Mud March', which occurred on 7 Feb. 1907.

where she found her vocation. While visiting America with her friend Ellie Rendel, she went on a speaking-tour with the Revd. Anna Shaw, a former Methodist minister; she then found herself ineluctably drawn towards national campaigning for the NUWSS, which needed her energy and enthusiasm at this time of rapid suffragist expansion. In a perpetual but pleasurable whirl, she helped launch the Young Suffragists (the NUWSS youth section) in 1909 and tactfully galvanized cautious non-militant elders into greater effort. She pressed the NUWSS to put up suffragist candidates at the general election of January 1910—probably mistakenly, because they were hopelessly defeated. 'We . . . rush wildly about interviewing people and pulling wires,' she wrote; 'it is great fun.' Her letters, often scribbled in pencil, flow forth from station waiting-rooms, train journeys, or committee meetings; 'she is one of those capable individuals who manage everything without a fuss', wrote Hannah, 'and who ask for no help'.[16]

But how should she react to militancy? It seemed so determined and courageous, and Ray was almost converted to it in 1907 when she saw Mary Gawthorpe confronting insurgent medical students. During 1909 she argued on the subject with her militant friend Winnie Buckley—her grandmother watching rather nervously from the sidelines.[17] She eventually pronounced the militants 'emotional unscrupulous unwise and dangerous', and pressed the NUWSS to condemn them. In the event its Cardiff conference, where she was active, simultaneously condemned both the government and the militants; 'I like these exciting things tremendously', she wrote, '—they are so full of incidents and surprises'.[18] A militant demonstration could still tempt her a year later; 'I wish I was a militant,' she commented privately. 'But one *can't*! They are so repulsive as well as so fine!'[19] Her rejection of militancy was crucial: it led her into feminist organizations that transcended Edwardian suffragism and pioneered new areas of inter-war feminist advance, and it gave her the type of political experience that made for influence later. Also important for her future, as champion of women's careers, were the lectures she attended on electrical engineering in Oxford: 'the mornings seem to fly away,' she wrote.[20]

[16] Smith Archives, Oxford: Ray to family, 2 Dec. 1909; Hannah to Mary, 13 Nov. 1909.
[17] Ibid.: Ray to Mary, 17 Dec. 1907; Hannah's superscription on letter from Ray to Mary, 13 Oct. 1909.
[18] Ibid.: Ray's diary, 16 Oct. 1909; Ray's postcard from Cardiff dated 'Wed.', postmarked 6 Oct. 1909.
[19] Ibid.: Ray's diary, 18 Nov. 1910.
[20] Ibid.: 19 Oct. 1910.

Ray was always more than a woman of action; a lifelong alternating pattern recurs of withdrawal and return, of secluded contemplation followed by almost frenetic public work. There were minor fluctuations within the week, month, or year, major fluctuations between phases of her life, and interactions between all of these. Whereas the years 1907–8 saw abundant action, the years 1909–10 saw contemplation; she was thinking hard about the long-term future. A continuous tension also moulds her personal relationships. In her diary for 1909 she finds it difficult to reconcile her dislike of individuals with her interest in human beings *en masse*, and she admires those who can dedicate themselves to a cause; 'to have personal ambition, or personal happiness as the only reason for life' would, she thinks, be 'awful'.[21] A reading of Carlyle stirs her distinct sense of personal destiny; she knows that it will involve women's suffrage and liberty, but is not yet clear whether it will involve writing; 'I *know* that there is something I have got to do', she writes, 'though I'm not sure what it is'.[22]

In December 1909 Ellie Rendel brought Ray and the Stracheys together for the first time; 'I do like them so much!' wrote Ray; 'they're literary and political just as I am'.[23] In reality, she liked them because they were so different. She was fascinated by these strange, long-faced, and studious young people—so united as a family, so indifferent to personal comfort, so fierce in defence of individuality. Her taste for the Stracheys, like her later taste for collecting Charlotte Yonge's novels, stems from her fascination with the unfamiliar experience of life in a large family. Furthermore Ray's outlook was still largely American, and her aims were far less intellectual, far more practical, than those of the Stracheys. She was quick-witted, of course, but much less verbal in her humour, less interested in juggling with words or ideas. She had no taste for stretching the mind as the athlete stretches the body; abstractions bored her, and even her sister's Freudian psychology seemed over-intellectualized. There they were, all peering short-sightedly into the books they held in one hand while gathering food with the other. What did it matter that they felt no obligation to entertain her? Here was a social life with (as she put it) 'no polite pretence about it'. Besides, the books were set aside when (as often happened) the conversation grew interesting. '*This* is the family I'm going to marry into,' she told herself.[24] She became specially devoted to Dorothy, Pippa, and Pernel, and married their brother Oliver.

---

[21] Ibid.: 24 Sept., 28 Nov. 1909.
[22] Ibid.: 24 Sept. 1909.
[23] Ibid.: Mary's typescript biography, viii. 18.
[24] Ibid. viii. 7. Interview with Barbara Strachey, 22 Jan. 1977.

Ellie's letters to Ray on hearing that she was to marry are tragic in their ferocious bitterness. She was not the only woman attracted to Ray; the Revd. Anna Shaw had competed with her for Ray's attention during the American tour. But Ray was deeply in love with Oliver, and because he saw himself as ineligible it was she who proposed to him. Thirteen years older than Ray, divorced, and with a nine-year-old daughter Julia, Oliver had just retired from working on the Indian railways, and seemed to have few prospects. It was an unconventional marriage for its day. They considered living together without getting married, and eventually married without their parents' knowledge; Ray gave her mother the news the week after. They at first proposed to live off collaborative writing, supplemented by Ray's allowance. But like most marriages, this one did not turn out as planned.

All this prolonged Ray's contemplative period. In 1912 she published her biography of Frances Willard; a biography of her grandmother, who died in 1911, followed in 1914. The idea of collaborating with Oliver on writing about India did not survive their contrasting literary styles, and *Keigwin's Rebellion, 1683–4* (1916) was their sole collaborative work. Extremely intelligent, very sociable, passionately interested in music, Oliver was a charming but lazy man; domesticity was not for him. He was no help in the house, and Julia was brought up largely by Ray's maternal aunt Alys. Ray managed the family finances, which were subsidized from I Tatti, and single-handedly brought up their two children, Barbara (born in 1912) and Christopher (born in 1916). Whereas Oliver's Strachey characteristics and sociability placed him nearer the centre of what came to be called the Bloomsbury Group, Ray did not advance beyond the sidelines, and did not enjoy literary discussion for its own sake. She appears only occasionally in Virginia Woolf's diary and correspondence, winning a sneaking admiration for her solid qualities; 'she makes me feel like a faint autumnal mist,' wrote Woolf in August 1915; 'she's so effective, and thinks me such a goose'.[25] Another reason for keeping away from Bloomsbury, as from I Tatti, was to shield the children from undue sophistication.

Ray too had little taste for domestic life, which she thought 'all abominably badly thought out'. There were the usual difficulties with servants, and Ray found it difficult to manage either the family finances or Julia, who was a difficult child and resented her stepmother. Ray's miscarriage in 1914 made things worse; 'I used to weep night after night, and my nerves were all gone to pieces,' she wrote.[26] She longed for a second

---

[25] V. Woolf, *Letters*, ii (1976), p. 63; cf. Ibid., *Letters*, i (1975), p. 457.
[26] Smith Archives, Oxford: Ray's diary, 23 Nov. 1914, 26 Mar. 1916.

child, and imaginary pregnancies and miscarriages followed. Alarmed at this uprush of an emotion she thought she had mastered, she kept a remarkable diary of her feelings, but a fibroid operation and a holiday abroad eventually brought these difficulties to an end. By 1915 contemplation could again give way to action, and Christopher's advent only briefly interrupted the transition.

As Oliver recedes within Ray's life, so Pippa advances. Ray had married Oliver, it was said, so as to be able to work more easily with Pippa. They often spent evenings and holidays together, and were already collaborating closely on suffrage business early in 1910. Though unmistakably a Strachey, Pippa like Ray wanted something more from life than literary talk, and Ray liked her reticence, so different from Mary Berenson's theoretical manner. This was the basis of a feminist partnership crucial for British inter-war feminist history. They laughed a lot when together, and their instinctive mutual understanding made them, in Hilton's words, 'like the two halves of a press stud as far as work was concerned'. Time eroded the importance of their contrast in age and feminist status, but enhanced the contrast between Pippa's birdlike form and Ray's growing size. 'Ray is becoming more and more the public woman,' wrote Virginia Woolf in 1919, '—floppy, fat, untidy, clumsy, and making fewer concessions than ever to brilliancy, charm, politeness, wit, art, manners, literature and so forth.'[27]

Pippa's major contribution to the partnership lay in her brilliant political sense; Hilton told me she had 'the kind of mind that not only saw the repercussions of an action, but saw the repercussions of the repercussions and the repercussions of the repercussions of the repercussions'. Pippa therefore became the long-term strategist behind the scenes while Ray's vigorous, extravert personality made her the executive arm. Whereas Ray was quick, positive, and rather impersonal, Pippa's decisions were wary and often painfully slow. From Pippa's political sense stemmed her brilliant drafting skills, for when writing to government departments she bore in mind not only the reply her letter would receive, but also her likely rejoinder to that reply. And whereas Ray was rather facile on paper, Pippa was a fine stylist. 'I should probably do very poorly in two hours, what you could do brilliantly in five minutes!' Astor told Pippa in 1937, asking her for yet another draft.[28] Nor did Pippa's reticence preclude skill

[27] Interview with Miss Hilton, 24 Feb. 1977. V. Woolf, *Letters*, ii (1976), p. 357.
[28] Interview with Miss Hilton, 24 Feb. 1977. Nancy Astor MSS 1416/1/1/1563: Astor to Pippa Strachey, 23 Apr. 1937. Author's tape-recorded interview with Mrs Gertrude Horton, 21 Mar. 1977, at 315 The Greenway, Epsom.

at managing staff; her patent interest in individuals gained their confidence, and so she got her way without provoking resentment.

Without this partnership, the LSWS would have lost most of its imaginativeness and drive between the wars, and might even have died in 1914. Equal pay and wider occupational opportunity would then have suffered severely, and we would now have no Fawcett Society, no Fawcett Library, and no National Advisory Centre on Careers for Women. Without these, the link between the feminist generations of the 1900s and the 1970s would have been tenuous indeed. In July 1915 Fawcett pronounced the Society's Women's Service Bureau 'extremely efficient' in training and assigning women for war-work. By January 1917 Ray was describing Pippa, Thena Clough, and herself as vigorously pulling wires in their dealings with the War Office, and 'going about like the three black ladies in the Magic Flute, setting everyone to work'. Fawcett, who was in a position to know, told Pippa in June 1928 that 'there never have been more splendid and *creative* colleagues than you have both been'.[29] The partnership also operated in family matters, and Ursula Wentzel affectionately recalls how they both backed her theatrical ambitions as a young woman, and made a point of attending her first professional performance: 'they both trotted round looking a little shaggy and totally out of place in a theatrical dressing-room.'[30] Pippa's self-effacement throws Ray into prominence in what follows, but Pippa's contribution towards Ray's successes must always be remembered.

Ray's major contributions to winning the vote were unobtrusive in 1916–18, but she did not shirk the less savoury and more public aspects of feminist work—whether in addressing open-air suffragist meetings or fractious feminist gatherings. In June 1913 we find her speaking for the non-militants at Greenwich, 'pelted with mud and things, clothes completely ruined, dirty to the skin' and taking refuge in a shop till the police told her it was safe to escape.[31] Three of her standpoints within the NUWSS between 1913 and 1918—all three fully in accord with its traditions—were crucial to her later career: resisting suffragist integration with the Labour Party; backing Fawcett in resisting pacifist entanglement during 1915; and upholding the autonomy of the LSWS, which she always

---

[29] House of Lords Record Office, Lloyd George Papers, D/20/1/48: Fawcett to 'My Dear Sir', 17 July 1915. Smith Archives, Oxford: Ray to Mary, 26 Jan. 1917. Fawcett Library Autograph Collection, IM/7172: Fawcett to Pippa Strachey, 29 June 1928.

[30] Interview with the Wentzels, 1 Mar. 1977.

[31] Smith Archives, Oxford: Ray to her family, 24 June 1913.

saw as something more than merely the London branch of a national suffrage body. Each can now be discussed in turn.

In 1912 the Union formed an electoral alliance with Labour as the party most sympathetic to women's suffrage; but suffragists had always shunned party connection, and many non-militants, including Rathbone, disliked this new move. In this internal argument during 1913–14 Ray showed her customary zest for intrigue; she eventually prevailed, largely because she chose the winning side on a second and more dramatic dispute—over pacifist affiliation in 1915, where she faced many of the same opponents. Feeling ran high, and Ray received abusive letters; but Oliver backed her strongly, and eventually it was the pacifists, who included some of the Union's most active members, who had to resign. 'We only did it by having the bulk of the stodgy members behind us,' Ray told her mother in April. During the June elections for office, Ray made her position clear: if the NUWSS supported the resigning executive committee members, she would cease to be a candidate.[32] The split greatly advanced her feminist career, like Rathbone's, by removing so many senior members from the Union.

Ray's close bond with Fawcett was now established, and in 1918 she discouraged overtures from the seceders: 'I daresay you do know how passionately we resented their behaviour to you,' Ray told her; 'certainly *they* know it. And now when they seem to be wanting to come in again I think you are absolutely right to oppose it.' From summer 1915 Ray was in a position to strengthen the Union's non-party outlook; national politics helped here, for coalition supplanted party government in May. 'I hold that things are so changed now that we must all start with a clean slate,' she told her mother in December, '. . . I have no doubt at all of winning in the end. We may shake off our extreme La[bour] people, which will do no harm at all'.[33] In 1918 she was still heading off dissident suffragists who were threatening to secede from the Union into a separate Labour suffrage society, but she triumphed again, partly because events since 1915 had greatly increased her influence.[34]

She replaced Catherine Marshall as the Union's parliamentary secretary in 1915, just before what turned out to be a crucial moment in suffrage history. At first her new post made few demands, but gave her good experience at co-ordinating voluntary and paid employees, handling

[32] Ibid.: Ray to Mary, 21 Apr. 1915. *Common Cause*, 4 June 1915, p. 124.
[33] Smith Archives, Oxford: Ray Strachey to Fawcett, 18 Feb. 1918; Ray to her family, 9 Dec. 1915.
[34] Ibid.: Mary's typescript biography, xv. 1.

committees, and surviving disputes. Then in autumn 1916 the whole suffrage question revived. The timing rather suited Ray because Christopher was born in November, the month when she told Oliver that now might be the time to revive suffragist demonstrations. She went on to admit that 'we are a horribly feeble lot to do it'; some extra-parliamentary pressure was required, but still more important at this stage were pressures of a more subtle kind, organized behind a political strategy that was shrewd in conception and execution. Ray excelled at this type of work; she became Fawcett's right-hand woman for mobilizing suffragists and Sir John Simon's for co-ordinating parliamentary support. She was in the thick of NUWSS efforts to cultivate *The Times*, and by February 1917 found herself 'parting from one cabinet minister at dinner time only to breakfast with another the next day'. Politicians had to be humoured, so she often had to conceal the fact that she was really in a rush. None the less, she admitted to her mother that '*I find this sort of work almost too fascinating*'.[35]

At the same time the NUWSS had to be kept united behind what was admittedly a very illogical compromise—votes for most women over thirty—and then other suffrage bodies had to be won over. The Pankhursts complicated the task, and success then seemed more precarious than it seems now; 'I often thank Heaven for my equable temper', Ray told her mother, 'for some of the[m] are extraordinarily trying'. Uniting all the suffragist organizations behind a deputation to Lloyd George in April 1917 was 'like trying to harness a pack of wild elephants—and wild elephants with years of private conflict behind them'.[36]

We do not know how far Pippa advised Ray on all this, but she certainly helped advance the third of Ray's standpoints within the NUWSS—the need to uphold the autonomy of the LSWS. The London Society, originally independent, had not joined the Union's federal structure till 1900. In 1913 Ray thought the LSWS would best ward off suffragette takeover by transforming itself into a federation of London branches, but still more effective for autonomy was LSWS work for women's wartime employment. This not only gave the Society a new role; it also helped push feminism forward from political to economic freedom. When war began, the LSWS set up a central clearing house to plan women's voluntary war-work. Early in 1915, this began organizing paid war-work for women; it later moved on to training them through classes in trades such as engineering. In 1916 the

[35] Smith Archives, Oxford: Ray to Oliver, 14 Nov. 1916; Ray to Mary, 4 Feb. 1917; Mary's typescript biography, xv. 6.

[36] Ibid.: Ray to Mary, 4 Feb., 1 Apr. 1917.

Women's Service work became financially independent, Ray became chairman of the Women's Service Employment Committee, and Queen Mary visited the Women's Service Workshops. The work grew fast in 1917, in which year Ray also began pressing the legal profession to admit women, and in 1918 she chaired the Women's Service committee on women civil servants. None of this was likely to endear her either to trade unions or to the Labour Party; indeed in January 1918 she privately thought women's admission to the Amalgamated Society of Engineers 'quite the most important thing that could happen for women in England now that the vote is won', and in the following year publicly described trade-union attitudes to post-war dilution as 'barbaric'.[37]

Ray's employment work was really her prime interest, and profoundly influenced her subsequent feminist strategy; by comparison she found suffragism, however fascinating in itself, rather a distraction. When the future of the NUWSS was being debated in 1919, she questioned whether there would henceforth be much spontaneous support for nationally organized political feminism, but she thought the Union could test the water by contracting into a mere co-ordinating and information-gathering body.[38] In the short term she lost this battle, but the gradual decline of national political feminism during the 1920s suggests that in the long term she was right. The NUWSS's successor, the NUSEC more closely resembled Oliver's rival scheme for a dynamic feminist pressure group. Although Ray was on its executive committee from 1919 to 1924, her heart was elsewhere, and she remained aloof during NUSEC's split of 1927–8 over family allowances; 'I can't pretend to care very much what happens to the NUSEC,' she privately confessed in March 1927.[39]

Instead, she channelled her feminist energies into the LSWS, whose history she published in 1927. At its annual meeting in February 1919 she overcame opposition and got its name changed to London Society for Women's Service; she felt she could encourage the Society to resume its one-time autonomy now that NUSEC was moving into new areas of feminist policy. In 1922 the Society decided to retain its traditional London suffragist role, but otherwise to concentrate entirely on employment work. In 1925 Ray proposed omitting 'London' from its title, so that as a national 'Society for Women's Service' it could affiliate to NUSEC but remain autonomous; she failed, but it was a foretaste of the future.

During 1919 Ray transferred her suffragist tactics to defending

---

[37] Ibid.: Ray to her family, 24 Jan. 1918. Smith, 'Sex vs. Class', p. 22.
[38] *Common Cause*, 19 Feb. 1919, p. 546.
[39] Smith Archives, Oxford: Ray Strachey to Fawcett, 10 Mar. 1927.

women's employment, and primed MPs to speak against indiscriminately restoring pre-war trade-union practices. Between 1919 and 1921 Women's Service Bureau interviews for work or training ran at an annual level of 13,000, and in 1920 a Yorkshire bureau was set up on the London model; late in 1921 the Bureau's register listed 48,800 women workers, and its classified index showed that 7,200 firms had so far been contacted. Yet this rapid growth was insecure. The depression threatened women's jobs; the labour movement, where Ray's tactics on suffragism and employment had made enemies, was on the counter-attack. Fund-raising proved difficult, and the Bureau's employment department had to be closed in 1922; the annual report thought closure at such a time 'a most distressing experience, which those who went through it will not soon forget'. Between 1923 and 1933 the Bureau's average annual number of interviews fell to 1,415.[40] Until the early 1930s the LSWS had to concentrate on working for women civil servants and equal pay, and on providing social facilities for London professional women.

Ray's feminist career was never linear in direction or undeviating in its short-term aims. There were also at least two potential distractions from feminism—a career in politics and family claims, and each will now be discussed in turn. In politics between 1918 and 1923 she operated at three levels. First she briefly acted as Astor's parliamentary secretary, keeping her on the rails and broadening her own political experience; the relationship was to be resumed later. In 1921 she also volunteered to help Wintringham hold the bores and cranks at bay, and to brief her on 'some of the inner histories, which is sometimes useful'.[41] At the same time she briefly ventured into politics on her own account. This took her beyond feminist circles, but her non-party position was a hindrance. Labour was impossible for her, yet she disliked Tory hostility to Germany and distrusted Lloyd George; the Liberals seemed the only refuge, but she shunned them too, and we can now see that in the short term they had no future. During 1921 she involved herself in trying to weld together a centrist combination based on union between Lord Robert Cecil and Viscount Grey of Falloden; 'a regular buzz of a life I lead,' she told Berenson, 'with one complicated semi-political intrigue after another'.[42] Yet England does not love centrist coalitions, and Ray's admiration for what she saw as Cecil's almost naïve idealism caused her to move off for a

[40] LSWS, *Annual Report, 1922*, p. 12. Statistics collated from LSWS annual reports.
[41] Smith Archives, Oxford: Ray to Mrs Wintringham, 24 Sept. 1921 (xerox copy).
[42] Ibid.: Ray Strachey to Bernhard Berenson, 15 May 1921.

time into working for that prize inter-war non-party cause, the League of Nations Union.

She stood as an Independent three times for Brentford and Chiswick— in 1918, 1922, and 1923. In three respects she faced difficulties experienced by many inter-war women candidates. First, lack of money; this nearly prevented her from standing at all in 1923. Second, she stood for an impossible constituency; the Conservatives held Brentford and Chiswick continuously from 1910 to 1945. Her Conservative rival on all three occasions was W. G. Morden, who held the seat from 1918 to 1931. Third, her career suffered from the Liberal Party's decline, for in two of her three elections she was the victim of a divided progressive vote; Brentford's Labour vote rose continuously from 1918 to 1929 inclusive, partly at her expense. She won only 1,623 votes (20.2 per cent of the votes cast) in 1918 and lost her deposit; she came nearest to success in 1922, the one election when the absence of a Labour candidate enabled progressives to unite, and won 7,804 votes (43.5 per cent). In 1923, however, when Labour stood again, her vote fell to 3,216 (27.3 per cent). On the votes actually cast, at no stage between the wars would a united Labour and Liberal or Independent vote have ousted the Conservative from this constituency. Liberal–Labour collaboration at the national level, how- ever, might well have boosted the anti-Tory vote, and would certainly have placed more winnable seats at Ray's disposal.

Ray's election addresses illuminate her political views. In 1918 she supports the Lloyd George coalition, the League of Nations, and social reform, but unemployment and foreign-policy questions disenchant her with the coalition in 1922. She refused to join the Liberals, and identified with centrist Conservatives, especially Cecil; 'I do not approve of extremes in politics,' says her manifesto; 'I distrust Revolution on the one hand and Reaction on the other'.[43] Free trade, social reform, and the League of Nations are her favoured causes, and both in 1922 and 1923 she privately anticipated victory. In 1923 she was surprised by the size of her defeat, and so disliked the tactics of her victorious opponent that she refused to shake hands with Morden when the result was declared.

At this point, her career changes direction. As she was accused at the 1922 election of neglecting her children, we must take stock of her family situation. During their first decade together Oliver and Ray collaborated on feminist work, but their interests gradually diverged and their married life became semi-detached. Ray disliked parties whereas Oliver was very

[43] Ibid.: Ray's 1922 manifesto.

sociable, so they inevitably drifted into different circles. By 1919 Oliver had taken up with Inez Jenkins, the first of his three longstanding liaisons; Ray was not unduly concerned, and ten years later decided to make things easier for him by agreeing to meet Inez socially. They held no parties at home between 1923 and 1938, but in 1938 Ray at last responded to Oliver's desire for three sherry parties, and held them at the LSWS headquarters. Their divergence should not be exaggerated: respect for people's individuality and independence was central to the Strachey canon, and Ray had fully accepted it from the start. She and Oliver never quarrelled, and although their social lives diverged, they were surprised but pleased whenever they found themselves dining together at home; Ray missed him when they were apart, nursed him when ill, enjoyed buying him surprises when out shopping, and liked talking things over with 'an old wiseacre', as she called him.[44]

On family finance as on everything else Ray was optimistic, and difficulties were in some ways compounded by her mother's substantial but unpredictable subsidies. Nor was Ray at all interested in housekeeping. She expressed mild surprise in 1939 when Barbara embarked on spring cleaning—something she had never gone in for. Instead she delegated to housekeepers and cleaners; Mrs Inwood ran things at the London end, and when the family stayed at Ray's Sussex cottage Mrs Glazier lived in, aided by a gardener/handyman. As any reader of Virginia Woolf's diary knows, engaging and retaining servants between the wars had become an organizational and diplomatic feat. Hence the unkempt state of the family house in Marsham Street, smelling strongly of Ray's thirty cigarettes per day. There were books scattered everywhere, a piano for Oliver, threadbare oriental rugs and bargain-basement furniture, though with the occasional valuable item. Ray rose above it all: other things were more important, one should relax at home, and life was far bleaker *chez* Strachey at Gordon Square. Indeed, when mushrooms sprouted in the dining-room after the great flood of 1929, guests were offered a choice of sweet or (pointing to the mushrooms) savoury.

If she had bothered with her clothes, Ray could have displayed her pleasant blue eyes and ample figure to striking effect. But she was bored by the whole subject, got Barbara to cut her hair, and rejected make-up. When dining out on one occasion, she noticed only in mid-meal that she was wearing her dress inside out. On another occasion Barbara told her before she left that her superb brocade evening dress, acquired from her

---

44 Smith Archives, Oxford: Ray to Oliver, 2 Feb. 1917.

mother, was on back-to-front, yet she swept off convinced that 'nobody'll notice'. 'I *am* glad to see you, Mrs Berenson!' Astor benevolently told Ray's mother at one of her grand parties. 'I've long wanted to meet the mother of the worst dressed woman in London.'[45] In all this Ray was simultaneously repudiating the woman-as-plaything concept, rebelling against her mother's values, imitating the Stracheys, and clearing time for things that seemed more important.

In The Mud House ('Mud' to the family), Ray's Sussex-thatched Fernhurst cottage on Friday's Hill, constraints were still more completely shed. There Ray could be found for most of the year wearing a sort of land-army khaki suit, breeches, a large loose coat with permanently over-filled pockets, and a very rudimentary straw hat.[46] In summer she relished nude bathing in a swimming pool which was large even by present-day standards; she would rush in, standing on her hands, and would then wave her legs—'such massive, such enormous legs', Barbara recalls—in the air. In a speech at Sheffield in 1919 she had dismissed the anti-feminists' 'physical force argument' by saying that she was physically much stronger than her husband, and in 1931 she was delighted at beating the whole of the LSWS 'junior council' of young professional women at style swimming.[47] Unexpected callers on Ray at Mud were stymied by her habit of fleeing into a locked lavatory—for she refused to mix in local society, let alone to return calls. Mud was the ultimate in repudiating her mother's values, a standing protest against constraints on women's freedom, a rural bolt-hole for a woman who if anything saw too much of people in her day-to-day urban life.

It was her own house in a double sense, for she had built it. In 1920 she launched 'Women Builders' to construct *pisé de terre* (rammed earth) houses, but the venture foundered on bricklayers' hostility and on the scarcity of suitable clay, leaving Mud as its memorial. Mary Dunlop, who went there as a child, remembers thinking it 'quite incredibly beautiful . . . like being in a fairyland'; it was set among sweet chestnuts in a copse wood invariably filled by wild flowers, and Mud's large main room opened on to a lawn through garage doors.[48] Inside, the usual shabby and untidy informality prevailed, together with a piano and a bizarre assortment of books. Ray later extended it, built a summer cottage near by,

[45] Ibid.: Mary's typescript biography, i. 14.
[46] M. A. Hamilton, *Remembering My Good Friends* (1944), p. 267.
[47] *Sheffield Daily Telegraph*, 11 Mar. 1919, p. 6. Smith Archives, Oxford: Ray to Mary, 13 May 1931.
[48] Interview with Mrs Dunlop, 25 Nov. 1984. Hamilton, *Remembering*, pp. 265–6.

and half-finished another (which still survives as 'the ruin') shortly before her death. Her Strachey guests gave Ray no help in her building works; noses in their books, they shuddered at this bizarre taste for the outdoor life. Her mother's visits, dutifully arranged at intervals, were difficult occasions; Mary usually claimed to be ill, the family all disliked her, she was helpless without servants, and required to be continuously entertained. But Ray was completely happy there, indulging her passions for digging, housebuilding, swimming, indoor games, and picking blueberries and mushrooms.

Ray organized her life so capably that Barbara never felt threatened by her public commitments. The children enjoyed Oliver, but respected Ray more. All three were so obviously Stracheys that Ray sometimes stood back almost as an onlooker, surprised but pleased to have produced two of them. 'I often think to myself with a real pang of pleasure', she told Fawcett during a moment of private patriotism in 1918, 'that I have married an Englishman and have English children.' Ray told her mother that 'if one has children one has to do it . . . to the best of one's ability'.[49] This remark captures Ray's strong sense of duty but gives too earnest an impression, for she positively enjoyed her children. Discipline was very relaxed, and she allowed each child one 'free week' of full authority at Mud during childhood. They called their parents by their Christian names and like Ray herself they acquired the Strachey habit of simultaneously eating and reading at mealtimes. Ray's resilient temperament, her skill at card games, and her love of outdoor and physical activity made her a good companion, and her children received ample warm affection.

Ray took great trouble in finding them the right schools, and wrote them pleasant unpompous letters which replied helpfully to questions and mixed good advice with family gossip, in-jokes, and nicknames. 'Darling Wretch', she wrote to Christopher in 1933, when he failed to instruct her on what to wear when speaking at his school: 'What do you mean by not writing to me and answering that all-important question about clothing? If you don't look out I shall appear and make my speech in my combinations.'[50] She never forced her feminist views upon her children, though she would have been delighted if Barbara had shared them; she was quite prepared to be teased about them and never bridled when her children pointed to an 'equal woman' in the London Underground—with her tweed suit, short hair, brogue shoes, and legs positioned rather far apart.

[49] Smith Archives, Oxford: Ray Strachey to Fawcett, 18 Feb. 1918; Ray to Mary, 8 Jan. 1928.
[50] Ibid.: Ray to Christopher, 31 Oct. 1933.

Barbara always felt backed up by her mother, whom her children nicknamed 'the Rock'; Ray was always honest when answering questions, gave helpful guidance, and was quick to assist in a crisis. When Barbara, beleaguered by imaginary difficulties in a Swiss boarding school, sent a coded message of distress, Ray got there within forty-eight hours; 'she was *totally* safe', Barbara told me, 'and she was always there when we wanted her'. When Christopher had sexual problems she was instantly sympathetic; 'count on me always for anything that I can do,' she wrote; 'you know all that, ugly one'.[51] Her qualities were certainly tested by what Mary called 'Barbara's Saga', the title of a chapter in Mary's biography of Ray. It discussed Barbara's brief and rather disastrous marriage in 1934 to Olav Hultin, a penniless, irresponsible, and somewhat drunken Finn whom she met on a cruise and rapidly married in Australia. Pregnant and unfunded in California, Barbara rang for money; Ray ensured that it arrived the next day. Barbara's debts, divorce, remarriage and mentally retarded son Roger now had to be coped with, yet Ray's excellent relationship with her daughter survived intact. 'I can't . . . wish to imagine a better mother than she was,' Barbara told Astor on her death; 'not only in every action and decision, but in person. She contrived to be that unique thing, a great woman, a truly wise parent and a very lovable person.'[52]

Barbara now makes only one criticism, though in its bearing upon her own life it is rather fundamental. Ray's letters more than once warned her against emotion, which (she told Barbara at about seventeen) is like onion in a salad: a little of it goes a long way. Here Ray was reaffirming both Hannah's and Strachey values, and no doubt over-reacting at the thought of her mother's emotionalism reappearing in Barbara; Ray certainly practised what she preached, because Barbara can now recall her losing her temper only once. Yet Ray's strong belief in self-determination both for herself and others left Barbara feeling 'morally uncorseted', without clear guidelines on conduct; her mother's outlook seemed to consist entirely of relaxations and tolerations, and offered nothing to react against. Ray had dedicated her biography of Hannah to Barbara, and in leaving Barbara to make her own decisions she was simply applying to the next generation the policy Hannah had applied to her; Hannah thought that older people should merely provide a background for the young, who in many ways are better-informed than the old, and told her niece Carey that she was 'not a believer in people interfering with young ones'.[53]

When asked, Ray of course gave advice; it was notably undoctrinaire for

[51] Ibid.: Ray to Christopher, 16 July 1937.
[52] Nancy Astor MSS 1416/1/2/211: Barbara to Astor, 29 July 1940.
[53] R. Strachey, *Quaker Grandmother*, p. 17.

its day. She was an early supporter of what became the Family Planning Association,[54] and when advising Barbara on relations with Wolf Halpern, later Barbara's second husband, she wrote a remarkable letter. Without opposing sex before marriage, she thought Barbara could perhaps tell people she was married; she need not in fact marry till children arrived, and, if the relationship did not work well, she could tell people she was getting a divorce without in fact needing it.[55] Whereas Barbara's response to Ray's pursuit of reason was to tell all, Christopher's was to defend his privacy against Ray's strong affection by becoming an oyster—thus ironically replicating Ray's relationship with Mary, but for a different reason.

Not content with family responsibilities, Ray more than once rescued relatives in distress—not a rare situation, given Bloomsbury's tangled emotional relationships. She may have failed with Julia, but she seems to have succeeded with the three children of her brother-in-law Ralph Strachey when their mother had a breakdown. 'I can hardly think of a time when she was not deeply involved in straightening out somebody else's troubles,' wrote her friend Mary Agnes Hamilton; 'or any when she suggested that she had any of her own.' Only once do her papers reveal personal anxiety—during what was for her a dreadful year, 1934. Barbara's baby was due in November, so ructions with Olav could not be risked; I Tatti had to be soothed with anodyne letters, yet financial problems were becoming acute; Astor was becoming peculiarly trying as an employer, and had publicly criticized Ray's professional competence; Ray's deadline for her book on women's careers was approaching; and crucial events were occurring on the women's employment front. 'I am beginning to think of you as a real standby,' she told Christopher in January; 'I don't think it's humanly possible', she told him in October, 'to do such an exacting job all through such a fierce domestic crisis.'[56]

These family distractions did not destroy Ray as a practical feminist. Her diverse talents reinforced two more of its dimensions—the literary and the economic—each of which will now be discussed. Even when in the thick of political achievement she was not always convinced of its value, and she had not enjoyed the 1923 election at all. The unexpectedly large Conservative majority at Brentford was emancipating: she would find

[54] National Birth Control Association, *1st Annual Report, 1930–1*, lists her as contributing one guinea.

[55] Smith Archives, Oxford: Ray to Barbara, 16 Feb. 1933.

[56] M. A. Hamilton, *Rachel Conn Strachey* [n.d.], p. 7. Smith Archives, Oxford: Ray to Christopher, 24 Jan., 9 Oct. 1934.

peace and quiet, and get on with some writing. It was her taste for solitude that induced her to write, rather than the other way round. Between 1923 and 1931 she produced two novels, a substantial biography of Fawcett, an edition of her grandmother's papers, a historical booklet and a classic history of British feminism, '*The Cause*'. This was far more than many scholars, undistracted and financially secure, produce in a lifetime—yet lack of money ensured that Ray was continuously torn between creative and journalistic work, and frequently interrupted by private and public commitments. She deeply appreciated Berenson's allowance which, as she told him in 1927, 'makes all the difference to me between just scratching along, and being able to live as I like to live without perpetual cares'; for about seven years, she told him in 1930, 'I have owed my liberty of spirit to you'.[57]

Fawcett's belief that '*The Cause*' 'ought to become "a classic"' has been fulfilled, and the achievement seems all the greater in the light of Ray's difficulties when writing it. She needed an hour to get going, yet when the children were at home this was difficult; she saw herself as a juggler keeping eight or nine balls in the air at once, or as trying to complete a jigsaw puzzle with too many pieces.[58] Yet by June 1926 she could tell her mother that she could sit down to '*The Cause*' 'with no unwillingness, and only rise up when my hand is cramped and my head turning round'.[59] Militancy was difficult to interpret, especially as Fawcett (to whom it was dedicated) and Pippa were scrutinizing her drafts; Ray herself acknowledged the militants' 'narrow unwisdom'. Yet in January 1928 she said she had been 'a good deal impressed with the militant side of it . . . I still think there were very unwise aspects of it: but it was a heroic affair.'[60] Given Ray's own history and the recency of militant events, her published account is remarkably fair, though she had to run the customary gauntlet of threatened Pankhurstian lawsuits and a review from Sylvia which saw her 'most serious failure' as 'her conspicuous lack of the impartiality so essential to the historian'.[61] The book prepared the ground well for the biography Fawcett had asked her to write in 1926; for Ray it was a labour of love, and she published it less than two years after Fawcett died.

---

[57] Smith Archives, Oxford: Ray Strachey to Berenson, 11 Aug. 1927, 11 Feb. 1930.
[58] Ibid.: Fawcett to Ray Strachey, 8 Oct. [1928]. See also Ray to Mary, 21 Aug. 1924, 8 Apr. 1928.
[59] Ibid.: Ray to Mary, 8 June 1926.
[60] BL Add. MSS 60729 (Strachey Papers) fo. 41: Ray to Pippa, 18 Feb. 1928. Smith Archives, Oxford: Ray to Aunt Carey, 2 Jan. 1928 (xerox copy).
[61] Institute of Social History, Amsterdam, Sylvia Pankhurst papers: typescript review of '*The Cause*'.

By this time there were signs of life on the women's employment front. Action was urgently needed, for inter-war Britain contained many women whose trapped mentality Winifred Holtby memorably portrayed in the disillusioned and overburdened science mistress Miss Sigglesthwaite: 'to begin every year with that financial load on one's shoulders. Never to dare to rest. Never to dare to be ill. Never, for a moment, to dare to dream of the sort of work one would really have liked to do . . .'[62] It was the section on careers that Ray most enjoyed when writing '*The Cause*', and among its photographs she particularly liked the one of the woman chimney-sweep. In 1929 she battled with Winston Churchill, Chancellor of the Exchequer, on the need for equal pay in the civil service, and in May 1930 she told Christopher she had 'practically written a whole book on . . . the Civil Service this week' for the Royal Commission. Ray and Pippa were embarrassed in 1937 when the Council of Women Civil Servants gave a dinner to celebrate their work in opening up the civil service to women; but they had earned the recognition; as Ray admitted to her mother, 'we *have* worked like blacks at it for 17 years'.[63]

In the late 1920s the LSWS found in Miss Clegg a rich backer who might at last fund it adequately, and there were high hopes when Ray at last got it made independent of NUSEC in 1929. But Miss Clegg died in 1930 before the money had been handed over, and hopes of developing the employment work once more crashed. The depression worsened things both for the LSWS and for Ray, whose allowance from Berenson could no longer continue; she therefore took paid employment as Astor's secretary in 1931. Her new post did not preclude feminist work, and she campaigned to get Indian women enfranchised, though like Rathbone she had her private doubts: 'I wonder what will happen if those very backward women do get the votes,' she speculated; 'perhaps nothing worse than the men having it.' In 1934 she saw herself as 'busily stage managing the evidence to be given' to a Foreign Office inquiry on appointing women to civil service posts.[64] In 1935 she published her handbook, *Careers and Openings for Women*, reissued in revised form in 1937, and in 1936 she edited an important collection of essays on feminism, *Our Freedom and its Results*.

Working for Astor was in some ways frustrating, and secretarial work is intellectually fragmenting, whereas Ray sought cumulative and personal achievement. 'I should like to get back onto a good long task to which a

---

[62] Holtby, *South Riding*, p. 174.

[63] Smith Archives, Oxford: Ray to Christopher, 16 May 1930; Ray to Mary, 26 Jan. 1937.

[64] Ibid.: Mary's typescript biography, section for 1933, p. 9 (entry for 28 July); Ray to Mary, 8 Feb. 1934.

little could be added every day,' she told her mother in November 1933, 'instead of the succession of badly done trifles which form the bulk of my work for Lady Astor.'[65] In 1934 Astor arranged for her to work part time and concentrate on what interested her, but even this did not last long; and nothing more than a file of notes and a shared train journey to Constantinople came of the idea that she should write Astor's biography. For some time Ray had been exploring other possibilities. Shortage of money forced the LSWS to scale down its more obviously attractive work in the hope of preserving the Women's Service Bureau; these changes 'were made with anguish', said the Society, 'and they left us with a crabbed, expert task whose importance was not easily grasped by the public.'[66] By 1932 it even contemplated closing the Bureau, but the Cambridge women's colleges and the Carnegie Trust came to the rescue. Ray chaired the Cambridge University Women's Appointments Board from its launching in 1930 till 1939, and the heads and former heads of women's colleges appealed in *The Times* for funds. This, together with grants from the Carnegie Trust, which had subsidized the LSWS library in the late 1920s, eventually created the WEF.

The Trust aimed to integrate the Bureau's work with the long-established but declining Central Bureau for the Employment of Women; 'gossip and scandals pour in every moment, which is great fun,' wrote Ray of the negotiations in December 1932. She told her mother she would relish working for the combined enterprise even without pay 'because it is *exactly* the job I am fitted to do, and all my previous work is relevant to it'. As usual she was too optimistic, for the Central Bureau resisted amalgamation so tenaciously that its progressive elements resigned *en masse* in 1933. 'It was a very stupid and tiresome affair, mismanaged all through,' wrote Ray in February; '. . . now the only thing is to wait till the old birds die off, or actually collapse.'[67] The controversy is well documented because the Carnegie Trust, whose records survive, financed both sides. After the split the Central Bureau was moribund, but this did not prevent it from living off the Trust in a most discreditable way for several more years.

All was not lost: Mrs W. L. Courtney, a seceder from the Central Bureau, staunchly backed Ray's applications to the Trust, which eventually agreed to finance WEF as a separate enterprise. At the beginning of 1934, with Pippa as honorary secretary of its executive committee, WEF

---

[65] Ibid.: Ray to Mary, 19 Nov. 1933.
[66] LSWS, *Annual Report of the Executive Committee, 1932*, p. 11.
[67] Smith Archives, Oxford: Ray to Mary, 16 Dec. 1932, 10 Feb. 1933.

took over the Women's Service Bureau and became financially independent. Ray was delighted at her new-found freedom, and disliked only its fund-raising aspect. WEF headquarters indexed and diffused information about careers, interviewed employers and potential employees, and sent out its officers on visits to schools, employers, and universities. Concentrating on careers for the middle-class woman, it aimed to supplement the labour exchange network, and—as the National Advisory Centre on Careers for Women—it still survives.

Ray brought to WEF at least three major qualities rarely combined in one person: a political sense, enthusiasm, and specialist knowledge. Her political sense was particularly needed early on, when WEF had to attract loyalty from members, clients, and staff. It was a genuine federation, not an autocracy, so Ray had to persuade autonomous bodies to collaborate. She was a good committee member—silent until her views were needed, but then forthright and practical in speech, effective at making a case and ready with her charm. As for the clients, her sister Karin noticed how tactfully she disarmed critics on the telephone by apologizing for things, whether she was to blame or not.[68] Her second quality, enthusiasm, was a great help in managing staff. She had to undertake the difficult task of co-ordinating paid with voluntary workers, and needed to boost the morale of employees who were at first inevitably underpaid. She was approachable, accessible, and a skilful interviewer who knew whom to select. Still more important, her enthusiasm and single-mindedness made the work enjoyable—more like a campaign or crusade. She knew how to delegate, when to share the drudgery, when to take a holiday. Her radiant expression remained vivid in Miss Hilton's memory after forty years. 'I do not know whether I was able to convey to you the really passionate eagerness with which we long to do our work well', Ray told the Trust in 1938; 'we are, in sober fact, enthusiasts.'[69]

Ray brought a lifetime's expertise to WEF. She was an excellent driver, could draft papers, handle correspondence, knew the world of women's careers backwards, had mastered the official statistics on the subject, knew how to cultivate the press, and could draw upon numerous relevant contacts. Furthermore the subject fascinated her—she was genuinely inquisitive about how things work. 'The whole thing has the *feel* of

---

[68] Smith Archives, Oxford: Mary's typescript biography, section for 1935, p. 6; Karin to Mary, 8 July 1935.

[69] Scottish Record Office, Edinburgh: Carnegie UK Trust Papers GD 281/82/139: Ray Strachey to Col. Mitchell, 5 Dec. 1938. This paragraph also draws upon the interviews with Miss Hilton, 24 Feb. and 23 Mar. 1977, at 12 Sydney House, Woodstock Road, London W4 1DP; the roneo'd typescript broadcast on 25 July 1940 by Mary Agnes Hamilton in Smith Archives, Oxford; and Hamilton, *Remembering*, p. 276.

success,' she told her mother in June 1935; it was exhilarating to be involved at last in an organization that—thanks to the Carnegie Trust— was not living from hand to mouth, and was (as she wrote in February 1936) 'definitely and obviously popular and on the up grade'. WEF impinged on ever-widening circles, so that Ray found herself chairing the Fashion Group's employment committee. 'They regard me, I think, as their pet oddity,' she told her mother; '. . . they *are* a queer pack of people—superficially very silly, and glittering, and as hard as nails underneath, with liberal doses of sentimentality, and not a glimmer of cultivation. But they are all earning pots of money . . . It is a liberal education of an odd kind to see how they function, and I enjoy it a good deal.' When a further Carnegie grant was announced at the end of 1938, the executive committee burst into applause.[70]

In these dangerous times Ray was of course defending only a small corner of democracy, but only she could have defended it so effectively; on a more wide-ranging platform she might well have achieved less. She admitted in 1936 that 'it seems all wrong to be so completely caught up in one single concern while the world is tottering so seriously. But actually, if it comes to rearming, the organization of women's employment is a necessary part of it.' WEF's consultations in person or by post ran at an annual average of 3,816 during the six years between 1935 and 1940, and the annual total rose in every year up to 1939; in that year there were visits from the Queen, who agreed to be a patron, and from the Duchess of Kent.[71] Then WEF was asked to compile a national register of women workers; 'it is a quite distinct problem of organization to do things on a really big scale', said Ray, 'and I find a technical interest in the job, as well as its intrinsic interest'. War reduced WEF's funds and employment work, but not the demands upon it; for instance, when war began, Ray opened an office to advise older women on how they could help. Although not very impressed with civil-service efficiency, Ray hoped by November 1939—in vain, as it turned out—that the Ministry of Labour would take WEF over.[72]

At Easter weekend in 1940 the family were for once all together, and Ray was able to observe as usual from the sidelines; Oliver, Barbara, and Christopher were 'making incessant music only interspersed by violent arguments, crosswords and paper games. It's really remarkable', she went

[70] Smith Archives, Oxford: Ray to Mary, 27 June 1935, 6 Feb. 1936, 28 Jan. 1936; see also Ray to Mary, 15 Dec. 1938.

[71] Nancy Astor MSS 1416/1/1/1409: Ray Strachey to Astor, 22 June 1936. Statistics calculated from figures in WEF annual reports in Carnegie UK Trust Papers.

[72] Smith Archives, Oxford: Ray to Mary, 29 Mar., 24 Nov. 1939.

on, 'how much alike all three look, and how similar their tastes and vocabularies are.' By now the nation was in real danger, and in May she reassured her mother that she had inherited her capacity for imaginative adjustment to whatever happens. Ray told her that at fifty-three she felt no older than she had felt twenty-five years before, 'except perhaps that I have less tolerance for pure theory, and that I'm not so ready to run or climb stairs'. She had a weekend at Mud in June, and found it 'a very quieting and soothing occupation' building a house while the world was reeling; 'I cut out 22 rafters for a roof', she wrote, 'and also spent a hot and lovely day on Blackdown picking whortleberries'. In her last letter to her mother, written on 18 June, she looked back over the past: 'whatever happens you know that we've all had enjoyable existences, packed with interest and good things, and even if we all snuffed out now, we should every one of us have had good worthwhile Times, and been glad to have been alive.'[73]

National and personal crises came together; Ray now required an operation for fibroid tumour. In a practical and unsentimental but affectionate note to Christopher, leaving all her property to him as sole executor, she said she did not expect to die, but thought it only sensible to simplify things in case the worst happened. Hilton last saw Ray when she looked round the door of the interviewing room on the second floor and said, 'Look after WEF for me; goodbye'; this helped make Hilton feel a personal responsibility for carrying on Ray's work as WEF's organizing secretary between 1948 and 1972. Among Barbara's last visions of Ray is the more mundane recollection of her gaining a quick entry into Bedford College, where she was staying at the time, by climbing in through a ground-floor window; the vision of her huge receding behind was, she recalls, 'a wonderful sight—typical, too'.[74] The operation at first seemed to succeed, but a second operation proved necessary and Ray died soon afterwards.

She died at her moment of greatest opportunity; the Second World War might at last have given her a job that measured up to her talents. By 1935 she thought she had 'got to a stage in my career where opportunities have begun to come my way'. What would she have done if she had lived? She would either have greatly expanded WEF's role, or she would have moved on. For some time she'd had her eye on succeeding Pernel as Principal of Newnham, and this might have reopened her writing career. In any event,

---

[73] Smith Archives, Oxford: Ray to Mary, Easter Sunday, 1 June, 18 June 1940.
[74] Interview with Miss Hilton, 24 Feb. 1977. Smith Archives, Oxford: Ray to Christopher, 3 July 1940.

the affection for England that had drawn her first to the Stracheys and then to Fawcett would have both encouraged and equipped her to find a constructive role. She told Fawcett that ever since early childhood she'd felt so strongly about England that she'd had difficulty in talking about it, 'but I've always thought it was one of the solidly good things in the world. Englishness I mean, and the characteristics of it.'[75]

Many criticisms of Ray can be made. Some may dislike her obvious ambition, and perhaps still more her taste for intrigue. Yet ambition is seldom undiluted by other motives, and its beneficial ramifications can be wide. Ray's apparent complacency or conceit when writing to her mother can be discounted, because her aim was to relieve Mary of worry and conceal difficulties. And at least Ray did not deceive herself, except perhaps in her perennial optimism—but without that, her energies might soon have run down. Furthermore, enjoyed intrigue is perhaps preferable, when motivated by high and consistently-held ideals, to Sylvia Pankhurst's mournful variant of it. Besides, what some see as intrigue, others see as the patient, painstaking, and down-to-earth process of co-ordination needed for democratic achievement. In practical affairs Ray knew the value of unobtrusiveness; 'somehow I love keeping my name out of things', she told her mother, when discussing one of her innovations in WEF during 1939.[76] As with Pippa, it is important not to allow Ray's tactical reticence to mask her real achievement.

Commenting on Ray's death in her diary, Woolf wrote of 'her immense activity, as if always trying to get what she could not', and attributed it to disillusion at the way her marriage had worked out; yet Ray's restless activity long antedates her marriage. Mary Agnes Hamilton says that in private discussion Ray 'hardly ever spoke kindly of anybody', and that her surface conversational gambits 'were cynical, pessimist, atheist, ruthlessly analytic and critical'. Yet she goes on to contrast this with Ray's generous and humane nature, and with her unwearying practical kindness to the very people she had been criticizing. Her 'verbal cynicism' was, in fact, only 'a protective covering for an unexpressed idealism that neither flagged nor faltered, once it had found its mark'.[77] The line between cynicism and realism is subjective, but political achievement rests more securely upon a rounded understanding of human nature as it is than upon a hopeful preference for human nature as it should be. Ray turned human

[75] Ibid.: Ray to Mary, 3 Mar. 1935; Ray Strachey to Fawcett, 18 May 1918; Ray to Mary, 27 Nov. 1933.

[76] Ibid.: Mary's typescript biography, section for 1939, p. 3 (26 Jan.).

[77] V. Woolf, *Diary*, v. 304. Hamilton, *Remembering*, pp. 268, 271; *Rachel Conn Strachey*, p. 4.

weaknesses to advantage for reforming purposes, never forgetting the talented women 'hidden in horrid little jobs, eating their hearts out for lack of a chance to show what they can do'.[78]

Virginia Woolf thought that Ray's plans for her life 'didn't altogether come off'; she 'wrote without stopping. No form, no fineness. Her life much of a scramble and a fight.' Yet Woolf's criticisms of Ray are always somewhat shamefaced. Ray, she said in 1918, 'tends to think us a set of good for nothing wastrels'; but she went on to admit that the day's work gave Ray 'some claim to look down upon us'.[79] Ray's feminism could never have produced the disgruntled cynicism of Woolf's *Three Guineas*; she never shared the Stracheys' negativism and pessimism. Shunning the social round, perennially short of money and beset by conflicting obligations, she did much for feminism and democracy at a time when both were vulnerable. She might occasionally take time off to show, in suffragist anniversary functions, that 'the militants did not have *all* the amusing incidents in that struggle', but commemorative gatherings could only be sideshows in a life that reached out into the future for new opportunities. 'Oh yes . . . ,' said Helen Darbishire, Principal of Somerville, 'Ray Strachey. Mmmm. She's someone who takes up lost causes and then they cease to be lost.'[80]

Her death left large holes in many lives. Many feared that WEF could not survive, though Hilton helped to ensure that it did. Oliver's last days were unhappy; his sociability eventually led him into excessive drinking, and he twice tried to kill himself. After a heart attack he entered a nursing home, often telling his visitors that he wanted to die; the end came in 1960. Christopher became a pioneer of computer language, Oxford's first professor of computing science, and died in 1975. Barbara worked for thirty years in the BBC, ending as programme planner of the World Service, and then embarked on a second career as author of several successful books.

Pippa was not one to reveal her feelings, but Barbara thinks that she was shattered by Ray's death; she certainly showed special affection to Ray's two children. She persevered with her feminism, and in her letters early in the Second World War she articulates the Stracheys' customary mock-horror at using political chicanery to promote a good cause—this time to extract spinsters' pensions from parliament.[81] In May 1939 she vividly

[78] Nancy Astor MSS 1416/1/1/1409: Ray Strachey to Astor, 9 June 1936.
[79] V. Woolf, *Diary*, v. 304–5; i. 155.
[80] WFL, *Bulletin* No. 187 (3 Mar. 1939), p. 5. Interview with Miss Hilton, 24 Feb. 1977.
[81] e.g. BL Add. MSS 60728 (Strachey Papers), fo. 273: Pippa to Pernel, n.d.

described a national service meeting at the Albert Hall which began with the singing of 'The Lambeth Walk'; no foreigner could have understood the occasion, she said—'I thought it perfection in its way'. At Gordon Square during the blitz she told Pernel she had the choice of two air-raid shelters, 'into which I betake myself at the sound of the Syreen as they call it'; one of them she had sampled night and morning, and found it 'quite a pleasant resort with rather a high class clientèle supplemented by a few taxi drivers and other passers by', and with plenty of light for reading if one chose one's seat carefully.[82]

In 1938 she welcomed what Ray called Woolf's 'glorious attack on the pomposity of men' in *Three Guineas*; 'thoroughly gratifying' was the thought of its discomfited male readers.[83] Her major public interest remained the LSWS; her annual reports were literary exercises in themselves, and still more fascinating when read aloud with her inimitable emphasis at annual meetings. In old age she became painfully slow in committees, but her mind and memory remained as sharp as ever, and when she retired as LSWS secretary in 1951 she continued for another decade as honorary secretary of the Fawcett Society. She was 'master alike of long-term statecraft and of short-term tactics,' said Vincent Rendel; 'the women of modern England are more indebted to her than most of them know'. Woolf once described the Stracheys as 'a prosaic race'; a Strachey, for her, was 'someone infinitely cautious, elusive and unadventurous. To the common stock of our set they have added phrases, standards, and witticisms, but never any new departure.'[84] Cautious and elusive Pippa certainly was, but unadventurous? This can hardly be said of a feminist so consistent and resourceful within a hostile climate; Woolf's analysis of the Stracheys seems more relevant to her own public life, for her personality and literary preoccupations kept her within safe confines.

Quietly but effectively, Pippa performed one further service for English women: throughout her life she and Ray kept alive an alternative, more balanced view on how the vote had been won than the Pankhursts ever provided. Pippa thought suffragism was moving inevitably to success, Pankhursts or no Pankhursts, and was restive under latter-day suffragette self-advertisement. 'I think individuals in the militant movement were heroic,' she told Ray, 'but I think the movement itself was unheroic to a

[82] Ibid.: fo. 234: Pippa to Pernel, n.d. [end. 14 May 1939], and fo. 243: Pippa to Pernel, n.d. [end. 25 Aug. 1940].
[83] Nancy Astor MSS 1416/1/2/190: Ray Strachey to Astor, 4 June 1938. BL Add. MSS 60728, fo. 231: Pippa to Pernel, 30 May 1938.
[84] M. Stocks, *Philippa Strachey, CBE, 1872–1968* (Fawcett House, 1969), p. 2. V. Woolf, *Diary*, i. 235–6.

marked degree—not to be respected in general.' Pippa may not herself have published on feminist history, but she influenced those who did. Roger Fulford was one of the earliest non-participant historians of British feminism; he collaborated with Lytton Strachey in editing Greville's diaries, and the Stracheys greatly influenced his *Votes for Women*.[85]

In 1937, entering a restaurant with Thena Clough after a late committee meeting, Pippa found herself accidentally trapped in the same room as militants celebrating Emmeline Pankhurst's birthday. Her description to Pernel of what followed—in a letter dated '14 Juillet (Taking of Bastille and birth of Mrs Pankhurst)'—can perhaps be fully savoured only by those who are well briefed on Edwardian suffragettery. 'Christabel made a quite incredible tub thumping oration full of God and Christ and victory through weakness—Jesus on his cross, Emmeline in her prison (but *not* Christabel) in a professional canting voice and with a large feathered hat on her head. It went on and on . . .' Thena made comic interjections *sotto voce* in a deep bass voice, but then Mrs How-Martyn got up, indicated that Pippa was sitting in the corner, and praised her recent efforts on spinsters' pensions. Applause followed. This, says Pippa, 'was altogether too ghastly for words. I never knew anything more shocking to the feelings!'[86] During the war Hilton asked Pippa to address some servicemen on her suffragist experiences: 'my dear', she exclaimed, 'they'd be *bored* to *distraction*. What would they want to listen to an old creature like me for?' She went under protest but was an instant success, and was kept up into the early hours of the morning; 'where *did* you find her?' the servicemen asked; 'what a *marvellous* person'.[87]

Pippa's home in Bloomsbury became even shabbier in the 1950s, with paper peeling off the walls and piles of correspondence stacked behind her chair; 'she'd got about 30 years behind,' Barbara recalls. Pippa took no offence when presented with a feather-duster by subordinates in the LSWS, but the situation became more serious later when a domestic accident caused the death of a resident niece; the death of Pippa's sister Dorothy soon afterwards upset her badly.[88] Though always ladylike in manner, Pippa could be capricious, impish, and very stubborn. When relatives struggled to get her to change her bank so as to avoid long journeys across

[85] Smith Archives, Oxford: undated pencilled letter dated 'Tuesday–Wednesday Feb' in file labelled 'Pippa'. Author's tape-recorded interview with Roger Fulford, 13 Apr. 1976, at Barbon Manor, Carnforth, Lancs.

[86] BL Add. MSS 60728 (Strachey Papers), fo. 226: Pippa to Pernel, 14 July [1937].

[87] Interview with Miss Hilton, 24 Feb. 1977.

[88] Interviews with Barbara Strachey, 22 Jan. 1977, and Mrs Gertrude Horton, 21 Mar. and 13 Apr. 1977.

London, there would simply be a long silence followed by a change of subject. Pippa was so indifferent to food that Barbara remembers seeing her cut a pea into four pieces and put each piece separately into her mouth; she eventually became undernourished, got rickets, and was carried off to hospital in a state of collapse. When she went blind she had to enter a nursing home. In preparing to go, she tortured her relatives with her slowness in sorting through her old papers, each of which stirred her fine memory into reflectiveness.[89] When well over ninety she tried to learn Braille, but her fingers were not sensitive enough. She struck up a very good relationship with her West Indian nurse, with whom she swapped nursery rhymes. Indeed, she remained so lively in her nineties that people visited her in order to be cheered up.[90] In 1968, she died.

[89] Interviews with Barbara Strachey, 5 and 22 Jan. 1977, and with the Wentzels, 1 Mar. 1977.

[90] Interviews with the Wentzels, 1 Mar. 1977, and Miss Hilton, 24 Feb. 1977.

PLATE 9. Margery Corbett Ashby at 91, in a delegation of women's organizations to the Prime Minister, 28 June 1973, asking for the anti-discrimination Bill to be enacted without delay (Press Association Ltd.).

7

Diplomat

MARGERY CORBETT ASHBY

ALL the chapters so far have emphasized the importance of diplomacy, in the sense of skill at minimizing opposition and getting people to work together. So rarely is this quality combined with conviction that the two are often seen as incompatible. Henry Harben, Mrs Emmeline Pankhurst, and her daughter Sylvia all display strong conviction, but frequently despise diplomacy; Astor and Billington-Greig also display strong conviction, but it is temperament rather than intention that denies them diplomacy, with consequent damage to their influence. On the other hand, Fawcett, Pippa and Ray Strachey, Hubback, and to a large extent Rathbone combine both qualities—with corresponding achievement. For the type of conviction that survives continuous contact with sceptics and opponents—that persists through the compromises and half-measures required by the political process—is tougher than conviction of a more flamboyant kind. Margery Corbett Ashby possessed conviction of this durable type. She epitomizes twentieth-century feminist diplomacy, if only because her diplomacy operated at more than one level. Her tact and charm enabled her to combine firm party loyalty with prominence in several British domestic non-party feminist organizations. And because she somehow combined her dedicated internationalism with a pronounced Englishness, she epitomizes the overseas links that were always important for British feminists, and especially so between the wars.

As with Pippa and Ray Strachey, family influences are integral to her feminism. Although born in Bayswater in 1882, she grew up in the family's large country house, Woodgate, in Danehill, one of the loveliest parts of Sussex. Danehill was then a very feudal society, and in old age she loved re-creating it for younger people who saw it as far-off history. As a lifelong and progressive democrat she hated class privilege, and was shocked to find feudalism still surviving at Bury St Edmunds when contesting a by-election there in 1944. Yet in later life she gave hints of feeling a lingering and private regret that the more attractive accompaniments of feudalism had vanished: the close relationships fostered between people of different social class, the mutual responsibilities between the deprived and the privileged, and a life lived at a slower pace in a relatively unspoiled countryside. 'It was a society', she told me, 'in which, as far as a child could tell . . . there didn't seem to be any antagonism or sense of inferiority on either side.'[1]

If anything went wrong in Danehill the villagers simply approached the big house for a remedy. Corbett Ashby delightedly recalled a letter her mother once read out over breakfast: 'Dear Mrs Corbett, We can't do nothing with our Jane, Yours Mrs Smith;' her father simply got into the pony-cart and sorted things out. Nothing gave her more pleasure than dwelling upon Woodgate's elaborate hierarchy of servants and complex pattern of housekeeping, and she enjoyed describing the half-mile family procession to church, 'followed by the train of servants of course' in their black afternoon clothes; on arrival, they were carefully segregated by social class—with a private staircase to the family pew on the first floor, a servants' pew on the ground floor, and carefully graded seating elsewhere for the rest of Danehill's community.

Her father Charles Corbett was her political mentor. Son of an architect who had established a successful property-developing firm in London, Charles was trained as a barrister, but as the eldest son he soon had to take over the family business together with the two family estates. The late-Victorian middle-class man with urban money who bought a country house could take one of two courses: become a Conservative and aim to join the local social hierarchy, or champion rural Liberalism and make a virtue of remaining an outsider. Charles chose the latter course, and so became a focus for local educational and progressive effort. He stood unsuccessfully as Liberal candidate for the East Grinstead division of Sussex in 1895 and 1900 and was boycotted by the local gentry for opposing the Boer War. The local agricultural labourers, still doubting the secrecy of the ballot, attended Liberal public meetings only in the evening for fear that their employers would identify them during the day. Charles was popular locally for his good works and for defending the rights of working men—their right, for instance, to object conscientiously to having their children vaccinated—and in 1906 his narrow election victory

[1] This chapter relies so heavily throughout on six tape-recorded interviews with Dame Margery—on 7 and 28 May 1974, 8 Apr. 1975, 21 Sept. and 23 Nov. 1976, 21 Feb. 1977—that reference to them has not been footnoted. Four took place at Wickens, Birch Grove, Horsted Keynes, Sussex, RH17 7BT; the others at 2 Stormont Road, London N6 (8 Apr. 1975) and at the University Women's Club, 2 Audley Square, London (21 Sept. 1976).

gave the constituency its one brief Liberal fling between 1885 and 1918. Local schoolchildren celebrated by taking a holiday and marching on to Charles's lawn to sing their congratulations.

Charles carried his Liberalism into the family, which Liberal visitors saw as 'a little green oasis of simple living and high-thinking', a genuine democracy where husband and wife respected one another, where master and mistress cared for their servants, and where parents brought up their children in liberal values.[2] It was from here, not from books, that Corbett Ashby acquired her Liberalism. Edwardian feminists often come from families whose lively political discussion cultivates a precocious sense of public responsibility. Her mother Marie Gray was the key figure here. Marie's father too had made a fortune in the City, as partner in a large confectionery business, and Marie was a trained singer with a fine voice, popular at charity concerts. She was also a keen feminist who helped launch one of Britain's earliest Women's Institutes, and a pioneer woman poor law guardian who for thirty-six years specialized in moving children from workhouse to foster parents.[3]

Charles fully supported Marie in her public work, and was one of Fawcett's most helpful parliamentary supporters between 1906 and 1910. Marie was tempted to join the militants, but Charles was so fond of her that he could not bear the thought of her going to prison, and because she was so fond of him she agreed not to do so; as Corbett Ashby explained, 'it was the happiest *possible* marriage, you see'. Her parents collaborated in the children's education. Charles had an encyclopaedic memory, and was the sort of man who read Xenophon for enjoyment when travelling to London in the train. He taught them Latin, Greek, and Mathematics; Marie taught religion and music; and there were governesses, one French and a sequence of German. It must have been a good system because Margery got to Cambridge and her sister and brother went to Oxford. It was her parents who launched her on public speaking, for Charles's election campaign of 1906 was almost a family affair. Margery made her first political speech at sixteen; Charles could not attend a meeting addressed by a supporter because he had to speak elsewhere, so the person next to her told Margery that she must propose a vote of thanks; 'I gasped "I can't"', she recalled, 'and at that moment my father's friend, who'd carried on the meeting, sat down and I got up. I'd never opened my mouth before.' A fortnight later she deputized for her mother in opening a Liberal bazaar.

[2] *Vote*, 21 Sept. 1923, p. 302.
[3] Obituary of Marie Corbett, *International Women's News*, May 1932, p. 86.

At Cambridge there was no point in reading modern languages because she was already bilingual in English and French and could speak fluent German; and though she knew the names of every wild flower she had done no science; the classics were therefore chosen. But her letters home say little about her studies, much more about the national political situation and about her debating successes. She was exhilarated by this, her first experience of communal living, and she made some lifelong friends (Mary Agnes Hamilton, for example) and broadened her political experience. She was prominent in Newnham's lively political society, with its alternating Liberal and Conservative governments, and its cabinet and parliament which debated Bills. Her speech on women's suffrage seems to have gone well. 'The Hall was immensely large and echoed rather', she told her mother in February 1903, 'so that it was rather a strain to fill it. I spoke for 20 min[ute]s and managed to keep to the course of argument I had meant to follow with only looking at my notes three times.'[4]

She also waged constant war with the authorities about the food; 'the cooking was a disgrace . . .,' she recalled; 'I led so many delegations that I was finally consulted in private as to remedies'. She worried about the dons' indifference to women's suffrage, and told her parents in 1903 that 'the most disappointing thing about college is the terribly low standard of public spirit and public intelligence in the women. I am sometimes so depressed by it.' She warned her parents not to expect a good degree; measles in her last year made things worse. Tempted to throw in her hand, she was restrained both by her father, who told her that 'obedience to authority is a virtue', and by what she called her 'prejudice against cowardice'.[5] She left Cambridge with a poor third in Part One of the Classics Tripos, and because Cambridge did not then give degrees to women she took her 'steamship degree' at Dublin. She thoroughly enjoyed her Newnham days, but was glad when they were over; 'looking back', she wrote long afterwards, 'I now see that I was a revolutionary at heart'.[6]

She took a short statistics course in London, but the subject was not at all in her line; then she spent a year at a teacher's training college in Cambridge. Her father thought women should get a professional

[4] City of London Polytechnic, Fawcett Library, Corbett Ashby Papers: Margery to her mother, 13 Feb. 1903.

[5] Ann Phillips (ed.), *A Newnham Anthology* (Cambridge, 1979), p. 52. Corbett Ashby Papers: Margery to her mother, 7 Dec. 1903; C. H. Corbett to Margery, 4 May 1904; fragment of letter from Margery, 3 May 1904.

[6] Phillips, *Newnham*, p. 51. She mis-remembered the class of her degree as 'a poor Second', whereas Newnham records show that in reality she obtained a poor Third. I owe this information to the Registrar of the Roll, Dr E. E. Mason.

qualification because, as she later pointed out, 'you couldn't be *sure* you were going to marry a good-looking millionaire'. She remembered this as 'the most, perhaps only, frustrating year of my life until the disarmament conference of 1932'. The courses seemed either trite or abstruse, her fellow students seemed dull and narrow, and she escaped to university dances; teaching, she decided, was not for her. Her forthright honesty was not yet laced with quite enough tact and charm, and she remembered infuriating the F. W. Hirsts about this time with her flippant rejoinders to their anti-suffrage homilies.

In 1905 and 1906 she ran two vacation courses for Hull dockside children, largely financed by a local shipping company and organized under Mary Murdoch, a successful surgeon and specialist in child diseases. This was Corbett Ashby's first experience of social work, and she was shocked at the poverty she saw there; there was poverty in Sussex, of course, but at least the Sussex poor could cultivate their allotments, rely on their pigs, and gather their free firewood. 'If I walked down to the docks', she recalled, 'the women would come out with their hair undone, the children would run out in the hot sun without any clothes on, but with marks of bites, you know. They were very, very poor.' Leila Montagu's London club for working girls made a similar impression; unable to buy decent underclothing, the girls shunned the sort of exercise that might publicly expose their poverty.

The road from social work to suffragism was direct; Edwardian women's social consciences would be still more effective if reinforced by the vote. Corbett Ashby regularly visited the House of Commons ladies gallery after her father's election. Although an aunt went to prison for the WSPU, Corbett Ashby was too deeply influenced by her father, too knowledgeable about the political system, to be in any way tempted. She paid a lifelong, down-to-earth but amused deference to maxims of political prudence. She wanted to get things done, and realized that this meant avoiding enmities and concentrating resources; in the 1970s she relished recalling the good sense in her father's advice—'if you want to reform anything else, do *not* reform your clothes'. 'Abstract theorems at no time have much interested her,' wrote a close observer in 1922; 'she has always been one of those whose way of helping the world on is to do the work that lies near to the hand, rather than to argue passionately about ultimates. The bent of her mind is altogether away from ultimates.'[7]

Her appointment as secretary of the NUWSS at £100 a year in 1907 came

---

[7] Xanthippe, *Westminster Gazette,* 25 Feb. 1922, p. 12.

as no surprise: 'I knew all the people on the executive, you see, and they knew me.' It was the beginning of a long career in non-militant feminism. Her week-day duties were nine-to-five, and involved managing the office staff, corresponding with important people, and compiling committee minutes. She stayed at Artillery Mansions during the week and went back to Sussex at weekends. Yet she did not last long as secretary because a minor administrative mishap gave Mrs Snowden the excuse for supplanting her by a Labour woman. Corbett Ashby refused to smooth things over by resigning and insisted on being dismissed. She derived some private pleasure from getting elected to the executive at the next annual meeting, and remained on it almost continuously till she became president of NUSEC in 1928.

Her recollection in old age of the exhilarating Edwardian suffragist mood echoes Ray Strachey's contemporary letters to her mother. 'This new political atmosphere thrilled me enormously', she later recalled, 'and I was a constant visitor in the Ladies Gallery' of the House of Commons.[8] She relished the absurdity of anti-suffrage argument, and recalled rebutting hecklers humorously so as to win round the audience. To the instruction 'get home and darn yer husband's socks', she replied that she'd done that already before coming to the meeting. When speaking outside Sussex she was once asked, 'Will the girls want to marry if they have the vote?' There were '*roars* of *delighted* laughter' when she replied: 'Well, young men in Sussex think far too well of themselves to suppose the girls wouldn't.' And in old age she could not suppress gusts of laughter while describing (in cultivated Edwardian tones) the anti-suffragist fear of enfranchising prostitutes, 'quite regardless of the fact that . . . for every prostitute there were thirty or forty dissolute men'.

Then there was the excitement of getting the Young Suffragists launched and of broadening out the freedoms of young middle-class women. In later life she became quite eloquent on how suffragism had transformed the expectations of a generation 'brought up on "don't" and "can't"', for the suffragists found 'that we were immensely loyal to other women instead of being proverbially catty, that we could organize, we could raise money, we could do all the things that we'd no *idea* that we *could* do, and you know the *exhilaration* was *terrific;* this new loyalty, this new opening-up of tremendous possibilities made it a most exciting time'. As she wrote in old age, 'these women aroused in me a passionate

---

[8] Corbett Ashby Papers: autobiographical chapter entitled 'Recollections between 1906 and 1910'.

admiration for women as women. They created a new loyalty which has stayed by me all my life. It is I suppose impossible for the young British women of to-day to realize the intoxication of belief in one's own and other women's capacity and responsibilities.'[9]

Her future husband Brian Ashby was a friend of her brother's at New College, Oxford; she first met him at a Christmas dance at Woodgate. He could not marry until he had established himself as a barrister, and in those days engagements were often long; they did not marry till 1910. They were very different; Brian came from a Conservative family, and had never thought about votes for women before meeting the Corbetts. Among the anti-suffragist arguments Margery ridiculed was the idea that marriage was an institution so fragile as to be vulnerable every four or five years if husband and wife voted for different parties. Her marriage was never at risk, and Brian was converted to Liberalism by a Roman Catholic padre during the war. In old age Margery could remember only one real quarrel with Brian in forty-nine years of marriage.[10]

The failure of children to arrive made her very unhappy; a pathetic letter to her mother, signed 'your very wretched child', survives from 1913: 'every baby I see makes me feel a real pain and I have shed gallons of tears. Work is the only opiate I have discovered.'[11] At last her only son Michael was born in November 1914 after Brian had joined his territorial unit; there followed all the worries associated with the war and with bringing up a baby on her own. She later recalled staying in lodgings at Windsor at a time when Michael would not sleep for more than three-quarters of an hour at a time. She felt exhausted and trapped; sometimes the landlady came to her rescue when she heard her pacing up and down in her flat, but 'I spent my days', she recalled, 'pushing the pram for what seemed miles, with a most cheerful infant'. Then Michael got tuberculous peritonitis, was operated on, and took a long time to recover.

In some ways her deep affection for Brian made things worse. His first posting was to Lowestoft. She accompanied him there with her young baby, and promoted local educational and hospital work; recognizing that needlework relieved the boredom of patients with tuberculosis, she inspired such good work that the mayor chaired her exhibition of it. Things became far more difficult when Brian went to France. She used to wake up at four in the morning, 'the time at which troops were liable to go

[9] Interview with Margery Corbett Ashby, 8 Apr. 1975. Corbett Ashby Papers: autobiographical fragment.

[10] David Mitchell's typescript of interview with Margery Corbett Ashby, 12 June 1980.

[11] Corbett Ashby Papers: Margery to her mother, 3 July 1913.

over the top, with a dreadful feeling of foreboding'. Her letters to Brian at the time show deep affection: 'I miss you here most dreadfully,' she wrote in December 1917; 'every place has such happy associations. Last night sitting in the study while Daddy held forth, it seems almost as if you must have gone into the drawing room to play the piano, or would wander in with a smile and a pipe. I can't remember you as ever anything but smiling at me, dearest heart. Whenever you came into the room or if I did there always was first that smile, just to establish connection, then we could go on without paying more attention perhaps. I do miss it so dreadfully.' She longed for him to come home on leave, and 'yet I almost dread your leave for how could I let you go again'.[12]

The armistice was an immense relief, and Brian began commuting to work in London (on war pension tribunals) from their house in Putney. Margery could then have chosen to lead a quiet but pleasant life as a suburban middle-class housewife and mother. Yet this would have betrayed her suffragist background and risked disappointing her enterprising mother, who survived till 1932. Besides, her father was prepared to finance her international feminist work even after she married. He lived on to 1935, 'a fine old English gentleman' according to his obituarist,[13] donating land for the Danehill Women's Institute, helping to build the village hall, and treating his son and daughters equally in his will; Woodgate was then sold to Harold Macmillan and the Corbett Ashbys settled in 1936 at 'Wickens', a secluded house in wooded country not far away. It had a superb view over the valley the family had once owned, and a garden on its slopes that was ablaze in spring with azaleas and daffodils.

Margery's immediate family eased her path into public life. Although Brian did not join in her campaigns, he shared her political outlook and gave her every encouragement. As for Michael, he was well able to entertain himself as a child, and never felt neglected by his mother despite her frequent absences. At first she vividly read stories aloud to him, but he soon became an avid and imaginative reader on his own. As for discipline, she did not fuss, and operated on her father's maxim: 'never say no if you can possibly help it, but if you say no, you mean it.' A maid-of-all-work lived in to do the housework, and Margery was always good at delegating to employees; only in her last ten years did she attempt housework of any kind. So she was free to follow her mother's example; she became active as a poor law guardian in Wandsworth and prominent in feminist

[12] Corbett Ashby Papers: Margery to Brian, 12 Dec., 4 Dec. 1917.
[13] *Mid-Sussex Times*, 26 Nov. 1935, p. 3.

international work. She sometimes had qualms. Writing from the SS *Arabic* in 1925, she told Brian that she missed him and Michael; she felt the conflict between family and 'interesting work', and admitted that 'I suppose like all of us I want to eat my cake and have it too'.[14]

Her international work must be seen in what is now a rather unfamiliar context. She had been brought up in the optimistic climate of Cobdenite Liberalism before 1914. Progressive people then envisaged a peaceable and harmonious world emerging from the decline of warlike aristocracies and monarchies; from the growth of free trade, commerce, and improved transport; and from the spread of democracy, education, and humane values, including feminism. Peace would spread quite rapidly and directly because the idealism of newly enfranchised men and women in the democracies would establish international political and judicial bodies; reason would settle such disputes as occurred through the growth of international arbitration. Speeding on this millennium were high-minded humanitarians whose international conferences established the contacts and structures from which the new international community would arise. In some ways these hopes were merely strengthened by the First World War, which seemed a mere aberration from Victorian optimism; its slaughter advertised the awfulness of the alternative. So the 1920s saw prosperity for the peace movement, the League of Nations Union, Esperanto and internationalism in all its forms.

Out of these idealistic, middle-class, and progressive circles emerged the IWSA. It was created by an American delegation at the International Council of Women's Berlin assembly of 1904, which Corbett Ashby attended with her mother; she attended all but one of its triennial international congresses till 1976. In those days overseas travel seemed cheap and easy to English people; fewer visas were required, and the old-style internationalism associated with upper-class life-styles had not yet vanished. But women rarely travelled abroad unaccompanied, let alone to their own international congresses; inevitably it was the well-to-do middle-class, liberal-minded woman with a sympathetic husband who went.

High hopes were placed in women's electoral influence after 1918, and like many inter-war British feminists Corbett Ashby transferred much of her effort from feminism into the League of Nations Union. Fawcett fully recognized the importance of women's international work, but had little

---

[14] Corbett Ashby Papers: Margery to Brian, 23 Mar. 1925. Michael's perspective comes from my tape-recorded interview with him and his wife Pamela, 15 Oct. 1982, at Wickens.

taste for it herself, so asked her to attend the Versailles peace conference in her place. Corbett Ashby immediately felt at home, for she knew most of the progressives gathered there. As a member of IWSA's executive and as its president from 1923 to 1946, she attended the League of Nations assembly annually at Geneva, and so carved out for herself a new and very demanding, though unpaid, career. Her common sense and balance were salutary in this world of heady idealism, cultural misunderstandings, and strong feelings. Her gentle but infectious sense of humour made an impact; as one observer put it, 'there is about her an atmosphere of serenity and harmony which makes the onlooker feel that she and life are friends . . . she was born with a natural tendency to like her fellow creatures'. Her unusual combination of sociability, humour, and modesty enabled her to bring people together. Her skills were certainly needed in IWSA; 'I wish we had a little more sense of humour and common sense,' she told her mother in 1922, when feminists were pressing impracticably for membership of the disarmament commission; 'I do feel weary of impractical persons'.[15]

Women's suffrage was now spreading so fast world-wide that IWSA broadened its feminist purposes, and renamed itself the International Alliance of Women [IAW] at its congress of 1926. Corbett Ashby's tact was particularly necessary if IWSA was to help rather than hinder feminism in the countries where it held its congresses. At this time suffragism was advancing in France, and would advance still further if the sister of the Archbishop of Paris became patron of the Association's French affiliate; over-eager American and British delegates endangered everything. 'The British delegation is awful', she told Brian, 'and gives me more trouble than any.' Although at the 1926 congress she gave the appearance of unruffled calm, her letters to Brian reveal the underlying reality; 'at all the moments of crisis and triumph', she wrote, 'I steady myself by thinking of you and him [Michael] . . . honestly without you both I should be desperately afraid'. None the less, she managed to impress at least one commentator with her 'wonderful gift for smoothing over a heated argument'.[16]

She impressed everyone at this congress with her remarkable command of languages. 'She could drop from one language to another so quickly that

---

[15] *Time and Tide*, 28 May 1926, p. 474. Corbett Ashby Papers: Margery to her mother, 22 Feb. 1922. See also Linda Walker's typescript of interview with Margery Corbett Ashby, 25 Mar. 1975.

[16] Corbett Ashby Papers: autobiographical fragment on the 1926 Congress; Margery to Brian, n.d. [1926]. Frances Taylor on IWSA's Paris Congress in *Argus*, 24 Sept. 1926.

it might be some seconds before one realised that she had changed,' wrote Frances Taylor. Both in 1926 and at Berlin in 1929 she also demonstrated that she could combine vigorous late-night sociability with resilience at difficult formal sessions the following morning. 'I could now occupy a throne in the Balkans without a tremor,' she told Brian in 1926.[17] One diplomatic feat, however, was beyond her; although the IAW and the International Council of Women were no longer divided on women's suffrage, they could not amalgamate without depriving women of one vote in the League of Nations.

She was now becoming known in government circles for her diplomatic expertise, and would have gained more recognition if Conservatives had not dominated British government between the wars. Recommended by Astor to MacDonald in 1931 as 'an absolutely A1 person',[18] she became substitute delegate for the United Kingdom at the disarmament conference. Apart from countering German propaganda during the Second World War in Sweden, where she said that for a month she was treated like a film star, this was the closest she ever came to governmental responsibility. By February 1932 she was telling her mother that the experience was 'really heartbreaking', and she later recalled this as 'the most unhappy period of my life'. 'A Prime Minister with no interest or knowledge of Foreign affairs and a brilliant Foreign Minister who could only work to a brief, which was never given to him, gave an impression of complete lack of leadership in world affairs by the British delegation . . . The last opportunity of securing international action for safe guarding peace was frittered away.'[19] As she told MacDonald when resigning, she had struggled in vain for three years to get the British government to support any practical scheme for mutual security as the basis for reducing armaments. When standing as Liberal candidate at Hemel Hempstead in 1935 she stressed the importance of recording every possible vote in favour of collective security.[20]

No wonder she was fierce when attacking Fascism and government policy from the mid-1930s. She took pride in the fact that the IAW, by refusing to accept Mussolini's Italian delegate, was the first international

[17] Frances Taylor, in *Argus*. Corbett Ashby Papers: Margery to Brian, n.d. [1926]. See also *Woman's Leader*, 28 June 1929, p. 163.
[18] PRO 30/69 (MacDonald Papers) 677/56: MacDonald's secretary Miss Rosenberg to MacDonald, 19 Nov. 1931, reporting Astor's telephone conversation.
[19] Corbett Ashby Papers: Margery to her mother, 7 Feb. 1932; autobiographical typescript headed 'Disarmament Conference 1933'.
[20] Ibid.: draft resignation letter, n.d., to MacDonald [endorsed 'as sent']. Printed election address, Hemel Hempstead, 1935.

organization to condemn Fascism; on trying to take over the German branch, the Nazis found that it had already disbanded. She knew how completely Fascism clashed with feminism: 'there can be no liberty for women', she told the IAW in January 1939, 'when liberty ceases to be a recognized right.' Her annual presidential messages became more and more gloomy. In 1937 she described Nazi doctrines as 'insidious and infectious', and as appealing to 'the vanity of men and to the laziness of women'.[21] She told Bradford Liberal women in March 1938 that the 'criminal farce' of British non-intervention in Spain should be abandoned; 'we have thrown away everything for which we fought the War, and now under far worse conditions we have only a little time left in which to build up again before it will be too late'. Chamberlain should call a conference of peace-loving powers to unite against aggression, she said; Britain, France, and Russia should collaborate in mutual defence. In her last peacetime presidential address she pointed out that 'a world governed by force, brutality and fraud will find no place for women, save as breeders of men and forced labourers'.[22]

As president of the IAW, Corbett Ashby was busy during congresses, but she had few continuing responsibilities in the intervals between them, so could take on other public work. She had always been active in British domestic feminism, and during the 1920s her international work reinforced her domestic feminist standing. She supported Rathbone within NUSEC on family allowances, and helped get them into the Liberal Party's 'Yellow Book' of 1928. When Rathbone wanted to retire as president of NUSEC, Corbett Ashby was her obvious successor, possessing what the Union saw as 'fine balance of judgement and . . . peculiar graciousness of personality'.[23] She was no mere figure-head; from 1928 she eased NUSEC's path towards another of its fruitful innovations—Townswomen's Guilds. The Women's Institutes had already demonstrated countrywomen's need for semi-recreational societies; the towns needed something similar, now that transport changes were transforming husbands into commuters and leaving their wives in the suburbs during the day. In her presidential address of 1927 Rathbone saw a vigorous branch life as the movement's 'first essential'; and though she admitted that some branches were neglecting feminism for 'more visibly produc-

[21] *International Women's News*, Jan. 1939, p. 25. WFL, *Bulletin* No. 125 (21 May 1937), p. 1.
[22] *Huddersfield Daily Examiner*, 29 Mar. 1938, p. 7. WFL, *Bulletin* No. 193 (28 Apr. 1939), p. 1.
[23] *Woman's Leader*, 15 Mar. 1929, p. 42.

tive' work, she thought branches should be 'kept in constant motion by the inflow of fresh currents'.[24]

NUSEC's council meeting of 1928 resolved itself into a committee to consider 'by what means the about-to-be-enfranchised women might be drawn into the women's movement'; at this committee 'Mrs Corbett Ashby made valuable proposals'.[25] Hubback's imagination lies behind the creation of the Guilds, but Corbett Ashby's close practical knowledge of the Women's Institutes provided an essential ingredient. She was on the key committee that devised the Guilds and helped enlist Alice Franklin, a childhood friend, to get them launched—a crucial move, for Franklin's enthusiasm soon became proverbial within the movement. Also important was Corbett Ashby's consistent presidential backing for the experiment. The cuckoo soon grew too large for NUSEC's nest, so the Union eventually separated its roles into two distinct organizations—NCEC and the National Union of Townswomen's Guilds. Without hesitation, Corbett Ashby agreed to preside over the Guilds, even though they were not yet fully fledged.

She succeeded for the same reason as Grace Hadow in the Women's Institutes. Her long feminist experience did not preclude a down-to-earth understanding of the problems faced by women much less fortunate than herself. She was dignified yet amusing, serious yet friendly and practical, with a lifelong interest in younger people, a lifelong skill at winning their confidence. She saw the Guilds as feminist in ultimate aim, but recognized that, for the moment, feminism was not enough; the Guilds must advance feminism more gradually and less directly than NUSEC. In her presidential address of 1930 she hoped to see the members 'so confident of equality that they can devote themselves to the improvement of their homes without feeling shut in by them'; the Guilds should 'rationalize cookery and homecraft as men rationalize their businesses, without fear of losing their university education or their claim to equal entry into industry and profession'.[26] They would be training-grounds for women who might later move into local government, voluntary organizations, and social work, and in 1934 she urged members to vote and exercise their rights as citizens.[27]

The Guilds' feminist founders probably hoped for faster feminist results than they obtained; to that extent the Guilds' feminist enemies within NUSEC were vindicated. It was not always easy to direct housewives visiting Switzerland away from apple brews and towards votes for Swiss women, or to prevent cooking and housekeeping from dominating Guild meetings.[28] Britain in the 1930s experienced a mild version of the 'appalling reaction against women in all spheres' in Europe that Corbett Ashby detected there in 1935, and in 1936 she complained that women had not sufficiently influenced the BBC, whose women's programme 'conforms too much to the so-called Woman's Page of our daily and weekly press'.[29] In reality the broadcasters—like the newspaper editors, the fashion designers, and the cosmetics manufacturers between the wars—were responding to demand. Something similar had happened within the Guilds, whose non-feminist members partially captured their feminist leaders.

The Guilds' growth-rate reminded Corbett Ashby of Edwardian suffragism, and at the annual meeting of 1933 (attended by 178 delegates from 83 Guilds) she saw the Guilds as having 'left behind the childhood stage' and as displaying 'the enthusiasm and self-confidence of vigorous youth'. She now encouraged them to raise enough money to become independent of grant-giving bodies.[30] Two factors accelerated the Guilds' divergence from feminism: the segregation of the political feminists into the NCEC, and the need for the Guilds to be non-political if they were to qualify for grants. This trend also endangered Corbett Ashby's presidency. When accepting the NUSEC presidency she had agreed to resign as president of the Women's Liberal Federation, but her Liberal allegiance was eventually made the excuse for ousting her from the Guilds presidency in 1935, the year when she stood as Liberal candidate for Hemel Hempstead.

Yet her charm made her so popular that a new domestic feminist presidency rapidly appeared in place of the old; Emmeline Pethick-Lawrence wanted to retire as president of the WFL, a far more political body than the Guilds, and who better than Corbett Ashby to succeed her? She did not intend to hold the post for long and was glad to hand over to Lady Pares in 1939. But she used her period of office to encourage British feminists to collaborate with the League of Nations when it requested information on the status of British women—an important development for the long-term evolution of British feminism.[31] The WFL gave her yet

[28] Author's collection: Corbett Ashby to author, 30 Nov. 1976.
[29] WFL, Bulletin No. 69 (1 Nov. 1935), p. 1; No. 87 (1 May 1936), p. 2.
[30] *Townswoman*, Apr. 1933, p. 1; Apr. 1934, pp. 5–6.
[31] WFL, Bulletin No. 80 (28 Feb. 1936), p. 2.

another platform for denouncing Fascism. Her presidential address of 1939 stresses that 'women can only attain the dignity of full human personality under Democracy', and that feminism can survive only if feminists join with men in upholding the basic freedoms; 'we have got to rouse ourselves', she said, 'to the urgent risk that . . . *all* human rights and human values will vanish'. Events since 1918 had shown not only that non-party feminism would fail in Britain, but that feminists must link up their cause with other humanitarian issues. In her message of November 1938 to the IAW she urged women to branch out beyond home duties and social reform: they must join and work for the political parties who stand against tyranny. 'We have not used the machine which controls us,' she went on. 'Let us awake and determine that women shall enter that machine to direct it for the defence of democracy.'[32]

She practised what she preached. Conservatism never tempted her. She had been an enthusiastic Liberal from the start, telling her mother in 1903 that 'Free Trade is so enormously and nationally important that I really would give up everything else for it'; she even thought suffragism should take second place to Liberalism at the coming general election. In 1909, unlike her mother and sister, she was ready to work for her father at the next election whatever the Liberal government's suffragist standpoint.[33] By her own conduct she falsified the belief of some Edwardians that one person could not simultaneously join the executives of the NUWSS and the Women's Liberal Federation, though she once had to rebuke the Federation's anti-suffragists for rudeness. She saw nothing progressive about the idea of a class-conscious party on the left, and told her mother as early as 1904 that she disliked the ILP's sectarian tactics and programme.[34] And whereas she thought suffragists should support suitable Labour candidates, she joined Rathbone and other suffragists in 1914 in condemning the NUWSS decision to oppose Liberal candidates at elections.[35]

Up to the First World War there was no necessary conflict between the Liberal and Labour parties, and Corbett Ashby might have got into parliament if the two had held together. As it was, her eight election and by-election campaigns as a Liberal candidate between 1918 and 1944 all

[32] Ibid. No. 183 (27 Jan. 1939), p. 1. *International Women's News*, Nov. 1938, p. 9.
[33] Corbett Ashby Papers: Margery to her mother, 7 Dec. 1903. Fawcett Library Autograph Collection 1F/6862: Margery Corbett to Miss Strachey, 25 Oct. 1909.
[34] Corbett Ashby Papers: Margery to her mother, 29 Jan. 1904.
[35] *Common Cause*, 23 May 1912, p. 104. Manchester City Library M50/1/1: Minute-Book of Manchester Society for Women's Suffrage, 7 Apr. 1914, p. 3.

ended in failure. In the first, at Birmingham Ladywood in 1918, she aimed only to show the women's flag and did not expect to get in, if only because her Conservative opponent was Neville Chamberlain. She pronounced the Lloyd George coalition dishonest for trying to combine the irreconcilable and for blurring genuine peacetime disagreement; as an Asquithian Liberal she stood for social reform (especially for better housing), the League of Nations, free trade, national self-determination, and equal citizenship.[36] She came bottom of the poll and lost her deposit.

Family responsibilities made Birmingham unsuitable, and her next constituency was Richmond, where she stood at the general elections of 1922 and 1923. 'First and foremost I am out to further the interests of my own sex,' she explained in 1920, hoping to attract women from other parties.[37] In 1922 she thought the chances of Liberal revival were good, and championed the idea of a centrist Liberal party that would moderate the extremes of right and left.[38] Unfortunately IWSA's claims prevented her from launching her campaign of 1922 in person, and her husband and her election agent faced one another forlornly over a table to discuss how to begin. Here again there was no chance of victory, but at least she found it easier to campaign from a home base. She was faced by 'an ex-boxer who fought on simple if unpolitical lines by offering 10s. a vote in all the pubs'; despite the split among Conservatives, whose Anti-Waste candidate triumphed over the official candidate, she still came third, though with a better proportion of the votes cast than at Birmingham. In the two-party contest of 1923 she lost again, though again raising her proportion of the votes cast.

Her next constituency was Watford in 1924, where she faced D. H. Herbert, a candidate unpopular with feminists at the time, but again came third. As a consistent inter-war advocate of the middle way, she saw the Liberal Party (with Asquith) as a moderating influence, not (with Lloyd George) as a radical alternative. In 1926 she thought both Conservatives and Labour had shown lack of leadership on the miners' strike, and for the rest of her life she regretted that the Liberals' Yellow Book of 1928 had never been implemented. When standing at Hendon in 1929 she saw public works schemes as 'surely common sense',[39] for they would increase employment and purchasing power, but she had no chance

---

[36] *Birmingham Gazette*, 20 Nov. 1918, p. 3. See also *Common Cause*, 13 Dec. 1918, p. 416.

[37] *Vote*, 30 Apr. 1920, p. 34.

[38] Corbett Ashby Papers: speech at Richmond in unidentified newspaper extract dated 17 July 1922; see also her letter of 22 Feb. 1922 to her mother.

[39] Ibid.: Election Address at Hendon, 1929.

against Sir P. Cunliffe-Lister's huge Conservative majority, and once more came third.

The only inter-war general election at which she failed to stand was 1931, but she signed the Next Five Years Group's *Essay in Political Agreement* (1935), and in the same year a prominent free-church leader got her to stand at Hemel Hempstead. Once again she faced a Conservative grandee, this time J. C. C. Davidson; she came second in a three-party contest, but was nowhere near victory. Ironically in the three-party by-election contest two years later she succumbed before the Conservative device of 'male equivalence'; when Davidson was made a peer the Party replaced him by his wife, who held the seat by a comfortable majority, and kept her rival in second place. Corbett Ashby's conduct at the declaration of poll shows how her tact sprang, not from a blandness of outlook, but from diplomacy's precarious triumph over strong feeling; her natural courtesy never tempted her to compromise on essentials in the hope of avoiding embarrassment. She complained indignantly that Viscountess Davidson had appropriated the Union Jack virtually as a party emblem at her meetings, thereby implying that patriotism was a Conservative monopoly. Her conduct gave Corbett Ashby the appearance of being a bad loser; it was an understandable but tactically unwise response from a deeply patriotic woman who was perhaps unduly rationalistic about how the electorate could or should be influenced.[40]

Both in public and private Corbett Ashby fiercely criticized National Government policy at this time; 'instead of Heil Hitler,' she wrote privately in February 1936, 'Blast Baldwin will do'. At Huddersfield in March 1938 she branded government foreign policy as 'appalling' and blamed the situation largely on 'the shiftless policy of large Conservative majorities in this country ever since the War, except for a few months of Labour democracy'.[41] In December 1940 she wished that the Liberal and Labour parties had thrown out 'the knaves and class ridden fools who have formed the H[ouse] of C[ommons] majority for 20 years'; a general election would have been better than a wartime coalition. Morrison at the Home Office seems at this time to have rejected her request for permission to travel in India and America—another example of the way 'so many people when they reach a high position become timid and lean on their officials and dare not say bo to a goose', 'another proof that those in power

---

[40] *Hertfordshire, Hemel Hempstead Gazette and West Herts. Advertiser*, 26 June 1937, p. 1.
[41] McMaster University Library, Brittain Collection: Corbett Ashby to Brittain, 24 Feb. 1936. *Huddersfield Daily Examiner*, 30 Mar. 1938, p. 10.

are already digging themselves in to prevent any real reforms domestic or foreign happening after the war'.[42]

In 1944 she broke the three-party truce by standing at Bury St Edmunds by-election; her platform was 'immediate acceptance of the Beveridge Report in full, and the immediate preparation of the measures necessary to bring it into effect'. Progressives, she argued, should unite against 'the Tory stranglehold', otherwise democracy would die; she demanded 'a square deal for the common folk', and wanted service people to return to 'a new Britain, a land where the material good things of life are shared out much more fairly than they ever were before'. Clement Davies described her aptly as 'upright and downright', and she won the support of the Common Wealth Party; but, as she later recalled, the Liberal Party 'disowned me, and was very angry with me'.[43] In this two-party contest, her last attempt to get into parliament, she won a higher percentage of the votes cast (43.8 per cent) than at any other of her elections, but victory still eluded her.

Two other things worried her at this by-election: first, the corruption— whereby local landlords coerced electors, free speech was restricted, evictions were threatened, some electors were prevented from voting, and her own campaign was generally obstructed. It all reminded her of Charles Dickens's Eatanswill, and she was still indignant about it when we discussed it in 1977. Her second disappointment was more personal: she was upset when Michael, then an Oxford undergraduate, failed to back her up in the campaign. She thought the family should stand together on such occasions, and said it would permanently alter their relationship, though it was not discussed afterwards. At the time Michael thought her unwise in her last-minute candidatures for hopeless constituencies; but he now thinks she had no strong desire to get into parliament, which would have greatly disrupted her family life, and that her main aim was to publicize her causes.[44]

Nobody could have struggled more gamely against more impossible odds to keep the feminist flag flying at elections between the wars. Why did she fail to get into parliament? After all, she had identified herself closely with a political party, and she was an excellent candidate—not better,

[42] Brittain Collection: Corbett Ashby to Brittain, 4 and 9 Dec. 1940.

[43] Corbett Ashby Papers: Election Address at Bury St Edmunds 1944; Clement Davies to Corbett Ashby, 3 Mar. 1944.

[44] The discussion of Dame Margery's family life in the later part of this chapter owes so much to discussions and correspondence with her son Michael and her daughter-in-law Pamela, and especially to a tape-recorded discussion on 15 Oct. 1982 at Wickens, that footnoting of individual points is not practicable.

perhaps, than Neville Chamberlain, J. C. C. Davidson, Cunliffe-Lister, or even Dennis Herbert, but certainly better than Keatinge at Bury St Edmonds, Becker at Richmond or, at Hemel Hempstead, Viscountess Davidson, who hardly spoke when she got into parliament. In speaking ability, political sense, relevant experience, and feminist commitment Corbett Ashby would have surpassed all but three of the thirty-eight woman MPs (Rathbone, Summerskill, and Wilkinson) between 1919 and 1945. 'That she has not been elected to our Parliament', said Lady Layton in 1936, 'is a reflection on the intelligence of democracy and a condemnation of our present electoral system.'[45]

This is too simplistic. Not only is there more to be said for the 'present electoral system' than Layton allows; she is also too harsh in blaming the individual elector for the outcome. For the major reason why Corbett Ashby never got into parliament is that she was offered a winnable seat only once, and on that occasion ill-health prevented her from taking it up. How could this occur? Because she chose the party with fewest safe seats at its disposal, and because she stood for constituencies in the South-East of England where Liberals were overwhelmed by large Conservative majorities and sometimes by well-known Conservative statesmen. Even if the Liberal and Labour votes cast in her elections had been united behind her, she would not have won any of her contests; indeed, in only two of her six constituencies were there any Liberal or Labour wins (both very narrow) between 1918 and 1945—at Hemel Hempstead in 1923 and at Birmingham Ladywood in 1929. Her career in some ways resembles her father's in Sussex: only in the most exceptional situation could she have won the seats she contested.

The outcome might have been different if the Edwardian alliance between Liberals and Labour had survived the First World War, for the unnecessary inter-war split weakened the morale of the left and diminished the number of its safe seats. The relative unity of the right and its skill at digesting new recruits from the left wrecked the careers of several promising Liberal and even Labour women MPs—those of Jennie Lee, for instance, Marion Phillips, Susan Lawrence, Margaret Win-tringham, and Mary Agnes Hamilton. A minoritarian Liberal Party and a class-conscious Labour Party deterred many able feminists—Ray Strachey and Eva Hubback, for example—from even offering themselves as candidates. And if the Lib–Lab split had to occur, it need not have been so damaging. Both the minority Labour governments could have won

[45] *Liberal News*, Oct. 1936, p. 2.

Liberal collaboration; Corbett Ashby thought later that, if MacDonald had taken up Asquith's offer of co-operation in 1924, 'we could have changed the face of the world'. In 1937 she was still urging Lib–Lab collaboration in 'The People's Front', with a programme of freer trade, collective security, arms reduction, and a Liberal domestic policy.[46]

By the 1940s the Corbett Ashbys' marriage had settled down into its final mould. Brian was a quiet, wise, and witty man who did not mind being thrown into the shade by his wife. Deeply fond of Bach, he was twice master of the Drapers' Company and active in promoting its educational work. They were an entirely unsnobbish couple, hospitable to relatives of the servants, refugees during the Second World War, and people down on their luck. They had religion, music, and gardening in common; as early as 1913 Margery had listed her recreations as 'digging and skiing',[47] and during the Second World War the garden was much extended. Brian contrasted the plight of the unhappy couple, 'together but not united', with their own situation, 'united but not together'. When she came home full of her adventures, Brian made a good listener; she sometimes wished he would be more inquisitive about her day's activities, but for him it was quite sufficient that she had returned. They were both happy in silent companionship, reading books in their chairs with a ritual game of patience before going to bed. Michael sees the marriage less as a union of opposites than as a complementary partnership, each respecting the independence of the other, and each 'really blissfully happy that the other one existed'.

Margery was lonely after Brian died, and Michael thinks she was so active in old age partly because she did not want to sit and think. She was an affectionate person, saddened by the loss of her parents, and deeply upset by the death of her grand-daughter Charlotte in a car accident at the age of twenty-one; years afterwards she told Pamela, her daughter-in-law, that nothing would ever be quite the same again. She was not fond of paperwork, though conscientious in dealing with it, and struggled to make progress with her memoirs. She did not like to be idle, and was never without her embroidery, crochet, or patchwork when she had nothing else to do. She long remained active in the garden, where the geese followed her about as she worked; all dogs were fond of her, though she was not very fond of them. In later life she became quite a keen reader of books on religion, travel, and biography. Her religious beliefs were strongly held, and she always gave up something for Lent. There was not much talk

[46] *Labour Monthly*, Feb. 1937, p. 91.
[47] *Women's Who's Who, 1913*, p. 214.

about religion in the family, but she was quite capable of holding her own in conversation with a bishop.

Two things became increasingly important to her in extreme old age—her family and her locality. She liked nothing better in later life than family gatherings, and during her last ten years her birthdays were always spent in this way, relatives taking turns to have a short talk with her. She was not afraid of disagreeing with her grandchildren on some things, but no bad feeling ever resulted because she was never censorious, and was always so obviously interested in their views and careers; she never assumed that the old are always right. Nor did she ever deploy her affectionate recollection of the past in grumbling reproach of the present; to the end she showed interest in, and concern about, current affairs.

Her relationship with Pamela could easily have been difficult, especially as Pamela did not share her feminist or political interests. But here too Margery's diplomacy was to the fore, for she never forced her views on others. Indeed, diplomacy is probably the wrong word, because Margery virtually adopted Pamela as the daughter she had always wanted; 'she became really like another mother,' Pamela recalls. When towards the end of Margery's life they shared the same house, Margery was happy to leave control of the domestic side to Pamela, yet never treated her as a housekeeper. It was a difficult balance to strike, but Margery was good at striking balances.

Anyone who met her in later life soon realized that she loved Sussex. She also loved the countryside, its birds and flowers, and although she might occasionally go up to London on business or to hear the Christmas Oratorio at St Paul's, she rarely went there for pleasure. She never turned down a local society's request for a subscription, and was always opening bazaars. In a way her life came full circle, for she became increasingly interested in the local causes her mother had taken up—the Women's Institutes, local Liberal Party work, and the local historical society of which she was the first president.

According to her *Times* obituarist, 'probably no-one has done more for the emancipation of women during the century'.[48] She was not an original thinker like Rathbone, nor even a prolific writer like Ray Strachey. She never got into parliament, nor did she ever influence feminist legislation as directly as Hubback or Ray Strachey. She was not an organization woman like Pippa Strachey, continuously influential behind the scenes, nor was she a charismatic leader like Emmeline Pankhurst. Yet at various times she

---

[48] *The Times*, 16 May 1981, p. 16.

presided over four major women's organizations, used her strong party connection and parliamentary candidatures to acclimatize the public to women's political participation, and helped to carry women into the heart of that male holy of holies: foreign policy. Her distinctive contribution to British feminism is best brought out by relating her diplomatic skills to her class background.

Her diplomacy owes much to her comfortable personal circumstances; patience and tolerance, charm and compromise do not flourish amid the desperation of poverty. She begins her memoirs by emphasizing her 'secret conviction that no one else can have been quite so happy and enjoyed life quite so much and so consistently as I have. That does me no credit since I have been sheltered by faith and love[,] by health and wealth all my life.'[49] Yet she did not use her resources primarily for enjoyment or to promote her own career. Like Fawcett and Rathbone she combined middle-class affluence with personal austerity and, like her mother, disliked buying anything for herself. She never travelled first class on a train, and could be persuaded to take a taxi only after falling down in a bus in her nineties. She had no interest in money matters, and although she loved her home and the things in it, her attachment was sentimental, not acquisitive. Her bedroom was almost spartan; at the end of her life she liked to sit in her husband's rather battered armchair, and regularly wore her mother's rather tattered shawl. She had no interest in clothes, used no make-up, and wore black for years after her husband died; it was only because Pamela occasionally insisted on taking her off to a dress shop in Lingfield that she looked nicely dressed in later life. Left to herself, she would have worn only old or battered clothes; new clothes might outlast her.

Joined to her personal austerity, never sanctimonious, was a firm but unsectarian integrity and a strong sense of public responsibility. She could express strong feelings both in private and in public, and her private correspondence shows that she could take a strong dislike to individuals, though she made this known only to intimates. But her father's influence and her Liberal and local government experience discouraged doctrinaire attitudes. Her diplomatic skills did not originate in lack of conviction. She thus acquired, as was stressed at her thanksgiving service in 1981, the unusual quality of being 'resolute without arrogance';[50] in this combina-

[49] Corbett Ashby Papers: autobiographical draft on early years.
[50] By the Dean of Westminster (14 July 1981).

tion, she epitomized the determined but pragmatic mood of British inter-war feminism.

Political as well as personal reasons prevented her last years from being entirely happy. In at least three respects the world seemed to be going awry. It was not so much the decline of the Liberal Party that concerned her, though this certainly harmed her career; it was more that liberal values seemed in decline. There was first the decline of internationalism as a popular cause and political priority; any late-twentieth-century advance here owes more to tourism and commerce than to international political structures. The great Liberal faith in free trade has withered, and the Cobdenite utopia—whereby democracy fosters internationalism and increased international contact banishes war—has been slow to arrive. Voluntary international structures like the IAW have faltered in this climate, and were badly injured by Communism and Fascism. In 1976 Corbett Ashby's tone still reflected her disgust when describing how Communists rigged the first meeting in Paris of the Democratic Federation of Women after the Second World War. 'I went without any prejudice,' she told me; '. . . they had real *gangsters*, ex-boxing toughs and that, and . . . I was watched from the moment I arrived . . . They wouldn't allow anybody to speak whom they hadn't got on their list.'

In some ways even more worrying was the apparent decline in Britain of the individual self-discipline that lay at the heart of Liberalism. She disliked the permissive society and the apparent decline in family values, and this was one of the two worries she discussed with her grandchildren. A related worry concerned the pursuit, modish in the 1970s, of instant political gratification; in her young days, she said, young people did not resort to militant demonstrations whenever their ideas failed to carry immediate conviction. Her concern emerges from the marginalia she scribbled beside a newspaper cutting about the violence of the so-called 'winter of discontent' in 1978–9, and her memoirs stress that the value of feminist militancy 'has been absurdly exaggerated' simply because it makes 'good dramatic reading'. In 1978 she said she had been unable to support suffragette militancy when it began hurting others besides the suffragettes themselves: 'you can't have the right to inflict suffering on other people for the sake of your own convictions', she pointed out, 'though I know that is not a fashionable view today.'[51]

In many ways she was a model of how to cope with extreme old age; in yet another of her skilful balancing acts, she somehow managed to remain

---

[51] Corbett Ashby Papers: autobiographical draft on early years. *Observer*, 28 May 1978, p. 4.

active and alert in her nineties without losing dignity and serenity. Acting on her maxim 'go when they want you to stay, and don't stay till they want you to go', she never clung to office. She enjoyed good health throughout her life, rarely catching a cold and never getting flu; but she hated growing old, slept badly at night, and had difficulty in getting warm. In her last years, she seemed to be holding herself to a daily timetable which, once abandoned, might never be resumed. She feared becoming a burden to relatives, and with characteristic honesty told David Mitchell at ninety-eight that 'just as babies progress in bursts, advancing suddenly then standing still, so in old age one does the same—in the opposite direction'.[52] These worries, together with political disappointment, help to explain why at ninety-nine she did not wish to reach her hundredth birthday. She would have seen it as one of her many blessings that this wish, too, was granted.

[52] David Mitchell's typescript of interview with Corbett Ashby, 12 June 1980.

8

Two Utopians

SYLVIA PANKHURST AND
HENRY HARBEN

'I AM a realist,' said Rathbone, recommending family allowances in parliament during 1944; 'I am never much concerned with what ought to be, I am concerned with what is and what will be, human nature and conditions being what they are.'[1] Most MPs would then have seen her not as a realist but as an idealist, for vision and imagination lie behind her reforming proposals. Besides, she was not contrasting her realism with idealism, but with utopianism: with the impossibilist reformer who mirrors on the left the impossibilist conservative on the right. Is the utopian reformer more idealistic than the realist reformer? Some would see the smaller reform as blocking the larger, whether deliberately or not; others would detect more idealism in the successful pursuit of a modest reform than in the impossibilist crusade for a larger. But in most practical situations, utopian and realist reformers are yoked somewhat awkwardly together, sometimes mutually reinforcing, sometimes mutually obstructing. This study of two utopians helps to set into context the realist reformers who dominate this book.

Pankhurst and Harben are by no means typical of utopians, who are eccentric almost by definition, though both qualify as utopians in the special sense of setting up ideal communities—Pankhurst with her welfare arrangements in the East End during the First World War, Harben on his estate in Newland Park. Both at first aimed at short-term practical achievement, yet with advancing age, instead of making the familiar transition from utopianism to realism, both moved in the reverse direction. Harben's abandonment of realist reformism was rapid. He defends modest and empirically based proposals for family endowment in 1910 by saying that the scheme must rest on existing family structures, for 'no ideals are worth much until in our imagination we have succeeded in linking them on the present state of things, until we have formed an idea of

[1] *HC Deb.* 3 Nov. 1944, c. 1174.

PLATE 10. Sylvia Pankhurst at Woodford (International Institute of Social History, Amsterdam).

how we are to make for them'.[2] Yet within two years he moved dramatically beyond the bounds of the practicable, never to return. Pankhurst's journey away from the British political mainstream was slower and less dramatic because she travelled more reluctantly and to a destination rather less remote from her starting-point.

Pankhurst's lifelong inspiration was her father, Dr Richard Pankhurst, whose election manifesto hung above her in Ethiopia when she died in 1960. But the rich account of her family she published in 1931—disguised as a history of the women's suffrage movement—shows how early her essential traits appeared. She was the Pankhursts' second daughter, born in 1882. Appalled as a child at the suffering in Dickens's novels, she acquired 'a longing, profound and constant, for a Golden Age when plenty and joy should be the gift of all'. Corporal punishment made so little impact upon her that Emmeline Pankhurst gave it up, and Sylvia was nicknamed 'little Briton' for not screaming when some burns were dressed. Longing to please her mother, she was disappointed to find that Christabel came first; Rebecca West later likened Sylvia's *The Suffragette Movement* to Gordon Craig's *Memories of my Mother* 'as an expression of the burning resentment that the child of a brilliant mother may feel at having to share her brilliance with the world'.[3]

Edwardian suffragism drew heavily on support from novelists, artists, and playwrights, if only because women enjoyed more opportunities in the world of art than elsewhere. The Actresses', Women Writers' and Artists' Franchise Leagues mobilized support of this type, and advertised it in eye-catching processions, while the Suffrage Atelier created striking posters and cartoons. So when as a young art-student she sought in 1906 to launch the WSPU in London, Pankhurst found sympathizers. Rejecting suffragist friends' offers of an artist's life in Italy, she saw herself always as the artist diverted from her true vocation by politics and suffering, and the key to much of her political conduct lies in her yearning to harmonize politics with art. For Emmeline Pethick-Lawrence, who first met her at this time, she resembled those late-nineteenth-century young Russian students who gave up all to prepare the people for revolution.[4]

Like Billington-Greig, Pankhurst was excluded from the centre of

[2] H. D. Harben, 'The Endowment of Motherhood', *Fabian Tract* No. 149 (1910), p. 3.
[3] E. S. Pankhurst in Asquith (ed.), *Myself When Young*, p. 262. E. S. Pankhurst, *Suffragette Movement*, p. 59. West, 'Mrs Pankhurst', pp. 483–4. See also Mitchell, *Fighting Pankhursts*, p. 322.
[4] E. Pethick-Lawrence, *My Part*, p. 149.

power when the WSPU began to grow, but unlike her she did not openly rebel; 'it was not in me to criticize or expostulate,' she wrote later; 'I would rather have died at the stake than say one word against the actions of those who were in the throes of the fight'. She later recalled the doubts she had repressed at the time: she thought her mother could have retained control of the WSPU without abrogating the constitution in 1907; she opposed the WSPU's dalliance with the moderate 'Conciliation Bill' (a non-party attempt at a modest measure of women's enfranchisement) in 1910–11 as unduly timid; and when asked by Christabel in 1912 to burn down Nottingham Castle she would go no further than fling a symbolic torch at it.[5] Her American tour of 1911 gave her some financial independence, by which time her mother and sister had decided she could be dispensed with. Sylvia felt that the WSPU was being mismanaged, and that Christabel, now exiled in Paris, was being badly advised. Again like Billington-Greig she regretted the WSPU's failure to embark on mass protest, and found 'calm thought and the sense of perspective' impossible within a movement whose members rushed to martyrdom while blessing 'as their truest saviours, the leaders who summoned them to each new ordeal'.[6]

Wider propaganda rather than accentuated militancy was her remedy, and she turned to the East End, 'the greatest homogeneous working-class area accessible to the House of Commons by popular demonstrations'. Keir Hardie encouraged her in this; 'now that my father was gone,' she recalled, 'he was my chiefest and dearest guide and leader', though Hardie did not at first know it.[7] After 1910 Pankhurst became the latest among several left-wing young women to have an affair with him. She regularly visited Nevill's Court alone and dined with him in London restaurants; an undated manuscript in her handwriting, kept with her Hardie letters, hints at some deep personal crisis involving him, and some of the poems she sent him from America are mildly erotic; in January 1912 she writes longing to take him into her arms and send him into a dreamless sleep. His example was for her 'a buttress against cynicism and spiritual despair', and she was disgusted when the WSPU attacked him.[8]

---

[5] E. S. Pankhurst, *Suffragette Movement*, p. 316; see also pp. 338, 396, 402. For 1907, see Fawcett Library: Sylvia Pankhurst, autobiographical memorandum prepared for Billington-Greig, p. 10.

[6] E. S. Pankhurst, *Suffragette Movement*, p. 316. See also Institute of Social History, Amsterdam, Sylvia Pankhurst Papers: unpaginated notebook for *Suffragette Movement*.

[7] E. S. Pankhurst, *Suffragette Movement*, p. 416. Sylvia Pankhurst Papers: unpaginated notebook for *Suffragette Movement*.

[8] E. S. Pankhurst in Asquith (ed.), *Myself When Young*, p. 278. For her relations with Hardie, see Sylvia Pankhurst Papers: undated MSS and poems filed with Keir Hardie

Through the East London Federation of the wspu she mobilized open and mass suffragist militancy—complete with drillings, armies, and processions carrying red caps on poles and singing the Marseillaise. This overt mood of revolution contrasted markedly with the conspiratorial and tactical militancy being organized by her mother and sister, whose drift towards sex-antagonism and destroying works of art she disliked. Family sentiment did not stand in the way of a clean cut: 'it is essential for the public to understand that you are working independently of us,' wrote Christabel in November 1913. In her somewhat theatrical account of the split, Sylvia points out in 1930 that 'it would have been impossible for me—constituted as I was—to do other than I did'.[9] Henceforth both the wspu's newspaper and Christabel's history of the movement ignored her work.

Sylvia's movement promised more than anything Christabel could offer. Mass militancy was bound to be more effective in alarming government than tactical violence, especially if reinforced by Sylvia's extraordinarily courageous, and in its later stages very public, hunger striking. The King feared that her published account of forcible feeding would rouse public sympathy; there was, he said, 'something shocking, if not almost cruel, in the operation to which these insensate women are subjected'.[10] Most important of all, Sylvia was moving towards a genuinely democratic route to women's suffrage, that is, towards adult suffrage.

She did not adopt this platform immediately or spontaneously: The East End pressed her into it. But she soon came to see how misleading and outdated were the old justifications for an apparently simple one-clause Bill whose sole aim was to remove the sex discrimination from the existing franchise. This was, in effect, what suffragists were still demanding, yet an 'equal franchise' which retained the old property qualifications was only nominally equal as between the sexes; and, as she later pointed out, it was 'too narrow, too tactical, for popular appeal; it might convince, but it did

correspondence, and letters to Hardie dated 22 Jan. [1912], 28 Jan. 1912. See also K. O. Morgan, *Keir Hardie: Radical and Socialist* (1975), pp. 12, 58, 165. For her resentment at suffragette treatment of Hardie, see Fawcett Library: Sylvia Pankhurst's autobiographical memo, p. 5.

[9] Rosen, *Rise Up, Women!* p. 219. Sylvia Pankhurst Papers: autobiographical notes sent with covering note dated 10 Dec. 1930, p. 7.

[10] Royal Archives, Windsor Castle, RA GV O 459/1: Stamfordham to McKenna, 27 Mar. 1913 (copy), quoted by gracious permission of Her Majesty the Queen. See also 'The Hunger and Thirst Strike and its Effects', a 4-page insert in *Woman's Dreadnought*, 4 Apr. 1914.

not enthuse; it had constantly to be re-stated and re-argued'.[11] Progressive Liberals, bidding for organized labour's continued allegiance, would now support nothing less than a genuinely democratic franchise for both sexes, and the reduced influence of back-benchers meant that only a government measure would do. The other suffragist organizations did not formally rule out adult suffrage, but in practice they opposed attempts to enact it, claiming that it diluted feminism and provided anti-suffragists with welcome distractions from the main issue. Yet the government's more radical leaders had been moving towards adult suffrage for some time, and its Reform Bill of 1912, which proposed a wider male franchise, would have allowed parliament to include women in it. Asquith told Pankhurst's deputation in June 1914 that if women were to get the vote, 'you must give it to them upon the same terms that you do to men. That is, make it a Democratic measure . . . If the change has to come, we must face it boldly, and make it thorough-going and democratic in its basis.'[12]

This was not the great suffragist breakthrough that Pankhurst later claimed, nor did suffragist newspapers then see it as such, though the *Vote* welcomed Asquith's 'altered tone'. Asquith's personal hostility to women's suffrage remained, and he was merely repeating what he had said in parliament's franchise debate of 12 July 1910.[13] But shortly after the deputation Lansbury arranged for Pankhurst to meet Lloyd George. Militancy must end before the Liberal machine could be won over, he said, and this would free him to introduce a women's suffrage Bill in 1915 on his own account; he would leave the cabinet if the government failed to support it. Sylvia both distrusted Lloyd George and doubted whether Christabel would concede a truce; and before she could advance things further, Harben—briefed by Lansbury—rushed over to Paris to brief Christabel, who at once repudiated the project.[14]

Sylvia felt liberated by London's East End. Not only had she jettisoned a mistaken WSPU policy: a pronounced personal emancipation was involved in shaking off for good her domineering sister so as at last to join her late father and her substitute father Keir Hardie in pursuing a radical route to women's suffrage. The war moved her further left. In May 1915 Hardie, dying in Caterham sanatorium, offered to return her letters and

[11] E. S. Pankhurst, *Suffragette Movement*, p. 242. See also my 'Women's Suffrage at Westminster', pp. 98–105.

[12] Rosen, *Rise Up, Women!* p. 236.

[13] *Vote*, 26 June 1914, p. 154; cf. *Common Cause*, 26 June 1914, pp. 244–5. *Votes for Women*, 26 June 1914, p. 598. See also *HC Deb.* 12 July 1910, c. 250.

[14] Sylvia Pankhurst Papers: typescript headed 'The Woman's Movement of Yesterday and Tomorrow', pp. 19, 22. E. S. Pankhurst, *Suffragette Movement*, p. 583.

one of her paintings, but asked to keep the painting which had hung over his fireplace because 'so closely associated with you, that I should not like to part with it'. In an unsigned and scrawled postcard to her, postmarked 28 July and addressed to 'Dear Sylphia', he sends love and adds that 'in about a week I expect to be gone from from [*sic*] here, with no more mind control than when I came'. On Hardie's death two months later, she wrote admiringly and at length about him in the *Woman's Dreadnought*, organ of the East London Federation.[15]

She was now becoming fierce in her class loyalties. In a chance encounter during 1915 McKenna, the former Home Secretary who had presided over forcible feeding, acknowledged her bravery, but she 'impetuously . . . rejected him; never would I surmount the barrier between the people and the governing classes whilst the masses starved on the other side!'[16] She now despised any propertied form of women's suffrage: the choice lay between progress and reaction. But if suffragists were to retain a hold on Lloyd George's government, formed in December 1916 and only precariously backing franchise reform, they needed to work in close collaboration. Henderson told her early in 1917 that he would have advocated adult suffrage in peace time, 'but . . . in war time this question could only be settled by having an agreed measure'. She was immovable: human suffrage was 'the only logical or practical political stand to take up'.[17] She mounted her own independent agitation for it during 1916–17, and struggled to prevent the Labour Party from accepting the age-restriction on women's votes. 'Can such an outrageous suggestion be intended seriously by any reasonably fair-minded person?' she asked; 'certainly no genuine democrat can possibly entertain the proposal for a moment!' Even the former militant H. W. Nevinson, active behind the scenes, exploded in his diary that Sylvia, like all the Pankhursts, was 'determined that nothing shall succeed without her control'; wrecking, he claimed, 'is in the Pankhurst nature'.[18]

Her impossibilism did not prevail, but her broadening horizons are reflected in a change of name: 'Workers'' replaced 'Women's' in the Federation's title. By December 1916 she wanted it to hold pacifist meetings,[19] and she hoped that a rent strike might promote a massive

[15] Sylvia Pankhurst Papers: Keir Hardie to Sylvia Pankhurst, 27 May 1915 and undated postcard [postmarked 28 July 1915].
[16] E. S. Pankhurst, *Home Front*, p. 219.
[17] Sylvia Pankhurst Papers: Minutes of the Joint Demonstration Committee, 9 Mar. 1917; letter from Sylvia Pankhurst to Mrs B. Ayrton Gould, 27 Mar. 1916 (copy).
[18] *Woman's Dreadnought*, 27 May 1916, p. 482. Nevinson Diary, 24 Sept., 26 May 1916.
[19] Sylvia Pankhurst Papers: Workers' Suffrage Federation, General Meetings Minute-Book, 18 Dec. 1916.

rehousing in the slums. Collectivism should grow up from below, she thought, not be imposed from above, and she later saw the Federation's maternity and infant welfare clinics as preparing the way for the government aid granted in 1918. But 1917 helped to push her forward from her local utopia—with its clinics, restaurants, and welfare centres— into utopianism on a larger stage.

After visiting Soviet Russia in 1920 she claimed to 'have seen wonderful things', and hoped to create 'a society where there are no rich or poor, no people without work or beauty in their lives, where money itself will disappear, where we shall all be brothers and sisters, where every one will have enough'.[20] Her socialism had already distanced her from her mother and sister and from non-party feminism. And whereas her mother and sister now wanted to work with the parliamentary grain, and urged women to move into the political mainstream, she now gravitated towards the non-parliamentary left. She knew that MPs had been self-interested in backing women's suffrage during 1917–18—'the old fogeys of Parliament . . . are saying "We must do something to popularize the old institution. Let us bring in the women"'.[21]—but she was determined not to succumb. Much to the disgust of her mother and sister, the cry of Sylvia's Stranger's Gallery demonstration in 1919 was 'We shall have no peace until we get a Soviet'.

Sylvia now joined a section of Labour's left that, in forming the Communist Party, entered a political ghetto; for within a Moscow-led Communist Party they could not wield their broad influence within the labour movement of earlier years. Lenin wanted Communists to permeate Labour by helping it into power; when Labour had failed in office, Communists could take over. Pankhurst disagreed, not because of the plan's cynicism, but because she thought Marxists who collaborated with Labour would themselves be tempted into gradualism.[22] So she retreated into forming a sect within a sect, and in 1921 served five months in prison for distributing subversive propaganda.

She now thought parliament could never solve the nation's problems, and announced in 1923 that it was 'past reform and must disappear'. In 1930 she said she could have had 'a score of good fighting opportunities' as parliamentary candidate, but pioneers 'are not inclined to be pliable . . . office for its own sake makes no appeal'. Women MPs seemed no better than male MPs; there they were, obediently toeing the party line, failing to

[20] Mitchell, *Fighting Pankhursts*, pp. 98–9.
[21] Ibid., p. 55; see also p. 73. *Daily Telegraph*, 16 Apr. 1919, p. 9.
[22] E. S. Pankhurst, *Soviet Russia As I Saw It* (1921), pp. 46, 48.

deliver the great reforms anticipated from the vote. The feminist societies, orientated towards parliament, were 'diminished relics of an earlier time'. Apart from occasionally hinting that feminists now needed 'the fire which lit the pre-war militant movement', she could now advance feminist aims only as a lone operator.[23] Yet given her independence, courage, dedication, and energy, this was no great limitation, and she contributed to inter-war feminism at three levels: each of which deserves discussion: as mother, as historian, and as utopian writer.

Influential on inter-war feminist critics of the family was Victor Margueritte's novel, *The Bachelor Girl* (1922), which encouraged unmarried women to bear children; by acting on its message in 1927 Pankhurst once more hit the headlines. There is a feminist dimension to her conduct here: she wanted to share the experience of so many other women, and Richard's birth led on to her *Save the Mothers!* (1930) and her campaign for better maternity care. On sexual matters she was by no means radical all round; communal child-rearing would deny the child parental love, she thought, and no socialist could ever see birth-control as a cure for poverty. But she correctly told the press (intensely interested in Richard's birth) 'that posterity will see nothing remarkable in our decision'; rightly or wrongly, the one-parent family is now commonplace, and many now share Pankhurst's view that marriage, too intimate a matter for a legal contract, should be terminable by mutual consent rather than 'after nasty, hypocritical proceedings in the Divorce Court'.[24]

Once more she paid the price of the pioneer. Her action divided the Pankhurst family still further, placed her in what was then the small and very suspect category of unmarried mother, and hampered the second of her inter-war feminist roles—that of feminist historian. An obituarist calculated that her books and pamphlets run to 1,850,000 words, not counting her numerous press articles. Some of these books were over-long, recondite, or hastily compiled; but as historian of British feminism, Pankhurst's place is secure. Her first contribution, *The Suffragette* (1911), a history of the WSPU up to 1910, is less a history than a well-informed propagandist weapon, and nowhere presents her subsequent adult suffragist critique of suffragette policy. It strains to make its readers grasp

---

[23] Mitchell, *Fighting Pankhursts*, p. 108. *Time and Tide*, 20 Sept. 1930, p. 1177. Sylvia Pankhurst Papers: typescript headed 'The Woman's Movement of Yesterday and Tomorrow', p. 33; typescript of 1934 (carbon copy) on 'Women's Citizenship', p. 7; cf. p. 3.

[24] *News of the World* clipping early in 1928 in David Mitchell Collection 73.83/20f. For her views of birth-control, see *Woman's Dreadnought*, 8 July 1916, p. 507. My tape-recorded interview with Mrs Annie Barnes, 18 Dec. 1974, at 8 East Ham House, Loxford Avenue, London E6, clarified Sylvia's feminist motives here.

what it is like to be on hunger-strike, but unfairly depreciates the non-militants, misleadingly plays down the WFL split, and endorses Christabel's 'keen political insight and . . . indomitable courage and determination'.[25]

Her *The Suffragette Movement* (1931) is in a different class, and, like Ray Strachey's '*The Cause*', its achievement is the more impressive given the difficult circumstances of its production. She had serious dental problems at this time, she was short of money, and was severely distracted by Richard. Her plight recalls Rebecca West's rather earlier complaint: 'I . . . love being with my work . . . I *hate* being encumbered with a little boy and a nurse.' It was difficult to get sustained bursts of writing done when she was fresh. 'When he is awake I cannot abstract myself', she complained; 'he is often needing something, cries etc, and keeping an ear open and constantly running to him sets my nerves on edge'.[26] None the less she managed to write over 600 large and invaluable pages. Publishers want quick results, she complained later, and 'do not at all realise that any work which is historical, unless it is to be full of errors . . . entails a considerable amount of labour'. She paid the price of her scholarship: *The Suffragette Movement* did not sell very well. But as she said in 1934, 'I wrote the book as I felt it ought to be. I did not accept the suggestion that it should be cut down, as I felt that I was writing for posterity.'[27] Students of British feminism will long be grateful to her for that.

Ray Strachey's review of the book distinguishes between 'a historical document' and 'a contribution to history'; Pankhurst, she thinks, has provided only the raw materials of history, not history itself. This is too harsh; but the book has many defects. It is unfair to the non-militants, inflates the Pankhurst family's importance, makes no effort to comprehend the anti-suffragist position, exaggerates the importance of the East London Federation, and adopts a rather bitter tone towards its conclusion. But Strachey goes much too far in saying that 'as a contribution to history . . . it is worthless', if only because Pankhurst interprets as well as describes. By thinking herself into the minds of Liberal politicians, and by criticizing the suffragists' failure to back adult suffrage, she joins up the earlier to the later half of her suffragist career. With hindsight, she says, it

---

[25] E. S. Pankhurst, *The Suffragette* (1911), p. 96. For her productivity, see *Ethiopia Observer*, Vol. 5, No. 1, p. 25, in David Mitchell Collection, 73/83/10.

[26] G. N. Ray, *H. G. Wells and Rebecca West* (1974), p. 94. David Mitchell Collection, 73.83/21(k): Sylvia to Mrs Walshe, n.d. [probably early 1929]; cf. Mitchell, *Fighting Pankhursts*, p. 245.

[27] BL Add. MSS 56769 (Society of Authors Collection), fos. 227, 162: Sylvia Pankhurst to D. Kilham Roberts, 13 Feb. 1935, 12 June 1934.

was 'obvious that a grave mistake was made in leaving the field of adult suffrage—the true field of the Labour movement—to those who were either hostile or indifferent to the inclusion of women'.[28]

Besides, Strachey's view of history is too austere, for whereas Pankhurst's successors could correct her bias, she alone could have contributed her vivid evocation of atmosphere, her panorama of personalities, her rich account of personal experience, and even at times her fine writing; good history can as readily emerge from involvement as from detachment. 'My desire has been to introduce the actors in the drama as living beings', she writes, 'to show the striving, suffering, hugely hopeful human entity behind the pageantry, the rhetoric and the turbulence'. In this she amply succeeds, and the book fully justifies its subtitle, 'an intimate account of persons and ideals'. Not only has posterity granted her wish of 1957 for a reprint; her book has been plundered by historians ever since.[29]

Political and other distractions prevented her from contributing to feminist history again on this scale. Her account of the East End during the First World War, *The Home Front* (1932), is more a compilation than a history, and her businesslike *Emmeline Pankhurst* (1935) has no new insights to offer. In later years she even obstructed historical writing by frequently threatening lawsuits instead of remaining quietly confident that the truth would emerge if left to make its own way. Among her victims were Ray Strachey, who had to modify her view of WSPU finance in '*The Cause*'; Vera Brittain, whose *Lady into Woman* allegedly made similar mistakes; and Roger Fulford, whose 'hideous distortions' in 'that horrible book' *Votes for Women* were excoriated in several angrily scrawled air-mail letters dispatched from Ethiopia to a long-suffering Fred Pethick-Lawrence in 1957.[30] Proposing a book on the Pankhurst family in 1961, Brittain rightly told Gollancz that 'there is much family material that is both humorous and ironic as well as tragic', but no such book could be written, she said, while Sylvia was alive, 'owing to her well-known litigious tendencies'.[31]

---

[28] *Woman's Leader*, 20 Feb. 1931, p. 19. E. S. Pankhurst, *Suffragette Movement*, p. 203; cf. pp. 205, 303–4.

[29] E. S. Pankhurst, *Suffragette Movement*, p. vii. Trinity College, Cambridge: Pethick-Lawrence Papers, Box 9, fo. 72: Sylvia Pankhurst to F. Pethick-Lawrence, n.d. [postmarked 25 June 1957].

[30] Pethick-Lawrence Papers, Box 9, fos. 71–2: same to same, n.d. [postmarked 24 June 1957]; n.d. [postmarked 25 June 1957]. See also Mitchell, *Fighting Pankhursts*, p. 244. Vera Brittain Collection: E. Pethick-Lawrence to Brittain, n.d. [end Jan. 1954].

[31] Brittain Collection: Brittain to V. Gollancz, 7 May 1961 (carbon copy).

Self-excluded from practical politics in the late 1920s and 1930s, Sylvia's utopian dreams could now be realized only in writing, on page after page of typescript. 'Drudge and drill! Drudge and drill!' her father had urged: 'if you do not work for other people you will not have been worth the upbringing!' Throughout her life she could work through the night when required, and Richard remembers often waking in the morning as a child to find her still at work in her study, meeting some printer's urgent deadline. The utopian thoughts rattling off her typewriter contrast strangely with the rather squalid untidiness of West Dene, Charteris Road, Woodford Green whence they came—with its wilderness of a garden, its disordered books and papers, and its lentil diet ('and oh, they did give her wind', Mrs Drake, who helped out, recalled).[32]

Her papers, now collected in Amsterdam, reflect an incessant and restless energy which begins many projects but completes few. They combine utopian socialism with a markedly individualist (not to say sectarian) reforming zeal, and with a recurrently optimistic small-scale entrepreneurship; her teashops, journalism, and publishing ventures reflect her desperate search for funds. She prepares multifarious articles, drawings, and poems for a wide range of causes, and all breathe that fierce commitment to truth and justice which plunges their author into one scrape after another. 'Oh my dear, why am I always in trouble?' she asks Norah Smyth when beset by a libel action; 'what hideous fate draws me to difficulty as surely as the sun rises?'[33]

Her books and articles frequently end on a note of utopian uplift; the peroration to *Delphos* [1927], her book on an international language, envisages 'a people cultured and kind, and civilized beyond to-day's conception, speaking a common language, bound by common interests, when the wars of class and of nations shall be no more'.[34] No troublesome party conflict disturbs her utopia, 'and contested elections with all their vulgar clap-trap, will be forgotten'. A Cobdenite complementarity between nations produces both peace and abundance, and there is an end to occupations parasitic on inequality, conflict, and competition: banking, advertising, debt-collecting. Universal co-operation at last releases the massive pent-up potential for abundance, wealth is distributed more fairly

[32] Mitchell, *Fighting Pankhursts*, p. 40. See also R. Pankhurst, *Sylvia Pankhurst. Artist and Crusader* (1979), p. 118. David Mitchell Collection, 73.83/42: Mitchell's interview with Mrs Charlotte Drake.

[33] Mitchell, *Fighting Pankhursts*, p. 248.

[34] E. S. Pankhurst, *Delphos. The Future of International Language* [1927], pp. 94–5; cf. the peroration to her *Home Front*, p. 447.

between the classes and sexes, and artificial distinctions of rank disappear. Cruel sports and time-wasting popular recreations like football fade away before artistic achievement, which becomes the highest pleasure.[35]

Communal housekeeping and vision of labour among women enable each utopian woman to realize her full potential, and housework becomes professionalized. Architects design houses for efficiency, with rounded corners and walls without cracks, and so reduce domestic chores; 'the hearth brush and dish cloth', she says, 'will disappear'. The utopian all-electric home receives its prepared meals from the communal kitchen, but contains waste-disposal units, washable table-tops, paper plates, and dishwashing machines. Scientific and simpler diet, a national medical staff, improved maternity services, swimming baths, gymnasia, and gorgeous flower gardens eliminate the doctor. Cosmetics, starched collars, boned corsets, and padded shoulders are cast away, fashion ceases to rule, and beauty animates dress 'as in the days of Ancient Greece'. 'My Utopians will step from flashing white buildings into green gardens,' she enthuses; 'their dwellings shall be open to the sun and air.'[36]

In some ways her feminist dreams are modest: communal child-rearing and birth-control play no role; women's emancipation comes through mechanization, not through male enlightenment; and domestic chores succumb, not to the house husband, but to the professionalized domestic servant and the domestic gadget. Her utopia is an odd mixture—at once seductively sybaritical and repugnantly puritanical, more alert than much inter-war feminist writing to the social impact of technical change, but self-indulgent in so far as it dwells on the need for political harmony without explaining how to get there. Utopia has become more a creed than a destination: 'I believe as firmly as in my youth', she says at the end of her childhood recollections, 'that humanity will surmount the era of poverty and war . . . I believe in *the Golden Age*.'[37]

She was soon diverted from these dreams to Ethiopia by her crusade against Fascism, in which Richard's father Silvio Corio was deeply involved. Ethiopia became the theme of the very long letters she wrote in green ink to the Ministry of Information during the Second World War.

---

[35] Sylvia Pankhurst Papers: typescript on 'The World I Want' (n.d.), p. 6; see also pp. 2–3.

[36] Ibid.: carbon-copy of typescript entitled 'What I Think the Future Holds for Women', p. 4; 'The World I Want', pp.1–2.

[37] Ibid.: 'The World I Want', pp. 1–2. E. S. Pankhurst in Asquith (ed.), *Myself When Young*, p. 312. See also Sylvia Pankhurst Papers: typescript headed 'The Woman's Movement of Yesterday and Tomorrow', pp. 38–40; carbon-copy of typescript on 'Ideal Homes Must Replace the Slums', pp. 5–7.

She went there twice—in 1943–4 and 1951–2—and settled there permanently in 1956. She was a distinguished resident. After all, she had befriended the Emperor when his supporters were few, and was a friend of his daughter; she also valuably publicized Ethiopia overseas as editor of the *New Times and Ethiopia News* from 1936 to 1956, and as author of her huge privately financed *Ethiopia. A Cultural History*; she was therefore given the privilege of retiring from the Emperor's presence without bowing or walking backwards.[38] Her house in Ethiopia was more a workshop than a home; there she wrote well over 500,000 words for the *Ethiopia Observer*, which she edited till her death. The paper, which Sylvia ran with Richard's help, dominated everything. Her life centred on her cluttered study, with its huge desk in the middle and books on Ethiopia all round the walls; her bedroom, austerely utilitarian, was used only for sleeping. Social life revolved around work. 'I don't think the concept of holiday exists . . .', Richard's wife Rita recalls of these years; 'work is a pleasure'. Her luxuries included only the fountain pens 'which she wore out almost as though they were pencils', the poetry that she continued to read and write to the end of her life, and the sight of her beloved eucalyptus trees and maskal daisies.[39]

There was little time for reminiscence or even for feminism. Rita assumed the woman's traditional role of running the household; Sylvia, too, perhaps partly because she was a guest in Ethiopia, fitted in with a traditionalist separation of sexual spheres. She kept clear of Ethiopian politics, refrained from political feminism, and confined her public activity to writing and philanthropy. She did occasionally write home on feminist history, contemplated publishing a biography of her father as 'an historical and filial duty' at her own expense, and thought of writing her own memoirs—but she died too soon.[40]

Although her digestion was not good, she showed remarkable stamina right to the end. Richard and Rita once tried to dissuade her from making and eight-hour landrover journey across rough country to a remote community centre; 'she turned and said "do you think I have come to the end of my active life?"', made the journey, and returned the next day little the worse for wear. In 1960 she thought of accompanying Richard and

---

[38] David Mitchell Collection, 73.83/17f: Mitchell's notes of interview with H. G. Molesworth. Mitchell, *Fighting Pankhursts*, p. 319.

[39] This account of Sylvia's final years owes much to my tape-recorded interview with Mrs Rita Pankhurst, 2 Feb. 1982, at 22 Lawn Road, London NW3. For the pens, see *Ethiopia Observer*, Vol. 5, No. 1, p. 43.

[40] Pethick-Lawrence Papers, Box 9, fo. 78 (2): Sylvia Pankhurst to F. Pethick-Lawrence, n.d. [end. 'early July 1959']; cf. fos. 82–3.

Rita on a weekend trip but eventually decided to stay at home; they returned to find her dead. Ethiopia was perhaps an appropriate place for her death, for there she brought off her most constructive achievement and witnessed her most satisfying victory. The women's victory had been only partial, and, as she put it, 'there was not a sufficiently large intelligent, progressive and active movement to make it as effective as one would desire'.[41]

As left-wing sympathizers with the WSPU, Pankhurst and Harben inevitably crossed paths. Harben helped to finance the East London Federation early in 1914,[42] and we have already seen how his impetuosity helped to wreck her negotiations with Lloyd George in June. Otherwise they shared only their utopianism, for on politics and personal conduct they diverged widely. Henry was grandson of Sir Henry Harben, president of the Prudential. Its chairman, Henry's father, was H. A. Harben, a gentle man, an artist and scientist, with a laboratory in his home at Newland Park, Buckinghamshire. Born in 1874, Henry seems to have been a charming but mischievous child, highly strung and subject to eczema; as eldest son of the eldest son he was led to think he could do no wrong. Educated at Eton, he represented the school at racquets and then went to Magdalen College, Oxford, where he read classics. He then studied philosophy at a German university, then law in Italy. At fifteen he had first been struck with the beauty of Agnes Bostock, six years younger than himself, and in 1899 he married her against her parents' wishes.

As a young man Harben embarked on several careers but persisted with none. The first was politics, where within twenty years he moved from right to far left. His first contest was as Conservative candidate in 1900 at Eye, a constituency which returned a Liberal continuously from 1885 to 1910; he vigorously defended the Conservative government but was soundly defeated. By November 1902 he was dining with the Webbs as 'a promising young Liberal Leaguer'.[43] When he contested Worcester as a Liberal in 1906 his Conservative rivals claimed that 'he fought in Suffolk and lost an Eye, and has since seen differently'. He attributed his conversion to realizing, as manager of schools in the East End of London, that the real problems lay at home rather than in the empire.[44] His

[41] Interview with Mrs Rita Pankhurst, 2 Feb. 1982. David Mitchell Collection, 73.83/21(i): Sylvia Pankhurst to Billington-Greig, 5 June 1956.

[42] BL Add. MSS 58226 (Harben Papers), fo. 96: typescript cyclo-styled letter from Sylvia Pankhurst to Harben, 2 Feb. 1914 causes him to give £150.

[43] B. Webb, *Our Partnership* ed. B. Drake and M. I. Cole (1948), p. 250.

[44] *Worcestershire Echo*, 11 Jan. 1906, p. 4. See also *Hampshire Telegraph*, 25 Nov. 1910, p. 3.

PLATE 11. Henry Harben and his first wife Agnes at the wedding of their granddaughter Gillian, Warnham Church, Sussex, 23 April 1955 (Mrs Naomi Lutyens).

campaign at Worcester was energetic and resourceful, and aroused great local enthusiasm. Agnes Harben sang the first verse of Annie Laurie at the start of one of his meetings, and the day before the poll there was 'loud and prolonged cheering' when he declared that 'if you vote for me tomorrow, when I get to Parliament, by Jove! I'll fight for you'. He then stood on a chair and recited the verse:

> For Freedom's battle once begun,
> Bequeathed from bleeding sire to son,
> Though baffled oft is ever won.[45]

Conservatives held the seat continuously between 1885 and 1910, but in 1906 Harben came within 130 votes of victory.

His Conservative rival was subsequently unseated for corruption, but a Conservative won the seat again in 1908. Meanwhile Harben was still moving left; he resigned from the Liberal League in 1907, claiming in this to be more consistent than Rosebery, its increasingly centrist chairman. In his letter of resignation his favourite theme once more appears: 'liberty is on the march at last; and no man, no group, no party in this country can stay its course for long.'[46] Harben had devilled for Travers Humphreys, but identified too closely with his clients to make a good barrister, and broke down; he was too conscious of the environmental pressures on impoverished offenders, and so practised at the Bar only between 1906 and 1910.[47] He compiled statistics for the poor law commission, sat on the Fabian Society executive from 1911 to 1920, and stood for his next constituency, Portsmouth, at the general election of December 1910. He did quite well, but the Conservatives held the seat.

Harben was no mere talker: philanthropy was in the family, for his paternal grandfather had given generously to hospitals, libraries, parks, mission work, and the blind in the London area. In running his 600-acre estate at Newland Park Harben tried to act on his principles: he paid his agricultural labourers above-average wages, provided cheap milk, and set up a lavish self-governing club-house with ample recreations. He was a prominent local figure—a short, stocky man who hunted with the Old Berkeley Foxhounds and played cricket for Buckinghamshire. He was also

---

[45] *Worcestershire Echo*, 17 Jan. 1906, pp. 2, 4.

[46] Letter dated 16 Aug. 1907 in unidentified newspaper cutting in a scrapbook about Harben owned by Mr and Mrs Hall, 44 Crowland Avenue, Hayes, Middx.

[47] All information about Harben that is not footnoted comes from the author's tape-recorded interviews with Harben's daughters, Mrs Molly Northey, 23 June 1976, at 3 Camellia Court, New St John's Road, St Helier, Jersey, and Mrs Naomi Lutyens, on 28 Mar. and 10 Apr. 1975, at 12 Rowland Close, Wolvercote, Oxford.

a JP and a lifelong freemason. He was not at first an active suffragist, and the proposals in his Fabian Society pamphlet of 1910 for family endowment are modest—about two months' wages for the mother while child-bearing—and are not cast in feminist terms.[48] But in 1912 he suddenly became a key supporter of the WSPU, paying several visits to Christabel in Paris, and providing both money and legal advice.

With his fourth candidature, at the Barnstaple by-election in 1912, he moved still further left. Adopted in February, he offended local Liberals in June by publicly condemning Asquith's handling of hunger-striking suffragettes and accusing him of 'moral incompetence to deal with the problem'. Lansbury's parliamentary protest in June against forcible feeding led Harben to tell him 'you're the only man with decent feelings in the House; and I honour you'. The previous day, he said, he'd decided to 'chuck' his candidature; the government had thrown away their 'glorious opportunity to do big things for the people'. 'I burn with impotence', he wrote, 'and long to be in Parliament: but I can't pretend to support any of the present blighters.' His sudden withdrawal in July before the poll—assuring the local party chairman that 'this policy of pusillanimous persecution is not my idea of Liberalism'—surprised local Liberals, though the local press thought it would not disappoint those who disliked his socialistic views. 'He has been a political chameleon,' wrote the *North Devon Herald*, 'assuming the colours of all the parties in turn. And in each instance he has only followed his convictions, the fact of the matter being that Mr Harben is a sentimentalist, not a politician.'[49]

Like many male champions of the suffragettes in their most militant phase, Harben's motives seem to have been as much sporting and chivalrous as feminist; when resigning at Barnstaple, he pronounced forcible feeding 'unmanly, ungentlemanly, unsportsmanlike, and uncivilised'. Conspicuously chivalrous towards women throughout his life, in the 1950s he could still quietly rebuke a woman guest at a restaurant for addressing the waiter directly instead of making her request through him.[50] Yet Edwardian feminists were beginning to see such chivalry as patronizing or even contemptuous towards women and in his private life, as we shall see, Harben's conduct was far from feminist.

[48] *London Budget*, 7 Dec. 1913, p. 5. Harben, 'The Endowment of Motherhood', p. 13.
[49] *North Devon Herald*, 4 July 1912, p. 1; cf. *Western Daily Mercury*, 6 July 1912, p. 12. London School of Economics, Lansbury Papers, vol. 5: Harben to Lansbury, 26 June 1912. [Exeter] *Express and Echo*, 8 July 1912, p. 7 (resignation letter). *North Devon Herald*, 11 July 1912, p. 13. See also *Devon and Exeter Gazette*, 6 July 1912, p. 5; *Western Morning News*, 6 July 1912, p. 3.
[50] [Exeter] *Express and Echo*, 8 July 1912, p. 7. Private information.

His money was useful to the WSPU, and he was prominent in its ally, the Men's Political Union. He was now close to Lansbury, and in 1912 joined the board of the *Daily Herald*. In November, when Lansbury resigned from parliament on the women's suffrage issue to stand for re-election at Bromley and Bow, Harben dispatched several large hampers of delicious food for the suffragette campaigners; and when Mrs Pankhurst wanted men to help finance the WSPU in December, Harben was among those approached.[51] In February 1913 he was ejected from the House of Commons gallery for protesting against forcible feeding, whose legality he challenged. But Nevinson doubted his consistency, noting in his diary in April that 'Harben after vowing to do all wonderful things . . . had forgotten all and gone for months to France'; in May Harben told Lansbury that he would stay in Paris (which he loved) till July so as to avoid arrest for assisting the WSPU periodical *The Suffragette;* 'one may as well have a good holiday', he wrote, 'if one is in for trouble'. 'Harben is flighty', wrote Nevinson in July, 'and domineers on strength of money.'[52]

Throughout all this, Harben was fully backed by Agnes—in Nevinson's words, 'so sweet and lovely'—who wore protective corrugated cardboard wrapping when on militant demonstrations, chained herself to a railing, and fought off the police in the hope of shielding him against arrest while speaking in Trafalgar Square. Newland Park became a refuge for released hunger-strikers, and C. E. M. Joad recalled the embarrassment of county visitors when they found 'haggard-looking young women in dressing-gowns and djibbahs reclining on sofas in the Newland[s] drawing-room talking unashamedly about their prison experiences'.[53]

In October Harben did his best behind the scenes to defend Mary Richardson, who was being forcibly fed in prison, and in November he 'spoke warmly' against government policy on suffragette prisoners when male suffragists questioned Lloyd George at Oxford. But he was becoming critical of Christabel's strategy, and was impressed in November when Sylvia linked up the suffragist and labour unrest at the Albert Hall meeting, though he realized that the labour movement was not yet strongly feminist.[54] Early in 1914 he wrote Christabel a dignified,

[51] David Mitchell Collection, 73.83/52: Mitchell's interview with Grace Roe, 22 Sept. 1965. BL Add. MSS 58226 (Harben Papers), fo. 6: Emmeline Pankhurst to Harben, 20 Dec. 1912.
[52] Nevinson Diary, 22 Apr. and 30 July 1913. Lansbury Papers, vol. 7, fo. 33: Harben to Lansbury, 6 May [1913].
[53] Nevinson Diary, 16 Mar. 1918. C. E. M. Joad, *Under the Fifth Rib* (1932), p. 41.
[54] *Oxford Chronicle*, 28 Nov. 1913, p. 4. BL Add. MSS 58226 (Harben Papers), fos. 57–9: Harben to C. Pankhurst, 5 Nov. 1913 (copy of typescript); for Richardson, see fos. 52–5: Harben to Mr Poole.

sympathetic, and powerful critique of her strategy; the WSPU would have succeeded better if other sympathizers had done the same. She was losing some of her best followers, he said, and was being kept ignorant of WSPU affairs. It was a friend's duty to warn her; 'I have felt myself wholly out of sympathy with some of the things which you have done, and which have made the blood of some of my friends boil,' he said; '. . . I am rapidly coming to the conclusion that I can only maintain any semblance of loyalty by keeping out of things altogether, and being silent.'[55]

In February he told Victor Duval, a fellow member of the Men's Political Union, that although he would remain as Treasurer for long enough to sign an appeal for funds, he disliked WSPU sectarianism and intended to go freelance for a time. Later in the month he was arrested with Nevinson and others for demonstrating at Westminster, and in Nevinson's diary we find him in a cell—together with Nevinson and Laurence Housman—'conversing and recounting with much laughter'; many years later Harben was to display a framed copy of his summons to Bow Street on his dining-room wall.[56] In 1912 the Pethick-Lawrences were expelled from the WSPU and formed the less militant United Suffragists; Harben does not seem to have joined, and apparently tried to prevent it from diverging too far from the WSPU, but his wife joined its original committee.[57] In June Harben was under threat of government prosecution for subscribing to suffragette funds, but his suffragist career was now drawing to its close. Nevinson vividly portrays its Indian Summer at a Newland Park fête in July—with about a thousand people consuming tea and witnessing Morris dancing, suffrage speeches, and sideshows of prison cells; Harben's wealth, he writes, 'is splendidly used'.[58]

Harben's *Daily Herald* connections and his perpetual quest for novelty were moving him still further left. It was not yet at all obvious that Labour would become an independent party or that the Liberal Party would break up, but he now began voting against Liberal candidates at elections. His political views made a Prudential post impossible for him, and his brother Guy occupied the role of deputy chairman that could have been his. His Labour interests reinforced his lifelong taste for presiding over people

[55] BL Add. MSS 58226 (Harben MSS), fo. 105: Harben to C. Pankhurst, n.d. [Pankhurst's reply is dated 15 Feb. 1914].

[56] Nevinson Diary, 25 Feb. 1914. See also Harben MSS, fo. 99: Harben to Duval, 11 Feb. 1914. For the framed summons, author's tape-recorded interview with Mr and Mrs Hall, 7 Oct. 1975, at 44 Crowland Avenue, Hayes, Middx.

[57] *Votes for Women*, 6 Feb. 1914, p. 281. Nevinson Diary, 16 July 1914.

[58] Nevinson Diary, 4 July 1914.

socially less elevated than himself. This involved him in some notable ironies, if only because servants abounded at Newland Park; 'I mean, you just *rang the bell*', his daughter Naomi recalls, 'and things happened'. Her elder sister Molly recalled the strangeness of a man who could angrily ring for the valet before dinner because the studs had not been put in his shirt, yet hold forth over the meal within the man's earshot about his belief in human equality. Beatrice Webb thought the same when she visited Harben in 1919, and was given 'too delectable food and wine for our ascetic digestion': 'His socialist opinions seem oddly out of place unless we regard them, like the pledge of the drunkard, as a hope of some way of curbing from outside his self-indulgent propensities.'[59]

It was Lady de la Warr who brought Harben into contact with the Lansbury circle; she shared his interest in hunting and theosophy, for Harben was chairman of the London Vedanta Society. He spent his own money to get the paper on a secure financial footing, yet refused to influence editorial policy; only Rebecca West's pregnancy prevented him from recruiting her as editor. He was also one of the four who contributed the initial total of £5,000 that was needed to set up the *New Statesman* in 1913.[60] His leftward tendency at this time emerges from comparing his heavily empirical and moderate *The Rural Problem* (1913) with his *Labour and the Land* (1921), which wants the game laws abolished, farmers and labourers equally represented on County Agricultural Committees, and the land nationalized. In 1920 he stood as a Labour candidate at Suffolk (Woodbridge), continuously Conservative between 1918 and 1945, and put up a good fight, but his 47 per cent of the votes cast was not enough to get him in. Parliamentarism was henceforth not for him.

In the First World War Harben was distressed when his eyesight ruled him out for military service; in April 1915 Nevinson found him 'restless and distraught, very spendthrift'.[61] He bought the Hotel Majestic in Paris for conversion into an English hospital, and when the Red Cross took it over he set up a rest-camp behind the lines at Étaples and a rehabilitation centre at Rouen. He also worked for MI5 in the Paris passport office, and there he met 'Baby'. At this point his private relationships with individual women become more interesting, for the purposes of this book, than his public defence of their sex, and henceforth move to the centre of the stage.

---

[59] B. Webb, *Diary*, iii (1984), p. 342. For Harben's voting habits see *Votes for Women*, 27 Feb. 1914, p. 328.

[60] Lansbury Papers, vol. 28, ii, fos. 2–4: Harben's confidential memo, 13 Nov. 1948. M. Cole, *The Story of Fabian Socialism* (1961), p. 156.

[61] Nevinson Diary, 25 Apr. 1915.

Chivalry is a consistent theme throughout his life, but whereas earlier it led him boldly to champion the emancipation of women in general, now it led him to cramp the horizons of the individual women with whom he chose to live.

As a young man he had been bowled over by Agnes's striking looks; he was an intensely emotional person, who readily shed tears at a beautiful sight, a moving poem, or a romantic song. Agnes kept his home beautifully, was an excellent mother to his two sons and three daughters, and remained in love with him till she died. But they had little else in common, and she was no match for him intellectually; she soon entered Harben's large category of people, sometimes including his own children, who were dismissed with the phrase 'third-rate mentality'. Family disputes soon caused trouble. Harben was vain, and liked his wife and daughters to be praised, but primarily as adjuncts of himself. He would command silence so that the precocious Naomi could be heard, yet there were scenes at mealtimes when his eldest son dared to defend Black-and-Tan actions in Ireland—Harben 'holding himself in, dilating his nostrils'. He was a hard man, and his daughter Molly recalled his impatience with anyone ill or lacking in courage; he forced his twelve-year-old daughter Naomi who had fallen from her horse and broken her collar-bone to remount at once, before receiving treatment, so as not to lose confidence.

Henry's recurrent crazes—for sport, health and dietary fads or odd cults—made things particularly difficult for Agnes; once he had mastered them he lost interest, and moved on. For tax reasons he sold Newland Park in 1921, and then suddenly deserted his wife and five children, making no provision for their welfare. 'He went off in the removals van,' Naomi recalls, 'sitting in the arm chair, smoking his cigar and reading the paper'. During her visit to Newland Park, Beatrice Webb had sensed that 'the life is clearly not a happy one for the wife', and on getting wind of the breakup she seized the opportunity to moralize about the effects of wealth when combined with 'following anarchic impulse': she recalled similar troubles among other young pre-war progressive intellectuals they had known. Harben seems simply to have forgotten to make financial provision for his family, who could not locate him for several weeks. He now saw them as fetters on his prized freedom; as he told Naomi, when urging her in 1939 not to allow children by an earlier marriage to prevent her from remarrying, 'the longer I live, the more I learn that freedom is all that matters'.[62]

[62] B. Webb, *Letters*, iii. 342, 400–1. Harben MSS owned by Mrs Lutyens: Harben to Naomi, 17 June 1939.

As so often, he refused to face unpleasant facts. 'You're not my daughter if you can't stand on your own feet,' he told Molly when she begged him to help the family. He treated his children equally, and encouraged them to look after themselves, perhaps partly because this was the quickest way to free his mind of them. None of his five children married happily the first time round, two of the daughters and one son were divorced, and one daughter committed suicide. Agnes henceforth devoted herself completely to her children, not divorcing Henry for fear of disinheriting them, and always hoping that he might one day return. Though he took her to the theatre once a year, he never came back.

Yet this is not the whole story, for Harben struck everyone as a charming man, a wonderful conversationalist, striking in dress and manner, generous, and full of boyish enthusiasm and energy; when golfing he would run from green to tee, and when driving a car he would simultaneously address his passengers in the back seat. He composed music for his daughter's ballets, and wrote the words and music for the plays produced by his younger son. 'Life with Daddy could not be anything but exciting,' Naomi recalled; '. . . anybody who was with him would always come away absolutely entranced by the brilliance of his mind, by the *fun* we all had . . . he was a *magnetic* personality.'

Within about three years Harben had decided that Miss Muloch, or 'Baby' as he called her, could make him happier than anyone else. Nobody knew where she came from. She had been a housekeeper in Liverpool, but when she first met Harben in Paris she was a nurse, and told him she had fled there because her Catholic faith was at risk from a Protestant suitor; she later made much of her family's alleged Irish landed connections. She was no intellectual—indeed, intellectuals found her conversation acutely embarrassing—but some saw her as astutely promoting her own interests. It seems to have been a father-daughter relationship, at least initially— perhaps always—and at first Baby enlarged upon her virginity. She called Harben 'Daddy', after the tall benevolent hero of the stage-play *Daddy Long Legs* and surrounded herself with religious accoutrements; 'you see, Daddy is Jesus Christ and I'm his Mary Magdalene,' Naomi once heard her say. Daddy and Baby had mysticism in common, for Harben was very interested in theosophy and wished Eastern philosophy was more widely understood. He consulted an astrologer on the timing of his prostate operation in 1937, and told a friend in the 1950s that he could levitate but thought it too dangerous to indulge.

Baby appealed to his romantic idealism, to his chivalrous protectiveness towards women, and his thirst for adulation. It was 'the breath of life to him', said Molly, to be at the centre of the picture and to be continually admired. When he had entered a room with Agnes, all eyes fixed upon her, but when entering a room with Baby, all eyes fixed upon him. Baby was a small person, and would sit in her small chair behind his large one, holding hands; she pleased him by repeating, as her own, remarks that he himself had made earlier but had since forgotten. She was assiduous in caring for him, but from the 1920s onwards friends and acquaintances gossiped about the precise nature of their relationship, incredulous that Harben could possibly fall for her embarrassing saintliness.

One of the gossips was Aldous Huxley, who portrays the relationship in his short story 'Chawdron' in *Brief Candles* (1930). Chawdron, nicknamed 'Nunky' in the story, is Harben; Maggie Spindell, nicknamed 'Fairy' in the story, is Miss Muloch. 'When she paraded the canonized kitten,' says the narrator, 'I felt sea-sick; but Chawdron thought she had the most be-yutiful character he'd ever met with in a human being.'[63] When Nunky and Fairy disagree, Fairy gets Nunky to resume his protective role by becoming ill. The denouement of the story describes how Chawdron, temporarily separated from Fairy, develops a boil on his foot, and later discovers from Fairy that she too has quite independently and simultaneously developed a similar blemish in exactly the same place. Huxley was only fictionalizing the stigmata that Daddy and Baby had reported to their friends, though these reports ceased after Huxley had published the story. Truth was, in this instance, stranger than fiction because whereas Nunky's infatuation was perhaps credible in Huxley's uneducated self-made presbyterian former businessman, it was incongruous in Daddy, the cultivated intellectual.

Brief Candles did not prevent Harben from presenting Huxley's *Brave New World* (1932) to Baby with the inscription 'for my dear Baby, with love from her Daddy' on 5 May 1932.[64] None the less most of his intellectual friends disliked Baby's company, and (whether intentionally or not) she distanced Harben from his children. Naomi, who in effect conducted an unobtrusive but sustained and ultimately unsuccessful struggle with Baby for her father's affection, found that whenever they met, Baby was there to prevent her from having a good talk with him. The family, in turn, partly from loyalty to Agnes, did not invite Baby to any family functions. Baby may even lie behind Harben's reluctance to speak to his children about their marital problems, though he eagerly fraternized with their estranged spouses. He 'could always put himself in somebody

<hr />

[63] Aldous Huxley, 'Chawdron', in his *Brief Candles* (1930), p. 37.
[64] This copy was owned by Mr and Mrs Hall when I saw it on 7 Oct. 1975.

else's shoes', Naomi told me, 'as long as it wasn't one of his own children'. Was Baby a hypocrite? Writing of Fairy, Huxley says that 'most hypocrites are more or less unconscious hypocrites. The Fairy, I'm sure, was one of them. She was simply not aware of being an adventuress with an eye on Chawdron's millions.'[65]

Daddy and Baby lived well in Paris between the wars. It was Harben, after all, who had taught C. E. M. Joad the importance of good food when dining at Kettner's in London in autumn 1914.[66] There was a brief essay in fiction with Harben's *Love Letters to a Dead Woman* (1923), but it was another of his false starts; for him, life was so much better than fiction. There were exotic places to visit, for instance; Harben was a connoisseur of wines and food, a walking Baedeker of European works of art, a past master in knowing how to behave in any social situation. Whenever Molly dined out with him, she always found a box of her favourite cigarettes set beside her place.

His political views seemed less and less compatible with his life-style. The heroes on the walls of his study in Paris were Cromwell, Wagner, Shaw, and Lenin. His links with Soviet Russia had begun as early as 1905, when he helped finance the coal ship chartered for Archangel which took off some of the Russian popular leaders; much to his surprise, the Russians made an unsolicited repayment to him in Paris after 1917.[67] During his visit to Russia in 1930, recorded for friends in his privately printed travel-diary, he found that rationing and curbs on luxuries made corruption 'practically impossible under the Soviets to-day', that workers' own committees prescribed working conditions, and that the Soviet economic growth-rate was increasing 'at a rate that is almost stupefying'. He wisely postponed writing about the Soviet political police until he'd crossed the frontier, and admitted that it was 'a blot on civilisation'. But similar institutions existed in countries like Italy and India, he said; the Russian police had at least been appointed by a popular regime. He thought the USSR so stable that only military defeat would overthrow it, and if the Russians succeeded it would be 'only a question of time for the rest of Europe to follow their example'.[68]

Harben's disillusion with British inter-war politics was complete. An observer rather more recently disaffected was Beatrice Webb, who with

[65] Huxley, *Brief Candles,* p. 37.
[66] Joad, *Fifth Rib,* p. 41.
[67] Harben's 7-page typescript on his links with Russia was consulted on 7 Oct. 1975 when in the possession of Mr and Mrs Hall.
[68] H. D. Harben, *A Diary written during a Visit to Russia in September and October 1930* (privately printed, 1930), pp. 96, 91, 92.

Sidney published the sympathetic *Soviet Communism* in 1935, and who described Harben's frame of mind in 1937, the year he inherited a million pounds from an aged aunt: 'he is extreme left, a devoted admirer of the USSR and incidentally of our book. As of old he is an agreeable cultivated man, talks loudly and well; reads all the newest books in three or four languages and travels extensively, picking up on the way the news of the world with avidity.' Even in 1964 MacDonald's conduct in 1931 could evoke Harben's indignation: his face 'flushed and he began to tremble with rage'. In December 1938 he denounced Neville Chamberlain, who was visiting Mussolini, for 'running around and slobbering to dictators'. Harben helped many Jews to get out of Hitler's Germany, and himself returned to England on one of the last boats back in 1939.[69] From his comfortable flat in Cavendish Square during the Second World War he promoted Citizens' Advice Bureaux in the East End, and came to admire the local people. But the Attlee government, and especially Bevin, disappointed him after 1945 for missing its socialist opportunities.

Distributing largess to so many grateful recipients, contrasting markedly in his spruce clothing with the company he kept, filling his Christmas card list with major figures on the British left, he and Baby always gathered a group around them at post-war left-wing gatherings. Well-tipped porters and regularly patronized shop-assistants were eager to serve them. Their opulent flat—the sort with mirrors behind ornaments in recesses—housed 10,000 books, many of them expensively bound and hand-illustrated in water colours. The flat quite often became the venue for high-level talks; for instance, J. F. F. Platts-Mills remembered a feast there for representatives of the newly Communist Cuba to meet ambassadors from Eastern Europe.[70] Harben, a friend of the British Communist leader Harry Pollitt, was convinced that the Communist countries were growing faster than the West, and although he never joined the Communist Party he justified his opulent way of living to himself by making large donations to it.

He was generous to the point of gullibility—not only to his left-wing friends, but also to employees and offspring requesting loans, poor parents hoping to educate their gifted children, tired people needing a holiday, and even complete strangers like the Morsons. This young couple felt they were being deliberately 'taken up' by him in the early 1950s; they first met

[69] B. Webb, *Diary*, iv. 389. Author's collection: David Mitchell to author, 4 June 1975. Harben MSS owned by Mrs Lutyens: Harben to Naomi, 10 Dec. 1938.

[70] Author's tape-recorded interview with J. F. F. and Mrs Platts-Mills, 16 Dec. 1976, at the Barbican.

him casually in the sort of inexpensive French hotel which alone could be afforded by British visitors in the days of tight exchange regulation. They vividly remembered their first glimpse of Harben in the restaurant, 'terribly English', upright and distinguished-looking with a rather loud voice, old-fashioned courtesy, and flamboyant gestures. He was always dressed for the part—Eton tie, pale-coloured thin suit for the summer, brown country suit when out of town—and enjoyed drawing attention to himself in public places.[71] Naomi recalls a hush descending on the foyer of the Haymarket Theatre when, on emerging from *The Second Mrs Tanqueray*, he said 'of course it's *dated;* I mean if everybody who had a mistress had to feel they had to commit suicide, why, the streets of London would be strewn with corpses'.

Baby was always in tow, well groomed and well dressed in black velvet, with Parisian handbags and a diamond or two, moving with small, rather mouselike steps. She fed Harben with cues for his best stories and laughed at only his jokes, but she was brushed aside if she ventured further, and stayed in the background. For Harben was a splendid and much-travelled conversationalist and raconteur who laughed at his own rather wicked or *risqué* stories, anecdotes, and reminiscences; he seemed always to have been present when interesting things happened. Indeed, the second of his travel books—*Japan and Back* (1936), a travel-diary of a journey with Baby in 1935–6—was not written for publication, but was printed, according to its preface, 'at the request of many friends'. Harben loved dining out and fed on human company, yet was a good listener, a master at giving his guests a good time, and gave the impression of being intensely interested in them. Russia was the one topic the Morsons avoided, because he did not seem open to reason on the subject, though he never tried to convert them. There was something decidedly odd about a revolutionary who attached such great importance to the minutiae of social etiquette.

Harben introduced Baby to the Morsons as his adopted daughter, and Pam Morson insists that she was never really anything more than that. They addressed her as 'Miss Muloch' and puzzled endlessly, like so many others, about what it all meant; as she recalled of the Harbens twenty-five years later, 'they were very bizarre'. The Morsons accepted Harben's invitations not only because they knew they would enjoy themselves, but 'because one hoped one would find the key to the mystery'. Towards the end of Harben's life, Baby rose in stature to become the polished hostess;

---

[71] Author's tape-recorded interview with Dr Basil and Mrs Morson, 13 May 1975, at the Hurlingham Club.

she no longer posed as the helpless orphan, though her sentimentality remained a constant social hazard; as Pam Morson puts it, 'sometimes you really felt like saying something really outrageous'. To the end, there were always two minds on whether Baby's devotion was genuinely fond or cleverly self-interested.

Towards the end of his life Harben prided himself on a personal regime whose self-discipline ministered to his self-indulgence. He regularly patronized high-class restaurants like Le Petit Savoyard in Greek Street; but if he was to remain healthy he must walk, run, swim, and leave long gaps between his high-quality meals. Third-rate cigars were reserved for the morning, second-rate for the afternoon, first-rate for the evening. 'In spite of my 90th year', he told Brittain in 1963, 'I manage to swim for about three-quarters of an hour every morning. Then after a really good french [*sic*] meal, I sleep half the afternoon.' He had moved from Cavendish Square, but the Harbens always chose a good address. In his old age young people found him invigorating. David Mitchell recalled Harben at the age of ninety-two as 'a most delightful character'—a short, slight man, with clipped white moustache, brightly coloured shirt, carnation in buttonhole, cigar and elegant suit, who 'still had something of the air of a boulevardier'.[72]

Intellectually he was still alert, interesting himself in the history of the Harben family and playing elaborate games with the Inland Revenue; much to his delight, he lived long enough to save his children from death duties. In his ninety-first year he still saw Russian employees as their own masters; 'one thing seems to remain true', he wrote, 'and that is the teaching of Karl Marx. The nations that follow him are growing stronger and those that oppose him are in greater difficulties every day.'[73] Mitchell found him still full of admiration for Christabel Pankhurst, despite their disagreements on policy, and he helped finance Brittain's biography of Fred Pethick-Lawrence, published in 1963. A few months after Agnes died he married Baby (in 1962). She devoted herself to his health but had little time for doctors, and preferred herbal remedies and vegetarian diets. When he was in another room she would call him to make sure he was all right; 'she would hover over him, you know, like a nanny', said Pauline

---

[72] Brittain Collection: Harben to Brittain, 31 May 1963. Author's collection: David Mitchell to author, 4 June 1975. David Mitchell Collection, 73.83/54: Mitchell's interview with Harben on 9 Feb. 1965. Author's interview with the Morsons, 13 May 1975.

[73] Harben's typescript on his links with Russia, fo. 5. For the Inland Revenue, see author's collection: Naomi Lutyens to author, 15 Dec. 1976.

Hall, his secretary, 'and she would insist on him drinking his tea very hot'. Only at the end did she move her bed into his room.[74]

Baby seems to have been shattered by Harben's death in 1967; Mrs Hall said she 'nursed his head for hours afterwards', and thenceforth always wore black. She placed a memorial notice in several papers annually and took Harben's bust and portraits with her when she moved to another flat, tastefully furnished as ever. 'I'll just go in and tell my husband that I'm going out,' she would say to Mrs Hall when leaving the flat; then she would go in to look at his picture, and sometimes talk to it. She looked forward to meeting him again after she died, but how would she cope with his first wife in the next world? She needed reassurance. She often talked about her life in Paris with Harben, wrote long letters, and conducted long phone conversations, but never invited anyone to visit, let alone to stay.

She was friendly with the Halls, but always drew a line beyond which friendship must not trespass; Mrs Hall gained the strong impression that she wanted to monopolize her and wanted her distanced from the neighbours. Yet Baby often upset Mrs Hall by leading her on and then setting her back with a critical remark. Sometimes she would bring out valuable books, yet when Mrs Hall admired them she would say 'don't touch, don't touch'. Baby remained in some ways a mystery to the end. She always dressed meticulously, with black gloves and a little veil on her hat, but soon became virtually a recluse. She lost any contact with left-wing views, strongly supported Edward Heath in his conflicts with trade unions, and became deeply critical of the Labour Party. The Harbens had supported the Big Ben Council for simultaneous prayer, and Baby became a follower of Brother Manders. In a cupboard she kept religious papers which she said she would show Mrs Hall when she was 'more spiritually developed'; at her death the cupboard was found to contain numerous copies of the monthly *Science of Thought Review*.

Baby visited convents and donated clothes; in letters and conversation she also painted elaborate pictures of her charitable work. She often told Mrs Hall she was going out 'to help my old people', and claimed regularly to go out in the evenings for this purpose, yet the housekeeper said she always stayed in at that time. Baby claimed to be doing important work for the poor in the East End, and dictated a totally implausible account of her good works at the strike-bound St George's Hospital in 1973.[75] As for her claim that the Salvation Army held committees in her flat, the Army knew

---

[74] Details not footnoted on the later life of Harben and Baby come from my tape-recorded interview with the Halls, 2 Oct. 1975.

[75] Mrs Hall retained her shorthand notes of the letter when I met her on 2 Oct. 1975.

nothing about them when inquiries were made after her death in 1974. Yet between the wars Baby was less eccentric than she now seems, for she was highly professional in pursuing the woman's traditional domestic, decorative, charitable and religious roles; at a time when men held the wealth, self-preservation and duty dictated a life-style like hers among many middle-class women. More surprising is the fact that such a life could be required of her by so vigorous a champion of the suffragettes as the young Harben had been.

Utopians are too miscellaneous a bunch for any firm generalizations to emerge from analysing only two. But a few parallels between Pankhurst and Harben are worth making in conclusion. Neither had much practical influence on politicians, or even on feminists, between the wars. During the 1920s Harben discovered in Soviet Russia a real-life utopia whose tragic history illustrates how elevated ideals can be used to justify a dangerous indifference to the methods employed for realizing them; Pankhurst fell back on imaginary utopias whose contemporary impact was small. As pioneers, both experienced an isolation that encouraged their search for endorsement from posterity; 'don't despair . . .', Harben told Lansbury when discussing forcible feeding in 1912, 'the world is for us in the end'. Pankhurst was conscious from her schooldays of being aloof from the crowd, and of taking decisions alone after much soul-searching. In the course of their careers, Harben and Pankhurst repeatedly deliver themselves from persons they regard as insufficiently progressive; as Pankhurst puts it, when breaking free from suffragist compromise during the First World War, 'to me it was essential to be able to voice my opinions spontaneously, and without fear or favour. To trim one's statements, in order to conciliate influential opinion, oppressed me with a sense of insincerity.'[76] The utopian's loneliness springs partly from an unusually penetrating vision, but partly from an intolerant impatience with fellow human beings.

With structures as with ideas, utopians are convinced protestants, perpetually on the move, never specializing, ever responsive to new pleas for help and to new humanitarian causes. They often limit their immediate influence by being 'advanced' all round, as did Sylvia and her father; their failure to confine their progressiveness to a single area of policy stems less from choice than from conviction that all evils are interlinked, and that

---

[76] Lansbury Papers, vol. 5: Harben to Lansbury, 26 June 1912. E. S. Pankhurst, *Home Front*, p. 154. See also Sylvia Pankhurst Papers: autobiographical notes (1930), pp. 3–4; E. S. Pankhurst in Asquith (ed.), *Myself When Young*, p. 268.

small-scale patching-up reforms will actually make things worse. For Sylvia, life was (as her father put it) 'nothing without enthusiasms', and she shows little of the realist reformer's economy in reforming commitment. 'I always feel that any protest is better than none,' she said in 1935, complaining that feminists did not organize protests against the Nazi concentration camps. 'When the need of others appeals to me as a matter in which I . . . ought to assist I must respond,' she wrote in 1930 of her Communist controversies; 'when a truth appears to me as one which it is my duty to state—I must do it. At such times I see everything very clearly . . . yet the inner judgment seat is a stern arbiter. I cannot escape the decision I believe to be based upon duty.'[77] Such conduct entails much sacrifice of self, but also suffering in others; adherence to principle can lead the utopian to see only a tempting potential for corruption in the loyalties and affections fostered by institutions, parties, family, and colleagues—and temptation must, in all conscience, be spurned.

When the utopian's courage leads to purism and sectarianism, it can become self-regarding in the most complex and subtle of ways, for then life itself becomes a work of art, self-consciously fashioned with posterity in mind. Amidst the excitements of histrionic politics—high ideals, romantic thoughts, dramatic events—the leading actor chivalrously rescues the weak and confronts the corrupt and the self-interested. It was through Max Beerbohm's eyes that Sylvia saw the court-room confrontation in 1908 between Christabel Pankhurst and Lloyd George: 'youth and an ideal, on the one hand, and on the other, middle age and no illusions left over,' and on meeting McKenna in 1915 she cast herself in Christabel's role. Harben's passion for self-dramatization went still further. Naomi described the memorably theatrical scene when, preparing himself for the removal of his prostate gland in 1937, he organized a sort of lying in state at Claridge's, his bed surrounded by solicitors.[78]

The utopian's integrity cannot be seen as necessarily selfless; it must always be assessed in the light of personal situation and contemporary comment. Pankhurst hinted at these complexities when telling the Workers' Suffrage Federation in 1916 about the happiness that results from altruism: 'we forget our own troubles if we try to lose our own identity in the troubles of others.' The utopian's ideals may even seem so

[77] Dr Pankhurst quoted in Asquith (ed.), *Myself When Young*, p. 259. Sylvia Pankhurst Papers: Sylvia Pankhurst to Miss M. Gellan (Secretary of the British Section of the Women's World Committee against War and Fascism), 11 Feb. 1935; E. S. Pankhurst's autobiographical notes (1930), pp. 11–12. See also Nevinson Diary, 17 Apr. 1915.

[78] E. S. Pankhurst, *The Suffragette*, p. 285. Author's collection: Naomi Lutyens to author, 10 Apr. 1976.

elevated as to justify tactics which might otherwise have seemed unduly devious. Lord Amulree provides a small-scale illustration of this; Pankhurst, he says, could be 'quite ruthless in a naïve way' when it came to fund-raising for Ethiopia. She regularly overspent, and 'it was always a sign that she had done something drastic when she arrived . . . hair all over the place, papers awry, flustered—and then confessed'.[79]

For all these reasons, the utopian can be a difficult colleague, whose innate or contrived distance from fellow human beings often fosters misunderstanding. 'I am sorry that you make your own difficulties by an incapacity to look at situations from other people[']s point of view as well as your own,' Emmeline Pankhurst told Sylvia in January 1914. Sylvia could be so single-minded on the telephone when roused against Fascism that a potential supporter could put down the receiver, answer the door, and pick it up again to find her still in full flood. In a letter of 1957 to Fred Pethick-Lawrence, she devotes a single line to congratulating him on his remarriage and then takes up ten sides with political matters.[80] Her gullibility caused her to be plundered by dishonest employees, whether at her Epping restaurant or at West Dene; in later life her limited range of human contacts caused her to be perennially rubbing her eyes at the persistence of views she had been challenging for decades.

Utopia gave both Pankhurst and Harben an excuse to shun the parliamentary career that they would have found personally uncongenial. Pankhurst's analysis of feminist history is often acute, but it never fully shakes off the WSPU's view of politicians as people who must be coerced, never fully understands or accepts their role in pursuing consensus. Neither Pankhurst nor Harben was capable of the collaboration, whether within or between parties, that is integral to the politician's trade, and when Pankhurst said that 'politicians . . . are always pliable',[81] her intention was not to praise. The failure to work continuously with others that Pankhurst owed to her temperament was reinforced in Harben by money, which enabled him repeatedly to evade difficulty merely by flouncing out. So both these utopians faced some embarrassment in the

[79] Sylvia Pankhurst Papers: Workers' Suffrage Federation, General Meetings Minute-Book, 15 May 1916. David Mitchell Collection, 73/83/17a: David Mitchell's interview with Lord Amulree, 27 Jan. 1965.

[80] Sylvia Pankhurst Papers: Emmeline Pankhurst to Sylvia, n.d. [sent shortly after her letter to Sylvia of 29 Jan. 1914, which had not produced the desired result]. See also David Mitchell Collection, 73/83/17b: Mitchell's notes on his interview with Mr Beaufort-Palmer, 20 Aug. 1965. Pethick-Lawrence Papers, Box 9, fo. 70: Sylvia to F. Pethick-Lawrence, 13 Feb. 1957.

[81] E. S. Pankhurst, *Suffragette Movement*, p. 605.

1930s when they wanted to resist Fascism yet had earlier repudiated parliamentarism, the major vehicle for resistance. Both in effect responded by vacating the domestic political field—Harben to enjoy himself in Paris and dream of revolution, Pankhurst to champion Ethiopia.

These two careers help to illustrate what seems at first sight a surprising feature of British dictionaries: their tendency to use the terms 'idealist' and 'utopian' pejoratively. Logic, personal consistency, idealism, courage, imaginativeness, and vision are fine qualities, but without the prudence and conciliatoriness of the Rathbones and Stracheys, political achievement dwindles. Yet reforming movements, political parties, and political systems must aim to harness rather than frustrate the utopian, for the terms 'realist', and still more 'pragmatist' can be used pejoratively too. If the utopian often subordinates means to ends, the pragmatist all too easily slips half-consciously into an exclusive preoccupation with means; and if compromise and bargaining fill the mind, idealism—and sometimes initiatives of any kind—can take their leave. The utopian's challenge to conventional conduct is sometimes salutary, for there is always room for argument about what is real and what is possible; human conduct is malleable, though less so than many utopians imagine. Nor does reforming dialogue take place only between contemporaries; the utopian often finds an echo in later generations. If a political system dominated by utopians would be unworkable, a society without them would indeed be impoverished and stagnant. Among the British political system's minor inter-war failures is the fact that it could not harness the talents of Pankhurst and Harben to better effect.

PLATE 12. Emmeline and Fred Pethick-Lawrence at the gate of Fourways, December 1949 (the photo, which they used as a greetings card, was taken by W. Start Walter).

9

The Politics of a Marriage

EMMELINE AND
FRED PETHICK-LAWRENCE

PARTNERSHIPS between women were important for inter-war feminists, as the careers of Rathbone, Wilkinson, and Pippa and Ray Strachey show. But for most women between the wars, the most important partner was male. Political relationships exist within families as within any other human institution whose members compete for influence, but we know little about politics at this level because so much of relevance occurs in private. Twentieth-century Britain's best-known and therefore most influential marriages have been those of monarchs and politicians. Film stars and popular entertainers, also influential, are rarely publicized as married couples; besides, they play many parts on the public stage, whereas the monarch and the politician normally play only one, and have been expected (at least until recently) to set an example in their married life.

Influential in a rather different way have been the marriages of significant couples on the left, where equality between the sexes is more likely to be valued than complementarity. The Glasiers, Snowdens, MacDonalds, and Coles exemplify the influential political partnership; the Webbs and Hammonds the scholarly partnership; the Pethick-Lawrences the feminist partnership. There are parallels between the last three of these marriages. All three were childless, but whereas the Webbs and the Hammonds were known for their collaborative scholarship, the Pethick-Lawrences were known for the quality of their marriage, and for the freedom each partner enjoyed within it; indeed, Fred was quite often asked for guidance on marriage, and once cited this as qualifying him to speak in parliament on family law.[1] The Pethick-Lawrences illustrate the problems and pleasures involved in modern marriage better than the Corbett Ashbys or the Billington-Greigs because both partners were

---

[1] *HL Deb.* 24 Oct. 1956, c. 1031.

active feminists and saw their marriage as embodying feminist values, and because both published autobiographies.

These do not of course reveal all; indeed, Emmeline's explicitly excludes her marriage. Nor do they reveal how much the marriage owed to their secretaries Esther Knowles and Gladys Groom-Smith. Emmeline's is thin on the years after 1914, and Fred (who published his in 1943) never acted on his desire to update it. Furthermore, although Fred's autobiography is remarkably reflective for a practising politician, it has its silences. It is an account of his public career, not of his private life; as Gladys Groom-Smith told me, 'I just felt that he was always afraid of revealing *himself*'.[2] As for Vera Brittain's biography of Fred, it was written too soon after his death to get him clearly into perspective, and says too little about his cast of mind, or about the way his special causes—feminism and India—interacted with his other interests and affected his career as a whole. Here the marriage itself must be discussed, both for its influence and for its intrinsic interest.

Neither Emmeline nor Fred enjoyed childhood. Fred Lawrence's father, a Unitarian, owned a prosperous London building firm, and Fred was born in 1871, youngest in a family of five. His boyhood was lonely because his father died when he was three and he was soon sent to boarding school. He disliked the whole status of childhood as restricting his freedom, especially when attempts were made to improve his handwriting by fixing a wooden instrument to his right hand; what he called 'my inherent resistance to mass psychology' prevented even Eton from taming him. Mathematics came to the rescue: 'I do not remember a time when I was not fond of figures', he wrote.[3] A double first at Cambridge brought him a fellowship at Trinity in 1897, and on the death of his only brother in 1900 he inherited his father's wealth.

Fred was tempted away from mathematics towards social reform by the inspiring lectures of the economist Alfred Marshall who, he said, 'stimulated my brain to ascertain the facts'—and by the influence of Percy Alden, Warden of Mansfield House University Settlement, Canning Town, who 'forced me to face them and, if I could, to justify them'; many years later he found Keynes's memoir of Marshall 'a masterpiece'. After a

[2] Like much else in this chapter, this comes from one of my two tape-recorded interviews with Mrs Gladys Groom-Smith, 9 June and 11 Aug. 1976, at Arden Loch, 121 Malthouse Lane, Earlswood, Birmingham. All information in the text that is unattributed comes from these two very fruitful discussions.

[3] F. P[ethick]-L[awrence], *Fate [Has Been Kind]* [1943], pp. 22, 15; see also p. 16. F. P.-L., in Sir J. Marchant (ed.), *If I Had My Time Again. An Anthology Contributed by Twenty Distinguished Men and Women* (n.d.), pp. 140–1.

world tour, Fred was called to the Bar in 1899 and settled at Mansfield House to study social conditions. At an amateur dramatic performance given there by working girls from the West London Mission he first met one of the two organizers, Emmeline Pethick; 'it was love at first sight'.[4]

Emmeline was born in 1867 into a middle-class family in Weston-super-Mare. Her autobiography is sensitive on how children think, perhaps partly because her own childhood was unhappy; by 1938, when she published it, she thought most children were happy, but fifty years earlier 'the majority were . . . often desperately miserable'. The reign in the Pethick nursery was harsh, and life 'was shadowed by fear'.[5] Her only comfort was Charlotte, the cook, who left after a dispute when Emmeline was only three; later, when Emmeline was ill with pneumonia, she kept calling for Charlotte, who was fetched from her new employers and thereafter became a much-loved member of the family—a fine teller of stories, who could attract Emmeline even as an adult to her room for Sunday tea.

A second major influence was her father, a born rebel who, as she wrote in her autobiography, 'is part of me still'. From him she inherited her passion for justice. In 1882 a Salvation Army captain was unjustly imprisoned for creating a local disturbance which had really originated with his rowdy opponents; Emmeline remembered her excitement while watching her father whip up a petition in Weston-super-Mare for the captain's release. 'In my dumb, childish fashion', she recalled, 'I simply worshipped him for it, and it forged our relationship for ever.' No doubt it was partly his influence that led her as a schoolgirl to brave a term in Coventry for refusing to confess to a sin she had not committed, and to defend the atheist Bradlaugh when attacked at her snobbish finishing school. On Emmeline's first arrest as a suffragette, her father was proud of her for championing the spread of democratic liberty.[6]

Like so many lapsed late-Victorian evangelicals, Emmeline subconsciously retained many evangelical ideas. Convinced that she was less attractive than her sisters, and determined not to accept the life of Weston's single girls, she was alerted by Walter Besant's *Children of Gibeon* to the economic plight of working girls, and went to work for the

---

[4] F.P.-L., *Fate*, p. 48; cf. p. 34. Marshall Library, Cambridge, Keynes papers, A24/1: F.P.-L. to J. M. Keynes, 19 Nov. 1924 (photostat copy located with the help of Ms Judith Allen, and quoted by permission of the Royal Economic Society, as are later citations from this archive). F.P.-L., *Fate*, p. 51.

[5] E.P.-L., *My Part*, pp. 350, 25.

[6] Ibid., p. 38; cf. pp. 34, 44, 47, 59. *Votes for Women*, 2 May 1913, p. 439.

West London Mission, where she made her first speech in 1891. Influenced by Whitman and Carpenter, she sought closer contact with working people and came under the influence of Mark Guy Pearse, 'a supreme influence in my life for ... twenty years'. His gentleness complemented her father's crusading for liberty and justice; 'sometimes throughout my life I have acted as the child of one', she wrote, 'and sometimes as the child of the other, and sometimes because of these two different moral standards I have been at conflict within myself'. Ideals of the simple Christian life led her and Mary Neal to move into artisans' dwellings among London working girls: as she later put it, 'we wanted to pay our debts'.[7] Intellectual influences—Carlyle's *Sartor Resartus,* the plight of Hetty Sorrell in *Adam Bede,* Mazzini and books on the Risorgimento—were much less important than her initial humanitarian impulse. At that time the folk-dancing movement was as preoccupied with social reform as with art, and in 1899 it led her to Mansfield House.

The correspondence between Emmeline and Fred in summer 1900 now appears intensely earnest. Her socialism seemed a major obstacle to marrying a Liberal Unionist candidate for parliament, especially when she saw the Boer War as 'organized murder for robbery'. When Fred suggested that compromise was possible on a moral issue she pronounced this deadly: 'place, position and any sort of purchase of power are dust and ashes to me compared with the integrity of one man's soul.'[8] With characteristic rationality and thoroughness, Fred toured South Africa to assess the justice of the war for himself; he returned a pro-Boer at a time when personal feeling on the question was intense, and abandoned his parliamentary candidature. These political entanglements perhaps mask difficulties at another level. As a child, Emmeline had been shocked when warned not to respond to friendly overtures from a stranger in nearby woods; after being rebuked as a schoolgirl for talking about childbirth after lights out, she repressed all thought of sex for several years. She later referred to 'the tangle of emotion which I and many others of my generation have had with much difficulty to unwind'.[9]

By summer 1901 she seems to have lost her doubts: 'my mate—my own beloved,' she writes in August, planning the furnishing of their house, 'I do love you. (I'm tookt all sudden like) ... I want you to be so happy in our sweet house.' Their views on the war deterred several of Fred's

---

[7] E.P.-L., *My Part,* pp. 100, 102. *Votes for Women,* 12 Mar. 1909, p. 429.

[8] Trinity College, Cambridge, P[ethick]-L[awrence] Papers, Box 7, fo. 49(2): E. Pethick to F. Lawrence, 'Thursday evening' [end. '?28 June 1900'].

[9] E.P.-L., *My Part,* pp. 56–8.

relatives from attending the wedding in October 1901, especially as Lloyd George was a guest; and when Fred changed his name to Pethick-Lawrence he sacrificed the chance of inheriting from a rich uncle. To judge from his intensely affectionate letters to Emmeline in 1902, the sacrifice was well worth while; their style now seems rather mannered in its elaborate chivalry—'I am your right arm, I am the coat of mail,' and so on—but the nicknames and childish language suggest much intimacy, and until the First World War their partnership dominated their public as well as their private life.[10]

'It was by a very extraordinary sequence of incidents', Emmeline recalled of her suffragette phase, 'that I, who am not of a revolutionary temperament, was drawn into a revolutionary movement.' With Fred as with Bertrand Russell, a wartime rejection of imperialism fostered a more general rejection of violence and a move towards social reform. Lecturing on socialism at Oxford, Fred could not decide whether to support or oppose it, but 'faced with my audience, I told them that socialism in some shape was inevitable, and that the important thing was to ensure that when it came it should take a good form'.[11] He bought a progressive newspaper, the *Echo,* and moved widely in trade-union circles; 'there is something about these great Trade Union men deep, life giving, satisfying,' he told Emmeline in 1905, '—a well of living water from which whosoever drinketh shall not thirst again'. Keir Hardie—for Emmeline, 'the greatest person we have ever known'—was their route into the WSPU in 1906; he encouraged Mrs Pankhurst in February to approach them for help in launching the Union in London, but Emmeline said she could not undertake more public work. It was the Lancashire mill-girl Annie Kenney—again sent by Hardie—who, Emmeline recalled, 'threw all my barriers down' with her breathless and trusting urgency; Emmeline agreed to become treasurer, and so was launched on the suffragette phase of her public life which dominates her autobiography.[12]

The mounting influence of feminist over labour pressures on the Pethick-Lawrences between 1905 and 1907 is clear from studying the *Labour Record and Review,* which Fred edited. Its number for November 1906 outlines his vision for the labour movement: 'three great movements are going on to-day in the world. The first is a rebellion against the domination of class. The second is a rebellion against the domination of

[10] P.-L. Papers, 7/135(1): E. Pethick to F. Lawrence, Saturday [end. 17 Aug. 1901]; 6/26(1): F. to E.P.-L., 1 Apr. 1902.

[11] E.P.-L., *My Part,* p. 148. F.P.-L., *Fate,* p. 56.

[12] P.-L. Papers, 6/105: F. to E.P.-L., 6 Sept. 1905. E.P.-L., *My Part,* pp. 129, 147.

sex. The third is a rebellion against the domination of colour. Socialism must be great enough to include all three.' Fred's own outlook was broad enough to embrace them all, but the second of the three took increasing priority. Emmeline's cloudily idealistic prose became a regular feature in the paper, and suffragette incidents became increasingly prominent until Fred announced in May 1907 that the paper would amalgamate with the *New Age,* thus freeing him for other work.

Defending the suffragettes against their critics within the labour movement in November 1906, Fred pointed out that 'they have no constitutional means of obtaining redress. They are outside the constitution, and as such must use unconstitutional methods to gain their end.' Earlier in the year he had stated his strong conviction 'that the women ought not to be left to fight this battle alone', since both sexes suffered under a system that kept one of them in permanent subjection.[13] He now saw himself as 'helping to prevent the disaster of a sex war'. The Pethick-Lawrence partnership fended off from the WSPU the sex-sectarianism which Christabel fostered after they left. He and Emmeline were disciples of Olive Schreiner, whose *Woman and Labour* Emmeline pronounced in 1911 'a necessity of everyday mental and moral life'; Schreiner saw the women's movement as 'not a movement on the part of woman leading to severance . . . but . . . *essentially a movement of the woman towards the man, of the sexes towards closer union*'.[14]

The Pethick-Lawrences lie behind the WSPU's rapid growth after 1906. They edited its important periodical *Votes for Women,* and subscribed £6,610 in identifiable donations between 1906 and 1912. They also brilliantly organized donations from others; Fred husbanded the accounts behind the scenes, while Emmeline's ingenuity and flair publicly boosted donations. Fred gave the WSPU cautious and well-informed advice on policy; Emmeline's high moral tone complemented Mrs Pankhurst's impulsiveness and Christabel's tactical manœuvrings. Emmeline lacked beauty, but she possessed charm, together with a sweet and attractive voice. Her oratory was uplifting, but often rather vague, theatrical, and sentimental—inspiring to some but embarrassing to others. H. N. Brailsford refers to her 'sort of spiritual exaltation, a wholly sincere if somewhat meridional absorption in the subjective beauty of big brave actions'. Asked on one occasion how to speak in public, she replied 'my dear, it doesn't matter a bit as long as you *feel* what you're saying'. Dramatic in her dress

---

[13] *Labour Record and Review,* Nov. 1906, p. 204; June, 1906, p. 86.
[14] F.P.-L., *Fate,* p. 92. *Votes for Women,* 3 Mar. 1911, p. 354. O. Schreiner, *Woman and Labour* (1911), p. 252 (Schreiner's italics).

and gestures, she was sometimes carried away. 'Maiden warrior!' she exclaimed to Christabel, released from prison in 1908, 'we give you rapturous welcome. Go forth with the fiat of the future, strong in the gladness and youth of your dauntless spirit to smite with your sword of destiny the forces of stupidity.' Virginia Woolf watched her closely at a suffrage rally in 1918: 'at best large indisputable platitudes, finely dressed and balanced, are the only things that can be put into speeches,' she wrote. 'I watched Mrs Pethick Lawrence rising and falling on her toes, as if half her legs were made of rubber, throwing out her arms, opening her hands, and thought very badly of this form of art.'[15]

The male suffragist, accused of betraying his sex and of effeminacy in accepting female leadership, needed both moral and physical courage at this time. And when the WSPU began to attack property, the authorities saw Fred, a wealthy man, as treacherous at a second level; the Pethick-Lawrences were 'the real villains, as to finance and violent words', said Asquith in March 1912. When Emmeline in May requested prison visits from her employees 'in view of the fact that I have three domestic establishments to supervise', a Home Office official minuted: 'people with 3 establishments and a lot of personal business ought to keep out of prison.' Fred and Emmeline saw their joint imprisonment in 1912 as accomplishing (in Emmeline's words) 'the purpose to which we were born and for which we were mated'.[16] She had been imprisoned five times before, and after hunger-striking she was forcibly fed in May; the prison doctor thought her 'very much excited, violent and resistive', and her personal doctors stressed that her health was in danger. She found the prison hymn-book 'a sort of life belt'; Fred had not been to prison before, and in letters highly mystical and poetic in tone he reassured her that he was well. He too hunger-struck and was forcibly fed; by 27 June his weight had fallen one and a half stones below normal and the weight-loss was accelerating; both were released.[17]

Fred seems to have worshipped Christabel from the start, and in common with many of Emmeline's working-class folk-dancing girls she

[15] Manchester City Library M50/2/1/315: Brailsford to Fawcett, 30 June [1910]. Author's interview with Mrs Lutyens, 28 Mar. 1975. *Votes for Women*, 17 Dec. 1908, p. 200. V. Woolf, *Diary*, i. 125.

[16] Fawcett Library Autograph Collection 1Jii/7016: Lady Frances Balfour to Fawcett, n.d. (reporting Asquith in Mar. 1912). PRO HO 45/24630: minute by 'C.B.' on 28 May 1912. V. Brittain, *Pethick-Lawrence. A Portrait* (1963), p. 64.

[17] PRO HO 45/24630: W. C. Sullivan to the Governor, Holloway Prison, 24 June 1912. P.-L. Papers, 7/169: E.P.-L. to F.P.-L., 25 June 1912. HO 45/24630: report on F.P.-L. by Dr Maurice Craig, 27 June 1912.

called him 'godfather'. Yet there had always been an 'atmosphere' between Fred and Mrs Pankhurst, who was far less deeply involved than the Pethick-Lawrences in the WSPU's day-to-day organization, and perhaps feared losing influence with Christabel. When Christabel was showered with tributes after addressing a suffragette meeting, Jessie Kenney remembered Mrs Pankhurst saying 'how godfather would like to have these'; even Christabel could hardly contain her boredom during his ill-delivered speeches. There were also divisions on policy, Mrs Pankhurst being keener to escalate militancy than were Christabel and the Pethick-Lawrences.[18]

During August, while the Pethick-Lawrences were holidaying in Canada, the government bailiffs began selling off their property, and in 1913 bankruptcy proceedings were begun. 'Hand in hand', Fred told Emmeline, 'we are stronger than tempests and avalanches and all the forces of evil . . . Your voice is music and your eyes are like the sentinels of heaven.'[19] But the Pankhursts now felt that the Pethick-Lawrences' wealth might enable the government to strike at the WSPU. When the Pethick-Lawrences returned home in October 1912, colleagues whom they had earlier taken into their own homes excluded them from the headquarters of the WSPU which they had done so much to create. In a meeting with Mrs Pankhurst and Christabel, a close friend for the past six years, it became clear that their expulsion had been carefully planned in advance.

The Pankhurstian ruthlessness which separated the 'Peths' from the 'Panks' in autumn 1912 never ceased to astonish the Pethick-Lawrences; 'many men and women who have made history have been cast in a similar mould . . .', Fred wrote charitably many years later. 'They cannot be judged by ordinary standards of conduct; and those who run up against them must not complain of the treatment they receive.' He was less philosophical at first, and told Lansbury in October that the situation 'at the time nearly stunned us'; in November H. W. Nevinson thought Fred 'felt bitterly hurt especially at the long underground preparation and sudden explosion upon their innocence'.[20] In July 1914 Fred privately attacked Mrs Pankhurst's meanness and play-acting for sympathy, and Nevinson thought him 'very violent' on the subject, which had become 'almost an obsession' with him. Emmeline's autobiography sees Mrs

[18] David Mitchell Collection, 73.83/48: Mitchell's interview with Jessie Kenney, 2 July 1965. See also E.P.-L., *My Part*, pp. 278, 283.

[19] P.-L. Papers, 6/120: F. to E.P.-L., 26 Nov. 1912.

[20] F.P.-L., *Fate*, p. 100. Rosen, *Rise Up, Women!* p. 174. Nevinson Diary, 25 Nov. 1912.

Pankhurst as 'fundamentally wrong' when she alienated public opinion by escalating violence from public to private property.[21]

The Pethick-Lawrences' public response was very different: with considerable dignity they avoided recrimination, repudiated criticism of the WSPU as treacherous, and refused to condemn militancy. Fred announced in October that he 'gloried in the window-smashing of last March', and Emmeline's uncompromising defence of it in December shows her rhetoric at its most cloudy; it 'was the breaking through of reality into a dream. It was the rending of the tomb by the bursting forth of the living spirit that had been imprisoned there . . . We must be prepared for the breaking up of the material substance of life before the spiritual force that is in this Movement.'[22] Although the Pethick-Lawrences founded a separate organization, the Votes for Women Fellowship (later renamed the United Suffragists), which encouraged collaboration between men and women, they never turned it against the Pankhursts.

With hindsight Fred thought the beginning of the Liberal Party's decline 'largely attributable' to its 'fast-and-loose method' on votes for women. In reality the Party split for quite other reasons, and if it had survived it could have accommodated Fred's lifelong liberalism more readily than Labour, whose statism and class-consciousness he sometimes found excessive.[23] As with so many of Labour's new recruits, it was the new party's liberalism that attracted him: its rationalistic optimism about human nature and its commitment to peace, free trade, and a liberal colonial policy.

The First World War strengthened the impulse towards Labour, and many of the ex-gaolbird politicians who joined Fred in a special dinner in 1924 owed their status not to suffragette militancy but to wartime conscientious objection. Fred and Emmeline seem to have responded similarly to the war. Although he thought failure to help France and Belgium would constitute a breach of faith, he condemned Grey for having reached surreptitious pre-war international commitments, and championed open diplomacy through the Union of Democratic Control, of which he became treasurer. In April 1917 he stood as a 'peace by negotiation' candidate at Aberdeen South, but came bottom of the poll with only 333 votes; called up in 1918, he became a conscientious objector and worked as a farm labourer. As Labour's Financial Secretary to the

[21] Nevinson Diary, 19 July 1914. E.P.-L., *My Part*, p. 284.

[22] *Votes for Women*, 1 Nov. 1912, p. 77; 20 Dec. 1912, p. 183.

[23] *HC Deb*. 20 Feb. 1925, c. 1531; cf. preface to his *Fate*, p. 7. See also Brittain Collection: F.P.-L. to Brittain, 14 Jan. 1940; *HL Deb*. 23 Feb. 1953, c. 622.

Treasury in 1929 he braved much criticism by ending penalties against civil servants who had once been conscientious objectors.[24]

In October 1914 Emmeline thought the outbreak of war 'the final demonstration of the unfitness of men to have the whole control of the human family in their hands'. She pleased the Anti-Suffrage League by recommending the old anti-feminist separation of spheres in a new guise: destroying the enemy should be left to men, she said, whereas 'the essential work of women lies in giving, maintaining, and saving the life of their own people'.[25] She backed the idea of a women's peace conference at The Hague in 1915 and from then until 1922 acted as treasurer to the Women's International League which grew out of it. She was still articulating her almost mystical hostility to war in October 1939; the new conflict was the Nemesis for earlier British injustice to Germany, she claimed, and Hitlerism could be broken only by a German uprising.[26]

By 1918 the Pethick-Lawrence marriage had settled into a mould. When together in public, they impressed everyone with their obvious mutual affection and thoughtfulness. Every 12 and 26 May they wrote special letters to one another, and on one of them they consumed what they called 'the feast of the spring', to which gooseberry pie was integral; Mrs Groom-Smith thought that the 12th was when Fred proposed, the 26th when Emmeline accepted. They exchanged daily letters (usually addressed to 'Partsy'—short for partner) when apart. Fred thirsted for companionship, while she found in him the idealism she craved and the qualities she had admired in her father and in Pearse. Fred referred in 1912 to 'the exquisite poise of your head', and said he found in her bearing 'my ideal of the perfect woman'. In 1944 he wrote: 'dear wife it has been wonderful to be married to you for 43 years, it has been delicious to love you and an inspiration to know that you love me.' 'My sweet love you are the apple of my eye,' he told her in 1948, and in 1950 he described their marriage as 'a pearl above all price'.[27]

The emotionalism of his letters, poems, and religion conceals the fact that Fred was the calm, organized, precise, and controlled partner who liked routine, hated personal upsets, and always took the initiative in resolving them. Emmeline was moody, impulsive, untidy, absent-minded,

---

[24] F.P.-L., *Fate*, pp. 118, 130. *HC Deb.* 5 Nov. 1929, cc. 825–6.

[25] *Votes for Women*, 16 Oct. 1914, p. 21; 28 Aug. 1914, p. 713. *Anti-Suffrage Review*, Jan. 1915, p. 3.

[26] Sylvia Pankhurst Papers: E.P.-L. to Sylvia, 14 Oct. 1939; see also same to same, 1 July 1940.

[27] P.-L. Papers, 6/116(1): F. to E.P.-L., 25 Apr. 1912; 6/143: same to same, 30 Sept. 1944; 6/194: same to same, 28 Jan. 1948; 6/198: same to same, 14 Aug. 1950.

disorganized, and sometimes difficult, but also warm, spontaneous, and far less pernickety. When she was in a bad mood or when bad news arrived, she would make this the excuse for avoiding tasks she disliked and take to her bed, sometimes locking the door behind her; Fred would not tackle the problem head-on but would complain mildly to his staff and then, when the time seemed ripe, encourage them to make an overture. Emmeline experienced the freedom of the emancipated woman but also the cosseting accorded to the woman-as-plaything. Though childless, she had no career, and left Fred to manage the finances (though she had income of her own and a separate banking account); she contented herself with running the household.

It was a semi-detached partnership, for which Emmeline had prepared Fred from the start; just before their marriage she described herself as 'an elemental earth-creature—a wild thing who has always found it hard enough to belong to the slow dull stuffy world of grown-up human beings'.[28] She liked her own company, and greatly valued her freedom within the marriage; she possessed the power to fascinate younger men, and her friendships included several platonic relationships with them. She and Fred exchanged ideas frequently, and they do not seem to have diverged politically after 1901; he would always consult her about forthcoming speeches. But she was not at all the politician's conventional wife, always beside him at public occasions and cushioning him against discomfort or inconvenience. Nor did he entirely live up to her hopes, for her notion of presiding over a salon foundered on Fred's tendency to fall asleep in it.

At Lincoln's Inn they originally had two flats, one for offices and one to live in, both on the same level but with no connecting door. The domestic flat was large, with a big drawing-room, separate bedrooms for Fred and Emmeline, and two rooms for a living-in housekeeper. Fred suggested making a door between the two flats, but Esther Knowles vetoed it because Emmeline's repeated demands would hold up the office work. So, as there was no question of Emmeline's descending and mounting the sixty-two steps between the flats, Gladys frequently found herself shuttling between the flats with the notes the couple exchanged during the day. Fourways, their Surrey house near Guildford, where they went at weekends, had four bedrooms, a billiard room, and huge gardens complete with bowling-green, tennis court, and miniature putting-green. In the garden was a cottage for Rapley, a living-in gardener and chauffeur adept at coping with

---

[28] Ibid. 7/132(1): E. to F.P.-L., Thursday morning [end. 8 Aug. 1901].

any emergency; his son assumed the role in later years. Even at Fourways Gladys once found herself repeatedly carrying notes between their bedrooms when both were ill, for Emmeline was by then too deaf to communicate by ear.

All this took some organizing, but Emmeline delegated the work at Fourways to a staff of eight, and was quite helpless at domestic tasks. Fred waited on her hand and foot, and always fell for her pleas of illness when there was something she did not want to do. She had the art of surrounding herself with people who doted on her, and she widened the circle of admirers by dictating long letters to relatives. She was a lazy woman who would allow people to do almost anything for her. When she dressed for an occasion she could look rather grand, but often she did not bother. After reading a letter or newspaper she would drop it anywhere; she felt entirely free not to eat a meal that had been carefully prepared; she was always losing things, and could almost go into a trance with a book when reading on her bed, forgetting all her engagements. When she was resting, Gladys was allowed to pat the pillow if interruption was necessary, but nothing more. It says much for her staff's devotion and for Emmeline's charm that the household ran so smoothly; she was not so much selfish as thoughtless, and for all her faults she was nice to work for because she was fun, and treated her employees as individuals, never talking down to them.

Unlike Harben, Fred applied his feminism consistently to both private and public life; Emmeline not only enjoyed much freedom, but received his help in the house. At Fourways he delighted in digging up new vegetables, cooking, shopping, and making jam, whereas Emmeline's cooking skills did not extend beyond mixing mayonnaise. Yet he too could be troublesome to employees, for he was a rather fussy man with fads—in his own words, 'a vintage crank'—though he found it easier to relax in Surrey than in London. Not that he was in any way extravagant: his London bedroom was austere, he was indifferent to clothes, hated wasting food, and stopped in mid-meal if he thought he'd eaten enough. He enjoyed food, but liked it plain, and disciplined himself not to eat between meals. He never drank tea or coffee, and Mrs Groom-Smith recalled his eating the same breakfast throughout the thirty-seven years she had known him: one-and-a-half pints of sweetened barley water, half a pint of hot milk, three pieces of toast, and half a pound of jam. Before visiting Laurence Housman in 1934 he explained that the menu must exclude garlic, onions, lemon, or marmalade pudding. He loved treacle pudding, and was so fond of apricots, unobtainable in Britain during 1947, that on the return journey from his India mission his aides foraged for them when the plane stopped at Sicily.[29]

Punctuality, routine, and the efficient use of time lay at the heart of Fred's demands on employees, and help to explain why he had fewer friends than Emmeline. He would interrupt even a casual anecdote to get its details right—though such fussiness became an asset during his Indian mission when vague Indian phraseology had to be pinned down. He could not stop himself from beginning each working day by going through the marriages, births, and deaths columns in the newspapers, and his letters of condolence were punctiliously dispatched. If casual visitors threatened the precise timing of his meals, they would not be encouraged to stay, nor were unexpected telephone callers well received, even when inquiring about Emmeline during her last illness. Fred hated his routine being interrupted—by long holidays, for example—but if holidays had to be taken they must be with the same person, such as Fred Hankinson; they went on river holidays together for years, with diminishing enjoyment on both sides.

Yet all this gives too cold an impression, and makes the devotion of Fred's staff inexplicable. In reality he was a rather lovable 'character', as childlike in his recreations as in his food—counting up his Christmas cards, and always relishing victory in a game or competition. He liked having spectators when playing billiards, and this was how his staff relieved his boredom on the Indian mission; always after dinner he would 'march me round the billiard table', Viscount Alexander recalled; 'he would owe me 50 on 100. He always won, and he would say, "It is all a question of mathematics".' Much to his enjoyment he would always beat his mission staff at guessing the temperature; his recipe was to guess the temperature in a cool tunnel and then add on a figure for the heat outside. He was so keen to receive birthday presents that he reminded his staff not to forget them. Such a man was inevitably good with children, never patronizing them, always ready to join in their games, songs, and nonsense rhymes, skilful at organizing tennis parties and eager for a picnic on the beach.[30]

Emmeline too was good with children; for example, a small spastic child

[29] Author's tape-recorded interview with Sir Frank Turnbull, 26 Oct. 1976, at 18 Aveley Lane, Farnham, Surrey. P.-L. Papers, 6/253: F.P.-L. to L. Housman, 18 Sept. 1934 (copy). Brittain, *Pethick-Lawrence*, pp. 96, 120, 144.

[30] *HL Deb.* 17 Oct. 1961, c. 324. See also interview with Sir Frank Turnbull, 26 Oct. 1976 and author's interview with the Misses Freda and Nancy Budgett, 25 July 1976, at 2 Elm Tree Cottages, Cranleigh, Surrey.

at Fourways, unintelligible to anyone else, established a strong rapport with her. This together with their childlessness helps to explain Fred and Emmeline's relations with staff, who often arrived as children and were virtually adopted. Employees enjoyed associating so closely with two such interesting and distinguished people; the Pethick-Lawrences were progressive for their time in their attitude to staff, and in their approach to social class generally. Two of their employees were integral to the Pethick-Lawrence life-style, yet feature only in the prefaces to the two autobiographies and nowhere in their indexes: Esther Knowles and Gladys Groom (later Groom-Smith). Although there were earlier regimes, this couple were at the centre of things from the 1920s to 1961.

Esther began as one of Emmeline's folk-dancing working girls, trained as an office-girl in the WSPU, then became Emmeline's secretary, then Fred's private secretary, and later also his parliamentary secretary. Self-improvement was the order of the day: the Pethick-Lawrences helped their employees to rise in society, and the employees helped each other. Fred often gave them instruction; Mrs Groom-Smith thought he would have made an excellent teacher—he was so clear, and had a fund of interesting information. Esther's devotion to her employers was complete. Emmeline 'was her lode-star', she used to say; but from the 1920s her loyalty was primarily to Fred, and if a parliamentary speech needed typing she would stave off a migraine with medicine from the Chancery Lane chemist and get it ready on time. She gave Fred companionship as well as devoted service: 'your spirit is a constant source of my delight and I love you for it,' he told her in 1947. As she wrote later, 'having worked so closely with P-L for all my secretarial life . . . I knew every "blink of his eyelids"!!!' The initials 'P-L' recurred in her conversation long after his death, for she was fascinated by her employers and kept talking about them.[31]

When Gladys Groom arrived in 1924 as a sixteen-year-old working-class girl she was almost fourteen years younger than Esther, who took her under her wing. Esther was then secretary to both Fred and Emmeline, but Gladys soon became Emmeline's own secretary. Gladys worked closely and harmoniously with Esther, who rebuked her at first for reading low-quality books, suggested better items and passed on cuttings from *The Times* to help her forward. Gladys was the kindest of women; Fred once referred to her as 'the radiant embodiment of courage and vitality', and she

---

[31] P.-L. Papers, 6/209: F.P.-L. to E. Knowles, 6 Nov. 1947. Brittain Collection: E. Knowles to Brittain, 10 Feb. 1962. See also author's tape-recorded interview with Mrs Nita Needham, 31 May 1976, at 14 Yarnton Road, Kidlington, Oxford.

became almost as happy at Fourways as in her own home.[32] When she discovered that Emmeline couldn't cook she took that on too, and genuinely enjoyed nursing her in old age, commuting to and from her Birmingham home at weekends. When Emmeline died in 1954 Fourways was sold, the Lincoln's Inn Office flat was vacated, and Gladys retired. For two years Esther coped on her own, but after her serious operation in 1956 Gladys returned to resume their partnership on a part-time basis. 'I made *them* my life', she said to me of the Pethick-Lawrences, 'simply because I was happy being with them . . . I don't know how I ever had the time to get married, really.'

Fred's secretariat is reminiscent of the resources of the nineteenth-century back-bencher. At a moment's notice he might need a letter received twenty years earlier, and a double-indexed filing system was devised accordingly. His time was closely organized on daily engagement-cards with the relevant documents attached, household accounts were cast up annually, and his speeches—all docketed in folders—were often reprinted and circulated to his 'encyclical list' of about eight hundred. When travelling to work, Esther marked up passages in *The Times* which he might find useful, and these were pasted on to sheets for him to read and were sometimes filed. Then there were Fred's annually-revised lists of seventy or eighty charities; donations were dispatched on 1 January to national charities, to former employees, and old suffrage workers. There were three Christmas card lists—'special', 'ordinary' and 'but if'; these were, respectively, for the 150 or so who received cards signed by himself, for other regulars, and for those who received cards only in return for cards sent. 'It was a mammoth job', Mrs Groom-Smith told me, 'and he was so serious with it.' The five or six hundred Christmas cards he received were sorted alphabetically and checked against the list of cards sent, which was then updated; changes of address were noted, and then the cards were sent down to Fourways to be savoured.[33]

Fred's civil servants found him conscientious, good at delegating, but demanding: he wanted punctuality, efficiency, accuracy, honesty, and industry.[34] He was often irritable, especially when interrupted while writing a speech. 'He never wasted half-a-minute, never', said Mrs Groom-Smith; '. . . he would say "come on, come on, come on", and in that *tone* too.' Yet he was a fair man who could take criticism from his employees, and respected them for standing up to him. He was

[32] P.-L. Papers, 6/213(1): F.P.-L. to E. Knowles, 10 Oct. 1948.
[33] Author's collection: Mrs Needham to author, 19 Feb. 1985.
[34] Interview with Sir Frank Turnbull, 26 Oct. 1976.

particularly difficult when Secretary of State for India (1945–7). One Christmas Esther and Gladys, thinking that he had left, rushed up to the office, delighted to be free; Gladys kicked her leg up, her shoe came off and flew up to smash the light. Much to their horror, Fred emerged from the inner office to investigate, but on being told what had happened he saw the humour of it and admitted that he had 'been very wicked, very naughty' with his bad temper. This was one advantage of working for him: he could joke with his secretaries, and he was a good raconteur who confided in them. How, for instance, was Emmeline to be handled today? Or should he, as Financial Secretary to the Treasury, put a tax on silk stockings? He could give credit when it was due, and once introduced them at a parliamentary dinner as the two best political secretaries in London.

Fred and Emmeline remained active inter-war feminists, but House of Commons life prevented their collaboration from being as close as before 1914. Emmeline stood for parliament only once, in 1918 at Rusholme for Labour, and was soundly defeated; she said later that 'one in the House and one out of it make the best team'. Both helped get Judge Neil over from the United States to promote widows' pensions in the early 1920s, and this was the theme of Fred's maiden speech in 1924.[35] But she rarely commented on politics between the wars; her autobiography is entirely slanted towards suffrage events, and she says almost nothing about her views on Labour Party affairs and inter-war politics. Her feminism was never as active after 1914 as before. In later life she doesn't seem to have wanted public recognition, but was disappointed that young women felt so little interest in the vote and made so little use of it. She had no links with the non-militants in NUSEC, the major feminist body of the 1920s, and was not active in the birth-control movement. She was not prominent in the Women's International League after 1925, and her role as president of the WFL from 1926 to 1935 was largely honorific, and is scarcely mentioned in her autobiography. She supported Sylvia and Richard Pankhurst financially and in other ways, and publicly asserted woman's right to a career, but did nothing for the LSWS or for WEF. Like the careers of so many former suffragettes, hers came to little after 1914.

The same cannot be said of Fred, who was an active and pioneering parliamentary feminist for the rest of his life. He contributed more on equal pay in parliament than all but two—Astor and Summerskill—of the thirty-eight women MPs between 1919 and 1945, and made major speeches in the equal-pay debates of 1936 and 1943. More than once he

---

[35] E.P.-L., *My Part*, p. 337. See also *HC Deb.* 20 Feb. 1924, c. 1899.

pointed out that government, by constructively responding to a reasonable campaign, could avoid the sort of sex war on this issue that had almost occurred over women's suffrage.[36] He was among the first to advocate feminist taxation reform, and thought it 'just silly' in 1949 to continue excluding women from the House of Lords now that they were so active elsewhere; in 1957, in one of his rare disagreements with his own party, he insisted on supporting equality, despite the danger of strengthening the hereditary principle.[37] In his eighties he acted as a sort of political agent for the ageing suffragettes; and despite the split of 1912, he stoutly defended their view of history when it was challenged by G. M. Trevelyan over dinner at Trinity in 1949 or by Roger Fulford's *Votes for Women* in 1957. He responded patiently and meticulously, though cautiously, to Sylvia's and Christabel's detailed complaints against Fulford, and helped to ensure that Christabel's memoirs were published in 1959.[38]

Brittain's biography portrays women's suffrage and Indian independence as the twin peaks of Fred's lifetime's achievement, yet in 1906 class domination had accompanied domination by sex and colour in his portrait of Labour's threefold enemy, and in reality it is the attack on class that dominates his career after 1918. In his entire parliamentary career from 1924 to 1961 only 5 per cent of his parliamentary contributions went on India and only 4 per cent on feminist issues (defined as franchise, family law, women's rights and status, women's employment, women's war-work, equal pay, and family allowances). He was no single-issue politician, and aimed to influence policy right across the board. After 1918 he was bent on making a career as a Labour Party politician, and devoted his main energies to economic questions.

He came bottom of the poll in a three-party contest at Islington South in 1922 with 30 per cent of the votes cast, but in 1923 in a three-party contest at Leicester West he defeated the Liberal candidate Winston Churchill, and retained the seat in 1924 and 1929. He was overwhelmingly defeated in 1931 after a straight fight with a Liberal candidate who supported the National Government, but in 1935 became MP for Edinburgh East after a narrow victory in a three-party contest, and won again comfortably in 1945 before being raised to the peerage. He was active in parliamentary debates from the start, and was always among the leading fifty MPs for the

---

[36] e.g. *HC Deb.* 1 Apr. 1936, c. 2043; 1 May 1941, c. 651.

[37] *HL Deb.* 27 July 1949, c. 594; cf. 30 Oct. 1957, c. 630; 21 Jan. 1959, c. 627.

[38] Brittain, *Pethick-Lawrence*, p. 218. P.-L. Papers, 9/49(1–4): notes headed 'Christabel's Criticisms of Fulford's Book', and written in response to her letter to him dated 25 May 1957 at 9/45.

size of his sessional debating contribution between 1925 and 1940; indeed, he needed to be active if he was to rise to the forefront, for on entering parliament he was already fifty-two.

He was a versatile parliamentary performer, both in mode of intervention and in subject-matter. He was active in asking parliamentary questions, and showed speed and grasp in the sort of debate which hammers out legislation in detail; like Susan Lawrence he was quick-witted and well informed in grappling with practical issues. This last quality was particularly valuable when he became Financial Secretary to the Treasury in 1929. Despite their later disagreements, Philip Snowden, his Chancellor of the Exchequer, pronounced him 'excellent' in the post, 'both in his Departmental duties and in the conduct of financial measures through the House of Commons'. He found his civil servants congenial, and coped efficiently with parliamentary questions over a wide area—from museums and civil service questions to banking and finance.[39]

During his Commons career he made on average a dozen major speeches a year, usually on economic matters, and these read well today in *Hansard*: his intellect was strong and well-informed enough to range widely over a question and produce a brilliant, economically argued, lucid synthesis, rather like a high-quality university lecture. Yet this was precisely the problem: his exact, mathematical brain tackles problems as though they are primarily matters of logic, and he sometimes has the air of the clever schoolboy correcting those around him, often at excessive speed and undue length. He is puzzled why so few MPs share his interest in rather dry and abstruse financial questions, and he has a dry and jerky speaking style; his speeches lack colour, liveliness, or imagination in content or manner. 'He can reel off figures,' wrote one experienced commentator, 'he can discuss intricate financial problems with confidence, but he has no charm, no imaginative background.'[40] Perhaps he tried too hard, for he wrote out his speeches in full beforehand, whereas Emmeline (a much better speaker) spoke only from a set of headings. 'It is only in the last year or two', he told the House in 1940, 'that I have risen to my feet without having a certain sense of nervousness in addressing this Assembly.' He was labelled 'Pathetic Lawrence' by the press gallery and was hurt by the criticism at first, but the actor Wilfred Walter gave him tuition, and he consulted his friends on remedies; his speaking manner improved somewhat, but it was never his strong point.[41]

---

[39] Snowden, *Autobiography*, ii. 766.
[40] Johnston, *A Hundred Commoners*, p. 200.
[41] *HC Deb.* 22 Feb. 1940, c. 1589. *The Times*, 12 Sept. 1961, p. 15. See Also F.P.-L. in Marchant (ed.), *If I Had My Time Again*, p. 141; F.P.-L., *Fate*, p. 140.

He had to win respect in other ways. One of these was his obvious affection for the House of Commons and devotion to its procedures; he curiously combined the rationalistic forward-looking reformer with the traditionalist stickler for routine. He relished parliament's rather clublike mood, enjoyed being involved in parliament's ceremony and traditions, and relished explaining them to visitors. Colleagues had to respect his integrity, intelligence, and conscientiousness behind the scenes. In him the mathematician's precision and abstraction were somewhat surprisingly combined with zest for the compromise that results from detailed negotiation between the parties, and he enjoyed the give-and-take of good debating for its own sake; he often praised the British capacity for resolving differences peacefully, and quite often at the end of a debate he would say that the time had been well and enjoyably spent.[42]

The main route to the respect of the House of Commons is through party; how did he stand there? In 1905 he denied that Labour was a class party, but admitted that 'because men with great possessions have their eyes blinded by wealth to the vital truth', most of its supporters came from working people. Yet here, as elsewhere in his career, he was building bridges; after 1924, as a rich and privileged person, he sought to achieve in the area of class, imperial, and international relations the reconciliation he had earlier sought between the sexes. As his *Times* obituarist puts it, he 'was a not uncommon type of English political life, a man of high and humane principle who employed his fortunate personal circumstances in the discharge of a scrupulous sense of public responsibility'.[43] After the decline of the Liberal Party, a progressive, rationalistic, humane, and conscientious politician naturally turned to Labour as the best route to appeasement in its widest and best sense. He saw the Labour Party as a stabilizing influence, a reason why Communism did less well in Britain than in France and Italy, and in parliament he more than once praised British gradualism.[44]

His outlook on practical questions flowed naturally from all this. Labour, if it was effectively to stabilize, must produce results. This located him, not in the centre of British politics as a whole, nor as an embattled moderate within the Labour Party, but securely and uncontroversially within Labour's mainstream. He seldom found it difficult to follow the party line, and kept aloof from party squabbles. He knew that MacDonald should take office separately from the Liberals in 1924, and unhesitatingly

[42] e.g. *HC Deb.* 11 Mar. 1936, c. 2268; 7 Dec. 1936, c. 1757; 26 Feb. 1941, c. 551.
[43] *Labour Record*, Apr. 1905, p. 48. *The Times*, 12 Sept. 1961, p. 15.
[44] *HC Deb.* 5 Feb. 1942, c. 1304. *HL Deb.* 3 Mar. 1948, c. 364; 8 Mar. 1950, cc. 145–6.

rejected MacDonald's suggestion that he should join the National Government in 1931.[45] He joined the Socialist League, but privately argued strongly against Cripps and G. D. H. Cole in 1932 when they wanted to commit the Party to nationalizing the joint-stock banks; the ground must be carefully prepared in opposition, he said, otherwise public support would be lost and 'we shall mess the job up altogether'.[46]

He hated authoritarianism, and preferred conciliation to confrontation; and his pursuit of harmony entailed painstakingly accumulating facts and rational argument. Hence his defence of conscientious objectors during the Second World War, his tendency in debates on penal questions to say 'there but for the grace of God go I', and his well-informed and well-argued speeches on capital punishment.[47] He refused to prosecute a burglar who stole jewellery from his Surrey house during his golden wedding celebrations in London, arguing that if the man wanted the jewellery that much he should keep it. His statesmanlike paper of 1927 on India strongly advocates commitment to self-government as a way of improving Anglo-Indian relations; quality of Indian government is, for him, a secondary question. The one burst of fury during his parliamentary debating career was provoked by Amery's authoritarian insensitivity to Indian opinion in the debate of 18 April 1944. As Secretary of State Fred believed in trusting the Indians, and tried to convince them of British sincerity; during his mission of 1946 he therefore made a point of assuming a judicial role.[48] Likewise with international relations: for him as for any mid-Victorian Liberal, free trade was the road to international harmony, and Keynes's critique of the Versailles settlement was 'of epoch making importance'.[49] He spoke rarely on diplomatic aspects but was very conscious of the economic dimension, and therefore closely scrutinized Conservative proposals for tariffs in the 1920s as the thin end of a protectionist wedge; when Britain's European Free Trade Association's negotiations seemed likely to bear fruit at the end of his career he welcomed the apparent impending decline of the protectionism whose revival his earlier career had witnessed.[50]

[45] F.P.-L., *Fate*, pp. 131, 136, 165–6. R. Bassett, *1931. Political Crisis* (1958), p. 164.

[46] P.-L. Papers, 5/43(3): F.P.-L. to Cripps, 28 Sept. 1932 (copy); cf. 1/167: F.P.-L. to G. D. H. Cole, 10 June 1932.

[47] *HC Deb.* 29 Nov. 1938, cc. 296–7; 22 Feb. 1940, cc. 1587–9. *HL Deb.* 28 Apr. 1948, cc. 496–9; 20 July 1948, c. 1038.

[48] PRO 30/69 (MacDonald Papers) 1172/399: printed paper dated 16 Jan. 1927 and headed 'Indian Problems', p. 5. *HC Deb.* 18 Apr. 1944, cc. 159–60. *HL Deb.* 7 Apr. 1948, c. 1182. P.-L. Papers, 6/160(2): F. to E.P.-L., 14 Apr. 1946.

[49] Keynes Papers, EC 1/2: F.P.-L. to J. M. Keynes, 23 Jan. 1920.

[50] *HC Deb.* 6 May 1925, c. 1034. *HL Deb.* 8 Mar. 1960, c. 881.

Yet he was keener than nineteenth-century Liberals to alter the balance of wealth within states; for him as for Emmeline, poverty caused war more than war caused poverty. So his hatred of war reinforced his domestic reasons for promoting a social conscience among the rich, and for trying to reduce class feeling. After 1918 he favoured a capital levy, and in the late 1930s a wealth tax; for him, the fate of France in 1940 illustrated how seriously a selfish upper class could endanger national unity.[51] He admired British courage (including that of his own secretaries) during the bombing, and often praised the taxpayer for bearing new burdens without complaint; imbued with the Attlee government's egalitarian mood, he welcomed Labour's erosion of class distinction.[52] All this fitted in with his personal austerity, and he disliked the Conservatives' preoccupation with affluence in the 1950s: 'I am terribly afraid', he said in July 1960, 'of the scramble in this country at the present time for personal prosperity and wealth.'[53]

An MP wins respect by making himself useful. Fred specialized in economic questions, which (when defined as including banking, taxation, tariffs, commercial questions, and government expenditure and accounts) take up 54 per cent of his parliamentary debating contribution. He was genuinely interested in economics, on which he published several books and learned articles; even in old age he gave it much of his leisure reading.[54] His expertise won the House's respect, and was invaluable to a party not always strong in the area. He could effectively tackle the Chancellor of the Exchequer on gold standard policy within just over a year of entering parliament; in 1939, after he had outgunned the then Chancellor Sir John Simon, Attlee told him that 'to the reader of Hansard the difference is plain between a man who understands finance and a man who has got up a brief, but does not really know his subject'.[55]

Like all socialists he defined economics very broadly to include the health, education, and happiness of a nation's human capital. When defending the national health service in the last year of his life he also stressed the socialist's strong sense of community and human interdependence;[56] throughout his career he wanted the budget seen, not as a narrowly financial operation, but as a device for promoting economic growth. He did not share Snowden's support for restoring the gold

---

[51] *HC Deb.* 24 July 1940, c. 916.
[52] F.P.-L., *Fate*, p. 203. *HL Deb.* 24 Feb. 1948, c. 47.
[53] *HL Deb.* 26 July 1960, c. 730; cf. 17 July 1961, c. 399.
[54] e.g. his speech in *HL Deb.* 17 May 1961, cc. 621–30.
[55] P.-L. Papers, 5/56: Attlee to F.P.-L., n.d. [end. '?Aug. 1939?'].
[56] *HL Deb.* 27 Mar. 1961, c. 7.

standard in 1925. He thought it would damage exports and so increase unemployment and lower wages, and always attributed the prosperity of the mid-1930s to the National Government's enforced abandonment of the gold standard which it had been set up to defend.[57]

In 1931 his position as Financial Secretary to the Treasury was crucial. Though in general he shared the Treasury point of view, he diverged on the higher financial issues where the civil servants tended to deal with Snowden direct. He denounced the National Government as 'formed for the express purpose of placing the neck of this country underneath the foot of foreign finance': it was all 'wholly unnecessary and infinitely degrading'. Budgets need not balance annually, he insisted, nor was the country verging on bankruptcy: overseas assets vastly exceeded liabilities. He would have mobilized the foreign investments of British subjects so as to peg the exchange rate; indeed, it would suffice merely to announce the intention.[58] If Labour had won the general election of 1931 he would no doubt have become Chancellor; as it was, the post eluded him and the electors gave him a holiday.

He was the ideal person for drawing Labour towards Keynesian remedies for unemployment, but although in 1959 he described himself as 'an unrepentant Keynes-ite'—claiming to have supported him 'all through' in favouring a budgetary deficit during a depression in order to stimulate the economy—his parliamentary speeches of the 1930s do not cite Keynes, perhaps partly because Keynes was a Liberal, and very little correspondence between them survives.[59] Fred cited Sweden in 1936 and New Zealand in 1938 as proof that prosperity can result from avoiding a deflationary policy during depression. He repeatedly argued in the late 1930s that 'finance should be the handmaid of economics', and that boosting purchasing power through welfare benefits would in itself boost the economy.[60] As the reach of the Treasury's arm extended, so his two major interests—taxation and banking—came together. He welcomed the institution of the exchange equalization account in 1932 as extending the government's control over the currency, and envisaged using its new-found monetary control to smooth out economic fluctuations; the nationalization of the Bank of England in 1946 was for him only the welcome culmination of a long process.

Whereas in the early 1930s the National Government accentuated the

---

[57] F.P.-L., *Fate*, p. 141. *HC Deb.* 22 Apr. 1936, c. 167.
[58] *HC Deb.* 10 Sept. 1931, c. 407. *Spectator*, 24 Oct. 1931, p. 527; 7 Nov. 1931, p. 596.
[59] *HL Deb.* 15 Apr. 1959, c. 645.
[60] *HC Deb.* 29 July 1938, c. 3546; see also 10 June 1936, c. 277; 14 Nov. 1938, c. 537.

trade cycle by cutting expenditure during a slump, in the late 1930s he was alarmed to see it failing to balance its budget during the run-up to a boom. Its motive was of course to finance the armaments made necessary by what he saw as a mistaken foreign policy. He wanted the increased taxation to be accompanied by an annual wealth tax, by restraints on luxury imports, and by effective planning to eliminate unemployment. His comments on budgets from the late 1930s onwards repeatedly stress the drawbacks of inflation as a random tax on the unemployed and on those with fixed incomes. He preferred taxation to loans as a way of financing the war, for loans would push up interest rates. In a courteous exchange of letters late in 1939 he contested Keynes's case for post-war credits, but in 1941 he welcomed the abundance of economic information provided with the budget, which did 'the highest credit to the able men whose services the Treasury can now command'.[61]

His economic outlook in the early 1940s was optimistic; 'the age of scarcity is past and the age of potential abundance has arrived . . .', he wrote in 1943. 'Poverty has become an anachronism, and nothing but prejudice and defeatism stand in the way of its abolition'; only technicalities seemed to prevent an immense expansion in national wealth.[62] Government planning could produce full employment, increase technical efficiency, encourage merit and promote education at the same time as women were becoming keener for paid work and the entire population was growing fitter. Larger industrial firms and managers' replacement of owners were tightening the links between industry and government. War demonstrated the constructive role the state could play, capitalism was being peacefully superseded, and nationalization would complete the process. Although he did not see nationalization as a panacea, Conservative denationalization in the 1950s made him very cross.[63]

He was still crosser about economic trends in the 1950s, for he thought the economy was being mismanaged. In his last parliamentary speech he admitted that he had been 'preaching . . . time and again' against the government's handling of bank rate.[64] Raising bank rate, he argued, tackled only short-term problems. It increased production costs, unnecessarily disturbed economic life, and reduced investment—thus slowing down Britain's relative economic growth and increasing

---

[61] *HC Deb.* 8 Apr. 1941, c. 1439; cf. 26 Apr. 1944, c. 802. Keynes Papers, HP 1/1: F.P.-L. to Keynes, 22 Nov. 1939, Keynes to F.P.-L., 11 Dec. 1939.
[62] F.P.-L., *Fate*, p. 7; cf. *HC Deb.* 13 Apr. 1943, c. 1099.
[63] *HL Deb.* 23 Feb. 1953, c. 622; 26 July 1960, cc. 729–30.
[64] *HL Deb.* 27 July 1961, c. 1103.

unemployment. He preferred physical planning of the economy, reinforced by consultation with the TUC; the choice did not lie between controls and no controls, he said, but between fine-tuned controls and controls that were clumsy and random in their impact. He never explained in detail how his controls would work, and British experience between 1961 and 1979 highlights the difficulties. For him the decade ended in disappointment; as he grumbled in his last speech, 'the same old dope, the same old quack medicines'.[65]

He was disappointed when his Indian mission of 1946 failed to get Hindus and Muslims to agree. He was thought to have been indecisive, and the major decisions on policy had anyway been taken by Attlee and Cripps; he was glad to retire in 1947.[66] Yet his Indian setback did not prevent him from becoming a highly respected figure in the House of Lords, whose less partisan mood probably suited him better; by 1945 his annual budget speech in the House of Commons had slipped into a non-party, largely technical mould, and the Lords found his rather academic approach more congenial. The balance of his interests did not change, and the three major events in his debating year during the 1950s all concerned economic policy: his speech on the Address at the start of the new session, his annual launching of the debate on the economy, and his speech on the Budget.

His lucid, logical, judicious, and wide-ranging synoptic economic analyses were often praised, and there was no tailing off with age in either the quantity or quality of his speeches; indeed, after Emmeline's death in 1954 he spoke more often. As a proportion of what was said by all members of the House, he contributed as much in the Lords as earlier in the Commons. While his intellect and expertise were respected, his obvious affection for the House and his enjoyment of debate made him popular, as did his unusual ability to combine courtesy and moderation with strongly held views and contempt for expediency. As Lord Hailsham writes: 'he was universally respected for the integrity of his character and the fearlessness and sincerity w[ith] wh[ich] he held relatively controversial opinions.'[67]

Why didn't he rise higher in politics? He had marked intelligence, money, fine political secretaries, expertise, range, self-discipline, loyalty to

---

[65] *HL Deb.* 27 July 1961, c. 1106; see also 2 May 1955, c. 665; 7 Mar. 1956, c. 138.

[66] *The Times*, 12 Sept. 1961, p. 15. Brittain, *Pethick-Lawrence*, pp. 149, 181, 187.

[67] Author's collection: Lord Hailsham to author, 30 Dec. 1983. I am most grateful to Lord Hailsham for permission to quote from his letter. See also *HL Deb.* 17 July 1961, c. 406 (Amory); 17 Oct. 1961, c. 327 (Layton).

party, and a distinguished wife. And he was conscientious: in eleven of his fifteen parliamentary sessions between 1924 and 1940 he was among the top hundred MPs for attendance in the division lobby. Bad luck played its part. He reached parliament late in life, and looked older than his age; 'old Pethick', or even 'funny old Pethick', is Hugh Dalton's phrase for him in his war diaries. 'Too old' was Attlee's reason for not pressing him into the cabinet in 1940. Fred's career also suffered by his absence from parliament between 1931 and 1935, when Attlee gained the leadership and Cripps (who eventually became Chancellor of the Exchequer) accumulated a parliamentary following. In 1942 he seemed sound enough to be made Leader of the Opposition, but as Dalton pointed out, the post was 'mostly honorific and ceremonial'.

There were other difficulties: to strangers Fred gave an impression of touchiness, and Brittain stresses his failure to push himself forward. More relevant is Attlee's comment: 'Very sound, but never really came over in the House of Commons.' Reading Fred's autobiography in 1943, Dalton noted that 'he has no sense of humour . . . and succeeds in making everything seem very flat'.[68] Furthermore Fred never really rooted himself in the Labour Party, and it was here that Dalton, his second usurper as Chancellor of the Exchequer, overtook him. Fred was not prominent in the Labour Party machine and spoke rarely in the party conference. He knew that influence on policy came less from speaking and voting in the House than from attending the parliamentary party's executive committee. But he had no trade-union or working-class background, and, although his loyalty to party was complete, he did not parade it.[69]

Still more important, Fred lacked the glamour and passion that move large gatherings. His exchange with Brittain in 1941, when diverging from her on pacifism, is revealing: 'I find that to allow my entrails to be lacerated by the distress of others', he told her, 'is to weaken and not to augment my power to help. I find this very much with my constituents. I will do anything I can to help them, but when they want love and sympathy and above all indignation I give them sparingly.' Such a man could never captivate the labour movement; predictably he clashed more than once with Aneurin Bevan. In February 1941 there was a chance of all-party agreement on reform of the means test, but Bevan joined the small left-wing dissident minority whom Fred attacked for posing as champions

[68] Dalton, *War Diary*, pp. 12, 351, 556. Attlee, *Yorkshire Post*, 27 June 1963, p. 4. Brittain, *Pethick-Lawrence*, p. 75.

[69] F.P.-L., *Fate*, pp. 136, 192.

of the oppressed and wanting 'to run with the hare and hunt with the hounds'. Fred seems to have got under Bevan's skin, for when they disagreed about Italian government four years later, Bevan retorted: 'that is the answer I might have expected from the crusted old Tory who still remains a member of this party.'[70] It was unfair, but it pinpointed Fred's image with the mass movement he could never hope to lead.

The career of so rational a man presents two further puzzles, less easily solved. First his consistent and lifelong defence of suffragette militancy as both effective and right. This led Emmeline's mentor Mark Guy Pearse to break off his friendship with her, and her autobiography admits the analogy between Mrs Pankhurst's militant structure and the Fascism that in the 1930s she herself loathed.[71] Fred's position jars with the humane values he and Emmeline stood for, and with the political methods he practised and so frequently defended in parliament after 1924. In May 1912 Fred thought politicians were treating the suffrage issue 'by methods of trickery and chicanery', and in October he described the House of Commons as 'one morass of intrigue and double-dealing on this question';[72] how could he retain such a standpoint after years of political experience? Not from wilful blindness, for he was a profoundly honest man who prided himself on confronting difficult facts.

In justifying what was done, Emmeline later made much of the fact that women's suffrage was won 'without a single case of injury to life or limb of its opponents being charged against it in the law courts';[73] this in itself constitutes no justification, nor does she offer any proof that it was militancy, however conducted, that won the vote. And the reasoning behind Fred's defence of the WSPU to G. M. Trevelyan falls below its usual high standard. He claimed that when anti-suffragists blocked the constitutional expression of a grievance, 'extraordinary and extralegal methods' are necessary.[74] Yet the blockage was far from complete, as the non-militant suffragists knew—especially if a practicable (adult suffrage) strategy replaced the equal-franchise objective for which in effect the WSPU campaigned. Nor is Fred convincing when he claims (without

[70] Brittain Collection: F.P.-L. to Brittain, 21 Feb. 1941. *HC Deb.* 13 Feb. 1941, c. 1561; 1 Dec. 1944, c. 307. See also Brittain Collection: Brittain to E. Knowles, 30 Oct. 1962 (copy); E. Knowles to Brittain, 1 Nov. 1962.

[71] E.P.-L., *My Part*, pp. 108–9, and Preface.

[72] F.P.-L., *The Man's Share. Mr Pethick-Lawrence's Defence of Militancy, delivered from the Dock of the Old Bailey* (Woman's Press, n.d.), p. 11. *Votes for Women*, 1 Nov. 1912, p. 77.

[73] P.-L. Papers, 7/37: speech by E.P.-L., 3 Mar. 1947, on the shooting of the film on 'Modern Wives'.

[74] Ibid. 6/280(2): F.P.-L. to G. M. Trevelyan, 3 Oct. 1949.

evidence) that 'extralegal methods' either roused public opinion after 1908 or coerced the government. A socialist's political inexperience, disrespect for property, and distance from the authorities may partly explain the Pethick-Lawrences' position between 1906 and 1914, but these cannot explain why for the rest of their lives they continued to defend what was done.

The second puzzle relates only to Fred. How could so rational a man content himself with so cloudy a religious faith? His remarkable lack of rancour at political setbacks owed much to a personal philosophy that he developed for himself. As a child he had sometimes cried himself to sleep puzzling over the idea of God continuing for infinite time in past and future, and the Unitarian minister Brooke Herford encouraged him to build up his own religion through persistent inquiry.[75] Fred was impressed by books on eastern religions, and eventually evolved a pantheistic, highly sentimental, and in some ways quietist faith which he tried to describe in the honest, reflective and penetrating self-analysis he published in the symposium *If I Had My Time Again.* The creed's objective, he said, was to integrate the personality through disciplining thought and will; 'if I were asked to sum up in a single phrase the main objective of individual life,' he wrote, 'I would express it as the enlargement of personality'. The individual should open out in response to the demands being made upon him. His creed produced passages like the following, when condoling Max Plowman on the death of his son Tim: 'nothing is ever lost. Nothing at any rate of love or beauty or joy. The rich stream of life flowing within the banks which you and Dorothy had formed from your bodies, the bright spirit which shone from its dancing wavelets ... these things are deathless.' Dalton found some of his autobiography's poetic parts 'quite blush-making, including the Song of Spring at the beginning, wherein he and the flowers in his garden burble to each other and send messages to her [Emmeline] in South Africa'.[76] Fred's beliefs may seem unsatisfactory in cold print, but his modesty would have prevented him from formulating their strongest justification: his lifetime of principled and substantial achievement. Two years before his death he described himself as an agnostic, but, said Lord Layton, 'as we walked out of his flat into Old Square he remarked, half in jest, half seriously, "I am the most religious-minded agnostic I know"'.[77]

[75] F.P.-L., *Fate*, pp. 16, 36.
[76] Ibid. p. 204. University College, London, Max and Dorothy Plowman Collection, Box 2: F.P.-L. to Max Plowman, 16 Apr. 1928. Dalton, *War Diary*, p. 556.
[77] *HL Deb.* 17 Oct. 1961, c. 327.

To the prison doctor in 1912 Fred at forty had seemed 'prematurely aged', looking quite fifty or fifty-five; and when at forty-three he was thrown from the platform at a Union of Democratic Control meeting, a young soldier called out: 'Don't hurt the old man.'[78] With his vivid gentian-blue twinkly eyes, and in later life his rather hunched body and large nose, he seemed to Mrs Groom-Smith 'just like Mr Punch'. Yet there was a boyishness about his habits and outlook that made him physically resilient. He did daily exercises and played tennis in Lincoln's Inn Fields till he was seventy-six. He liked walking, and ten years later he was still walking from Holborn to Westminster and sometimes walking back.

Emmeline was less fortunate. After Fred's career became so firmly centred on London she sometimes felt lonely at Fourways, and deafness increased her isolation; she was quite open about it, and used to place a large and (to others) embarrassingly noisy deaf-aid on the table in front of her when speaking in public.[79] Then she broke her hip, had it in irons for a year, and had to give up her beloved gardening; but she could still enjoy flowers and natural beauty, and loved being taken out for drives. A heart attack followed, and by 1951 she was virtually bedridden, Fred referring in a letter to 'her break up of personality'. He was sometimes impatient with her deafness and slowness, and eventually Elizabeth Kempster joined the Pethick-Lawrences' extended family to nurse her. She had herself been handicapped by polio, and found her new employers very sympathetic; they encouraged her to overcome her difficulties, and she felt almost like an adopted daughter.[80] Despite being at Fourways all the week, Gladys was quite often summoned back from Birmingham at weekends to help out.

A few months before she died Emmeline was afraid that Fred would be lonely after her death; 'Esther dear', she said, 'will you remember this—when I'm gone I don't want my Fred to be lonely'. Esther Knowles passed the message to Fred, who was much reassured; as she wrote afterwards, 'I knew and she knew that I knew what she meant without putting it into words'.[81] He was a man who could not live alone and had recently become

---

[78] PRO HO 45/24630: medical report to the Governor of Brixton Prison, 27 June 1912. F.P.-L., *Fate*, p. 114.

[79] Author's tape-recorded interview with Miss Marian Lawson, 20 Nov. 1974, at 44 Mount Street, London.

[80] P.-L. Papers, 6/220: F.P.-L. to E. Knowles, 26 Mar. 1951. I also draw here upon my tape-recorded interview with Miss Elizabeth Kempster, 24 June 1976, at the Horizon Hotel, St Brelade's Bay, Jersey.

[81] E. Knowles, autobiographical memoir in *Calling All Women*, 1975, p. 16. Brittain Collection: E. Knowles to Brittain, 16 June 1962.

very dependent on Esther, referring in 1951 to 'the wonderful personal relationship that there has been between us'.[82] She and Gladys were therefore less surprised than the rest of the world when Fred remarried in 1957. He had known Helen McCombie (née Craggs) as a suffragette, and she had been one of the friends who accompanied him on his annual visit to Kew Gardens to look at the magnolias. She was a less intellectual, less gentle character than Emmeline, and Esther thought Fred set about adjusting to her 'sometimes . . . as an algebraic and mathematical problem'. Esther mediated, and the couple soon settled down; Helen brought colour to Fred's life and much enjoyment, and he regretted that poor health prevented her from accompanying him more frequently to public functions. 'There was quite a lot of warmth in their relationship to each other', wrote Esther in 1962, 'and Gladys and I and Helen and Freddie all worked together as a very contented quartette.'[83]

Gladys played a crucially important role at the end. She was present when—unbeknown to the public—Fred had a stroke about four years before he died; so successfully did she encourage him that he recovered almost completely. She quite often entertained him at her Birmingham home and took trouble to make small comforts available to him there; 'I really and truly loved them,' she said of the Pethick-Lawrences. Esther said that after his last speech in the House of Lords in 1961 'he simply "folded up"'; 'the loss of our "little Freddie" is irreparable and Gladys and I are heart-broken'.[84]

Vera Brittain told Esther in 1962 that she felt 'more and more that some day there should be a really big biography about both him and Emmeline', and wanted as much of his correspondence preserved as possible. Discussing the Pethick-Lawrences' suffragist role, Esther in later life used to say, 'I want to see them vindicated', and 'they've never had their full due'.[85] Unfortunately Esther and Gladys could not prevent Fred and Helen from destroying papers that might have guaranteed the vindication Esther envisaged and the big biography Brittain wanted; the draft of Emmeline's autobiography, far longer than the published version, would alone have been precious. Only a fragment now survives of the Pethick-Lawrence papers Esther and Gladys so loyally created and filed away.

---

[82] P.-L. Papers, 6/219: F.P.-L. to E. Knowles, 17 Jan. 1951.
[83] Brittain Collection: E. Knowles to Brittain, 30 Aug. 1962. The Fawcett Library now holds the memoir of the second Lady Pethick-Lawrence sent by her daughter Sally Walker to the author in 1983.
[84] P.-L. Papers, 4/67: E. Knowles to 'Madeleine', 18 Sept. 1961 (copy).
[85] Brittain Collection: Brittain to E. Knowles, 19 June 1962 (copy). Author's interview with Mrs Needham, 31 May 1976.

Given Fred's systematic working methods and the wide range of the Pethick-Lawrences' interests, the archive might have become a major source for modern political history. More important, it might have illuminated still further what was surely one of the most significant marriages twentieth-century Britain has so far seen.

10

Catalyst and Facilitator

EVA HUBBACK

DEMOCRACY prescribes only a limited role for government, and draws heavily upon the spontaneous initiative and collaboration of individual citizens. Democracy also relies heavily upon the type of citizen who can identify and bring together the people whose voluntary co-operation is needed, and who knows how to influence government and public opinion through operating a network of voluntary bodies. Eva Hubback earns a chapter in this book with her abundant initiatives, and with what Stocks describes as her 'singular talent for combining pertinacious attack with friendly and reasonable co-operation'.[1] The last chapter is appropriate for her because she draws together so many of the book's earlier themes, organizations, and personalities.

She is interesting for other reasons as well. Her career illustrates the many new and useful directions that an imaginative suffragist could take in her public work after 1918, and shows how the tension between private and public responsibilities could become creative in the hands of a feminist with imagination. As a widow with three young children, she somehow managed to harmonize feminism with enthusiasm for motherhood more effectively than many of her contemporaries. Rathbone's feminist initiatives closely resemble Hubback's but owe less to personal experience, whereas motherhood stimulated Hubback to think hard about how to make child-rearing attractive to the emancipated woman.

For several reasons Jews were prominent in early twentieth-century British feminism; a Jewish League for Women Suffrage was founded in 1912, and suffragism owed much to the Zangwills, the Löwys, and the Franklins. Because their political rights had been won so recently, Edwardian Jews naturally sympathized with other groups seeking emancipation, and Jewish libertarianism was reinforced in the 1930s when Jews and feminists confronted the same Fascist enemy. The Jewish culture of education and self-improvement sent many Jews into the

[1] Stocks, *Rathbone*, p. 109.

PLATE 13. Eva Hubback, *c.*1947, photographed by Robin Adler (Mrs Diana Hopkinson).

artistic and intellectual circles that sympathized with suffragism, and eventually tempted some to leave the Jewish community altogether. By the 1880s wealth was turning some Jews towards Conservatism, but many progressive-minded Jews could still be found in the suffragist middle-class suburbs of Edwardian London and Manchester. One could root oneself more deeply in British society through social reform which, as we have seen, frequently led on to suffragism. This transition was all the more likely within those Edwardian Jewish families who ran the elaborate system of Jewish charities; none was more active here than the Spielman family into which Eva was born in London in 1886.

The later career of her father Meyer Spielman—a stockbroker as a young man—was artistic, idealistic, and retiring; he was knighted in 1927 for his work on behalf of juvenile delinquents. His wife Gertrude, eldest daughter of the banking millionaire George Raphael, was more practical than her husband; within the Jewish world she anticipated the role Eva later played within a wider circle. Gertrude was the first woman in many posts; she formed the Union of Jewish Women in 1902, and remained active on its executive committee till 1946. Spielman wealth did not preclude a strong sense of duty; Gertrude took cold baths till her fifties, made a point of answering letters on the day of receipt, and stayed up half the night dealing with her public work so as not to neglect her family during the day. For, though strict with her children, she was affectionate and understanding towards her family; 'though not an intellectual, she had any amount of native shrewdness', Eva recalled, 'and good judgment in daily life'.[2]

Eva was brought up in the Jewish faith, learned Hebrew, and attended the synagogue regularly. Her childhood was marred by monotony and governesses, and Gertrude fought a continuous and losing battle with her about tidiness and punctuality; but Eva admired her mother, and her letters home from St Felix School, Southwold, suggest an easy relationship with her parents. Burning her hair accidentally at the age of eighteen she hastened to correct Gertrude on how it had happened: 'as if you thought that your daughter would ever CURL her HAIR . . . What I meant was that I caught it by mistake on a candle!'[3] She was not keen on the elegances of social life and set her heart on going to Cambridge. This was an unusual ambition for a Spielman girl, and her parents tried to

---

[2] Hopkinson, *Family Inheritance*, p. 187. See generally W. Raphael, *Gertrude Emily Spielman, 1864–1949. A Memoir* (privately printed, 1950).

[3] Eva Hubback Papers (in the care of her daughter, Diana Hopkinson): Eva to Gertrude, 27 Feb. 1904.

divert her with a finishing school in Paris and a year of social life in London. But these were not to Eva's taste, and she went up to Newnham to read economics in 1905.

'I have simply heaps to tell you', she wrote on arrival, 'as something happens almost every minute although at the same time, the days pass like wild-fire;'[4] her letters continue in this breathless vein, for it was an exciting time to be at Cambridge. The emancipation involved in moving out from a somewhat restricted Jewish circle into a wider world of art, literature, and politics shaped the rest of her career and launched her on lifelong friendships. She fell in and out of love with Frank Joseph, a cousin at Oxford, and her Jewish faith gradually slipped into an unobtrusive agnosticism.

She was very shy on formal occasions, and her enthusiastic bursts of talk on social or political issues alternated with periods of silence. With her mop of frizzy hair, usually untidy, she was unsophisticated in the directness of her questions, but friends liked her lively spontaneity. Many years later a friend recalled her at Young Fabian picnics: 'what struck me most about her then was her intense enjoyment of everything—the views, the sandwiches, the bathing, the breathless talk on cycles as we battled along against the invariable fenland winds.' But her letters reveal zest for her studies too, and after getting an upper second in part one of her economics tripos she obtained a first class in part two, surpassing all the men in her year. Alfred Marshall's reference praised her individuality, her spontaneity, and her clear and methodical mind: she was 'firm of purpose', with 'a strong sense of duty'.[5]

Basing herself at home, she now embarked serious-mindedly on care-committee work in Whitechapel for the London County Council, becoming a poor law guardian for Paddington in 1910. She began arguing with her two more conservative brothers. 'Art and literature are splendid things,' she told her Cambridge friend Bill Hubback, 'but they are not the most important things to me *at present*. They will be when man's material welfare is assured.' She told him she wanted first 'to know facts, facts, facts, about the way people live now and about political psychology', about government and how it could be improved. But like so many Edwardian progressives, she was critical of the working people she wanted to help. 'I don't *like* a London crowd amusing itself,' she wrote in 1911. 'It is good tempered enough, but so silly and ugly and vulgar, and such squirmy

[4] Hubback Papers: same to same, 21 Oct. 1905.
[5] Ibid.: Olwen Campbell's typescript memoir. Marshall's testimonial is enclosed in his letter to Hubback, 4 Dec. 1909.

people. A really damned thing was to see some drunken women carrying tiny babies (one of them feeding hers) and dancing.'[6]

Bill was a university lecturer in classics who later ventured into economic history. He was a wildly untidy, vigorous, optimistic, gregarious, and carefree young man, still prone to turn cartwheels and leap over stiles. Friends were delighted at his engagement to Eva, but the Spielmans were alarmed. Gertrude was in tears when she brought the news to Eva's younger sister, Winifred, for Eva was the first of her extended family to 'marry out'.[7] Outraged relatives shielded their marriageable daughters from her contamination. Yet by marrying Bill in a register office in 1911, Eva set a precedent, and many cousins later confided in her when agonizing over whether to follow the same path.

She retained much of her Jewish past. Particularly important were the complex and contradictory feelings of family security and Jewish insecurity. Unusually in the circumstances, her parents provided a generous marriage settlement; they also gave her large money presents and helped out in emergencies. She always had the feeling that she would be backed up in a crisis by her wealthy family and her numerous first and second cousins. Though she had little in common with her two brothers, she was always interested in their doings, and to Winifred she was very close. Then there was what Winifred called the 'emotional insurance' provided by the Spielmans' self-confidence as big fish in the Jewish community's small pond; in her larger pond later, Eva always knew that people would listen to her and carry out instructions. Stocks may be right in detecting a Jewish component in her 'kind of matriarchal belief in the family'.[8] Her long widowhood reinforced such feelings, and her strong sense of family deeply influenced her feminism; she liked family celebrations and birthdays, and often took the children to visit her parents on Saturdays. Her Jewish background also nourished her strong sense of public duty, backed by a lifelong personal moral code which she taught her children. In what she called 'Sunday school' she read them poetry and extracts from the Bible and ethical books on Sunday mornings, then played the piano and they would all sing; she also read them Quaker essays and for a time they attended a Quaker Sunday School.

At the time of her engagement she thought that 'being married would be

[6] Hopkinson, *Family Inheritance*, pp. 51, 67.

[7] Author's tape-recorded interview with Mrs Winifred Raphael, 2 Mar. 1976, at 28 Clareville Grove, London SW7 5AS.

[8] Hubback Papers: Mary Stocks's script for a talk on Hubback on the BBC Light Programme, 13 Oct. 1952.

like a prolonged reading party with the additional attraction of babies'.[9] The babies soon arrived—Diana (named after Meredith's feminist heroine, and later Eva's biographer) in 1912, Rachel in 1914, and David in 1916. And in 1913 the Hubbacks moved into Threeways, their Cowles Voysey home in Hampstead Garden Suburb, which Eva loved. This handsome William-and-Mary style house adjoining the Heath still stands confidently in Wellgarth Road. Inside, 'there was a sort of Heal's decency about it', Olivier Bell recalls—with comfortable, well-made furniture.[10] Eva was artistic, but inherited something of her mother's personal austerity, so the design of the house reflected her taste for light and air; for Diana it remains 'one of the coldest and draughtiest houses I have known'.[11]

The marriage at first went well, but Bill was a sociable, easy-going character, less serious-minded than Eva. She told the children almost nothing about the marriage, though she suggested to Diana that it might have run into difficulties if Bill had returned from the war.[12] He died of a head wound in 1917, which left her a widow with three young children and a war-widow's inadequate pension. She had resumed social work after Rachel was born, and (with a relative) launched the first infant welfare clinic in South Islington. From 1916 to 1917 she was temporary lecturer in economics at Newnham, and then spent six weeks reading science with the idea of becoming a doctor until she decided that science was not for her.

Suffragism made her known to a wider public. At first she supported the suffragettes, but had become lukewarm by 1910, and was put off altogether by their arson and hunger-striking. She remained keen on the vote; when voting for the first time in 1918 she took Diana with her into the polling booth and impressed on her the importance of the event by making her put the cross on the paper. She began work for the NUWSS information bureau shortly before the vote was won, then took over from Ray Strachey as Parliamentary Secretary, and retained the post till 1927. Her predecessors Catherine Marshall and Ray Strachey had made the post the hub of the non-militant suffragist machine, and she continued the tradition. There was nothing inevitable about the many family and welfare reforms which so advanced women's interests in the early 1920s, nor about the advent of

---

[9] Ibid.: Evelyn Radford's typed memoir.
[10] Author's collection: Mrs Olivier Bell to author, 28 Jan. 1985.
[11] Hopkinson, *Family Inheritance*, p. 75.
[12] All personal information about Hubback that is not footnoted in the text comes from my two tape-recorded interviews with David and Diana Hopkinson, 15 Feb. 1976, 2 Oct. 1984, or from Diana's biography of her mother.

the equal franchise in 1928. These reforms required from their promoters tact, a sense of timing, sensitivity to political situations, as well as persistence and skill in unobtrusively accumulating contacts, influencing the press, gathering facts, and drafting policy proposals. At the same time friends had to be held together and recruited through rousing public opinion when necessary. As Hubback recalled in 1938, 'we had . . . to learn a new technique, to enter into questions of law and of policy far more subtle and complicated than in the old suffrage days. And we had ourselves to become experts.'[13]

At all this she was adept, and was reinforced by her political partnership with Rathbone. They worked well together. Both had powerful intellects, and Hubback's organizing genius complemented Rathbone's experience and presence. Most of NUSEC's important decisions were reached over lunch at Rathbone's house in Romney Street between Hubback, Rathbone, and Macadam.[14] In her presidential address of 1923 Rathbone gave Hubback almost all the credit for the Matrimonial Causes Act: she had suggested the idea to NUSEC's executive, drafted the Bill, and got the Liberal lawyer and MP Major Cyril Entwistle to sponsor it. In the same year NUSEC's annual report found it 'difficult to overstate how much the Parliamentary work of the Union owes to her judgement and political sagacity'. So close was this partnership, that she must receive some of the credit for Rathbone's even greater achievements. 'I am so bad at expressing affection,' Rathbone told her in 1941. 'I don't think I ever shew how much your friendship means to me.'[15]

In the mid-1920s Lady Rhondda and the Six Point Group repeatedly grumbled in the feminist weekly *Time and Tide* about NUSEC's timidity and delay; in 1923, for instance, a correspondent complained that NUSEC's 'pettifogging measures' were 'always a little less than is fair and right'. In 1924 Rathbone and Hubback agreed that the measure then going through parliament did not yet equalize guardianship rights, but said that accepting half a loaf now would not preclude later gains, whereas widening amendments would wreck the measure. *Time and Tide* thought half-measures should be accepted only if compatible with an important principle, whereas this Bill was 'an insult to the women's societies'.[16] The

---

[13] Hubback Papers: Hubback's typescript presidential address, 16 Mar. 1938, to the annual council of the NCEC.

[14] Author's interview with Mrs Gertrude Horton, 13 Apr. 1977.

[15] NUSEC *4th Annual Report, 1923*, p. 30. Hubback Papers: Rathbone to Hubback, 2 Sept. 1941. Rathbone, *Milestones*, p. 21.

[16] *Time and Tide*, 21 Sept. 1923, p. 957 (Nina Boyle); 20 June 1924, p. 587; cf. Rathbone's letter on p. 597.

Six Point Group liked labelling politicians black or white, whereas (as Hubback pointed out) 'most of them, we find, are grey or piebald'. In 1926 Rathbone saw events in 1925 as having 'strikingly justified the policy and methods of the NUSEC'; making uncompromising 'demands' and then expecting the walls of Jericho to collapse was 'not the way to get things done'.[17] Pressure groups find it difficult enough to influence the pace of legislation at the best of times, and over-enthusiastic extra-parliamentary campaigners thirsting for enemies can easily slow it down. In the Conservative governmental climate of the 1920s, Hubback was surely right to stress the need for prudence if anti-feminists were to be kept at bay.

British feminists in the mid-1920s argued about policy as well as tactics. Rathbone acknowledges Hubback's help in the preface to her *Disinherited Family,* and Eva joined Rathbone in pressing inter-war feminists to cater more fully for the wife and mother. Exchanging views with Winifred Holtby in 1926, she admitted that it was easier to mount an agitation on a single-issue egalitarian basis, but as full legislative equality was 'undoubtedly in sight' she thought it time to move on. The 'new feminists' whom she supported wanted to ensure 'that the whole structure and movement of society shall reflect in a proportionate degree the experience, the needs and the aspirations of the women, as well as the men of the community'; family allowances and birth-control were 'not a side show, an excrescence on feminism, but part of its very core'. As most women then spent their best years on housekeeping, bearing and rearing children, sex differentiation 'must prevail in that most important of women's occupations, maternity'. Hubback also diverged from the 'old feminists' on factory legislation, and in 1929 she and several Labour women publicly urged special legislative provision for women on hours and working conditions.[18]

She combined her work for NUSEC with teaching economics to various classes, especially in the sixth form of Streatham Hill High School for Girls, and in 1927 she was chosen from 130 applicants as Principal of Morley College, a well-known evening college in Lambeth. But she remained chairman of NUSEC's parliamentary sub-committee, and stayed on its executive committee; 'I am torn in two between gratitude and regret,' Fawcett told her. 'We cannot over-estimate the value of your service to the Women's cause.' She had yet to crown her contribution to

---

[17] *Time and Tide,* 30 July 1926, p. 700. Rathbone, *Milestones,* p. 31.
[18] *Yorkshire Post,* 12 July 1926, p. 6. *Time and Tide,* 20 Aug. 1926, p. 761. See also *The Times,* 1 Feb. 1929, p. 13.

NUSEC, for she seems to have been a key figure in ensuring that it set up the Townswomen's Guilds in the late 1920s. Corbett Ashby recalled being questioned by Hubback, then in hospital, about the Women's Institutes; Hubback's idea was to revive NUSEC by applying the Institutes' methods to urban women. Hubback was on the key NUSEC committee which devised the Guilds; it was partly through her family connection with the Franklins that the Guilds recruited their most enthusiastic promoter, Hubback's cousin Alice Franklin, and it was through Hubback's birth-control connections that Lady Denman's help was enlisted.[19]

Hubback could not herself be active in the Guilds, if only because she had agreed to carry on the egalitarian aspect of NUSEC's programme when it divided itself into the National Union of Townswomen's Guilds and the NCEC in 1932. As president of the Council—seen by a knowledgeable commentator in the mid-1930s as 'a very small body, but active and progressive'—she linked it up with several other 'Middle Way' reforming causes. Yet the commentator went on to say that there was 'now no strength behind' the NCEC. In 1938, when resigning its presidency, Hubback admitted the need for more members, but said she could not herself give the necessary time; her energies in the 1930s were in fact going elsewhere.[20] Picton-Turbervill succeeded her, and the transport and other difficulties experienced by most voluntary bodies during the Second World War accelerated a gentle decline that dates almost from the Council's foundation.

Rathbone once described the NCEC as 'a power station of ideas'. It helped widen the franchise for Indian women and promoted improved children's nutrition; its diverse role may explain why it spent so much time reporting work done by other bodies, so little describing its own. There were complicated interactions here between bodies that were nominally separate yet drew on the same personnel; the Children's Minimum Committee (or Council, as it later became) was itself, as Hubback pointed out, 'a temporary meeting ground for the many organizations whose concern is largely or mainly with child welfare'.[21] The Committee aimed to prevent parental poverty from denying any child the minimum diet required for full health, and joined nutritionists in campaigning for things

---

[19] Hubback Papers: Fawcett to Hubback, 10 Sept. 1927. For Hubback's role in creating the Townswomen's Guilds I have drawn on my interviews with Margery Corbett Ashby, 8 Apr. 1975 and 23 Nov. 1976, and with Mrs Horton, 13 Apr. 1977.

[20] Nancy Astor MSS 1416/1/1/1437: carbon copy of typescript [by Ray Strachey?] on leading women's organizations. Hubback Papers: typescript address, 16 Mar. 1938, p. 6.

[21] Rathbone quoted in Hubback's address of 16 Mar. 1938. J. Lewis, *The Politics of Motherhood. Child and Maternal Welfare in England, 1900–1939* (1980), p. 176.

like free milk at state schools, compulsory school meals for poor children, and better allowances for the children of the unemployed.

In addition to promoting family allowances and children's nutrition, Hubback made an unobtrusive but important contribution to the birth-control movement in the early 1930s. Her marked alertness to new ideas is very apparent here. She joined the Malthusian League in 1910 but never liked its strong emphasis on the economic arguments for birth-control, and later left it to join the Society for Constructive Birth Control and Racial Progress, founded by Marie Stopes in 1921. 'The matter should be dealt with from the humanitarian standpoint', she later emphasized, 'rather than that of economic theory which was divided in the matter'.[22] She joined the Eugenics Society in 1929 and began serving on its central committees in 1932; its links with the birth-control movement at this time were strong, and at the general election of 1929 she formed a joint committee of women's organizations to question MPs on their views about birth-control. Out of this grew the Birth Control International Informa-tion Centre, which in 1930 took over the work of the International Federation of Birth Control Leagues; from this grew the International Planned Parenthood Federation which has since become so influential overseas. But more important was the way Hubback brought medical and lay people together within the National Birth Control Association, later the Family Planning Association.[23]

She needed all her diplomatic skills if the various birth-control bodies were to federate under the Association's umbrella without offending Stopes; the outcome differed markedly from Billington-Greig's attempts at feminist amalgamation during the 1940s. Hubback worked closely with the pioneer birth-control doctor Helena Wright, who was determined to prevent the Association from alienating Stopes too early. Wright told me that Hubback was the sort of person to whom people listened in committees: she was quietly courageous, efficient, good at fund-raising, and knew what she wanted. Her tact was also needed to press politicians, local authorities, and the Ministry of Health into financing birth-control information and making it accessible; the Association would ultimately have been happy for government to take over its activities entirely.[24]

[22] David Owen Centre for Population Growth Studies, Cardiff, Family Planning Association Archive A5/1: NBCA minutes, 24 Sept. 1931. See also Lewis, *Politics of Motherhood*, pp. 200, 205.

[23] See Houghton's 'The Rise of the International Planned Parenthood Movement', *Family Planning*, Apr. 1962. These paragraphs owe much to my tape-recorded interviews with Dr Helena Wright, 27 Feb. and 24 Apr. 1977, at Brudenell House, Quainton, Bucks.

[24] Interview with Dr Wright, 24 Apr. 1977. See also B. Evans, *Freedom to Choose. The Life and Work of Dr Helena Wright, Pioneer of Contraception* (1984), p. 145.

Hubback was simultaneously acting as an imaginative and energetic Principal of Morley College. Her predecessor Barbara Wootton had prepared the ground with helpful staff changes, and without the dedicated support of her secretary Margaret Cowles and the bursar-administrator George Cottrell, Hubback would have achieved much less. Cowles and Cottrell worked well together; Cottrell was happy to remain in the background, while Cowles held the fort for Hubback when away. Evenings were Hubback's Morley hours, and she spent much time away from the College during the day making contacts; the College was a good launching-pad for other activities, which in turn benefited the College. Effective subordinates ultimately shed credit on the employer who selects, motivates, and trusts them; Cowles's loyalty was almost legendary, and Cottrell told me that Hubback 'had a genius for choosing the right people'.[25] She introduced distinguished visiting speakers to the College and obtained royal patronage. In 1928 a sports ground was bought at Eltham, and she instituted an annual College dinner with well-known guests; in 1929 these included Ramsay MacDonald and William Rothenstein. In 1928–9 she launched the College's public lectures and an annual open day. Enrolments rose fast, and a long-postponed extension was opened in 1937. Hubback was alert to new opportunities, and rose fully to the challenges of the depression and the Second World War— promoting army education, efforts for child welfare, discussions on the Beveridge Report, and so on.

She also carried forward what was perhaps the College's most important early twentieth-century artistic achievement—Holst's distinguished musical tradition. She loved music, especially Hebridean folk songs, and sometimes carried the children off to chamber music concerts. She first encountered Michael Tippett when promoting education for the unemployed—work which eventually made her prominent in the London Council for Voluntary Occupation during Unemployment. Tippett was then promoting children's choirs and musical activity among Cleveland ironstone miners, and came to her notice through Alan Collingridge who (like Hubback) had a wide range of contacts. Tippett began lecturing at the College in the mid-1930s and built up the South London Orchestra. The war made it necessary for Morley to appoint a new Director of Music in 1940; Tippett got the job, and remained there till 1951. When Tippett—then in his prime, lively and unorthodox—came forward during the war with numerous ideas of his own, Hubback was the first to respond.

[25] Author's tape-recorded interview with George Cottrell, 3 July 1976, at Westwyns, Longdogs Lane, Ottery St Mary, Devon. Interview with Mrs Horton, 28 Feb. 1977. See also D. Richards, *Offspring of the Vic. A History of Morley College* (1958), pp. 223, 231, 233.

Once she had appointed staff, she believed in trusting them completely. 'I was obviously her favourite . . . ,' he told me; 'I could do what I liked.'[26]

The war had dispersed much of Holst's choir, and the music library was bombed, so there were many opportunities. Tippett worked on madrigals, got interested in Purcell, fostered appreciation of Monteverdi, and helped arrange a memorable concert by Myra Hess. He drew fully upon the rich musical talent then available in South London, especially upon aliens and war service rejects; indeed there were complaints, backed even by Vaughan Williams, that he was departing from the College's British musical tradition. On this as on everything else, Hubback defended him. She was, says Tippett, 'a very liberal-minded woman *indeed*', and 'a tower of strength' in 1943 when he was imprisoned as a conscientious objector, despite not sharing his views. She also helped to ensure that Norbert Branin was protected from work that would damage his hands.

There was more to this than delegating or providing administrative help: Hubback gave Tippett moral support and encouragement. 'We got *very* close,' he recalled; 'I mean I was, I should think, the only person of my age that called her by her Christian name.' Morley College was a very informal place then, and Tippett could easily drop in for quarter of an hour's chat with her in her office quite regularly. He confided in her as a warm, stimulating, generous, and approachable person at a difficult time in his life; 'she was one of the remarkable . . . figures in my life altogether,' he says. When she died he did not wish to stay, and so in 1951 he left.

All the threads of her career—as liberal-minded, Jewish-born educationist, suffragist mother, founder of the Townswomen's Guilds, and patriotic opponent of Fascism—come together in the Association for Education in Citizenship [AEC]. Women's fight for the vote was itself, she said, 'the fight for democratic citizenship', and NUSEC always saw itself as helping to politicize the new voters. In 1929 the Townswomen's Guilds aimed 'to encourage self-education, independent thinking, and effective action among women voters on all questions concerning their citizenship'. Its founders wanted it to provide 'a training in democracy' through its own democratic structure, and hoped it would tempt its members into standing for parliament and local councils.[27]

Another root of the AEC lay through Hubback's long-standing friendship with Ernest and Shena Simon. As a young man Ernest had been

[26] Author's tape-recorded interview with Sir Michael Tippett, 29 Aug. 1981, at Littlecote, Church Green, Burford, Oxon.

[27] Hubback Papers: typescript address, 16 Mar. 1938. *Woman's Leader*, 15 Mar. 1929, p. 44. NUTG, *Annual Report, 1934*, p. 6; cf. p. 8.

shy of women yet wanted a wife who could play Beatrice to his Sidney Webb; at a dinner-party in 1911 Hubback introduced him to Shena, a friend she envisaged as an ideal wife. Hubback, the Simons, and the Laytons moved freely among those creative inter-war progressive intellectuals who gave the Liberal Party such a long afterglow; the final drafts of its Yellow Book emerged from a holiday taken by these five in the Alps. The AEC also originated on a holiday, for the pamphlet *Education for Citizenship* was written at the Simons' country cottage in the Langdale valley during 1933; on this subject, Ernest once told her, 'you are my second mind'. Nor was it a purely intellectual partnership, for Ernest acted as guardian to the Hubback children after 1917, and financed holidays and medical treatment for the family. When Eva was receiving blood-transfusions during her last illness he insisted on making his own blood available too.[28]

A combination of patriotism, secularized morality, and strong belief in democracy lay behind the AEC. The Simons were distinguished but late exponents of the provincial civic consciousness which achieved so much in Victorian Britain, and which deeply influenced young Edwardian Fabian intellectuals like Hubback. Yet by the 1930s this tradition was being eroded by centralized government and welfare, the spread of mass entertainment, the growth of the popular press, and the cult of domesticity. Hubback had already organized a survey of the literature on citizenship, and her collaborators merged with the AEC on its formation. 'The most fundamental of all our problems is . . . how to evoke civic consciousness,' she wrote. 'The accumulation of knowledge and the development of reasoning power will by themselves be useless if an active motive force be not first generated.'[29]

Rule by the few was unacceptable, so school and university teachers must act as a secularized but evangelical priesthood. In 1947 Hubback complained that 'at present the subjects chosen for research frequently do not appear to be selected on account of their intrinsic importance. They are often frivolous in relation to the urgent need for enlightenment in so many of the problems which have baffled the shattered world of today.' Citizenship must be consciously mobilized. 'The child's social education,' she wrote, '—his relationships with the communities of which he forms part—has been, comparatively speaking, neglected'. The AEC aimed at creating a national organization to promote democratic ideas; concentrating

[28] M. Stocks, *Ernest Simon of Manchester* (Manchester, 1973), p. 105; see also pp. 25, 33, 85. Interview with the Hopkinsons, 15 Feb. 1976.
[29] Hopkinson, *Family Inheritance*, p. 129.

on the teenager, it sought 'to advance the study of and training in citizenship, by which is meant training in the moral qualities necessary for the citizens of a democracy; the encouragement of clear thinking in everyday affairs; and the acquisition of that knowledge of the modern world usually given by means of courses in history, geography, economics, citizenship and public affairs.'[30]

The *Townswoman* recommended *Education for Citizenship* as something which 'should be read and thought over by every woman in the movement',[31] but here—as at Morley College—Hubback was skirmishing well beyond feminist frontiers. The persecutions of the late 1930s caused her to move on still further when, both in her own home and in her public work, she responded to the claims of refugee immigrants. In a part-time *tour de force*, she and Ernest directed AEC policy, drew support from a wide political spectrum, and brought together teachers in the relevant subjects. They organized conferences, prepared bibliographies, published books and pamphlets, wrote frequently in the press, and later founded the *Universities Quarterly*. The AEC was never her sole preoccupation, and Ernest would have liked more of her time; yet it went downhill after her death when denied even a portion of her initiative and energy, and in 1957—though the need for some such body is still felt—it was wound up.

This remarkable career in a widow without wealth but with three young children poses at least two questions: how did she reconcile her public and private duties? And how was she able to achieve so much in the public sphere? Her methods of work are of special interest. Her London base was Threeways, capacious and comfortable—despite the cold—with its books, pictures, artistic and comfortable furnishings. She was not interested in cooking, and was rather absent-minded even when eating. Diana resented her tendency to buy the cheapest food, the cheapest theatre-seats, the cheapest clothes. Two things shielded Eva from many of the modern career-woman's conflicting loyalties. Firstly, domestic help was still widely available, and she was good at delegating. Originally she had a nurse and nursemaid, followed by a nursery governess, as well as household staff. Later she had a couple living in—the wife responsible for cooking, the husband working at his own job. And later still Gunhild the Danish housekeeper lived in, supplemented by a daily who came in to clean; as Eva often had a lodger it was hard work, and the dailies usually didn't stay long. Secondly her variant of feminism grew out of her

---

[30] E. Hubback, *The Population of Britain* (Penguin edn., 1947), pp. 181–2, 165. *New Statesman*, 14 July 1934, p. 63.

[31] *Townswoman*, May 1934, p. 31; cf. Oct. 1935, p. 154 (Corbett Ashby).

domestic experience instead of cutting across it. Campaigning to reward motherhood was but one of several ways in which, as Diana puts it, her 'threads of private and public life were closely woven'.[32]

Though by modern standards firm with her children, she was a liberal parent by the standards of the time; young people holidaying in Cornwall with the Hubbacks enjoyed the family's informal way of living, and were intrigued by a mother who combined a taste for sea-bathing before breakfast with insistence on a high standard of mealtime conversation. As teenagers, David went to school as a weekly boarder at Westminster and Diana to St Paul's, staying with her grandmother during the week; only Rachel was based at home. Eva recognized the potential conflict between her public and private obligations. 'Do you feel neglected?' she sometimes asked Rachel; as Rachel was busy in the evenings, her mother's absence at Morley College did not worry her. Yet she recalls Eva noticing (when she was about nine) that her new pencil-box needed naming; Eva suggested she might write the name on: 'I said "yes", and as she wrote my name, I thought "oh, you're being like an ordinary mother, the kind who makes jam and things"'.[33]

Eva always seemed too tired to listen when Diana wanted to talk; as a young woman, Diana 'actively resented' the pressures upon her mother, and reacted against them by showing only a lukewarm interest in feminism. She remembers comforting her eleven-year-old brother when he worried about Eva returning from Morley College late at night.[34] But Eva was careful about selecting schools for her children, and her influence on their careers was so great that Rachel simply grew up with the idea of being a doctor, just as David simply assumed that he would be a civil servant. Eva's choice was correct only for David, for Rachel soon found that medicine was not for her, and Diana was not suited to a university course. Eva applied in the family sphere the techniques that were so successful in public life—seeking the best advice on their careers, making use of contacts, and sending the children to acknowledged experts for guidance. Graham Wallas, for instance, advised Diana on methods of study before she went to university.

Not content with responsibility for her own family—and but for Bill's death in the war she might have reached her target of six—Eva delighted in her five grandchildren, had many godchildren, and was intensely

[32] Hopkinson, *Family Inheritance*, p. 15.
[33] Author's tape-recorded interview, with David and Rachel Hubback, 2 Feb. 1976, at 15 Park Drive, London NW11. Private information.
[34] Hopkinson, *Family Inheritance*, p. 97. Interview with the Hopkinsons, 2 Oct. 1984.

interested in other people's offspring. Diana says she 'would travel a great distance to see a new-born infant',[35] and stopped mothers in the street to talk about their children; before the Second World War she ran the Hampstead Heath Babies Club from Threeways nursery. She also took into her home lodgers, students, refugees, and the children of friends who were in difficulties, and was one of the few people regularly to visit Margery Olivier, a Cambridge friend who became mentally ill, over thirty years. Margery's sister Brynhilde when dying asked Eva to be guardian to her three younger children, and Eva took them out or had them for holidays.

Young people appreciated her unusual combination of dependable common sense and open-minded intellectual vitality. In one holiday at Treyarnon, Olivier Bell remembers her intervening only once, when summoned to deal with an emergency, but she immediately acted 'with her usual solid calm and good sense and imperturbability'. More than one young person found her a 'second mother'. One lodger of the late 1920s was the economist Thomas Balogh, a Hungarian student alone and rather lonely in London. He found her sensitive, helpful, and interested in his subject; 'she made people feel secure,' he recalled.[36] If young people were in difficulties, she would not weigh heavily in, but would concentrate completely on what they were saying and then clear-headedly suggest what, if anything, could be done. To her cousin Catherine Joseph and her fiancé, who as a gentile had been coldly received by the family, she could hardly have been more understanding or helpful. 'The word "generation-gap" meant really nothing to Eva,' Peggy Jay recalls. She was refreshingly unshockable, and Jenifer Hart saw her as 'one of the few people one would go to to consult about one's life and work and really want to know what they thought'.[37]

Friends stayed with her at her two holiday homes—Trethias Cottage at Treyarnon Bay in Cornwall and Maes Caradoc in North Wales. The first, jointly owned with her friend Mary Moorhouse, was comfortable and (after 1930) all-electric; the second had been discovered by Bill and was rented. Maes Caradoc—less frequently visited by the family—was wild

---

[35] Hopkinson, *Family Inheritance*, p. 125.

[36] Author's collection: Mrs Olivier Bell to author, 28 Jan. 1985. Author's tape-recorded interviews with Mrs Catherine Dennis (née Joseph) and Peter Joseph, 28 Jan. 1981, at 33 Bedford Row, London WC1; and with Lord Balogh, 3 May 1977, at the House of Lords.

[37] Author's tape-recorded interview with Mrs Peggy Jay, 11 Jan. 1977, at 12a Well Road, London NW3. Hubback Papers: J. Hart to D. Hopkinson, n.d. This discussion also owes much to my tape-recorded interview with Mr and Mrs Dennis, 19 Apr. 1980, at 59 Belmont Road, Portswood, Southampton SO2 1GD.

and primitive, with water from a mountain stream, coal fire, oil lamps, primus stoves, outdoor lavatory, and no electricity. Eva loved them both, the first for its walks and cliffs and swimming all the year round, the second for its mountain rambles and early morning cold swims in the freshwater pool near by. These places catered for the impulsive spontaneity that once led her to leap out of a train in the middle of the night in Sicily when she suddenly found it stopping at a place she wanted to visit.[38]

She often worked on holiday, but after sprawling in a chair for an hour or so she would suddenly get up and say, 'now we're all going for a walk'; after walking she would work for an hour or so, and then say 'well, now we'll go and see if we can't have lunch'. Routine was not to her taste; spontaneity was important. There was more to this than a mere pursuit of pleasure: a personal philosophy lay behind it—a belief in seizing life's fleeting opportunities, in grasping moments for seeing new sights and meeting new people that might never recur. She would rather see half a play than no play at all. Indeed, she once burst in upon Marjorie Green, secretary to the Children's Minimum Campaign Committee, saying 'Miss Green, I want to go out on the town', and carried her off to the best bits of three separate plays. 'She was always trying to get into the latest film, you know, between two committees,' Diana recalls. She would read only the best bits of the novels delivered by the Times Book Club, and Diana says that in the middle of writing an article she would get up 'because there was a miraculous sunset to be seen. "Come out *now*," she would say . . .'.[39]

Her zest for freedom and spontaneity perpetuated in her friends' minds their image of the Edwardian Cambridge undergraduate, with her fuzzy hair and clothes merely thrown on. She had fine features and expressive brown eyes, and in later life looked imposing on the rare occasions when she bothered with her appearance. She was, as she herself said, 'well upholstered'. This did not make for a graceful carriage or for nimble climbing at Maes Caradoc, but it helped her bear degrees of cold at Threeways or in the sea at Treyarnon that some found astonishing. Clothes she saw as a nuisance, and she would try to get all she wanted during a rushed visit to the sales. Diana once searched seven different shops for the exact shade of green silk she needed for a dress: 'but life is too short for that kind of thing,' Eva exclaimed.[40] So she looked large, floppy,

[38] Interview with Mrs Raphael, 2 Mar. 1976; cf. Hubback Papers: Evelyn Radford's typed memoir.

[39] Interview with the Hopkinsons, 15 Feb. 1976. Interview with Mrs Soper, 22 Feb. 1977. Hopkinson, *Family Inheritance*, p. 21.

[40] Interview with Mrs Dennis and Peter Joseph, 28 Jan. 1981. Hopkinson, *Family Inheritance*, p. 23.

and soft in loose, comfortable but unfashionable clothes, her stockings often rumpled. She used to describe how she once found her waist petticoat descending when walking down Whitehall with Sir Thomas Inskip; nipping into a doorway, she stepped out of the garment, pushed it into her shabby and commodious leather bag (invariably bulging with books and papers) and walked on, apparently without Inskip noticing. *En route* to Buckingham Palace on one occasion, she rang up her secretary saying, 'I've got one brown shoe and one black shoe; you must either bring one or the other'.[41]

Somewhat unkempt to look at, rather clumsy in her movements, careless about humdrum matters, superficially untidy in her paperwork, always losing things on the Underground though usually getting them back—she was none the less extremely well organized on things that mattered. 'She might (and often did) lose a glove, an umbrella or a spectacle case,' said her secretary Elizabeth Neville, 'but a paper—never;'[42] however chaotic her office, she could always find what she wanted. Anyone distracted by her clothing soon responded to her smile and to what Wright called the 'brown velvet voice' which had impressed her at their first birth-control meeting. She was as good with people on public as on private matters, and knew that the effective reformer must operate on two fronts simultaneously—through converting significant individuals, but also through rousing public opinion. Her speeches did not always convey her enthusiasm. She learned to project her 'unassertive, rather tentative voice', but it was not musical, and she was not noticeably fluent.[43] On the platform she had no sense of drama or of rhythm, found it difficult to tell jokes, and possessed no natural eloquence; she did not publicly display the lightness of touch she had in conversation. She was always at her best behind the scenes.

She had a clear head and a good memory for the arguments on any issue, and her drafts were highly professional. A friend's comment on how she advised individuals applies equally to her public work: 'Eva would always go for the essentials in someone else's work or problems, clarifying a question or reducing perplexity to a manageable choice of alternatives, even where the subject was one of which she had no direct knowledge.'

[41] Interview with George Cottrell, 3 July 1976. Author's tape-recorded interview with Mrs M. S. Stephens, 30 May 1976, at The Forge, Hollow Lane, Wilton, Nr. Marlborough, Wilts.

[42] Hopkinson, *Family Inheritance*, p. 148.

[43] Interview with Dr Wright, 27 Feb. 1977. Author's collection: Mrs Olivier Bell to author, 28 Jan. 1985.

Then there was her dynamic energy; she thought that people could and should both interpret and change the world. 'I like and respect Mrs Hubback in all ways,' said a young demographer staying at her house, 'but I do wish she wouldn't talk about population at breakfast.'[44] She was too forthright always to be tactful. Her causes seemed too pressing for administrative incompetence or academic indecision to be tolerated, and she would sometimes shift obstacles by exploding, though her storms soon passed. Like Rathbone she expected staff to work as hard as she did. Employees who shared her dedication, as at Morley College, had no difficulty, but subordinates sometimes saw their work as only a job, nor could volunteer colleagues be treated as subordinates. Lady Clark remembered helping her canvass at North Kensington in 1946; though Hubback was well able to enlist the loyalty of her helpers, 'she was never grateful, however hard you worked'.[45]

Her gusto for facts reflected her public spirit, her idealism, and what some saw as her unsophisticated zest for improvement. She 'never doubted that obstacles *could* be removed,' writes Diana. 'Knowledge and the intelligent use of knowledge were her answers to all such problems. The facts had first to be uncovered, examined, arranged in logical pattern. When that pattern had emerged . . . the right course of action could be laid bare.'[46] Her facts came from the three dailies and half dozen weeklies she stacked on her sitting-room table at Threeways; from the London Library books she carried round wherever she went under her arm or in her big bag, and which she read whenever she snatched a free moment; and from talking to people—for she was interested in how other people lived, and passed on their comments to others.

Her son-in-law David Hopkinson speaks of her 'ability to . . . live in different worlds and bring them together, and to get strength from different parts'. She was a good listener, a telephone-exchange or entrepreneur between ideas and personalities as well as between institutions and movements, a person who enjoyed arranging introductions and who always asked herself, when faced by a problem, whom she could consult and which expert would know. Conversations at Threeways were always being interrupted by the telephone, which she kept in the sitting-room instead of the hall. 'She always knew the latest theory about

[44] Hubback Papers: Evelyn Radford's typed memoir. Hopkinson, *Family Inheritance*, p. 22.

[45] Author's tape-recorded interview with F. Le Gros and Lady Clark, 6 Apr. 1976, at Flat 16, Park Close, Templar Road, Oxford.

[46] Hopkinson, *Family Inheritance*, p. 13.

almost anything . . .', Jenifer Hart recalled, 'and usually thought there was something in it . . . it was refreshing and stimulating and made one feel she would never ossify.'[47]

Friends and relatives were both a pleasure to her and a help in her public and family life. Some may have been put off by her Jewish background, but her Jewishness was never obvious to outsiders, and the Jewish cousinhood brought her many contacts. During her long widowhood, friends (as Diana puts it) 'collectively . . . made up something like a spouse'. Her Cambridge contemporaries were especially important to her, and she would make use of them, together with her educational contacts, her feminist colleagues, and anyone else she knew, and would expect them to use her in the same way. 'I feel sociable,' she would say, and grasp the telephone to round people up. She collected a group of Liberal and Labour Hampstead people of all ages around her, and often had guests to Sunday lunch. Every year she held two summer parties at Threeways on consecutive nights, each for about 150, lubricated by punch; one was for relatives, one for friends, and the guests spread out into the garden under the Chinese lights.

She had no secretary of her own for most of her career, and until she established an office and secretaries at Threeways during the Second World War she used the secretaries of her various organizations. She was approachable and informal in manner, and as a good democrat she encouraged suggestions. She was interested in individuals, and really cared about their problems; some of her employees stayed for years. She was good at drawing on qualities in colleagues that she did not herself possess, and combined two talents rarely united: the imaginativeness needed to initiate fruitful projects, but also the organizing ability needed to get them launched. 'Once she'd got a thing going,' David Hubback told me, 'she would pull out and get someone else to run it while she went on to the next thing.' She marshalled her energies and alighted upon essentials with a notable sense of proportion, a quality she often recommended to Rachel. She was good at switching quickly and frequently between interests, yet amid the mêlée she kept a firm hold on priorities. She had a strong sense of what was worth doing and what was not; the word 'worth' recurred in her conversation and in her advice to the children. Her economy of time was almost obsessive, and she thought Diana immoral for reading novels in the morning.

Her day began early. She did not usually get back to Threeways from

---

[47] Hubback Papers: J. Hart to D. Hopkinson, n.d.

Morley College till ten or eleven at night, yet the next morning she usually worked between five and eight, and then cleared her head with a walk on Hampstead Heath. When visiting her friend Olwen Campbell she was usually up at six; Campbell would draw her bedroom curtains to see her 'even on quite chilly mornings, sitting on a deck chair on the dewy lawn', reading a book or typescript.[48] Except when preoccupied with an individual's personal problems, she was always in a hurry, always late. She snatched most of her meals hastily at odd times, and did not take trouble over them. At the Spielmans' Saturday lunches, Gertrude would become increasingly restive when Eva failed to appear; arriving breathless and untidy, with her entourage of children, she often had to leave early in order to squeeze in something else. When moving about the country she organized her engagements in such a way as to meet the maximum number of people with the minimum expenditure of time and money. A two-day visit to Campbell would be planned; later it would be reduced to one day; Campbell would expect her for dinner, but after all had been prepared she would ring to say that she must stay for supper where she was lecturing but would arrive later. Her visits 'were always the same in their variety— amusing, tantalising, interesting, disappointing, hurried . . . We would have a host of things we were planning to talk about, but so much would be fitted into her day that most of the talk would happen hurrying on the way to catch a bus.'[49]

Friends might understand, others did not. In 1933 a subordinate in the birth-control movement, arranging for her to meet the sympathetic MP, Dr A. B. Howitt, asked him to phone through his preferred time 'as Mrs Hubback is a terribly busy woman'; understandably he took offence. Diana says that Eva 'had a complete illusion that she was a punctual person' and would say 'well, I am really a *very* punctual person, but just occasionally things do make me late, outside my control'. In reality, the punctual person takes care to arrive on time and keeps events as far as possible under control. Those who were punctual for committees understandably objected when she wanted to go over business already transacted before she arrived. She sometimes made things worse by falling asleep at committees or on the platform, though she usually seemed to wake up at the crucial moment.[50]

[48] Hopkinson, *Family Inheritance*, p. 184.

[49] Hubback Papers: Olwen Campbell's typed memoir.

[50] Family Planning Association Archive A8/1: Miss Holland to A. B. Howitt, 29 June 1933 (copy); Howitt to Holland, 29 June 1933. My interview with Mrs Horton, 28 Feb. 1977, discusses Hubback in committee.

She enjoyed discussion but disliked verbal fencing for its own sake; David Hopkinson says she 'could be impatient with people who seemed to her impractical or unable to relate their thoughts to any actions'. Likewise the smaller social conventions seemed unimportant or irrelevant to her. The single-mindedness of her public work sometimes led her to neglect the small talk that puts people at their ease, or the encouragement and banter that create goodwill; she saw public work as a serious matter. Her directness made her seem rather overpowering to those who failed to perceive the rather shy person underneath; 'when you were arguing with her', says Michael Stewart, who worked with her in the AEC, 'she had a massive confidence that she was right'.[51] In this she was rather like Rathbone, whose combination of shyness and dedication led some men to flee for cover. On the other hand, she never put on acts, and was always the same person with different people. And in her leisure moments she was excellent company, with a taste for light opera and light-hearted things like the Cochran reviews in the 1930s and *Oklahoma*.

Like many progressive people of her generation she had high hopes of a population policy, and devoted much of her last decade to demographic issues. For her as for Rathbone, family allowances offered a cure for the falling birth-rate, and in 1944 she published *Population Facts and Policies*. She was justifiably disappointed when not invited to join the royal commission on population, but she submitted much written evidence and greatly helped Peggy Jay, who did join it, and who therefore now sees her as 'a kind of spiritual member' of it.[52] Her Penguin book, *The Population of Britain* (1947), dedicated to Rathbone's memory, begins by disclaiming expertise: it is 'an endeavour to sum up for the ordinary man and woman, in an all too brief space, the present situation with regard to population problems'. The book first explains why the birth-rate is falling and then, in the section that gave her most difficulty, sketches out the problems it will create, for she sees the post-war baby boom as only temporarily interrupting a long-term decline. No doubt with the Spielman cousinhood in mind, she stresses how smaller families will in some ways impoverish childhood.[53]

Her patriotism leads her to warn against eroding the demographic basis for British world influence: 'the British people have traditions and standards of value—ethical, religious and political—derived from a

---

[51] Author's tape-recorded interview with Lord Stewart of Fulham, 29 Mar. 1978, at 11 Felden Street, London SW6 5AE.

[52] Interviews with Mrs Jay, 11 Jan. 1977, and with the Hopkinsons, 15 Feb. 1976.

[53] Hubback, *Population*, p. 7; see also pp. 64, 273.

conviction of the value of each individual as a person. These democratic ideals of freedom, of kindness, of justice, of reason and of the rule of law are needed more than ever in a world in which many countries have not as yet discovered how to combine freedom with order.' She denies that birth-control will reduce unemployment, which she attributes more to faulty organization than to over-population; a declining home population will actually reduce demand and leave houses empty and derelict. And by shifting the population balance towards the old, it also threatens to overload the social services and erode progressive political opinion.[54]

As for remedies, she wants the ordinary parent to recognize that 'the number of children he has is not *only* his own affair, but the affair of the community as well', so she hopes from public opinion 'a change of values, a greater robustness of outlook and simpler ways of living'. Furthermore government must act quickly to prevent the decline from accelerating. It must discourage young couples from emigrating, encourage assimilable immigrants, and boost family size through rent subsidies, family allowances, scholarships, better health care, family planning clinics, and day nurseries. She also wants government to promote sterilization of the mental defective and to 'make it easy for those *parents who are above the average* physically, mentally and morally to have many children'.[55]

Some of these ideas, particularly the last, are not fashionable now, and feminists have become less preoccupied with rewarding the woman who chooses to stay at home than with making it easier for women to pursue full-time careers. None the less, the book is highly practical and common-sensical in approach, lucidly written, economically argued, wide-ranging in perspective, and lent impact by its clear headings and summaries. In retrospect her predictions are sometimes right, sometimes wrong, but invariably interesting and her own.

All this achievement did not save her from much unhappiness during the 1940s. There was of course plenty in this decade to depress a rationalistic Edwardian meliorist, especially one born into a Jewish family; yet some of her disappointment was more personal. Her leftish views did not preclude a profound patriotism. She liked pageantry and monarchy and regretted that government did not draw fully upon her talents during the war. She studied the honours list closely, and punctiliously congratulated her friends when they appeared in it; she would have liked to be there herself, but despite all her public work she did not appear,

---

[54] Ibid., p. 114; see also pp. 122, 127, 144, 272.
[55] Ibid., pp. 273, 154, 284.

perhaps partly because she was active in so many spheres that she was difficult to pigeon-hole.

Her career also suffered from lacking any firm party attachment. She worked on the Yellow Book and was asked to stand as a Liberal candidate for the LCC in 1928. In 1932 her cousin Lord Samuel wanted her to stand as a Liberal candidate for parliament,[56] but she turned down both opportunities, and first stood as a Labour candidate in 1932 for Hendon borough council. Like so many progressive inter-war intellectuals and feminists she hovered between Liberals and Labour, signed the Next Five Years Group's *Essay in Political Agreement*, and called herself a 'Lib–Lab'. Richard Titmuss resembled her in this, and helped Rathbone with *The Case for Family Allowances* (1940); socialism became for him the way to keep up the birth-rate, and one of Hubback's most fruitful suggestions was that he should be invited to contribute to the war histories.[57] To her son David, she was 'more anti-Tory than pro-Labour', yet in 1945 her admiration for Churchill caused her to think twice before voting Labour. She became increasingly enthusiastic for the Attlee government, and after her Middle East tour for the British Council in 1947 she wrote to *The Times* to deplore 'the unnecessary and unwanted sympathy' she had received from British overseas residents for having to live in the United Kingdom; Britain's difficulties were far less serious, she said, than they seemed to those living overseas.[58]

Her last years show no loss of momentum. Her work for the neglected child brought together all her interests: concern about poverty, love of children, belief in the education of both mother and child. She chaired the sub-committee appointed in 1945 by the Women's Group on Public Welfare whose report was published as *The Neglected Child* in 1948. 'Reading this report', wrote J. B. Priestley in his introduction, 'is like following a small group of stout-hearted explorers through a dense and steamy jungle. The subject is appallingly complicated.'[59] In its inquiries and recommendations, the committee operated within Hubback's familiar world of pressure groups, voluntary workers, academics, and civil service experts. Its practical and empirical mood, its questionnaires, and its expert evidence on legal, administrative, sociological, and welfare questions reflect all the zest for facts she'd felt over thirty years before. It is a

[56] Hubback Papers: Herbert Samuel to Hubback, 10 Mar. 1932.
[57] M. Gowing, 'Richard Morris Titmuss, 1907–1973', *Proceedings of the British Academy*, 61 (1975), p. 7; see also pp. 6–7, 10.
[58] *The Times*, 3 June 1947, p. 5. See also Hopkinson, *Family Inheritance*, p. 165.
[59] Women's Group on Public Welfare, *The Neglected Child and his Family* (1948), p. ix.

characteristic product of what now seems a far-off post-war world where collaboration in 'planning' between high-minded and progressive intellectuals and interventionist agencies would shortly produce prosperity and happiness for all. Hubback combined all this with local government work, joining the London County Council in 1946 as Labour councillor for North Kensington. She was co-opted on to the education committee, and became chairman of its primary and secondary schools sub-committee, focusing on curricular reform and child-care questions but also promoting art therapy at LCC mental hospitals. Her immensely hard work did not prevent her being defeated in 1949.

There is an element of escapism in all this. She once told a friend that she would not be happy in a world where everything went right, because she needed to help people in trouble. 'I must be active and busy the whole time', she told Diana late in life, 'otherwise I feel so terribly depressed by my own sad thoughts.' This was nothing new, for she had told Bill shortly before marriage that her social work was 'a safety valve for any irritation or unhappiness'. What her sister Winifred called Eva's 'spread maternal feeling' led her to take responsibility for other people's troubles and often to blame herself for what went wrong, or to reproach herself for taking what later seemed to be wrong decisions, even on small matters.[60]

In October 1940 she blamed herself for being absent from Morley College when the bomb dropped. In 1941 she regretted being away from home when her artist–lodger Charles Grave died from a heart attack; they had been introduced by Wright, who thought both were emotionally lonely. They had grown very attached to one another, and Grave's death was a major reason for her frequent depressions in later life; she resumed the interest in extra-sensory perception that she had briefly shown after Bill's death on the prompting of a sister-in-law. In a curious way, the fact that she was always educating or being educated placed a barrier between herself and other people, so that she was simultaneously approachable and remote. Yet she often warned her children against self-pity, and her response was constructive.

Shortly before her death she was investigating the outlook and situation of the English housewife, and both her family and colleagues at Morley College thought she was burning herself up with eagerness to get things done; perhaps she sensed that she had not long to live. 'I always longed for her to take life easier,' Diana told me, 'not only because one would have seen more of her . . . but because she would have lived longer and enjoyed

[60] Hopkinson, *Family Inheritance*, pp. 185, 67. Interview with Mrs Raphael, 2 Mar. 1976. See also Hubback Papers: Olwen Campbell's typescript memoir.

old age.' Upset by Gertrude's death six weeks before her own, Eva was saddened to see her mother's possessions being dispersed: 'I hate the flat going as it was all so beautiful and serene and full of memories,' she wrote. Eva had suffered great pain from indigestion in middle age, but an operation for duodenal ulcer had succeeded, and otherwise she enjoyed good health. Her family did not suspect anything serious until she entered hospital in 1949, and even on the day of her death they thought she would probably recover. She knew there were still so many things for her to do; as she told Winifred, 'I don't think it would be a good thing if I died now, do you?'[61]

Her sudden death after an operation on a stomach haemorrhage shattered not only her family but the many people who relied on her. Mrs Stephens, her secretary, felt safe walking through the bombing raids as long as Hubback was beside her; 'you know, she was an incredible *power*; you felt, if you trotted along beside her . . . that nothing could happen to you. She was quite immortal'; bombs would surely never dare to descend on *her*. When the news reached Erna Nelki, for whom Hubback had found a job as a refugee from Hitler in the late 1930s, she felt a great sense of loss; 'oh dear,' she said to herself, 'what now? in England, you have lost your great protector.'[62]

Where does Hubback belong in feminist history? Very much in the non-militant tradition of working closely with men. 'Though she was at heart a feminist', writes Stocks, 'and really cared about the position and wellbeing of women—she didn't always appear to be a feminist . . . because unlike some feminists of her generation, she really liked men. She liked working with them and talking to them. She liked the way their minds worked.' Men, in their turn, liked her for the rounded, harmonious quality of a personality that sought to reconcile family and feminist roles. Her public work grew naturally out of her experience as wife and mother, and family responsibilities were more a stimulus to public work than a distraction from it. 'She was not that type of reformer in whom absence of human ties and sympathies finds compensation in public works,' writes Diana. 'For her, the fullness and completeness of an individual life depended in large measure on the degree to which it embodied an active service on other people's behalf.'[63]

---

[61] Interview with the Hopkinsons, 15 Feb. 1976. Hopkinson, *Family Inheritance*, p. 187. Interview with Mrs Raphael, 2 Mar. 1976.

[62] Interview with Mrs Stephens, 30 May 1976. Author's tape-recorded interview with Mrs Erna Nelki, 9 Mar. 1976, at 43 Nightingale Lane, London SW12.

[63] Hubback Papers: Mary Stocks's BBC talk, 13 Oct. 1952. Hopkinson, *Family Inheritance*, p. 175.

She would now be surprised to know that a distinct feminist movement had revived so long after her death, for she did not envisage any continuing need for it; as Diana writes, 'the underlying assumption of all her work was the need for active and intelligent participation in the perpetual process of reforming and improving social organization'. Enfranchised women could be expected to merge their feminism into a more generalized interventionist, educational, and progressive movement for public welfare. She was not restive under a continued separation of roles; in 1947 she thought 'public opinion should emphasise that *the bearing and rearing of children* is the finest of all professions for women', and welcomed the fact that 'for most women, work in the home is likely to come first'.[64]

The 'new feminism' of the 1920s, to which she contributed so much, knew that feminism could survive only by reducing its preoccupation with the single woman and increasing its concern with the practical needs of the housebound mother—territory already occupied by the two most prosperous inter-war women's organizations, the Mothers' Union and the Women's Institutes. The advent of the modern life-cycle had reached the stage where marriage was becoming almost universal, but where birth-control had not yet firmly established the two-child family; where mechanization had made only preliminary forays within the home; and where divorce and changing sexual attitudes had not yet proliferated the single parent. It is hardly surprising that a suffragist like Rathbone, addressing early twentieth-century women's meetings, should find maternity questions cropping up 'on all occasions, irrespective of what the subject immediately on hand may be'.[65]

In her personal life Hubback showed courage and resource, and here she resembles Ray Strachey, whose political methods and outlook she largely shared, though the two women do not seem to have seen much of one another. For much of their lives, both lacked support from a husband and received financial help from friends and relatives. Both combined an energetic public career with taking sole responsibility for bringing up a young family. Both combined conscientiousness as a mother with imagination and energy in public work. Family background and gender made both at first in some sense outsiders in British public life, yet both became adept at tactics that involved operating very much from the inside. Both died prematurely after an operation, and both deserved more recognition from contemporaries and posterity than they have received.

[64] Hopkinson, *Family Inheritance*, p. 175. Hubback, *Population*, pp. 283, 219.
[65] Rathbone, *Disinherited Family*, p. 83. See also M. Anderson, 'The Emergence of the Modern Life Cycle in Britain', *Social History*, Vol. 10, No. 1 (Jan. 1985), pp. 82, 86.

But the essence of Hubback does not really lie in committees or public meetings or drafts or dossiers; she spent time on these primarily to remove injustice and unfairness, in the hope of freeing others to share the spontaneous self-realization and fulfilment that she herself so relished. As a disciple of Meredith and a devotee of Housman, she retained throughout her life the Edwardian progressive's pursuit of the simple life through strenuous outdoor holidays, rambles over rough country, and scalings of the heights. Diana affectionately recalls summers in the early 1920s when Eva was working for NUSEC and arranged for the children to stay with a governess at Treyarnon. Eager to see more of her family, she would take the Friday night train from London to Newquay, breakfast at a hotel and set off for Treyarnon by the strenuous twelve-mile cliff path. On the way to meet her, 'we used to see her in the distance hurrying along and very happy and pleased, and then she used to throw out both her arms when we arrived . . . terribly pleased both with us and being on the cliffs again and being by the sea which she loved'. Catherine Joseph, who never forgot her generous sympathy at a difficult time, likes to think of her walking out in old clothes with friends along the top of a mountain ridge near Maes Caradoc, for it was in mountains and wild countryside that Eva always felt happiest.[66]

[66] Interview with the Hopkinsons, 2 Oct. 1984. Interview with Mr and Mrs Dennis, 19 Apr. 1980.

CONCLUSION

'CONCLUSION' is hardly the word, because this book aims only to provide interim signposts through some rather rough country: besides, each biographical chapter contains its own conclusion, in more senses than one. Yet one theme does run throughout the book: the strategic and tactical problem facing the first generation of enfranchised women. Tentative answers can now be offered to three rather large questions on which discussion has hardly yet begun, and which later generations will answer more conclusively: what did the vote achieve for British women between the wars? why didn't it achieve more? and would different tactics have speeded things up?

The first question isn't easily answered, if only because Edwardian suffragists never attained their aim of getting women enfranchised through a distinct measure. There were 8,479,156 women who first qualified as electors in December 1918, but there was simultaneous and major change on the male side too; whereas there had been only 7,709,981 male electors in December 1910, there were 12,913,166 in 1918. Yet this did not deter inter-war suffragists from confidently pronouncing upon the distinctive impact made by women's votes. Their reasoning was simplistic: they listed the legislation affecting women passed after 1918, and left the reader to deduce that women's votes had produced it. Rathbone, for instance, claimed in 1936 that the vote had ensured 'far readier and more abundant attention . . . to questions of housing, of public health, of every aspect of child welfare, even of international peace'.[1] Of course women made major gains between the wars. From 1918 they could stand for parliament, and the first woman went there in 1919; women became eligible for all branches of the legal profession and for jury service in 1919; in the early 1920s several family and welfare reforms extended women's rights and benefits; and the equal franchise arrived in 1928. But it is a rather elementary error in logic to assume that two events are causally linked simply because one chronologically follows the other. Many other factors could have produced some of the effects that allegedly followed from the cause; welfare reforms, for instance, could have been a

---

[1] E. Rathbone, 'Changes in Public Life', in R. Strachey (ed.), *Our Freedom*. p. 74. Figures from F. W. S. Craig (ed.), *British Electoral Facts, 1885–1975* (3rd edn., 1976), pp. 75, 78.

response to a feeling that wartime casualties must be recouped, to a patriotic solicitude for war widows, to the accelerated wartime rise of organized labour, or to Labour's subsequent dominance of the British left.

More sophisticated analyses dwelt upon the pace of legislation benefiting women; Rathbone, for instance, noted that whereas during the twenty years up to 1918 only six laws specially affecting women were passed, the next seven years saw twenty such laws.[2] Yet the pace of legislation on all social and economic questions had been increasing for decades; Rathbone seems never to have felt the need to balance off feminist influences against the many other long-term pressures making for state welfare, still less does she move on from absolute to proportionate figures and ask whether women gained a larger share of the total legislation enacted after 1918. Besides, parliament did not need the stimulus of the women's vote to enact feminist legislation; Edwardian anti-suffragists had always argued that women, amply protected by a solicitous male parliament, did not need the vote. Edwardian suffragism, by diverting feminists from social to political priorities, and by introducing all the distractions of militant tactics, may even have reduced perceived demand for feminist legislation—a demand which was free to revive after 1918, when these distractions had been removed. Developments in the 1930s reinforce doubts about any one-to-one connection between votes and legislation. Women rose steadily as a percentage of the electorate from 39.6 in 1918 to 52.8 in 1931, and first attained a majority in 1929; yet after the mid-1920s feminism weakened as a parliamentary influence.[3] In reality, the vote's impact can be discovered only from closely investigating the history of particular Bills.

Astor often made a rather less grandiose claim for the women's vote: that it had transformed parliament's approach to women's questions. 'When I stood up and asked questions affecting women and children, social and moral questions, I used to be shouted at for five or 10 minutes at a time,' she said in 1928, contrasting the situation she had faced in 1919.[4] Yet this argument, too, is unconvincing. Her initial reception could as much have reflected a very personal hostility to herself and (as Chapter 3 suggests) to her methods; besides, even on her own argument the vote had

---

[2] Rathbone Papers, XIV 2.5(44): typescript of speech, 8 Oct. 1934, on 'The Women's Movement. At Home and in the British Commonwealth', p. 3; cf. Astor, *HC Deb.* 29 Mar. 1928, c. 1453; 8 Apr. 1935, c. 927. See also V. Douie, *The Lesser Half* (Women's Publicity Planning Association, n.d.), p. 5.

[3] As even Rathbone admitted, in R. Strachey (ed.), *Our Freedom*, pp. 51–2. Figures from Craig, *Electoral Facts*, p. 78.

[4] *HC Deb.* 29 Mar. 1928, c. 1452.

not immediately changed MPs' mood, for women began voting in 1918. In reality it is long-term social change, not franchise reform, that transforms parliamentary manners. Slow but profound shifts in popular morality and manners—partly feminist in inspiration but also owing much to industrialization—had been refining attitudes towards women for a century. No political reform produced the changes witnessed by Emmeline Pethick-Lawrence during her lifetime, for example: 'I lived in the days when the mention of maternity occasioned a laugh or a leer,' she wrote in 1938; 'when women were referred to as "the sex"; when "the old maid" was the butt of ridicule; and when the term of opprobrium directed on a man who was a fool was "old woman"! These things have changed . . .'[5]

Christabel Pankhurst, in her millennial phase by 1924, was not concerned that the vote had so little impact; 'who would exchange the grandest of our old illusions concerning what the votes of women could do', she asked, 'for the assurance of what the Lord Jesus Christ will do in time and eternity?' Yet Rathbone was worried as early as 1920,[6] and with reason. Even by 1930 there were only 2,000 women among the 23,000 justices of the peace in England and Wales, and in 1929 women lost an important niche in local government when the poor law guardians were abolished. There were only 323 women among the 10,312 candidates at general elections before 1945, and the number of women MPs before 1945 peaked at only fifteen for a few months in 1931.[7] By 1928 Brittain thought it widely believed 'that "feminists" . . . are spectacled, embittered women, disappointed, childless, dowdy, and generally unloved'.[8] Why was progress so slow?

No explanation confined to British feminism will do, because women's suffrage has nowhere produced any far-reaching short-term change in the balance of political forces, or even in the relative influence of parties.[9] Nor is the problem peculiar to women's votes because, as Fawcett pointed out, 'many years passed' before the widened male franchise of 1867 and 1884 'produced any visible effect on the type of MP sent to Westminster'. Political power no more rested in middle-class hands after 1832 than in

[5] E.P.-L., *My Part*, p. 347.

[6] C. Pankhurst, *Pressing Problems of the Closing Age* (n.d.), p. 48. Rathbone, *Milestones*, p. 3.

[7] Statistics cited by Rathbone in R. Strachey (ed.), *Our Freedom*, p. 37; D. E. Butler and A. Sloman, *British Political Facts, 1900–1979* (5th edn., 1980), pp. 206–8, 230. For the impact of poor law reform, see *HC Deb.* 29 Apr. 1930, cc. 155–8.

[8] *Manchester Guardian*, 13 Dec. 1928, p. 8.

[9] M. Duverger, *The Political Role of Women* (UNESCO, 1955), p. 140.

working-class hands after 1867 and 1884. Surveying reformers' disappointments in 1874, the radical John Morley questioned the value of prayer when 'to have our prayers granted carries the world so very slight a way forward'.[10]

More helpful are explanations offered by Bagehot and Mill. Bagehot thought that a new constitution produces its full effect only when both statesmen and people have grown up under the reformed conditions. J. S. Mill argued that power depends on three elements—numbers, property, and intelligence—but also on how far these are organized; 'the advantage in organisation', he said, 'is necessarily with those who are in possession of the government'.[11] New voters do not immediately oust an elite, if only because its members, according to Sidney Low, 'are always calling on each other, or lunching, or dining, or attending receptions together; they have been at the same schools and colleges; they have shot together, hunted together'. Rathbone rightly noted that, by contrast, a newly enfranchised class 'is always naturally timid and uncertain of itself', and 'likes to cling on to the shoulders of the more expedient classes'. Women were still excluded from many male centres of power after 1918: from professional and political clubs, formal and informal, as well as from the male colleges in Oxford and Cambridge. And even when women entered the most important male club of all—the House of Commons—they perpetuated the separation of spheres by segregating themselves from men intellectually, and even at first geographically.[12]

Why did British feminists expect any other outcome? Partly because, like earlier franchise reformers in Britain and elsewhere, the campaign for the vote developed a momentum that led them both to exaggerate the present sufferings of the unenfranchised and the gains to be made from emancipation, a term suffragists used synonymously with enfranchisement. In Britain as in the United States, therefore, many assumed after enfranchisement that women's emancipation was now complete, and moved on from feminism to other things. Several prominent Conservatives foresaw the vote's limited impact, for their Party rarely exaggerates the social effect of political change. In a pre-war women's suffrage debate,

---

[10] *Woman's Leader*, 24 Nov. 1922, p. 337; cf. Rathbone, *HC Deb.* 20 May 1931, c. 2016. J. Morley, 'On Compromise', in his *Works*, iii (1921), p. 4. See also W. F. Monypenny and G. E. Buckle, *The Life of Benjamin Disraeli* (2 vols., 1929), i. 501.

[11] J. S. Mill, *Representative Government* (1861; Everyman edn., 1910), p. 183. See also W. Bagehot, introduction to the 2nd edn. of *The English Constitution* (Fontana edn., 1963), pp. 268, 279.

[12] S. Low, *The Governance of England* (1914 edn.), p. 187. *HC Deb.* 20 May 1931, c. 2016. See also my 'Women in a Men's House', pp. 633–644.

Balfour questioned whether there had been any clear causal link in the nineteenth century between political and social reform: trade unions had existed before 1832 and working hours had been restricted long before working men won the vote. Lord Hugh Cecil told parliament that on women's suffrage he was neither a pink nor a white: that is, his face grew neither pink nor pale when discussing the matter; he rejected the idea that 'the great forces of human passion, which religion and civilization have struggled against for centuries, can be affected one way or another because women once in three or four years enter the polling booth and mark a voting paper.' Baldwin told NUSEC in 1928 that he expected only modest improvements from the equal franchise: 'I have been too long in politics', he said, 'to take the Apocalyptic view.'[13]

In arguing like this, Conservatives were for their own purposes making the distinction drawn by Liberals in earlier franchise debates between politics and society, but were drawing the opposite conclusion. Macaulay in 1831, like J. S. Mill during parliament's first women's suffrage debate in 1867, claimed that votes should be attached to a social and economic power that had already been won.[14] Liberals wanted to ensure that the electorate mirrored a social change that had already occurred, whereas Conservatives doubted whether votes could of themselves change society very much; the same point was being made from different directions.

The Conservative analysis gains credence from investigating the motives of the politicians who conceded votes to women, for their aim was to stabilize society, not to change it. Like earlier franchise reformers they hoped that by enlarging the electorate they would strengthen the existing political system in two ways: by eroding the extra-parliamentary ranks of the disaffected, and by ensuring that reformers continued to orientate themselves towards parliament. They knew that by removing grievances they would undermine the case for wider political change, and they knew it was important to demonstrate the system's responsiveness. In the year of the Russian revolution, they wanted to strengthen their claim to be representative; as Lord Durham had said during the crisis over the first Reform Act, 'to property and good order we attach numbers'. And when in the aftermath of the General Strike Baldwin faced a cabinet divided on equal franchise, he found the reform extensively backed within the party

[13] Cecil, *HC Deb.* 24 Jan. 1913, c. 916; cf. 19 June 1917, c. 1660. Baldwin, *The Times,* 9 Mar. 1928, p. 16. Balfour, *HC Deb.* 12 July 1910, c. 257. For the USA, see C. N. Degler, *At Odds. Women and the Family in America from the Revolution to the Present* (Oxford, 1980), p. 437.

[14] In *HC Deb.* 5 May 1913, c. 1716, on women's suffrage, Lord H. Cavendish-Bentinck cites Macaulay on the 1831 Reform Bill. J. S. Mill, *HC Deb.* 20 May 1867, c. 821.

in the country. Analysing the reformer's plight, when addressing ageing suffragettes in 1932, Harold Laski was concise but jaundiced: 'privilege never retreats until the purpose of its retreat has already been won.'[15]

Feminists did not offer these reasons for disappointment at the time. As so often with reformers who move only among their own kind, some blamed the party system; some even saw party conflict as a doomed relic of the old politics. The mid-Victorian case for feminists staying outside the parties was strong because non-party causes profited from the fact that party discipline in mid-Victorian parliaments was loose; besides, pioneer feminists wanted to avoid being divided along party lines. Non-party feminist organizations drew all feminists together, generated ideas, and boosted morale. But when the late-Victorian parties developed their machinery for moulding opinion and tightened their grip on back-benchers, the non-party strategy entailed sacrificing major parliamentary and other opportunities for influencing both sexes. NUSEC was still persisting with a non-party stance in the 1920s, yet the idea of a woman's party foundered with Christabel Pankhurst's defeat at Smethwick in 1918 and, as we have seen, Rathbone's parliamentary situation was entirely exceptional; even Astor's political influence suffered from her wavering party loyalty. Women's continued political segregation would risk perpetuating the separation of roles between the sexes that lay at the heart of the anti-feminist philosophy, whereas partnership between men and women had always been the dominant mood within British feminism. Ray Strachey, for one, realized that women MPs must now carry this partnership into parliament: 'the interests of men and women are so closely bound together that they cannot be divided', she said in her general election address of 1918, 'and . . . what is for the good of one sex must certainly be for the good of the other.'[16]

Yet when they joined political parties, feminists faced a new dilemma; 'we have to remember that, when women are first enfranchised, they will find a political system established which has been made by men,' wrote Bertrand Russell in 1910, 'where the parties are divided according to the divisions of opinion among men, where all the candidates are men'. Furthermore in a two-party system, political parties are wary of minority opinions; a political party must aim to cover the whole range of public

[15] Durham quoted in N. Gash, *Politics in the Age of Peel* (1953), p. 16. H. Laski typescript on 'The Militant Temper in Politics' (Museum of London Suffragette Collection Z 6061), fo. 19. On Conservatives and the franchise, see Sir R. Sanders, in *HC Deb.* 29 Mar. 1928, cc. 1412–3.

[16] Strachey quoted in Brookes, *Women at Westminster*, p. 11. See also T. Hunter, 'Australian Women', *Australian Quarterly*, 35 (1963), pp. 81–2.

policy, and feminism required drastic redefinition before it could do that. No loyal MP wanted to trouble the party with what it would regard as side-issues; 'sex should not be dragged into politics,' Marion Phillips told Dora Russell, who pressed birth-control on the Labour women's conference in 1924; 'you will split the Party from top to bottom'. Whatever the merits of birth-control, Labour candidates knew that their Catholic supporters disliked it. Likewise the Conservative Thomas Inskip warned Astor, due to speak in his constituency in 1926, against pursuing feminist themes; what Bristol's poor women wanted was 'help in discovering a reason for the faith that is in them. They are Unionists more by instinct than by conviction . . . these women are so childlike in many ways, that it seems almost unfair to talk politics to them.'[17]

Inter-war feminist leaders were only beginning to establish the wider political connections needed to influence a major political party, and were often surprised at attitudes encountered outside their ranks. 'Truly, one rubs one's eyes in amazement,' wrote Sylvia Pankhurst, on hearing in 1935 that the Oxford Union had excluded women from its new dining-room; it carried her back, she said, to the early Victorian period. More perceptive was Ray Strachey's response in 1934, when confronted in a public inquiry by people who opposed admitting women to the diplomatic service: 'I live so much among sensible people', she wrote, 'that it comes as quite a shock to find them hardly speaking the same language.'[18] The parties had yet to be convinced that the feminists represented views widely held among voters of both sexes. In 1936 Rathbone adduced bribery and distractions to explain why working-class voters did not capitalize upon their electoral majority,[19] but neither explanation is required for women voters, few of whom had been feminists in the first place; when Edwardian anti-suffragists had proposed a referendum of women, suffragists prudently opposed it. In 1934 Rathbone claimed that 'the whole attitude of Parliament' had changed on women's questions now that women made up more than half the electorate; but her problem as a feminist lay in the fact that women electors were by no means always feminist in outlook. One suffragist in 1931 even claimed that 'the vote desired by only a small number of people has been thrust on millions without preparation,

---

[17] B. Russell, 'Anti-Suffragist Anxieties', in *The Collected Papers of Bertrand Russell*, 12 (1985), p. 314. D. Russell, *The Tamarisk Tree* (1975), p. 172. Nancy Astor MSS 1416/1/1/807: T. Inskip to Astor, 5 Dec. 1926.

[18] Sylvia Pankhurst Papers: typescript of letter, 11 Mar. 1935, to *The Times*. Smith Archives, Oxford: Ray Strachey to Christopher, 16 Mar. 1934.

[19] *HC Deb.* 26 Feb. 1936, c. 508.

explanation, or any idea that to understand voting and all it implies to the welfare of the community does not come by the light of nature'.[20]

Once committed to a party, the feminist found herself being prised apart from feminists in other parties. When Emmeline Pethick-Lawrence stood at Rusholme in 1918 as a Labour candidate, six Liberal women told the *Manchester Guardian* that she was splitting the progressive vote; eight Labour women then wrote in to brand the Liberal Party as standing 'for a half-hearted bolstering up of the old competitive system', and six Conservative women wrote in to stress the Conservative candidate's attraction for women voters.[21] Feminists who joined parties in the 1920s found themselves drawn into supporting rival sets of ideas and building up rival mass party machines.[22] Parliament's adversary structure accentuated partisan feeling, and Astor could seldom persuade feminist MPs to work together. Foreign policy and class relationships were so central to inter-war political debate and aroused such strong feeling that they soon pushed feminism (together with other domestic and non-class political issues— Welsh and Scottish nationalism, for instance) into the shade, and woman MPs like Lawrence and Astor were sucked into confrontation. On questions such as strikes, Ireland and foreign affairs the *Woman's Leader* admitted in 1920 that 'women as women have no solidarity of opinion'; both sexes favoured peace and good government, neither was unanimous on how to get them. Florence Horsbrugh spoke for many in 1934 when she claimed that there were no 'women's questions' as such. Another of Balfour's prophecies (in 1910) was being endorsed: that 'if there is no division of opinion on matters of general policy corresponding to the division between the sexes, an extension of the Suffrage would have no important effect either on legislation or administration'.[23]

A further (and related) difficulty was the simple-majority electoral system, which discouraged women candidates. Proportional represen-tation originally attracted J. S. Mill as an aid to minority interests, and one of the best arguments for it has always been the hope that it will encourage

---

[20] Rathbone Papers, XIV 2.5(44): Rathbone's typescript of speech on 8 Oct. 1934, p. 3. *Woman's Leader*, 3 Apr. 1931, p. 69 (Edith How-Martyn). On referenda, see my *Separate Spheres*, pp. 158–60.

[21] *Manchester Guardian*, 4 Dec. 1918, p. 7; see also 2 Dec. 1918, p. 8; 5 Dec. 1918, p. 5.

[22] Women's growing role in the Conservative and Labour Party machines is conveniently set out in *Woman's Leader*, 30 Jan. 1925, p. 5; 13 Feb. 1925, pp. 19–20.

[23] *Woman's Leader*, 5 Nov. 1920, p. 868; cf. 24 Mar. 1921, p. 116. Horsbrugh, *Edinburgh Evening News*, 7 Aug. 1934, p. 3. BL Add. MSS 49793 (Balfour Papers), fo. 123: Balfour to Annie Kenney, 3 Jan. 1910 (copy); cf. Lytton Papers, Knebworth (in the care of Lady Cobbold): Balfour to Lytton, 17 Mar. 1910.

a more balanced slate of candidates. As it was, women MPs did not reach their twentieth-century peak, or hillock, of twenty-nine (4.6 per cent of the total) till 1964. Women's admission to parliament in 1918 reproduces on a larger stage what happened in the trade-union world after 1921 when the National Federation of Women Workers amalgamated with the National Union of General Workers; they were all too easily absorbed, neutralized, or digested by the men.[24] So the early women MPs, instead of justifying the nervous predictions (from Lord Hugh Cecil, for example) that they would transform parliament's mood, soon accepted its values and its party priorities. Proportional representation might have benefited feminism in a second way—by prolonging the strength of a third party with humanitarian connections and strong links with peace and welfare, eager for political participation and energetic in making converts to parliamentarism. Liberalism was an outlook naturally aligned with feminism, and the Liberal Party's survival would have moderated the class loyalties that cut across inter-war feminism. Liberals adopted a higher proportion of women candidates than Labour or Conservatives between 1918 and 1979, yet Liberal decline ensured that a much smaller proportion of them were elected;[25] Corbett Ashby's fate was but one of many between the wars.

Further difficulties confronted the feminist who saw that public opinion must be shifted before parliament would move. The depression, reinforced by fissures on the left, helped to produce in Britain what was by European standards a mild anti-feminist reaction. Ideas, like trade, have their cycles, and the concerns of one generation often diverge from those of the next. There have been six British feminist booms of varying size (in 1866–72, 1879–84, 1903–12, 1916–20, 1940–45, 1964–76), all coinciding with advance on the left; these alternate with slumps in feminism during the five intervening periods and since 1976, all coinciding with advance on the right.[26] After 1920, NUSEC's council meetings were increasingly dominated by grey hairs. Ray Strachey in 1936 thought 'modern young women' showed 'a strong hostility to the word "feminism"', and all which they imagine it to connote'. Inter-war women MPs quite often publicly disclaimed feminist views, and in 1937 Brittain referred to the 'mildly contemptuous' attitude towards the women's revolution among younger people who did not think it fashionable to be 'earnest', 'serious', or

[24] Soldon, *Women in British Trade Unions*, pp. 117–20.
[25] Calculated from the figures in my *Separate Spheres*, p. 236.
[26] For more on this, see my 'Women's Suffrage at Westminster', pp. 87–91.

'intense'.[27] Younger relatives of leading inter-war feminists—the daughters of Billington-Greig, Ray Strachey, and Hubback, for instance, or Corbett Ashby's daughter-in-law—were quite often indifferent to feminism. Rathbone in 1936—noting the feminist slow-down since 1928—commented philosophically on the 'periods of action and reaction . . . common to all great movements'; when wind and tide are contrary, she argued, 'it is sometimes wisest to take shelter and sit tight'.[28]

Much British inter-war feminist energy was channelled overseas. The movement had always been international in outlook, and overseas evangelism seemed the next priority—as witness Corbett Ashby in IWSA or Emmeline Pethick-Lawrence in the Women's International League. It seemed urgent to get Indian women the vote, abolish female circumcision in Africa, and end Mui Tsai in Hong Kong. For some (like Kathleen Courtney) feminism led naturally towards crusading for peace and internationalism, and so into the League of Nations Union and hostility to Fascism. Even when British women were the feminists' main concern, there was the problem that (as Rathbone told NUSEC in 1925) many desirable reforms—equal pay, opportunity for work, equal moral standard—would gain less from legislation than from general shifts in public opinion.[29] After feminists had formally repudiated what she called 'the Turk complex'—the male distaste for seeing women in positions of authority—their attack could be pushed home only by trying to make windows into men's souls.

Furthermore inter-war feminists found it difficult to agree on a programme. Edwardian suffragism, like earlier extensions of the franchise, temporarily united people who disagreed on other questions. Suffragism and feminism overlapped but they were not identical. Some suffragists had never been feminists; they supported women's suffrage only as Liberals, democrats, socialists, or humanitarians, and when freed from the distraction of campaigning for the vote resumed woman's more traditional artistic, philanthropic, or family priorities. They were—in the phrase William O'Neill applies to an American context—'social feminists', mainly preoccupied with service to others; apart from the vote, women's distinctive needs had not been their main concern.[30] Could enfranchised

---

[27] Strachey in *Our Freedom*, p. 10. Brittain's review of *Our Freedom* in *Fortnightly Review*, Jan. 1937, p. 120; cf. Women's Local Government Society, *6th Annual Report since Incorporation, 1920–1, p. 11. For women MPs and feminism, see my 'Women in a Men's House', pp. 641–4.

[28] Rathbone in R. Strachey (ed.), *Our Freedom*, p. 56.

[29] Rathbone, *Milestones*, p. 26; cf. *HC Deb.* 3 Aug. 1943, c. 2130.

[30] Degler, *At Odds*, p. 326; cf. W. E. S. Thomas, *The Philosophic Radicals. Nine Studies in Theory and Practice, 1817–1841* (1979), p. 336.

feminists be unified by any other reform? In October 1917 Fawcett told Swanwick that when women had won the vote the NUWSS would need to organize the women's vote for women's questions: 'I remarked on the difficulty of organizing what doesn't exist,' Swanwick recalls, 'and she said very cheerily: "Oh I shall retire and watch you all floundering."' Unity could be temporarily preserved by campaigning for the equal franchise; in her presidential address of 1927 Rathbone saw it as 'not so much . . . one among other reforms, but . . . the key position which gives access to them all'.[31] But 'votes for flappers' was less exciting as a crusade than the enfranchisement of a sex; nor could it be mounted immediately after the Act of 1918.

The *Woman's Leader* admitted that the vote had 'brought . . . immense new difficulties. We had to make a kind of mental effort which hitherto had not been required of us—we had to think in correct proportions'; feminism had become more 'a problem of thought rather than a problem of action'. Brittain argued in 1928 that 'the woman's movement of to-day requires a high degree of intelligence and reason in each one of its followers', whereas 'the feminism of the suffragettes demanded such intellectual standards only from their leaders'.[32] NUSEC and the Six Point Group responded by agitating for several reforms simultaneously, but this blurred the feminist focus and fomented continuous dispute about priorities.

The very term 'feminism' needed closer definition. It does not appear at all in the volume of the *Oxford English Dictionary* published in 1901, but the *Supplement* draws its first citation (in inverted commas) from a French context of 1895, and defines it as 'advocacy of the rights of women'. The NUWSS, humanitarian in mood and keen for support from men, disliked using a term with sectarian connotations; 'humanists we are, not feminists,' wrote the editor of its periodical *Common Cause* in 1912. 'I am not a feminist . . . ,' Despard told a pre-war Glasgow audience: 'it is my earnest hope that the present women's movement will prove to be a passing phase and that the day is not long distant when it will merge with the men's movement.'[33] By the mid-1920s the term was familiar enough for commentators to apply the American categories of 'new' and 'old' feminist to current British feminist debate, and one of Rathbone's major

---

[31] Catherine Marshall MSS, Box 22: Swanwick to Marshall, 10 June 1917. *Woman's Leader*, 4 Mar. 1927, p. 28.

[32] *Woman's Leader*, 12 Mar. 1920, p. 125. P. Berry and A. Bishop (eds.), *Testament of a Generation. The Journalism of Vera Brittain and Winifred Holtby* (1985), p. 101.

[33] *Common Cause*, 16 May 1912, p. 82. A. Linklater, *An Unhusbanded Life. Charlotte Despard. Suffragette, Socialist and Sinn Feiner* (1980), p. 164.

services to British feminism was to encourage constructive discussion between them.

They diverged, she said, not on the need for equality, but on how best to attain it; as a 'new feminist' she wanted the term 'to embrace also the securing for women of certain rights which are not at present possessed or desired by women as such, but which are necessary to enable women to attain the same freedom of self-development or self-determination which men enjoy'.[34] The 'new feminism' resembles T. H. Green's 'positive Liberalism' in being less concerned with formally endorsing the aspiration, more with ensuring its wider realization. 'New feminists' thought women would enjoy real freedom only with the aid of discriminatory measures such as family allowances and special legislation for women on working hours and conditions; only thus could women's distinctive social role be reconciled with genuine equality of opportunity. Given that by the mid-1920s recent legislation had met most of their equalitarian demands, the 'old feminists' never revealed their remedy for the effective subordination of women, especially of mothers.

Yet the 'old feminists' had a case, for the long-term programme of the 'new feminists' was obscure. They might precariously unite behind family allowances, but what came next? Women's sexual emancipation? Campaigns for more birth-control information, free abortion on demand, and removal of welfare discrimination against unmarried mothers? This might have recruited the forthright feminist who shocked the Bishop of Durham, Hensley Henson, in 1930; contraceptives, she said, could free unmarried women to enjoy sexual relations instead of shrivelling into old maids. 'Why should they not have lovers', she asked, 'and by the help of contraceptives, have no children? Who would be injured by their doing so? And, if no one was injured, why was it wrong?' Yet such a policy would at once have antagonized important sections of public opinion. In 1937 the National Birth Control Association consulted sympathetic MPs on whether to test opinion by mounting a parliamentary debate on birth-control, but eventually decided that 'while a favourable vote would have excellent results an unfavourable vote would be disastrous', and opted for delay.[35] Only in the mid-1950s, after the Family Planning Association's long period of discreet pressure, was this barrier broken down with help

[34] *Time and Tide*, 25 Feb. 1927, p. 192.
[35] H. H. Henson, *Retrospect of an Unimportant Life*, ii (1943), p. 270. Family Planning Association Archive A 5/2: Executive Committee minutes, 27 Jan. 1937; cf. A 5/3: Executive Committee minutes, 22 Sept. 1937.

from Iain Macleod the Health Minister; even then, the birth-control case was carefully distanced from any notion of increased promiscuity.

Besides, feminists disagreed about birth-control. Ever since being embarrassed by Wollstonecraft's personal life they had been cautious on sexual matters. Some inter-war feminists hoped to end the double standard of morality by extending to men the restrictions imposed on women, and not by relaxing restrictions for both sexes. Feminists implicitly disagreed on this even within the covers of the same book. In Ray Strachey's symposium *Our Freedom and its Results* (1936), Mary Agnes Hamilton points out, apparently without disapproval, that middle-class women are now imitating working-class women on pre-marital intercourse. Alison Neilans, by contrast, sees birth-control as having 'placed the woman, if she chooses, in almost the same position of irresponsibility as the man', and is worried by the fact that although the end of the double standard is 'definitely in sight . . . it is not ending in the way anticipated by the pioneers who fought for it'.[36]

Fairer welfare provision was in theory a second potential line of 'new feminist' attack: better maternity leave, more infant schools, family allowances, and equal claim to national insurance benefits. Both Edwardian suffragists and anti-suffragists had expected women voters to promote welfare measures; 'every extension of the franchise has been followed (at a respectful distance) by a modification of the orthodox economics,' wrote Bertrand Russell in 1910. Fred Pethick-Lawrence agreed, yet when looking back in 1943 he had to admit that, though some aspects of feminism had advanced faster than expected, 'in the main matter of economic equality it has not gone so far or so fast'.[37] This was partly because inter-war Conservative predominance, reinforced by the depression, curbed welfare expenditure of any type. But also responsible were feminist divisions on this question: to push welfare forward among feminists' priorities would risk splitting them along party lines. It would be difficult to extract more state intervention from a feminist movement that had been initially libertarian and emancipatory in objective. Even family allowances seriously divided NUSEC in the 1920s. On the other hand Bondfield, Lawrence, and Wilkinson saw feminism and the Labour Party as advancing together. 'In the economic world', wrote Charlotte Gilman, 'excessive masculinity, in its fierce competition and primitive individu-alism; and excessive femininity, in its inordinate consumption and

---

[36] In R. Strachey (ed.), *Our Freedom*, pp. 268–9, 222.
[37] B. Russell, 'Anti-Suffragist Anxieties', p. 309; cf. F.P.-L., *Standard*, 24 Jan. 1913, p. 13. F.P.-L., *Fate*, p. 106.

hindering conservatism; have reached a stage where they work more evil than good'.[38]

A third theoretical option was for 'new feminists' to step up pressure for more and better-paid women's careers. Women needed adequately paid jobs not just for their own sake but because money was the key to advancement elsewhere. Virginia Woolf thought her career profited more from her legacy than from the vote; shortage of money helps to explain Ray Strachey's failure to persist as a parliamentary candidate, and perhaps also Christabel Pankhurst's move into evangelism.[39] Yet here war and economic depression stood in the way. So fierce was the depression's onset in 1920, so entrenched were the trade unions, so recent was women's occupational advance, and so strong did the ex-serviceman's moral claim on jobs seem to be—that feminists could conduct only a rearguard defensive action. Nor was family life then as compatible with mothers' full-time employment as it is now. Many families were large by present-day standards, and housekeeping was relatively difficult; if a family was to keep out of poverty, it needed a 'good manager'. So it often seemed sensible to separate the male and female roles.

Progress on equal pay and opportunity was difficult, said Rathbone in 1929, because 'exceptional unemployment has intensified masculine jealousy and against the barriers of trade union and professional exclusiveness the methods we are wont to use in Parliament are well-nigh useless'. As she pointed out later, 'when there was work for all, it was relatively easy for men to be magnanimous'.[40] During the depression women's employment increased, but only in the relatively under-unionized service and light-industry sectors; the depression arrested women's wartime advance within the more strongly unionized heavy industries. As Mary Macarthur put it: 'women are badly paid and badly treated because they are not organised and they are not organised because they are badly paid and badly treated.'[41] Only in particular areas where the case was strong or the enemy vulnerable—in the civil service, for example, or in the professions—could much inter-war progress be made. Even then, feminists were sometimes divided; Rathbone, for instance, thought

---

[38] C. P. Gilman, *Women and Economics. A Study of the Economic Relation between Men and Women as a Factor in Social Evolution*, ed. C. N. Degler (first published 1898; Harper Torchbooks, New York edn., 1966), pp. 139–40.

[39] V. Woolf, *A Room of One's Own* (first published 1929; Harbinger edn., New York, 1957), p. 37. Smith Archives, Oxford: Ray Strachey to her family, 20 Nov. 1918; Ray to Mary, 10, 16, and 17 Nov. 1923. For Christabel, see Mitchell, *Fighting Pankhursts*, p. 123.

[40] Rathbone, *Milestones*, p. 45. Rathbone in R. Strachey (ed.), *Our Freedom*, p. 55.

[41] Quoted in Soldon, *Women in British Trade Unions*, p. 55.

that equal pay without family allowances would curtail women's chances of work.

Inter-war feminism therefore embraces several distinct positions. First there were the women who exerted a feminist influence despite themselves: inter-war anti-feminists in public life (such as Atholl), whose sheer competence reproduced the old anti-suffragist paradox whereby women entered public life in order to prove their incapacity for it. Then there were suffragists (such as Bertrand Russell) who saw themselves not as feminists, but as democrats, humanitarians, or socialists. There were feminists (such as Christabel Pankhurst) who sought the vote simply as a mark of status, and who thought the campaign for it at least as important as the objective itself. There were 'social feminists' (such as Kathleen Courtney) who thought women needed the vote if they were to be more useful in non-feminist spheres of work, and felt free to leave organized feminism after 1918. And there were 'welfare feminists' (such as Bondfield or Astor), some of whom repudiated the feminist label altogether; they wanted discriminatory welfare benefits for married women which would increase the attractions of a domestic role. Feminists of this type overlapped with the 'new feminists' (such as Rathbone) who formalized and generalized the argument by claiming that nominal equality was not enough; they gradually diverged from 'old feminists' like Fawcett, whose individualist and equalitarian variant of feminism aimed primarily at removing discrimination against women. Within each category, individuals differed over specific feminist priorities.

Divisions were even more rife among inter-war women in general: between women in different political parties and generations; between feminists and anti-feminists; between the woman who aimed to enter occupations hitherto confined to men and the married woman who stayed at home and wanted her husband to hold down a well-paid job; and between women (whether feminist or not) who were fragmented into family groups. Nor should geography's importance be ignored. Suburbanization was segregating many women from the centres of power where their husbands worked, and fragmenting women one from another. Unlike earlier newly-enfranchised groups, inter-war women were not a horizontally stratified group, and did not therefore enjoy all the political influence that comes from work-based trade unions, professions, and pressure-groups. Most were home-based or in jobs that were part time in the double sense of hours worked and proportion of lifetime absorbed. They were also tied far more closely to men than were male employees to their employers. Their relationship with men, like that between consumer and producer, denied them the institutions that aggregate views and press them on the politicians. Denying the analogy between a sex and a class in 1910, Lord Hugh Cecil explained that 'a class is in its very idea a separate thing with common interests. Sex is just opposite. Sex is a body whose members are essentially interested in the members of the other sex.'[42]

Fragmentation was intellectual as well as geographical and political. 'How any woman with a family ever put pen to paper I cannot fathom,' Virginia Woolf exclaimed in 1930; 'always the bell rings and the baker calls.' Domestic distractions and physiological obstacles hampered inter-war women far more than earlier enfranchised groups. 'Looking back on my own life,' wrote the former suffragette Hannah Mitchell during the Second World War, 'I feel my greatest enemy has been the cooking stove—a sort of tyrant who has kept me in subjection.'[43] Sylvia Pankhurst's difficulties in bringing up Richard, and Ray Strachey's in rearing Barbara and Christopher, have already been discussed. Annie Kenney told Christabel that her *Memories of a Militant* (1924) had been written 'under *very* difficult conditions', and that some of the best bits were thought up while taking her son Warwick out in the pram. Many inter-war women therefore experienced what Rosamond Lehmann called a 'shredding out of one's personality upon minute obligations and responsibilities'.[44]

Ideas of 'associated living'—that is, of professionalized and communal cooking, laundering, child-rearing, and housekeeping—were propagated by socialists, were taken up by Charlotte Gilman, and attracted some Edwardian feminists;[45] but the inter-war tendency lay away from communal living and towards the fragmented suburban estate of semi-detached homes. At the same time, married women were pressed into cultivating a type of professionalism that did not enjoy the profession's financial rewards or corporate structure. Child-rearing is one of the earliest areas where this appeared. Public health officers from the Edwardian period onwards publicized the need to instruct mothers in

---

[42] *HC Deb.* 11 July 1910, c. 102.

[43] V. Woolf, *Letters*, iv (1978), p. 176. H. Mitchell, *The Hard Way Up*, ed. G. Mitchell (1968), p. 240.

[44] David Mitchell Collection, 73.83/34: Annie Kenney to Christabel Pankhurst, n.d. (typescript copy, end. '*c.*1942'). Lehmann, *A Note in Music* (1930), quoted in N. Beauman, *A Very Great Profession. The Woman's Novel, 1914–39* (1983), p. 95.

[45] e.g. Annie Besant in *Fabian Essays* (1889; Jubilee edn. 1948), p. 144; C. Cross, *Philip Snowden* (1966), p. 91. See also Gilman, *Women and Economics*, pp. 237–45, 267, 284, 297–8; B. Harrison, 'Women's Health and the Women's Movement in Britain, 1840–1940', in C. Webster (ed.), *Biology, Medicine and Society, 1840–1940* (Cambridge, 1981), p. 42.

their craft, and were reinforced by the inter-war child psychologists who pressed the mother to rear her own child. This was but one aspect of the continuing twentieth-century campaign for domesticity which encouraged women to spend more time and thought on the new (but unpaid) profession of housekeeping; cookery experts like Elizabeth David carried the process further in the 1950s. Professionalism of an unpaid and intellectually distracting type extended even to clothing and appearance. Cosmetics firms, fashion designers, and editors of women's magazines encouraged a trend away from public life and towards acquiring expertise in hairstyles, make-up, and personal relationships. Sylvia Pankhurst noticed about 1934 that there had been a reaction from emancipated womanhood towards 'painted lips and nails, and the return of trailing skirts which impede progress, and other absurdities of dress and deportment, which betoken the slave woman's sex appeal rather than the free woman's intelligent companionship'. She complained that 'amongst crowds of young women, the emancipation of today displays itself mainly in cigarettes and shorts'.[46]

One feminist palliative was the partnership in public work between women with complementary qualities—between Lady Denman and Margaret Pyke in the Family Planning Association, for instance, Hubback and Rathbone in NUSEC, Bondfield and Macarthur in the National Federation of Women Workers, Pippa and Ray Strachey in the LSWS, Gertrude Horton and Alice Franklin in the Townswomen's Guilds. Or the partnership could take the form of Rathbone's with Macadam, Maude Royden's with Evelyn Gunter, Hubback's with Cowles, or Ellen Wilkinson's with her sister Annie—whereby one woman takes on the public role while the other, like 'loyal and dependable' Annie, hovers in the background as 'a practical, unobtrusive and invaluable back-up'. Domestic service institutionalized this type of female partnership. Swanwick's feminism, for instance, flourished on her partnership with her suffragist servant Agnes: 'I can't write and speak myself,' Agnes once told her, 'but I can set you free to write and speak.'[47]

Higher taxation, however, and the decline of domestic service reduced such options. Nor could the major household aids—detergents, refrigerators, washing machines, frozen and convenience foods—yet be afforded; some had not yet even been invented. Ray Strachey's analogy between her

---

[46] Sylvia Pankhurst Papers: typescript headed 'Women's Citizenship', p. 2 (carbon copy).
[47] Vernon, *Wilkinson*, p. 119. H. M. Swanwick, *I Have Been Young* (1935), p. 208.

life-style and the juggler keeping all the balls in the air[48] applies equally to Rathbone, Astor, and Hubback—for even where servants were present or children were absent, women (whether they had jobs or not) were expected to do more than men: caring for relatives or aged parents, taking more time with their appearance, developing their skills as cooks and housekeepers. 'All my life I have tried to do too many different things,' writes Dora Russell; 'I wonder if this is not a perpetual dilemma for women.' It is not surprising that many women made a virtue of apparent necessity, and opted out of public life—as witness the inter-war successes of the Women's Institutes and the Townswomen's Guilds, both traditionalist on women's role. Clementine Churchill's *Times* obituarist thought that 'marriage was her vocation', and many humbler women displayed her pride in guaranteeing 'a contented home and warm family affections' to breadwinning husbands.[49]

If inter-war feminism progressed only slowly, and if the parliamentary road bristled with difficulties, was there another road? Militant tactics, for instance? Fred Pethick-Lawrence sometimes hinted as much in parliament. Sylvia Pankhurst even claimed that the campaign for the vote had done more than the vote itself to broaden our women's careers between 1911 and 1921. Edwardian suffragists, she claimed, had secured equality in old age pensions, and under the National Insurance Acts inequality towards women was 'certainly less than it would have been but for the strong woman's movement then existing'.[50] Yet this analysis is to say the least controversial, and between the wars nothing approaching WSPU militancy occurred—nor was such a course advocated by Sylvia's mother and elder sister.

The memory of suffragette militancy has certainly inspired twentieth-century women to resist oppression. It also destroyed some of the sillier aspects of the anti-feminists' 'physical force argument'. But suffragette folklore could not be allowed to guide inter-war feminists seeking practical reforms, for militancy had in reality been counter-productive for much of the period between 1906 and 1914, if only because it entangled debate on long-term objectives with dispute over short-term tactics. It would have been still more counter-productive between the wars, if only because enfranchised women with their own MPs could not plausibly have claimed that militancy alone would get them a hearing. Furthermore militancy's

---

[48] Smith Archives, Oxford: Ray to Mary, 8 Apr. 1928; cf. Stocks, *Rathbone*, p. 184.

[49] D. Russell, *Tamarisk Tree*, p. 167. *The Times*, 13 Dec. 1977, p. 17 (leading article).

[50] Sylvia Pankhurst Papers: typescript headed 'The Woman's Movement of Yesterday and Tomorrow', fo. 29; cf. fos. 27–8.

reintroduction would have submerged inter-war feminist argument on objectives (inevitable, and relatively fruitful) by feminist dispute on tactics (distracting, and relatively sterile). Even non-militant feminist organizations could make only slow progress between the wars.

Militancy had never attracted the sort of woman who worked closely with men in the labour movement, and would certainly have repelled the type of woman most active in public life after 1918. She gained her self-confidence from class background or organizational connection. Then as now she often came from a politically articulate family like the Corbetts,[51] and knew how to 'work' the existing political machinery. If she was a newcomer to public life, she was likely to have come up through the democratic structure of the non-militant suffragist organizations. But she could well be an anti-suffragist like Atholl or Violet Markham, whose honour in 1954 caused Sylvia Pankhurst to advocate a protest to the BBC 'by every woman who cares for her citizenship'.[52]

In many countries the vote arrived as a result of war or revolution, and owed little to any preceding feminist activism,[53] but in Britain between the wars the long pre-war history of non-violent feminist organization paid handsome dividends. Several former non-militant suffragists feature prominently in this book, and certain characteristics recur: a rationalistic outlook, firm curbs on emotion, strict economy of time, a marked sense of public duty, and strong political and personal self-discipline. Stocks, for instance, was completely indifferent to personal comfort. Her family feared that in old age she might part with all her furniture; possessions were an encumbrance. While giving away quite large sums, she was too economical to eat out, take taxis or travel first-class, and was completely indifferent to food; her daughter Helen spent some gloomy times down at West Bay with her, living off an egg.[54] Of the fourteen women discussed in this book, only Emmeline Pankhurst, Astor, Wilkinson, and (on occasion) Emmeline Pethick-Lawrence showed any interest in dress. In NUSEC's annual council meeting of 1931, Stocks carried a motion deploring the return of long skirts by a large majority.[55] Swanwick angered younger

[51] Vallance, *Women in the House*, pp. 61–2. Brookes, *Women at Westminster*, p. 239.

[52] David Mitchell Collection, 73.83/44: Sylvia Pankhurst to Mrs Drake, 1 July 1954.

[53] Duverger, *Political Role of Women*, pp. 10, 124, 139. T. Lloyd, *Suffragettes International. The World-Wide Campaign for Women's Rights* (1971), p. 101.

[54] This discussion of Baroness Stocks owes much to my tape-recorded discussions with her daughter Mrs Ann Patterson, 18 Dec. 1975, at 42 Campden Hill Square, London W8; with her daughter Miss Helen Stocks, 24 Jan. 1977, at 44 Regent's Park Road, London NW1; and with her granddaughter Miss Kate Patterson, 15 Dec. 1975, at Corpus Christi College, Oxford.

[55] *Woman's Leader*, 20 Mar. 1931, p. 53.

readers in 1932 by attacking undue preoccupation with cosmetics. 'Can they really follow a difficult scientific demonstration or a complex piece of music,' she asked, 'can they feel the intensities of admiration or love when a good part of their thoughts is concerned with the question "Is it time to powder my nose again"? Their triviality is tragic.' Sylvia Pankhurst was equally indignant: 'who cares . . . how Churchill dresses or whether he has a handsome nose or a lovely complexion!'[56] Feminists' distaste for cosmetics and constricting clothes owes something to concern for women's health, free movement, and uncluttered time. But their distaste has deeper roots: in a middle-class puritanism and high-mindedness that was by no means confined to feminist women. Hubback and Rathbone were not at all unusual within their class in fearing a national tendency towards extravagance and false materialism.

The inter-war feminist leaders, whether politically on the right or the left, drew on deep reserves of patriotism and religion. The two world wars showed that their patriotism could transcend party ties and unite a Rathbone to an Astor, a Wilkinson to a Fawcett, a Ray Strachey to a Corbett Ashby. Feminism of course required resistance to Hitler, but here again the primary impulse lay deeper: in a commitment to parliamentary government, to political pluralism and humane values that was much more widely held—indeed, had become part of the national self-image by the late-Victorian period. This feminist patriotism was seldom crudely chauvinist, largely because so deeply penetrated by religious sentiment. Like so many modern British reforming movements, feminism owed much to evangelicalism, and in its early years much also to nonconformity. With Bondfield, Astor, and Corbett Ashby, religious inspiration was direct. And when—as with Billington-Greig, Wilkinson, and Hubback— parental religion was rejected, much of religion's serious-mindedness, moralism, personal austerity, and missionary drive remained.

Given the inter-war prominence of such people, why the steady inter-war advance of suffragette views on how the vote had been won? H. W. Nevinson predicted that the non-militants would reap the credit for what had really been achieved by the suffragettes, yet as Rathbone pointed out in 1936, 'in fact, it has been rather the other way'. By 1974 Kathleen Courtney had given up all hope of getting the public to appreciate the non-militants' achievement: 'if that's what people want', she told me, 'well, let them have it.'[57] The explanation does not lie in any

---

[56] *Manchester Guardian*, 24 Aug. 1932, p. 6. Fawcett Library: Sylvia Pankhurst's autobiographical memo written for Billington-Greig, p. 5.

[57] Rathbone in R. Strachey (ed.), *Our Freedom*, p. 24. Author's interview with Dame Kathleen Courtney, 22 Apr. 1974, at 3 Elmtree Court, Elm Tree Road, London NW8.

non-militant reticence, for non-militants wrote abundantly on feminist history. Stocks repeatedly stressed its drawbacks, and even claimed in 1924 that its impact on the intellect had disqualified former suffragettes for further achievement. 'In my view, militancy . . . came within an inch of wrecking the suffrage movement, perhaps for a generation,' wrote Rathbone in 1936. 'Then, just in the nick of time, came the outbreak of the Great War.'[58]

Rathbone attributed the suffragettes' historiographical success to the fact that 'sensational methods always impress the popular imagination more than those which are quieter',[59] but this cannot suffice. At a very general level their success stems from the fact that shorthand analyses of past events suit the lay public, who cannot afford the time and perhaps even lack the desire to appreciate the full complexity of the political process. The apparent triumph of the brave brings a reassuring sense of poetic justice, especially when later experience seems to refute contemporary fears about militancy's long-term consequences. Besides, by the 1950s the suffragettes' own increasing age and respectability made it seem incredible that anyone could ever have thought them dangerous. But another level of explanation lies in reasoning more specific to inter-war feminist history. Suffragette historiography was used by impatient people (by the Six Point Group, for instance, or by Sylvia Pankhurst) as a stick with which to beat a feminist establishment which they thought slow and timid. Dorothy Thurtle of the Workers' Birth Control Group grumbled privately in 1928 about NUSEC: 'I went through the Suffrage fight and I remember repeatedly feeling exasperated with them as I do now. Very few positive helpful suggestions were ever forthcoming but when any one else wanted to do something there were a thousand reasons why it should not be done.'[60]

Furthermore, suffragettes' relative distance from public life after 1918 paradoxically increased their *esprit de corps*, and therefore their preoccupation with the past. Inter-war non-militants were so deeply involved in practical activity that they were too busy to imitate the suffragettes' recurrent commemorative gatherings. By 1935, the year when Ray Strachey was getting WEF launched, the Suffragette Fellowship was trying to get the authorities to return the banners the police had seized from the WSPU in the raid of 1913. In 1945, the year when Rathbone's family

---

[58] Rathbone in R. Strachey (ed.), *Our Freedom*, p. 24. Stocks, *Woman's Leader*, 31 Oct. 1924, p. 321.
[59] R. Strachey (ed.), *Our Freedom*, p. 24.
[60] Nancy Astor MSS 1416/1/1/309: D. Thurtle to Astor, 14 Dec. 1928.

allowances finally triumphed, the Fellowship was busily planning an archive for suffragette records. In 1955, when NUSEC's successors had at last committed a British government to the principle of equal pay, the Fellowship was industriously collecting prisoners' names for its suffragette roll of honour.[61] In the following year even Christabel Pankhurst questioned these suffragette priorities: 'do our men voters spend their time, thought and tongue on how, and through whom, they got the vote? No, they do not. They have more sense. They concentrate on how to *use* their vote.'[62] This book aims to help redress the historiographical balance. It focuses on a neglected period of feminist consolidation—on a period when feminist leaders' prudence risked incurring neglect by posterity. Their prudence does not signify mildness of feminist commitment; on the contrary, they envisaged a new society very different from the old—transformed not just in its political system, but in the details of family life. Their achievement was considerable and at no stage inevitable.

'The truth is that shock troops do not make good statesmen,' Mrs Swanwick pronounced in 1930, 'and that those who uncritically follow a leader . . . are often useless for reconstruction.'[63] The roots of non-militant achievement lie in the structure of the NUWSS, which, according to a supporter in 1912, 'has, while agitating for power, never ceased to be the finest training ground for the wise use of power: the system of popular election, the decentralisation of our work, the responsibility thrown upon every individual member, not only to act but to think, have all tended to a steady growth in political knowledge and sagacity and to that balance of mind which comes from free discussion and criticism'. This was a firm basis on which to extend women's political participation after 1918. From the outset NUSEC was closely linked to the Women Citizens Associations, eighty-two of which were affiliated to the central body by July 1921, and we have seen the emphasis given to citizenship by the early Towns-women's Guilds. Non-militants were active after 1918 in running their committees, handling procedural problems, and practising outside the feminist movement the tactics they had learned inside it.[64] Condemning the militants in 1909, A. M. Allen was prescient in claiming that 'it is in

---

[61] D. Mitchell, *Queen Christabel* (1977), pp. 367–8. Suffragette Fellowship, Manchester City Library M 220 (Hannah Mitchell MSS), 3/2/1: Suffragette Fellowship, *News Letter for 1945. Calling All Women*, Feb. 1955, p. 7.

[62] David Mitchell Collection, 73.83/32: C. Pankhurst to Billington-Greig, 13 Nov. 1956.

[63] *Manchester Guardian*, 3 Nov. 1930, p. 6.

[64] *Common Cause*, 29 Feb. 1912, p. 795. See also Stocks, *My Commonplace Book*, pp. 76–7. *Time and Tide*, 8 July 1921, p. 639.

great measure how we have fought which will determine what we shall win'.[65]

Yet merely to operate at the local level would have been to endorse the anti-suffragist position that women should leave national politics to the men. The non-militants engaged in significant national effort in all directions—from the Townswomen's Guilds to the National Birth Control Association, from children's nutrition to the enfranchisement of Indian women. Politicians' attitudes to women could permanently improve only when it became clear that women's votes were compatible with parliamentary government. This placed a heavy responsibility on inter-war feminist leaders, who helped to render MPs more accessible and got party programmes of the 1920s alerted to women's needs. Nearly half the women candidates at the general election of 1922 were former suffragists,[66] mostly non-militants, who also contributed six of the thirty-eight women in parliament before 1945 (Bentham, Phillips, Picton-Turbervill, Rathbone, Wilkinson, and Wintringham); the adult suffragists, by contrast, contributed only Bondfield, and the suffragettes none. The woman MP—however outnumbered by men, and whether feminist or anti-feminist in outlook—offered all women a new model; she made one more breach in male professional exclusiveness, struck one more blow at the philosophy of separated spheres. There were achievements in policy as well, many of which this book has already discussed. Equal franchise was an important success, but significant progress was also made on opening up the professions to women, making equal pay a live political issue, and establishing a firm historiographical foundation for future feminist achievement.

All this achievement took place within a most unfavourable political, international, intellectual, and economic climate; it must not be judged by some abstract standard, but in relation to the difficulties faced, and must focus as much on anti-feminist perils averted as on the feminist gains made. Nor was anything like the full range of inter-war women's talent ever mobilized. The study of British women's history during this period leaves behind an impression of unrealized potential and wasted talent. There are Corbett Ashby's eight unsuccessful parliamentary candidatures, for example; Ray Strachey's long struggle to get WEF launched; Susan Lawrence's prematurely terminated parliamentary career; and the inability of Billington-Greig and Hubback to find in later life a post that

---

[65] *Common Cause*, 12 Aug. 1909, p. 228.
[66] *Woman's Leader*, 3 Nov. 1922, pp. 314–7.

really measured up to their talents. Feminists will struggle to find ways of preventing such waste in future, but partly because inter-war feminists prepared the ground so well they will operate with greater resources and in a more favourable political, intellectual, and economic climate. Their chances of success will depend heavily on how far they can rival their inter-war predecessors in striking a judicious balance between revolutionary aims and prudent action.

FURTHER READING

Introduction and Conclusion

The best introduction to the history of British feminism is still Ray Strachey's '*The Cause*'. *A Short History of the Women's Movement in Great Britain* (1928), but it is inevitably inadequate on events after 1918. Sylvia Pankhurst's *The Suffragette Movement. An Intimate Account of Persons and Ideals* (1931) complements Strachey on the militant side. A. E. Metcalfe's *Woman's Effort. A Chronicle of British Women's Fifty Years' Struggle for Citizenship (1865–1914)* provides much valuable factual information not obtainable elsewhere. Margaret Barrow's *Women 1870–1928. A Select Guide to Printed and Archival Sources in the United Kingdom* (1981) is full and scholarly. A valuable reference work is *The Europa Biographical Dictionary of British Women*, ed. A. Crawford *et al.* (1983). Olive Banks's *Biographical Dictionary of British Feminists Volume One: 1800–1930* (1985) covers fewer people but in greater detail, and provides memoirs of all but four of the sixteen people discussed in this book. Two good textbooks provide an international dimension: Richard J. Evans's *The Feminists. Women's Emancipation Movements in Europe, America and Australasia, 1840–1920* (1977) and Olive Banks's *Faces of Feminism. A Study of Feminism as a Social Movement* (Oxford, 1981); Banks is particularly useful for comparing the British and American feminist experience. Maurice Duverger's *The Political Role of Women* (UNESCO, 1955) is stimulating for its international comparisons. On social and economic context, R. M. Titmuss's 'The Position of Women' in his *Essays on 'the Welfare State'* (2nd edn, 1963) pp. 88–103 is excellent, and can be supplemented by Jane Lewis's *Women in England, 1870–1950. Sexual Divisions and Social Change* (Brighton, 1984).

There is as yet no general textbook on the history of British feminism between the wars. The subject is best approached through Mary Stocks's excellent *Eleanor Rathbone. A Biography* (1949), and can be followed up by reading the useful collection edited by Ray Strachey, *Our Freedom and its Results. By Five Women* (1936). Unfortunately Lady Rhondda's *This Was My World* (1933) was too discreet and published too early to shed much light on her prominent inter-war feminist role, but Mary Stocks shows her customary balance and good judgement in her two autobiographical volumes, *My Commonplace Book* (1970) and *Still More Commonplace* (1973).

Those who want fuller detail on inter-war feminist organizations should consult the annual reports of the following organizations: the NUSEC, the NCEC, The Six Point Group, the Open Door Council, and the LSWS. The leading inter-war feminist periodicals contain a wealth of detail. They are the *Woman's Leader* (successor to the non-militants' *Common Cause*) which survived till 1933; *Time and*

Tide, founded in 1920, which was sympathetic to the Six Point Group in the 1920s but lost its feminist preoccupations early in the 1930s; and the *Vote*, organ till 1931 of the WFL, and succeeded by the League's scarce and cyclostyled *Bulletin*. The ageing suffragettes foregathered in the Suffragette Fellowship's occasional *News Letter*, and later in its *Calling All Women*.

Feminist classics of the period are Eleanor Rathbone's *The Disinherited Family* (1924) and Virginia Woolf's *A Room of One's Own* (1929). The literary background is important, and is best followed up through Virginia Woolf's *Letters* (6 vols.; 1975–83) and *Diaries* (5 vols.; 1977–84), and through the writings of Winifred Holtby and Vera Brittain; a useful introduction to the latter is P. Berry and A. Bishop (eds.), *Testament of a Generation. The Journalism of Vera Brittain and Winifred Holtby* (1985). Valuable on women's popular fiction is N. Beauman's *A Very Great Profession. The Woman's Novel, 1914–39* (1983).

Much more important as influences on women, at least in the short term, were non-feminist organizations like the National Union of Townswomen's Guilds and the National Federation of Women's Institutes, both of which published annual reports and periodicals (the *Townswoman* and *Home and Country*, respectively). Nobody has yet systematically explored the wealth of material in women's magazines on cosmetics, dress, cookery, etiquette, and on the decoration, furnishing, and mechanization of the home; Caroline Davidson's *A Woman's Work is Never Done. A History of Housework in the British Isles, 1650–1950* (1982) badly needs supplementing towards the end of her period. The complex relationship between feminists and the medical profession is explored in my 'Women's Health and the Women's Movement in Britain, 1840–1940' in C. Webster (ed.), *Biology, Medicine and Society, 1840–1940* (Cambridge, 1981), pp. 15–71.

1. Two Models of Feminist Leadership: Mrs Fawcett and Mrs Pankhurst

There is no good modern biography of Fawcett, but Ray Strachey's *Millicent Garrett Fawcett* (1931) is adequate, and Fawcett's disappointing *What I Remember* (1924) adds little to it. The best evocation of the non-militants' mood is the fifth chapter of Mary Stocks's *My Commonplace Book* (1970), but Leslie P. Hume's *The National Union of Women's Suffrage Societies, 1897–1914* (New York, 1982) chronicles in detail the earlier history of the organization which Fawcett led. Constance Rover's very full *Women's Suffrage and Party Politics in Britain, 1866–1914* (1967) pioneered the scholarly study of British feminism at the parliamentary level, and can be supplemented by my 'Women's Suffrage at Westminster, 1866–1928', in M. Bentley and J. Stevenson (eds.), *High and Low Politics in Modern Britain* (Oxford, 1983), pp. 80–122.

The best introduction to Pankhurst is Rebecca West's excellent biographical study in the collection published by Ivor Nicholson and Watson entitled *The Post Victorians* (1933). Sylvia Pankhurst's *The Life of Emmeline Pankhurst* (1935) is concise but rather jejune. Much richer on the background and personalities of the militant leaders is her excellent *The Suffragette Movement* mentioned above.

Emmeline Pankhurst's autobiographical *My Own Story* (1914) was ghosted, and is inaccurate and disappointing. David Mitchell's *The Fighting Pankhursts. A Study in Tenacity* (1967) collects valuable information about Emmeline Pankhurst's career after 1918. The best and most up-to-date book on the militants is Andrew Rosen's *Rise Up, Women! The Militant Campaign of the Women's Social and Political Union, 1903–1914* (1974), but the most penetrating evocation of the suffragette mood was published in 1911 and is now scarce—Teresa Billington-Greig's *The Militant Suffrage Movement. Emancipation in a Hurry* (Frank Palmer, [1911]). Also evocative is Emmeline Pethick-Lawrence's *My Part in a Changing World* (1938). My 'The Act of Militancy. Violence and the Suffragettes, 1904–1914' in my *Peaceable Kingdom. Stability and Change in Modern Britain* (Oxford, 1982), pp. 26–81, focuses on the organizational dynamic behind militancy, and Chapter 9 of my *Separate Spheres. The Opposition to Women's Suffrage in Britain* (1978) describes the hostility it evoked.

2. Woman of Ideas: Teresa Billington-Greig

There is no biography, but the Fawcett Library holds a rich collection of autobiographical manuscripts. I have supplemented them by interviews on 24 Aug. 1974 and 19 Sept. 1984 with Teresa's daughter, Miss Fiona Billington-Greig, and on 19 Sept. 1974 with Teresa's niece, Mrs Blackman. The best introduction to her written work is her *Militant Suffrage Movement* mentioned above, but her *The Consumer in Revolt* [1912] and *Commonsense on the Population Question* (Malthusian League, [1915]) are characteristically trenchant. Episodes in her career can be followed up in sources relating to the WFL, whose minutes and periodicals survive in the Fawcett Library.

3. Publicist and Communicator: Nancy Astor

The best biography is C. Sykes, *Nancy. The Life of Lady Astor* (1972), but M. Collis, *Nancy Astor. An Informal Biography* (1960) has value. Although John Grigg's *Nancy Astor. Portrait of a Pioneer* (1980) lacks footnotes, it contains original material and presents a rounded portrait with abundant illustrations. Rosina Harrison's *Rose. My Life in Service* (1975; Futura paperback edition, 1976) and Michael Astor's *Tribal Feeling* (1963) both provide perspectives whose value comes from illuminating informal and domestic situations. No study has so far done full justice to the feminist and parliamentary dimension of Astor's career. This can be achieved only through quarrying the large collection of Nancy Astor MSS at Reading University and her many contributions to *Hansard;* both have been drawn upon heavily here. John Ramsden, *The Age of Balfour and Baldwin, 1902–1940* (1978) provides the best background on the Conservative Party during this period. For the parliamentary background, see my 'Women in a Men's House. The Women MPs, 1919–1945', *Historical Journal*, 29, 3 (Sept. 1986), pp. 623–54.

4. Constructive Crusader: Eleanor Rathbone

The small collection of personal papers in Liverpool University Library is disappointing, and no larger collection seems to have survived, though Mary Stocks had access to some such collection when writing her *Eleanor Rathbone;* a new biography is now much needed. The best introduction to Rathbone's political outlook is *Milestones. Presidential Addresses* (Liverpool, 1929), her collection of speeches to NUSEC, but her important contribution to Ray Strachey's *Our Freedom* is also illuminating on this aspect. Here again, *Hansard* provides a rich insight into publicly expressed opinions, and can be supplemented from the feminist angle by the *Woman's Leader*. Rathbone's *The Disinherited Family* (1924) provides the best insight into the impressive range and power of her intellect. On family allowances, see J. Macnicol, *The Movement for Family Allowances, 1918–45. A Study in Social Policy Development* (1980). This portrait also owes much to the employee's eye-view provided in interviews by Mrs Cox, Mrs Schaerli, Mrs Soper, and Mrs Wolff. Arthur Marwick's 'Middle Opinion in the Thirties. Planning, Progress and Political "Agreement"', *English Historical Review*, Apr. 1964, pp. 285–98 provides valuable political context. For parliamentary background, see my 'Women in a Men's House' mentioned above.

5. Class Politics: Margaret Bondfield, Susan Lawrence, and Ellen Wilkinson

The relations between women and the labour movement have been little studied in this period, but see H. Smith, 'Sex vs. Class. British Feminists and the Labour Movement, 1919–1929', *Historian*, Nov. 1984, pp. 19–37. This chapter's emphasis on the parliamentary career of its three subjects means that *Hansard* is the main source used, though Beatrice Webb's diaries provide invaluable informal insights. There is no good biography of Bondfield, perhaps because she is a rather unexciting subject. M. A. Hamilton's *Margaret Bondfield* (1924) was published before the denouement, and Bondfield's autobiography, *A Life's Work* [1949] is disappointing, but Marion Miliband provides valuable information on her in *Dictionary of Labour Biography*, ii (1974), pp. 39–45.

Although there is no biography or autobiography of Lawrence, C. D. Rackham's short memoir in *Fabian Quarterly*, Spring 1948, is first-rate; see also D. E. Martin's contribution on her in *Dictionary of Labour Biography*, iii (1976), pp. 128–132. Margaret Cole rightly pointed out as early as 1949 that a biography of Lawrence was much needed, but nobody noticed.

Wilkinson's contribution to the Countess of Asquith's collection, *Myself When Young* (1938) shows how valuable her autobiography would have been if she had lived to write it. Betty Vernon's *Ellen Wilkinson, 1891–1947* (1982) collects useful material, and can be supplemented with Stella Davies's 'The Young Ellen Wilkinson', *Memoirs and Proceedings of the Manchester Literary and Philosophical Society*, 107 (1964–5), pp. 34–9. There is a lively essay on Wilkinson in K. O. Morgan's *Labour People* (Oxford, 1987). The *Dictionary of Labour Biography* has not yet published a memoir, and a full-scale book-length political study would be justified. For parliamentary background on all three women, see my 'Women in a Men's House' mentioned above.

6. *Two Organization Women: Pippa and Ray Strachey*

No biography exists of either. Interviews (especially with her daughter Barbara and her colleague Miss Irene Hilton) have greatly enriched my understanding of Ray, but Pippa cannot now be recaptured through this device, and her charming letters show what a serious loss this is. Ray does not reveal herself much in her numerous publications, of which the best are '*The Cause*' (1928) and *Millicent Garrett Fawcett* (1931), but Barbara Strachey's *Remarkable Relations* (1980) clarifies the family context and provides much entertainment *en route*. Virginia Woolf's diary sheds a fitful, sometimes distorting, but sometimes illuminating, light on Ray; unfortunately she does not seem to have trained her probing spotlight on to Pippa. Most valuable of all as a source are the Smith Archives, to which Mrs Strachey gave me generous and unstinted access. These can be supplemented with the Carnegie UK Trust papers in the Scottish Record Office, all too little of whose abundant information on WEF could be presented here.

7. *Diplomat: Margery Corbett Ashby*

In this chapter, too, interviews (most notably with Dame Margery herself) have been of central importance. No biography has been published, though Arnold Whittick has written one which I have not seen. The Corbett Ashby Papers are in some ways disappointing, partly because their subject was so self-effacing and so uninterested in herself. They consist largely of newspaper cuttings, but there are a few revealing family letters, and the autobiographical drafts contain valuable material. Danehill Parish Historical Society published some of this material in its '*From the Feudal to the Jet Age*'. *Dame Margery Corbett Ashby DBE 1882–1981* (1982). Background reading on the non-militant suffragists is listed in the bibliographies for Chapters 1 and 4. For the Townswomen's Guilds see Mary Stott, *Organization Woman* (1978). There is no adequate history of the WFL. There are two histories of the International Alliance of Women, the feminist organization which claimed Dame Margery's lifelong dedication: Adele Schreiber and Margaret Mathieson, *Journey towards Freedom* (Copenhagen, 1955) and Arnold Whittick, *Woman into Citizen* (1979).

8. *Two Utopians: Sylvia Pankhurst and Henry Harben*

Patricia W. Romero's *E. Sylvia Pankhurst, Portrait of a Radical* (1987) was published while this book was in proof, and is the only full-scale biography; although it presents new material, it is inaccurate on details and weak on the overall British political context. The Sylvia Pankhurst papers in the Institute for Social History, Amsterdam, are a large and rich collection, and can be supplemented by Pankhurst's abundant published writings. Of these, the most revealing is *The Suffragette Movement* (1931); Ray Strachey rightly told the readers of the *Woman's Leader* on 20 February 1931 that it is 'in its way, as complete a revelation of its author's character as the most exacting student of psychology could desire'. Pankhurst also contributed a penetrating autobiographical essay to Margot Asquith's symposium, *Myself When Young* (1938). Chapter 1's bibliography lists background reading on militant suffragism, and for later years David Mitchell has gathered a wealth of material into his valuable *The Fighting Pankhursts. A Study in Tenacity* (1967); much of his raw material is now in the Museum of London's David Mitchell Collection, and is well worth consulting.

Harben was not one to hide his light under a bushel, but he was too eager for audiences in his own day to bother much with posterity, and the flatness of his published writings gives no hint of the personality who obviously fascinated his hearers. There is no biography. Nor was Harben successful enough in a worldly way for people to preserve much of his correspondence, though the British Library holds a useful volume of Harben Papers. By no means all the most interesting personalities, however, enjoy worldly success, and it is fortunate that this chapter has been able to draw heavily upon interviews with Harben's daughters, with his employee Mrs Hall, and with his friends the Morsons.

9. The Politics of a Marriage: Emmeline and Fred Pethick-Lawrence

Both the autobiographies are revealing. Vera Brittain's biography of Fred is disappointing, but in writing it she generated some interesting manuscript material which is now in the Vera Brittain Collection at McMaster University, Hamilton, Ontario. Fred contributed a penetrating essay on his personal philosophy to the symposium edited by Sir James Marchant, *If I Had My Time Again* (n.d.). The Pethick-Lawrence papers in Trinity College Library, Cambridge, are revealing on the personal side, but weak on the political dimension; a large proportion of the Pethick-Lawrence papers were destroyed towards the end of Fred's life. On the other hand, the public aspect of Fred's political career is fully outlined in his many speeches in *Hansard*. Very helpful for the Pethick-Lawrences' domestic life were my interviews with Mrs Groom-Smith, Miss Elizabeth Kempster, and Mrs Needham. An interview with Sir Frank Turnbull contributed a civil servant's valuable eye-view. Chapter 1's bibliography provides background reading on the militant suffrage movement.

10. Catalyst and Facilitator: Eva Hubback

Family Inheritance (1954), Diana Hopkinson's biography of her mother, is excellent. I have supplemented it by studying the Hubback Papers, a small collection which Mrs Hopkinson used when compiling the book. Two interviews with Mr and Mrs Hopkinson were invaluable, and led on to interviews with Eva's sister, Winifred Raphael, of whom Eva was very fond, and with Eva's two younger children David and Rachel Hubback. Interviews with her former colleagues, Mrs Gertrude Horton, Mrs Peggy Jay, Mrs Erna Nelki, Mrs Soper, Mrs Sprince Stephens, and Dr Helena Wright, and with her cousins Catherine and Peter Joseph, were helpful on specific aspects. Much of the bibliography for Chapter 4 is also relevant for Hubback, but it should be supplemented by Jane Lewis's *The Politics of Motherhood. Child and Maternal Welfare in England, 1900–1939* (1980), and by B. Evans, *Freedom to Choose. The Life and Work of Dr Helena Wright,*

Pioneer of Contraception (1984). Interviews with B. A. Howard and Lord Stewart of Fulham clarified the role of the Association for Education in Citizenship, as did Guy Whitmarsh's 'Society and the School Curriculum. The Association for Education in Citizenship 1934–1957' (Birmingham School of Education M.Ed. thesis, 1972); a full-scale published study of the Association is much needed. See also Denis Richards, *Offspring of the Vic. A History of Morley College* (1958).

INDEX

Where an entry has sub-headings, these are alphabetized by key-word. Entries for the book's major themes are doubly sub-divided. In such cases, the following broad categories are employed for personalities: biography, characteristics, opinions, and relationships. These categories are then themselves sub-divided alphabetically by keyword, except that in each case the section on biography is arranged in rough chronological order. Major institutions are subdivided as follows: history (chronologically arranged), characteristics, personalities, policies, and relationships. To ensure that the Index fully plays its part in drawing together the book's major themes, institutional and personal entries are supplemented by the following major analytic headings, the more important of which are also sub-divided:

INDEX

Major entries appear in bold